LORD WOLSELEY.

ÆTAT 48.

Drawn and Engraved by W. H. Gibbs.

LONDON RICHARD BENTLEY & SON 1883.

GENERAL

LORD WOLSELEY

(OF CAIRO),

G.C.B., G.C.M.G., D.C.L., LL.D.

A MEMOIR.

BY

CHARLES RATHBONE LOW, I.N., F.R.G.S.,
AUTHOR OF
'THE HISTORY OF THE INDIAN NAVY,' ETC.

LONDON:
RICHARD BENTLEY AND SON,
Publishers in Ordinary to Her Majesty the Queen.
1883.
[*All Rights Reserved.*]

Printed and bound by Antony Rowe Ltd, Eastbourne

PREFACE TO THE SECOND EDITION.

THIS Memoir of Lord Wolseley, so far as it deals with his career up to the time of his proceeding to Cyprus in the summer of 1878, was published in that year. His conduct of operations in Egypt appearing to call for a new edition, I have written a sketch of his services from that date up to the present time.

This volume contains the first published account of Lord Wolseley's administration of Cyprus. It was his intention to write an official report of his doings during the first twelve months the island was under British rule, when he organized the administration and guided the tottering footsteps of this, the youngest of the Mother Country's Colonies. But his hurried departure to Natal, to supersede Lord Chelmsford, prevented the execution of this design. The account of Lord Wolseley's conduct of affairs in South Africa, including the operations in Zululand, his dealing with the Boers, and the Secocoeni Campaign, are also published in this volume for the first time, and, as with the Cyprus chapter, the details may be relied upon, his lordship having kindly revised the proof-sheets.

As with the Cyprus and South African chapters, the last, giving an account of the Egyptian Campaign, has been

PREFACE TO THE SECOND EDITION.

written without any assistance from previously published works, for mine is the first in the field. This will, perhaps, be taken into consideration by critics and an indulgent public, whose pardon I crave for any shortcomings. These will be amply atoned for when Colonel Maurice, R.A., the accomplished writer and correspondent of the *Times* in Egypt, has published the official account of the campaign, in which I understand he is engaged. I take this opportunity of specially thanking him,* and also Colonel Herbert Stewart, C.B., A.D.C. to the Queen, Major R. C. Lawrence, who commanded the detachment of cavalry that occupied the citadel of Cairo—one of the most dashing feats of the war—and other officers who have afforded me information when writing this portion of the work.

In the previously published chapters of this volume, we have seen Lord Wolseley as a Regimental officer in Burmah, leading a storming party and narrowly escaping with his life; as an Engineer in the trenches before Sebastopol, fighting and toiling, suffering and shedding his blood; as a Regimental and Staff officer, participating in some of the most stirring scenes of the Indian Mutiny; and on the Staff in the China Campaign of 1860;—thus building up that thorough acquaintance with the art of war, which he has turned to such good account. We have followed him as leader in the Red River and Ashantee Expeditions, in both of which he displayed his remarkable aptitude for command, his energy, resource, and unflagging determination to succeed when everything was against him, and failure appeared imminent to the most hopeful.

In the last five years of his eventful life we shall see him as an administrator and lawgiver in Cyprus, which afforded a virgin field for constructive statesmanship. We shall see

* Colonel Maurice was kind enough to peruse the proof-sheets of the Egyptian chapter, and says, in a letter to me: 'I must congratulate you upon the accuracy with which the account of the Egyptian Campaign is written.'

PREFACE TO THE SECOND EDITION. v

him in Zululand, as the soldier who, by his combinations and pertinacity, hunted down the Zulu King in the depth of his African jungle, and as a Constitution-maker, partitioning his kingdom, and dictating the terms of settlement. From Zululand we shall follow him to the Transvaal, and his duties change from coercing Zulus to the impossible task of striving to conciliate Boers. But at least he kept the peace, and the magic of his name awed the sturdy farmers into submission. Again the scene changes, and we find him once more leading British soldiers to victory. Secocoeni, the Basuto chief, who had defeated the attempts alike of Zulus, Boers, and British soldiers to capture his stronghold, met his conqueror in Lord Wolseley, whose brief but brilliant and successful campaign against that dreaded chief astonished alike Native and European in South Africa, and raised British prestige to a height it had never before attained.

From South Africa, and the peaceful precincts of the Horse Guards, where he guided the military reforms instituted by Lord Cardwell and Mr. Childers, at the call of his country he once more buckled on his sword, and having organized the force that was to restore the authority of the Khedive and put an end to military despotism in Egypt, he carried through, to the letter, the programme of operations he had marked out before leaving this country. This punctuality is not the least surprising feature of his conduct of the war, but it is one that has always marked his military career.

In the Red River Expedition he took a force of 1,200 soldiers and 500 non-combatants, over an untrodden wilderness, to Fort Garry, a distance of 1,200 miles from the point of departure, and arrived at his destination within twenty-four hours of the time fixed before quitting Toronto. He marched into Coomassie on the day he designated before quitting Cape Coast Castle; and, as he told us, drank his afternoon tea in the fortress of Secocoeni, in the wilds of the Lulu Mountains in the Transvaal, on the very day he indicated, months before, in letters to the Secretary of State for War and the Field-Marshal Commanding-in-Chief. Finally, as we have seen, he fought the decisive action of the war and entered the capital of Egypt on the dates marked out by him while in England;—thus conducting the movements of armies and the combinations of war with the regularity of clock-work. As far as we are aware, in no age and by no general has the practice of the art been reduced to such conditions of mathematical precision, and been made so closely to conform to the will of the Commander.

Before the victories of Prussia over Austria in 1866, and of the combined German army over France four years later, it was the custom in this country to sneer at studious officers as *doctrinaires*, but few now will be bold enough to gainsay the truth of Don Quixote's saying, 'The sword hath never blunted the pen, nor the pen the sword.' Lord Wolseley has ever been one of those ardent but judicious reformers who, while recognising with the Duke of Wellington the superiority of the British officer to the same class in any other army, and approving generally our regimental system, have sought to remedy defects in our military organization, which, if permitted to exist unchecked, would land this country in disasters more dire than those she met with in the Crimea. An advocate of short service, not only with its concomitant of young non-commissioned officers and soldiers, but of young officers also, he dared to lay a sacrilegious hand on the constitution of the British army, hitherto regarded as the very Palladium of aristocratic privilege, and placed by a constitutional figment under the direct control of the Crown. When the new system did not, apparently, work well, as during the Zulu War, when some of the battalions were notoriously inefficient, he bluntly asserted that the cause of the failure lay not in the system, though that was not sufficiently developed to be fairly tested, but to the half-hearted manner in which it was worked by the Horse Guards. This assertion aroused a storm of abuse on the head of the bold innovator, but the high state of discipline, and the marching and fighting powers displayed by the army under his command in Egypt, and the greater ease with which the complicated machine having its motive-power in Pall Mall, now moves under his guiding hand, proves that he had warrant for his assertions.

It is easy, after success has been won, to make light of the difficulties encountered by our army in Egypt, and to depreciate the fighting qualities of the men opposed to us; but the former were very great, and afforded to an incompetent general—and recent events in South Africa have shown the race is not extinct—vast possibilities of failure and disaster, while the resistance made by the Egyptian army during the brief struggle at Tel-el-Kebir, when it was surprised out of sleep by the fierce onslaught at all points of an apparently endless line of British red-coats, was by no means so despicable as was made out. Sir Edward Hamley does justice to the gallantry of the enemy opposed to his Highlanders, who, at one point, actually gave ground, and were driven back to the first line of the intrenchments they had carried.

It was on all grounds, political no less than military, essential that the campaign should be 'short, sharp, and decisive.' Delay meant not only vast expenditure, but increased probabilities of political complications with Turkey, France, and Russia, no less than a great uprising of the Arab race. Had Arabi won even a partial success, or held his opponents temporarily in check, the power of the movement he headed would indeed have become more than national, and the Mussulmans of the Arabian desert, and of Tunis and Tripoli, no less than the malcontents from the Soudân, would have thrown in their lot with the leader of the rebellion. Then the physical difficulties were great, and the time of year was unfavourable; and when we consider the heavy sick-list of our troops in Egypt, the result, according to the doctors, of the hardships of the brief campaign, some calculation may be made of the losses we must have encountered had it been prolonged. Thus while the croakers, who always make their voices heard on the outbreak of a war, had many grounds for their pessimistic vaticinations, the most sanguine never anticipated such a rapid and complete success.

Marching and fighting under a tropical sun in the strip of desert between Ismailia and the cultivated Delta was nothing to the Indian Contingent, some of whom had accompanied Sir Frederick Roberts in his celebrated march through Afghanistan; but it was otherwise with the soldiers fresh from Aldershot and the Wellington Barracks. Fainting under the stifling heat, the Guards and the rest of the army marched and worked like navvies with an unmurmuring spirit worthy their ancient renown. Like the immortal 'Ten thousand' Greeks,—' whose glory,' says the poet Thomson, 'not the prime of victories can reach :'

'Deserts, in vain, opposed their course.'

Not the least brilliant operation of the war was the seizure of the Suez Canal, which was exclusively the work of the British navy. M. de Lesseps acted on the impression that his *non possumus* and bluster would paralyze the action of the British commanders so far as operations on the Canal, the offspring of his genius, were concerned. But he exaggerated the extent of his power, and his indignation was almost ludicrous when Admiral Hoskins and Captain Fitzroy met his hysterical protests by courteously but firmly carrying out their orders. As matters turned out, the eminent French engineer not only rendered incalculable service to civilization and his Canal, but conduced to the rapid success of the campaign, by hoodwinking Arabi into the belief that his guarantee of the neutrality of that passage would be respected by the British commanders, for a small portion of the 7,000 labourers whom Arabi impressed to throw up the lines of Tel-el-Kebir could, in a few hours, have rendered the Canal impassable to the transports conveying the troops.

When the difficulties of transport had been overcome, and the force was massed at Kassassin, the critical moment for proving his capacity had arrived for Lord Wolseley. He had to decide by the light of insufficient information—for he had no reliable intelligence of the real strength of the army concentrated behind the lines in his front—the method by which he was to assault the works—whether by shelling them preparatory to an assault, by turning them, or by surprise. A doctrinaire general would have adopted the first course, which would have prepared his enemy to give him a warm reception, and might have ended in a failure. The second method, even if successful, would have involved tedious movements and the dispersion of his force, and both courses would have been attended with a prolongation of the campaign. The assault with the bayonet, delivered as a surprise, was the course that alone remained, and its adoption showed military genius of a high order, which was not belied by the manner in which it was carried into execution. No such feat has been performed in recent times, except at Shenovo, when Skobeleff stormed the Turkish intrenchments; but that was after the capture of Plevna had demoralized his enemy. In adopting this method of attack, Lord Wolseley displayed the judgment which forms a correct estimate of the resistance to be overcome, the self-reliance which is willing to risk the chance of failure in order to attain an adequate result, and the confidence in his troops which induces a reciprocal feeling.

It was said by the Duke of Wellington that there were not half a dozen generals in the British army who could march a body of 10,000 men into and out of Hyde Park without confusion; and if this is so, few indeed are the generals in ours or any other army who would undertake to march a force of 14,000 men and 60 guns, forming a line nearly four miles in length, for a distance of eight miles over the trackless desert, guided only by the glimmer of the stars. To perform this operation so that, at the moment of attack, the whole line should have taken up their assigned positions with absolute accuracy, is a feat unprecedented in ancient or modern warfare. With such judgment was the time for the final rush selected, that had it been a few minutes earlier it would have been too dark, and had it been a few minutes later the surprise would have failed; while, as planned, the exact moment was chosen when the assault could be delivered with the smallest loss, the distance to be crossed under fire was moderate, and the leaden hail mostly passed over the heads of the stormers.

Again Lord Wolseley displayed his military genius,[*] which in him is almost an instinct, in dividing his operations into two distinct attacks, so that in the event of one failing, the chance of the second succeeding would not be lessened. Between the two attacks the artillery was massed; on the right flank was the whole of the cavalry, to profit by success or cover a retreat; and on the left flank, south of the Canal, marched the Indian Contingent, which moved one hour and a half after the main body, in order that it might

[*] A writer of acknowledged originality and graphic power, Mr. Kinglake, in his latest published (the seventh) volume of the 'Invasion of the Crimea,' goes out of his way to compliment Lord Wolseley and his army for their achievements in Egypt. The passage is as forcibly and picturesquely written as anything from the pen of the author of 'Eothen.'

press home its attack only in the event of success. Lord Wolseley knew that if one of the attacking brigades could establish a footing within the enemy's works, all would be lost for the Egyptians; and so it proved when the Highlanders crossed the ditch and scaled the intrenchments.

It was the chief characteristic of Napoleon that he gave no time to a beaten enemy to rally, but followed up a victory with crushing effect. In this crucial test of a great general Wolseley is not wanting. Having defeated the Egyptian army, he gave no thought to his rear or transport—these had been sufficiently provided for in the busy days since landing at Ismailia; but he directed his undivided attention to crushing the enemy in his front beyond the power of his again rallying, and seizing the strategic points, above all the capital, menaced with the fate of Alexandria. Within forty-eight hours of his victory, he had reaped the full fruits of that surprising success. The country had been overrun, the army dispersed, and, with the surrender of Cairo and of the rebel leaders, the resistance to the authority of the Khedive collapsed.

Lord Wolseley has had to pay the penalty of greatness, and cavillers have sought to detract from the credit due to him for the uniform success he has achieved; but since his last surprising performance the voice of envy and detraction, which, in former campaigns, attributed success to fortune, or to his staff (who repudiated the honour), has been silent under the unanimity with which foreign as well as home critics have lauded the originality of his plans for the conquest of Egypt, and the boldness and promptitude with which he put them into execution. From a political point of view the services he has rendered to his country by the rapidity and completeness of his success can scarcely be exaggerated, and will become more apparent with the lapse of time. That trite phrase of Julius Cæsar—*Veni, vidi, vici*—has never been more aptly applied than to the conquest of Egypt by the British General. To have overrun and subdued in twenty-five days the country of the Pharaohs and Ptolemies—the classic land that has witnessed the glories of Alexander, Cæsar, and Napoleon—must be a proud recollection to Lord Wolseley, to the brave army he has led to victory, and to the country that gave them birth.

C. R. LOW.

KENSINGTON, *January,* 1883.

PREFACE TO THE FIRST EDITION.

SOME explanation appears necessary in publishing the Biography of a man still living. On the 6th of May, 1874 immediately on the return of Sir Garnet Wolseley from Ashantee, I commenced to write this Memoir of his military services. The task was a difficult one, for Sir Garnet had lost all his papers and journals. During the Indian Mutiny they were stolen, and what remained to him were burnt at the great fire at the Pantechnicon, where all his furniture and effects were consumed. When, therefore, I applied to him for assistance, he expressed his regret that he had no private papers whatever in his possession, but consented to give me all the information in his power. Thus, at numerous interviews, whenever he had a spare hour from his duties at the War Office, as head of the Auxiliary Forces, he told me

> 'The story of his life,
> From year to year; the battles, sieges, fortunes,
> That he had passed.
> He ran it through, even from his boyish days,
> To the very moment that I bade him tell it.'

As I was not unfamiliar with the military events of the wars in which he had participated, I was enabled to put to him what lawyers call 'leading questions;' and these, as he frequently owned to me, assisted a naturally retentive memory in reviving his recollections of the past. In this story of an eventful life, he

> 'Spoke of most disastrous chances,
> Of moving accidents by flood and field;
> Of hair-breadth 'scapes i' the imminent deadly breach.

By correspondence and personal acquaintance with officers of his Staff, and others who had served under his orders, I learned anecdotes illustrative of traits of character, which will lend an additional interest to the narrative. In this manner the book was written, and Sir Garnet Wolseley, after perusal, testified to its absolute veracity in a letter addressed to me. The Memoir, especially the earlier portion, may, therefore, almost be regarded as an Autobiography.

The Memoir was passed through a military magazine, but it was not until early in the present year, when war with Russia was imminent, and Sir Garnet was placed under orders as Chief of the Staff to the Expeditionary Army, that I decided to republish, in book form, the military experiences of an officer whose name was in everyone's mouth, as that of a General of established reputation, from whom great things were expected. The Press and periodicals of the day were full of speculations as to his chances of success, and the events of his past career, so far as they were known, were eagerly discussed, thus showing the public interest in him. I accordingly revised the work, and completed it up to date, including an account of the Natal Mission, derived from papers supplied by Sir Garnet Wolseley. However well or ill, from a literary point of view, I may have acquitted myself of the task, at least I may claim for the book the merits of authenticity and completeness, and trust it may be found interesting, as the hero's life has been a changeful scene of adventure, such as falls to the lot of few men in this prosaic age.

In writing of one still among us, it would be unseemly to

speak in the terms of eulogy warranted by the circumstances of his career; but it is allowable to quote despatches and the opinions of those who have served with him. As a young officer, wherever the danger was greatest and the fire hottest, there he was to be found. In Burmah he led two storming-parties in one day, and was dangerously wounded at the moment of victory. In the Crimea he was once so severely wounded, that the surgeon passed him over for dead, and he was twice slightly wounded, while he was, perhaps, oftener in the trenches than any officer in the British army.

At the Relief of Lucknow he again led a storming-party; and, in the China Campaign, he was in the thick of the fire at the capture of the Taku Forts. The bare enumeration of the occasions on which he courted death and won 'the bubble reputation,' shows that he was possessed in a conspicuous degree of the first of military virtues. More admirable than the fierce courage which inspires during the heat of battle is the calm lofty spirit that retains its equanimity when failure appears certain and all men despair of success. That Sir Garnet Wolseley possesses this noblest of the attributes of those who claim to be leaders of men, is testified by those who served with him in the Red River and Ashantee Expeditions. A distinguished officer assured us that when, in the advance through the Canadian wilderness, everyone resigned all hope of reaching Fort Garry, so many, and seemingly insurmountable, were the natural obstacles, the Commander alone retained his sanguine anticipations of success, and nerved all hearts by his encouraging words and example. The same we know was the case in the Ashantee Campaign, when, at one time, it appeared that the task of reaching Coomassie and returning to the coast within the limited period available for hostilities, was an impossibility. But his indomitable will surmounted all obstacles, and the campaign was a brilliant success.

We are accustomed to applaud such acts of heroism and devotion when told of the warriors of Greece and Rome, but they are not less worthy of chronicle and admiration when narrated of our fellow-countrymen and contemporaries. Moreover, the narrative of deeds such as we are about to recount is useful as an example to the rising generation of young Englishmen, who will learn that the age of chivalry, notwithstanding Burke's magnificent lament, is not yet over, but will last as long as there are brave hearts to illustrate the page of our history, and generous instincts to applaud them.

Sir Garnet Wolseley carries self-reliance almost to a fault, if that is possible; though the absolute confidence he inspires in his Staff, who rally round him as he passes from one triumph to another, willing tools in the hands of the master workman, shows that it is founded on just appreciation of his own powers. Swift to form his plans, he executes them with unfaltering tenacity of will, and the correctness of his judgment amounts almost to instinct.

C. R. LOW.

CHELSEA, *July*, 1878.

CONTENTS.

CHAPTER I.

THE BURMESE WAR.

Introduction.—Parentage.—Early Life.—The Burmese War.—The Advance on Myat-toon's Position.—Ensign Wolseley leads the Storming Party on the 19th of March, 1853.—Is wounded.—Returns to England 1

CHAPTER II.

THE CRIMEAN WAR.

The Crimean War.—Captain Wolseley proceeds to Sebastopol.—Work in the Trenches.—The Bombardment of the 9th to the 17th of April. —The Attack on the Quarries.—Gallant Services of Captain Wolseley. —The Assault of the 18th of June.—The Third, Fourth, and Fifth Bombardments of Sebastopol.—The Affair of the 30th of August.— Captain Wolseley is severely wounded.—Service in the Quartermaster-General's Department.—Return to England . . . 22

CHAPTER III

THE INDIAN MUTINY.

Captain Wolseley proceeds on Service to India.—Wrecked at Banca.— Arrival at Calcutta.—Proceeds up-Country.—In Action near Cawnpore.—March to Alumbagh.—The Relief of Lucknow.—Wolseley storms the Mess-house.—Occupies the Motee Mahul, and effects Communication with the Residency of Lucknow.—The Defence of Alumbagh.—Campaigning in Oude.—Actions at Baree and Nawabgunge.—Service on the Nepaul Frontier 66

CHAPTER IV.

THE CHINA WAR.

The Occupation of Chusan.—The Disembarkation at Peh-tang.—The Action at Sinho.—The Capture of the Taku Forts.—The Advance on Pekin.—Narrow Escape of Colonel Wolseley from Capture.—The Looting of the Summer Palace and Surrender of Pekin.—Colonel Wolseley's Visit to Japan and Mission to Nankin.—Return to England 119

CHAPTER V.

SERVICE IN CANADA.

The Trent Affair.—Colonel Wolseley embarks for Canada, and is employed on Transport Duty.—His Visit to the Headquarters of Generals Lee, Jackson, and Longstreet, and Impressions of the Confederate Armies.—Colonel Wolseley's Services during the Fenian Invasion in 1866 154

CHAPTER VI.

THE RED RIVER EXPEDITION.

The Red River Expedition.—The Organization of the Force, and Start for Thunder Bay.—The Road thence to the Shebandowan Lake.—Down the Lakes, and across the 'Portages' to Fort Frances.—Running the Rapids of the Winnipeg River to Fort Alexander.—The Arrival at Fort Garry.—Success of the Expedition.—Return of Sir Garnet Wolseley to England 185

CHAPTER VII.

THE ASHANTEE WAR.

Preparations for the War.—Arrival at Cape Coast.—Operations South of the Prah.—The Action at Essaman.—Defence of Abrakrampa, and Retreat of the Ashantees.—Illness of Sir Garnet Wolseley.—Preparations for crossing the Prah.—The Advance into Ashantee.—Battle of Amoaful.—Action at Ordahsu.—Capture of Coomassie.—Return to Cape Coast.—The Treaty of Fommanah.—Sir Garnet Wolseley returns to England.—The Welcome Home 241

CHAPTER VIII.

THE NATAL MISSION.

Visit to the Cape.—Reception at Durban and Maritzburg.—Natal Politics and Parties.—The Constitution Amendment Bill.—Triumph of Sir Garnet Wolseley's Policy.—Progress through Natal.—Return to England.—Is appointed High Commissioner and Commander-in-Chief of Cyprus 328

CHAPTER IX.

THE ADMINISTRATION OF CYPRUS.

Occupation of Cyprus by the British Troops.—Condition of the Island and its Inhabitants. — The Reforms introduced by Sir Garnet Wolseley.—His Opinion of the Healthiness of Cyprus.—Sir Garnet Wolseley recasts the Administration of the Island.—Visit of some Members of the British Government to Cyprus.—Sir Garnet Wolseley and the War in Afghanistan.—Condition and Prospects of Cyprus.— Sir Garnet Wolseley returns to England in May, 1879 . . 347

CHAPTER X.

SERVICES IN ZULULAND AND THE TRANSVAAL.

Sir Garnet Wolseley is appointed to the Chief Political and Military Command in Natal and the Transvaal.—Arrival in Zululand.—Pursuit and Capture of Cetewayo.—The Settlement of Zululand.—Departure of Sir Garnet Wolseley for the Transvaal.—His Reception at Pretoria and the other Towns of the Transvaal.—Declaration of British Policy with respect to the Country, and its Effect on the Boers. —The Campaign against Secocoeni.—Capture of the Chief's Stronghold on the 28th November, 1879.—Sir Garnet Wolseley and the Boers.—His Opinion on the Basuto Question.—Return to England of Sir Garnet Wolseley 361

CHAPTER XI.

THE EGYPTIAN CAMPAIGN.

Sir Garnet Wolseley as Quartermaster-General.—Attends the German Autumn Military Manœuvres.—Is appointed Adjutant-General.— Nomination of Sir Garnet Wolseley to the Command of the Expedition to Egypt.—He proceeds to Alexandria.—Change of the Base of Operations to Ismailia.—Transport Difficulties.—Advance of Sir

Garnet from Ismailia.—The Action at Tel-el-Mahuta.—Capture of Mahsameh.—The Action at Kassassin of 28th August.—Preparations for the final Advance.—The Action of the 9th September.—The Night March on the 12th September.—The Battle of Tel-el-Kebir.—The Surrender of Cairo.—Operations of the Cavalry.—Sir Garnet Wolseley in Cairo.—Return to England.—Conclusion 399

GENERAL

LORD WOLSELEY

(OF CAIRO),

G.C.B., G.C.M.G., D.C.L., LL.D.

CHAPTER I.

THE BURMESE WAR.

Introduction.—Parentage.—Early Life.—The Burmese War.—The Advance on Myat-toon's Position.—Ensign Wolseley leads the Storming Party on the 19th of March, 1853.—Is wounded.—Returns to England.

LORD WOLSELEY is one of the foremost and most trusted of England's soldiers. In his conduct of the Ashantee and Egyptian Expeditions he presented a rare combination of dash and foresight, patience and energy, strategical skill and administrative capacity. These pages will show that, alike in the planning and execution of both these campaigns, he took a just view of the difficulties to be encountered, and of the time and measures necessary to overcome them.

But not only for the skill with which he conducted the Ashantee and Egyptian Wars does Lord Wolseley merit the thanks of his countrymen, and the commendation of military critics. He had seen much and varied service since he entered the Army, and the galaxy of medals and stars he

wears on his breast, attests the fact that in every quarter of
the globe, and in every great and almost every 'little' war
in which the British soldier has been engaged since his entry
into the Service, he has participated; while the official records
of these campaigns and sieges show that he has always earned
the encomiums of his commanding officers and the thanks
of his Government.

Lord Wolseley served as a subaltern officer in the Burmese War of 1852-53, and showed in his 'first appearance' on that stage where soldiers achieve distinction—the
field of battle—that he was made of the stuff of which
heroes are fashioned. Again, in the trenches before Sebastopol, which ran with the blood of some of England's
bravest sons, he manifested, under the most trying circumstances, a calm intrepidity which extorted the admiration of
all witnesses. He participated in some of the most striking
episodes of that terrible struggle known as the Indian
Mutiny, which, doubtless, future historians will regard as
exhibiting in their strongest light the patient endurance and
stubborn valour of the British soldier; and again, the
orders and despatches of the General Commanding in the
China War of 1860, show the estimation in which he was
regarded by his military superiors. In the Expeditions to
the Red River and the Gold Coast, when Lord Wolseley
was first entrusted with independent command, he manifested talents for organization and practical knowledge of
the art of war, as well as that peculiar aptitude for inspiring
confidence in those under his command which is among
the chief attributes of military genius. His successful conduct of these arduous operations placed him in the foremost
rank of that small band of Generals from whom any Government, jealous only of the honour of its country, without any
regard to aristocratic connections or political claims, would
feel bound to select the Commander of an army, in the

event of political complications embroiling this country in an European war.

Lord Wolseley is the eldest son of the late Major G. J. Wolseley, of the 25th King's Own Borderers, and was born at Golden Bridge House, County Dublin, on the 4th June, 1833.

The family of Wolseley is one of the most ancient in the county of Stafford, the manor of Wolseley having been in their possession before the Conquest. Among their progenitors was Sewardus, Lord Wisele, fifth in descent from whom was Robert, Lord of Wolseley in 1281; and Ralph, another descendant, was a Baron of the Exchequer in the reign of Edward IV. There are two baronetcies in the Wolseley family. The senior title was among the first creations of James I., and dates from the year 1628. Sir Charles Wolseley, the second baronet, represented the county of Stafford in the Parliaments of Charles I. and Charles II.; he was also high in favour with the Protector, and was a man of much consideration in those times. Richard Wolseley, a younger son of the second English baronet, was a captain in the service of King William III., and had three sons, the eldest of whom, on the death of his uncle, succeeded as fifth baronet to the English title and estates. Captain Wolseley devised his Irish property to his youngest son, Richard, who, in 1744, was created a baronet of 'Mount Wolseley, Carlow,' in Ireland. His eldest son, Sir Richard, succeeded to the title and estates; and the younger, William, Sir Garnet's grandfather, entered the Army and became a captain in the 8th Hussars, in which regiment he served on the Continent. Subsequently he retired from the Service, took holy orders, and became Rector of Tullycorbet, County Monaghan.

Lord Wolseley is not the first of his family who has won military fame; his ancestor, Colonel William Wolseley, having greatly distinguished himself during the Irish war *temp.* William III. This officer,* on the 29th of July, 1689, relieved the hardly pressed garrison of Enniskillen, defended by General Gustavus Hamilton, and advancing with the Enniskilleners, numbering about 3,000 men, defeated the Irish army, 5,000 strong, with guns, commanded by Macarthy (Lord Mountcashel) at Newtown Butler. In those fanatical days 'The sword of the Lord and of Gideon' was the watchword alike among Protestants and Papists; no quarter was given by the stout colonists of Ulster, and 1,500 of the enemy fell by the sword, and 500 were driven into Lake Erne, where they perished miserably. Colonel Wolseley also commanded the Enniskilleners† at the ever memorable battle of the Boyne, on the 1st of July, 1690, when the star of King William, of 'pious, glorious, and immortal memory,' rose in the ascendant, and that of his pusillanimous rival, James II., set for ever in defeat and ruin.

Lord Wolseley was educated at a day-school near Dublin, and later had private tutors. As a boy he was remarkable for his studious habits, and when a mere child had read all

* Lord Macaulay (see his 'History of England,' vol. iii. p. 242) writes of Colonel Wolseley: 'Wolseley seems to have been in every respect well qualified for his post. He was a staunch Protestant, had distinguished himself among the Yorkshiremen who rose up for the Prince of Orange and a free Parliament, and had, if he is not belied, proved his zeal for liberty and true religion, by causing the Mayor of Scarborough, who had made a speech in favour of King James, to be brought into the market-place and well tossed there in a blanket. This vehement hatred of Popery was, in the estimation of the men of Enniskillen, the first of all qualifications of command; and Wolseley had other and more important qualifications. Though himself regularly used to war, he seems to have had a peculiar aptitude for the management of irregular troops.'

† The Enniskilleners commanded by Colonel Wolseley consisted of horse and foot, and are now known as the 6th Dragoons and 27th Regiment. They were raised, respectively, by Colonel Cole (afterwards Earl of Enniskillen) and Gustavus Hamilton (son of Sir Frederick Hamilton, one of the Generals of Gustavus Adolphus, the great Protestant champion), who, for his great services as Governor of Enniskillen, at the Boyne, and the capture of Athlone (which he effected by surprise), was raised to the peerage as Baron Hamilton and Viscount Boyne. The author may perhaps be forgiven for noting his own descent from this nobleman, with whom Wolseley's ancestor was so closely associated, Richard, fourth Viscount Boyne, being his great-grandfather.

EARLY LIFE.

the chief works on military history. It was always his own wish and that of his parents that he should enter the military profession, and his name was put down for a commission when fourteen years of age. His predilection for study was not confined to a liking for one branch of learning, and he was remarkable for proficiency in mathematical studies, and used regularly to go out four or five times a week surveying and acquiring a knowledge of the art of military engineering. He was also versed in fortification and astronomical science, and exhibited his versatility by the proficiency he acquired in such practical pursuits as carpentering and the use of the lathe. His aptitude for military engineering and fortification, and the practical knowledge he acquired of these sciences, as well as of the cognate study of land-surveying, were of great service to him during his career in the Crimea, where he performed the duties of Assistant-Engineer during the siege of Sebastopol, and afterwards when employed surveying in the Quartermaster-General's Department. A high historical authority has said that no 'commander-in-chief is fit for his post who is not conversant with military engineering,' and certainly the successes achieved by Lord Napier in Abyssinia, and Lord Wolseley in the Red River and Ashantee campaigns, may be greatly attributed to their practical knowledge of the science of military engineering.

Lord Wolseley's military career commenced in March, 1852, when he was appointed Ensign in the 80th Regiment, at that time engaged in the Second Burmese War. As reinforcements were required for the regiment owing to the great losses it had sustained by disease more than at the hands of the enemy, he was ordered out from the depôt to the seat of war with a detachment of recruits. Ensign Wolseley, therefore, had not been many months in the Army before he left England on foreign service.

Since those early days in his career, the subject of this memoir has voyaged over many seas, to China and India, to America, the West Coast of Africa, Cyprus, Natal, and Egypt; but at this period of his life, the sea, with all its terrors and fascinations, was novel to him. This his first voyage was made in a sailing-ship, steamers as transports being at the time unknown, for the *Himalaya*, the first of the class, was yet in the ship-builder's yard. His experiences of this long voyage were therefore similar to those of most of us who have voyaged to India by the Cape route in a sailing-ship, and are well summed up by Lord Macaulay in that passage in his biography of Warren Hastings wherein he gives the monotony of the sea as the reason for the first of the famous Viceroys of India doing anything so commonplace as falling in love with the Baroness Imhoff.

'There are few people,' says the great essayist, 'who do not find a voyage which has lasted several months insupportably dull. Anything is welcome which may break that long monotony—a sail, a shark, an albatross, a man overboard. Most passengers find some resource in eating twice as many meals as on land; but the great devices for killing the time are quarrelling and flirting.'

As regards our hero, he passed his time in neither quarrelling nor flirting; for as to quarrelling, though a very fire-eater in the presence of the enemy, he was far from being of a quarrelsome disposition; and as to flirting, why that was out of the question, for the sufficient reason that there were no ladies to flirt with.

Ensign Wolseley arrived in Burmah at a time when the almost unbroken series of successes achieved by the British land and sea forces was dimmed by a sad disaster—the failure at Donabew, which necessitated retributive operations, in which Mr. Wolseley first exhibited those soldierly

ARRIVAL IN BURMAH.

qualities which have made his name renowned in our military annals.

A noted Burmese leader, Myat-toon by name—whom it was the fashion of despatch-writers to style a 'robber-chieftain,' though his countrymen doubtless regarded him as a self-sacrificing patriot—having established himself near Donabew, a force of 272 seamen and marines and 300 Sepoys, under Captain Loch, C.B., of H.M.S. *Winchester*, was despatched against him. On the 3rd of February, 1853, the column marched through fifteen miles of jungle, and on the following morning, after advancing five miles, came to a deep and broad nullah, from the opposite bank of which the enemy, concealed behind a breastwork, opened a heavy musketry fire. Captain Loch made repeated but unavailing efforts to cross the creek, and received a mortal wound; at length, when Mr. Kennedy, First Lieutenant of the *Fox*, and many brave men had fallen, the force retired, and after a fatiguing march of twelve hours, reached Donabew.

General Godwin and the whole army were eager to wipe out the stain of this disaster, and to that able soldier, the late Brigadier-General Sir John Cheape, of the Bengal Engineers (the same distinguished corps that has produced Lord Napier of Magdala), was entrusted the arduous task. Every European soldier that could be spared from Rangoon or elsewhere was hurried up to Prome, and Ensign Wolseley, who had arrived in November with a detachment of about 200 men of his regiment, chiefly recruits, found himself under orders to embark from Rangoon. On the 18th of February, previous to Wolseley's arrival at Prome, Sir John Cheape had left that place, with 800 men, for the purpose of attacking Myat-toon's stronghold; and four days later quitted Henzadah, on the Irrawaddy, some thirty-five miles north of Donabew, and began the march inland, but owing to defective information, and a failure of supplies, he was obliged to fall back on the river, and reached Zooloom on the 28th of February. Thence, on the following day, the greater part of the force moved to Donabew, where they were joined, on the 6th of March, by reinforcements, including 130 men of the 80th Regiment, under the command of Major Holdich,* with whom was Ensign Wolseley.

Again, on the 7th of March, the Brigadier-General started to beat up the quarters of Myat-toon, who had shown himself the most redoubtable of all the leaders of the 'Golden Foot,' as the monarch of Burmah styled himself. The British force consisted of about 600 Europeans and 600 natives, 2 guns, 3 rocket-tubes, and 2 mortars, with a detachment of Ramghur Horse, and 70 Sappers. Being now assured that three days' march would bring them in front of Myattoon's stronghold, General Cheape started at two p.m., on the 7th, taking seven days' provisions with him, but without tents.

About five p.m. the column reached the bank of a broad nullah; at least 130 yards wide, seven miles distant from Donabew. Here the enemy opened a fire of jingals and musketry, and Ensign Wolseley first smelt powder in earnest. The guns having silenced the enemy, the troops passed the night behind a belt of jungle parallel with the nullah; and rafts having been put together by the Sappers, the following day was occupied in passing across the guns and baggage, which operation was not concluded till late at night. The force marched on the 9th, but, about noon, it was said they were on the wrong road; the guide was accordingly flogged, sent to the rear, and another one called up to take his place. The new guide turned to the left, and, after a most tedious round, under a glaring sun, brought the wearied troops back to the identical spot from which they had started. After a halt of two hours, the column

* Now General Sir Edward A. Holdich, K.C.B.

MARCH ON MYAT-TOON'S POSITION. 9

marched to a nullah at Kyomtano, where they encamped. During the night the Burmese showed themselves from the jungles on the left, but the guns opening on them, they soon disappeared; they then came down under cover of the fog, and fired into the camp at a point where the nullah was about fifty yards wide. On the following morning a bridge was extemporized by connecting the rafts with planks, and the troops and baggage were passed across.

On the 11th, the force started at the usual hour (nine a.m.), and everyone expected to reach Myat-toon's position that day. During the march the rear-guard was attacked. The road lay through a thick forest, where the Burmese had only to throw down a tree or two with their usual skill in such matters in order to require a new road to be cut round the obstacle. As they had done this in several places, there was very hard work, and the advance was tedious. Shortly after entering the forest, a small breastwork was taken, and at length, as the Artillery horses were staggering in their harness, the General determined to encamp near some water. Cholera made its first appearance in camp this night.

Myat-toon's position was said to be only two miles to the left, but no reliable information could be gained of the road through the jungle. As provisions were failing, it was thought prudent to return to Kyomtano, about nine miles from Donabew. On the 13th March, all the hackeries (as also the sick and wounded) went into Donabew for provisions, and, on the 16th, returned with ten or twelve days' rations.

It would be hard to exaggerate the difficulties and obstacles encountered on this march. When the small force had, with infinite toil, and suffering severe privations owing to the intense heat and want of water, commenced to close in towards Myat-toon's stronghold, it was found that the approaches had to be made through a dense forest, or thick jungle and heavy brushwood, through which it was necessary to cut every inch of the paths along which the hackeries (or bullock-carts), the guns, and the troops had to pass. This dangerous and fatiguing duty had to be performed under a hot sun, for throughout the entire time occupied by the operations, it was impossible to march until nine a.m., on account of dense fogs, which rose about two in the morning, and wet the men's clothes as effectually as rain, and as there was no such luxury as a change of linen in the camp, the clothes had to be dried on their wearers' backs, only to be drenched again on the succeeding night. There was not a single tent with the force, and the men bivouacked in the fog and dew all night, and marched and fought under the tropical sun all day. But all was of no avail, and owing to the unwillingness or treachery of his guides and the failure of provisions, Sir John Cheape was compelled to retrace his steps to Kyomtano. The heat and hardships the troops had endured during this trying march, induced fever, dysentery, and, worse than all, cholera; 13 succumbed in one day, and over 80 perished from this fell disease, which is the invariable accompaniment of Indian campaigns in which the troops are much exposed.

While halting at Kyomtano, Sir John Cheape ascertained that the jungle to the westward was quite impenetrable, and that there were only two routes to the position occupied by Myat-toon at Kyoukazeen, one to the southward, and the other to the northward by Nayoung-Goun. As there was no choice between these routes as regarded distance, and the same obstacles and opposition were to be anticipated, Sir John resolved to adopt the northerly route.

As Sir John Cheape considered it desirable to give the enemy as little time as possible to strengthen his almost im-

AN ARDUOUS MARCH.

pregnable works, he directed Major Wigston,* of the 18th Royal Irish, to occupy a position of importance some three miles in advance, so as to enable the main force to move early on the following morning. Major Wigston accordingly marched at two p.m., on the 17th of March, with the right wing, consisting of 9 officers and 200 men of the 18th Royal Irish, 3 officers (including Ensign Wolseley) and 130 men of the 80th Regiment, 3 officers and 190 men of the 4th Sikhs, and 33 Madras Sappers. A breastwork in the forest was carried in good style by the 18th Royal Irish, who were leading, supported by the Sikhs, and the column bivouacked here for the night, and was undisturbed.

Sir John Cheape moved early on the morning of the 18th, with the left wing, consisting of 6 officers and 200 men of the 51st Light Infantry, and 8 officers and 380 men of the 67th Bengal Native Infantry, followed by the guns—the entire force† carrying seven days' provisions.

After going about two miles through the forest, and passing breastworks from which only an occasional shot was fired, the guides, instead of proceeding farther by the road which had been followed on the 11th, turned sharp off to the left, along a path bristling with obstructions and felled trees, so that it occupied two hours to perform the distance of one mile.

As they drew nearer to Myat-toon's stronghold, it was found that his dispositions for defence exhibited considerable skill, and were admirably adapted to the nature of his position. The entire country, or rather forest, was defended with strong works, such as stockades, abattis, stakes or fences, according as the nature of the ground seemed to require, while the presence of the enemy was constantly made apparent by a straggling and worrying fire on every side.

* The late Colonel Wigston, who died in September, 1882.
† The total force engaged was 605 Europeans and 22 officers; 608 Sepoys and 12 officers.

They had not proceeded more than a mile from their midday halting-place when a sharp fire opened from the left; but the troops, advancing with great gallantry, carried a breastwork. In this affair Ensign Boileau, of the 67th Native Infantry, was killed, but the enemy suffered severely, though, unfortunately, Myat-toon, who commanded in person, effected his escape to his main position about midway between the Bassein river and the Irrawaddy.

Sir John Cheape lost no time in following up the enemy; but, after proceeding along the road for about a mile, thought it advisable to halt at a piece of water, the surrounding jungle being reported as full of Burmese. At eight p.m. the General fired three rockets as a signal to Commander Rennie, I.N., who, with 80 blue-jackets from his ship, the Honourable Company's steam-frigate *Zenobia*, and Captain Fytche, with his Native levies, was acting in co-operation in the neighbourhood. The rockets were replied to by guns. All that night cholera raged in the camp, and the position of affairs looked very gloomy.

At seven a.m. of the 19th of March the force moved, the right wing leading, with the 80th as the advance-guard, followed by the Sappers clearing the road; the left wing being in rear of the Artillery. This eventful day was not to close without some warm work, in which young Wolseley was destined to play a prominent part. In his life had arrived that most critical and anxious time for which every soldier yearns—the hour had struck in which he was to receive his 'baptism of fire.' Every man who has worn a sword knows full well how many gallant hearts there are in both Services, who have prayed for this most honourable opportunity, but have been denied the distinction they would have earned had a hard fate been more propitious. In his incomparable 'Elegy,' Gray sings how

> 'Hands that the rod of empire might have swayed,'

are bent only on the plough in the painful struggle, continued day by day, to gain a bare subsistence. So, in some remote country town or cheap watering-place, may be seen gallant gentlemen on the Half-Pay or Retired List, who drag out their remaining years in obscurity, 'unhonoured,' as far as medals and decorations go, and 'unsung' by the Muse of History, but who, had they been born under a luckier star, would have been immortalized in history as the possessors of qualities that we recognise in a Napoleon, a Wellington, and a Lee.

If Ensign Wolseley was fortunate in the circumstances of his military career, it is equally certain that he never missed an opportunity. Whenever a chance offered for earning distinction, he eagerly grasped at it, and—being blessed with a sound constitution and an equable temperament, the *mens sana in corpore sano*, so much lauded by the Roman poet—was enabled to pass with unbroken health through the hardships of campaigns conducted in the most deadly climates of the world, and to return to duty after receiving severe wounds.

A storming-party was told off, consisting of the 80th Regiment, supported by the 18th Royal Irish and the 4th Sikhs. On coming opposite the enemy's left flank, the firing commenced, and the rockets were advanced and opened fire. The Sappers worked away at the path, which was much entangled with wood, and the guns were shortly got into position and opened fire. Then the storming-party advanced, but were met by so heavy a fire that both the senior officers, Majors Wigston and Armstrong, and many men, were wounded. 'On reaching the front,' says the General in his despatch, 'I found that Major Armstrong was also wounded, as well as many other officers and men, and that the fire of the enemy on the path leading up to the breastwork was so heavy, that our advanced party had not succeeded in carrying it; the most strenuous exertions were made, and Lieutenant Johnson,* the only remaining officer of the 4th Sikh Local Regiment, persevered most bravely, but it only increased the loss. The 80th and Sikhs then went on in the hope of getting round the extreme right of the enemy. The jungle, however, was so thick, and the abattis so strong, that our men got dispersed, and could not get through it.'

Ensign Wolseley's personal share in this first effort to storm the enemy's works was cut short, doubtless fortunately for himself, by an accident. He speaks with admiration of his associate in the perilous honour of leading the stormers, young Allen Johnson of the 4th Sikhs. He himself being well in advance of his men, had reached within twenty yards of the breastwork, when, suddenly, the earth gave way under him, and he found himself precipitated into a covered pit (technically known as a *trou de loup*), having pointed stakes at the bottom, with which, among other obstructions, the Burmese had studded the narrow entrance to their position. When his men were beaten back, he was in great danger of being killed by the enemy; but after a time he managed to rejoin the detachment, which had fallen back and got scattered. The task allotted to the 80th was certainly a very trying one for a body of men consisting almost entirely of recruits who had never before been under fire; to carry an almost inaccessible position, held by a numerous and invisible enemy, was a duty that was calculated to put to the test the steadiness of veteran soldiers.

The General now determined to try the 18th Royal Irish, but the fire of musketry and grape was so heavy, that they also fell back having sustained loss, including Lieutenant Cockburn,† who was wounded. Although it was difficult, from the dense smoke, and under so heavy a fire, to discern

* Now Major-General Allen Johnson, C.B., Military Secretary to the Secretary of State for India.
† This gallant young officer died shortly after of his wound.

exactly what lay between the assailants and the breastwork, the General—who was now joined by Major Holdich, of the 80th, who succeeded to the command of the right wing on Major Wigston being wounded—at length ascertained that there was no water, and no obstacle that could not be easily surmounted, if only the troops could pass through the enemy's fire, a distance of some thirty yards. The 'assembly' was, accordingly, sounded, with a view of getting together as many men of the right wing as could be collected.

In the meantime, Major Reid, of the Bengal Artillery, brought up, in the most gallant manner, his 24-pounder howitzer, which was dragged through the bushes by hand (chiefly by volunteers from the 51st Regiment), and opened with canister within 25 yards of the enemy, with deadly effect. The gun was, however, in a much exposed position, and Major Reid was almost immediately wounded, upon which the command devolved upon Lieutenant Ashe, who kept up the fire with spirit.

'Finding,' says the General, 'the right wing much weakened from the loss they had sustained, and the number of men it was necessary to employ as skirmishers on the banks of the nullah for the purpose of keeping down the enemy's fire, I ordered a reinforcement from the left wing; they were joined by the men of the right wing that had been collected by Major Holdich, and who were led by Ensign Wolseley, and the whole advanced in a manner that nothing could check. The fire was severe, and I am grieved to say that gallant young officer, Lieutenant Taylor, 9th Madras Native Infantry, doing duty with H.M.'s 51st Light Infantry, fell mortally wounded. Ensign Wolseley, H.M.'s 80th Regiment, was also struck down, as well as many other gallant soldiers; but the breastwork was at once carried; and the enemy fled in confusion, the few who stood being shot or bayoneted on the entrance of our men.'

In this second attempt to storm the enemy's position, which ended in a complete and glorious success, the chief honours were borne off by Lieutenant Taylor, who fell a sacrifice to his gallantry, and Ensign Wolseley, who nearly shared a like fate, though, happily for his country, a merciful Providence bore him through that terrible fire to increase his renown on many battlefields. Taylor led the men of the 51st, and when Major Holdich called for volunteers from his own regiment, Wolseley immediately responded, and, though much shaken by his accident, offered to lead the storming-party. In a few minutes he had hastily collected such of his men as were within call, and was ready for a second attempt. The two young officers, without a moment's hesitation, made a rush up the path leading over the breastwork, which was so narrow that but two men could advance together. Almost at the same moment, while well in advance of their men, and racing for the honour of being first in the enemy's works, they were both shot down, and, strange to say, were wounded exactly in the same spot. A large iron jingal ball struck Wolseley on the left thigh, tearing away the muscles and surrounding flesh. Feeling the blood flowing from the wound, with great presence of mind he pressed his fingers on the veins, and so slightly staunched the bleeding. Fortunately, in his case, the artery, which was laid bare, was not severed, whereas with poor Taylor the artery had been cut, and so he bled to death in a few minutes before assistance could come.

As Wolseley lay helpless on his back, he, with unabated resolution, waved his sword, and cheered on his men, and though some of them offered to carry him to the rear, he refused, and lay there until the position was gained by the gallant fellows, who emulated the example of their youthful leader.*

* Speaking of his own men, Wolseley says that, after he received his wound, Sergeant-Major Quin greatly distinguished himself by the intrepid

Mr. Wolseley received the most prompt attention at the hands of Assistant-Surgeon Murphy, who immediately applied a tourniquet to the wound, and to his skill and care he attributes, under Providence, his recovery. For six months he had a soldier in constant attendance upon him, as there was great danger of his bleeding to death. During all that time his constitutional strength was severely taxed, owing to the suppuration, which was constant and profuse, and he was given to understand that his condition was one of grave anxiety, for had the sloughing extended to the artery, which was much apprehended, nothing could have saved his life. But, thanks to a sound constitution, unimpaired by youthful excesses or hard living, he gradually gained strength, and though he had to use crutches for some time after his arrival in England, no permanent injury was sustained either to his general health or to the limb affected.

In the captured works were found the 2 guns which fell into the enemy's hands on the 4th of the previous month. They had been well served to the last, and in attempting to carry off one of them, 12 Burmese were killed by a well-directed discharge from a nine-pounder gun. The enemy sustained heavy loss in killed and wounded. His whole force and means were concentrated in this position, and the General was of opinion that he must have had about 4,000 men in the breastworks, which extended some 1,200 yards in length. Myat-toon, the Burmese leader, escaped with

---

manner in which he led the detachment. This gallant soldier, who afterwards served in the 78th Highlanders, was offered a commission for his bravery on this occasion, which, however, he declined. The General wrote in his despatch: 'Lieutenant Trevor, of the Engineers, with Corporal Livingstone, and Private Preston, of the 51st Light Infantry, first entered the enemy's breastwork, the two former each shooting down one of the enemy opposing their entrance. The lead devolved on them and on Sergeant Preston, of the 51st, and Sergeant-Major Quin, of the 80th, when Lieutenant Taylor, Ensign Wolseley, and Colour-Sergeant Donahoe fell in the advance.'

about 200 followers. Owing to the assistance of Captains Tarleton, R.N., and Rennie, I.N., by one p.m. of the 21st, a sufficient number of boats was ready in the nullah for the conveyance of the artillery, and the sick and wounded, Ensign Wolseley being of the party. The whole were shipped on board the steamer on the following morning, and arrived at Donabew the same day. Mr. Wolseley, with all the bad cases of the sick and wounded, was then transhipped to the *Phlegethon*, which was despatched to Rangoon.

On the evening of the 24th of March, the whole force had arrived at Donabew, and thus ended the last service of importance of the Burmese War. The loss in killed and wounded during the operations, between the 27th of February and the 19th of March, was 2 European officers* killed, and 12 wounded; 1 Native officer killed, and 1 wounded; 18 non-commissioned officers and rank and file killed, and 93 wounded. Of these casualties, 11 were killed, and 9 officers and 75 men were wounded, in the action of the 19th of March, when the fire was pronounced by Sir John Cheape—a veteran who had conducted the engineering operations at the second siege of Mooltan in 1849, and was present at the 'crowning mercy' of Goojerat —to be 'the most galling he had ever seen.' Myat-toon, styled a robber, and for whose head a reward of 1,000 rupees was offered, though he asserted that he had a commission from his sovereign, displayed military capacity of a high order in the choice of his position, the manner in which he

---

* The following were the officers killed and wounded :—Killed : Lieutenant Taylor, 9th M.N.I. ; Ensign Boileau, 67th B.N.I. Wounded : Bengal Artillery, Major Reid, severely. Madras Artillery, Lieutenant Magrath, slightly. Bengal Engineers, Lieutenant Trevor, slightly. 18th Royal Irish, Major Wigston, severely; Lieutenant Cockburn, mortally; and Lieutenant Woodwright, slightly. 80th Regiment, Lieutenant Wilkinson, severely ; Ensign Wolseley, severely; and Assistant-Surgeon Murphy, slightly. 67th B.N.I., Lieutenant Clarke, severely. 4th Sikhs, Major Armstrong, severely ; and Lieutenant Rawlins, severely.

strengthened it, and the resolution with which he withstood the assaults of a disciplined force with guns. He inflicted on the first Expedition the severest check and the heaviest loss we had experienced throughout the war, and was not routed by Sir John Cheape without heavy loss, and then confessedly only by a final desperate effort. Though the arena of the encounter was in a remote jungle, where special correspondents, unknown in those days, had not penetrated, it is certain that British gallantry has not often received a brighter illustration than in the stubborn efforts, at length crowned with victory, made by that handful of soldiers.*

This service, which was the last performed by Sir John Cheape, was also the first seen by young Wolseley, who received here a scar which he will carry to his grave, the first of those honourable mementoes of valour and patriotism. It was a service that merited the Victoria Cross; and had the order 'For Valour' been instituted in those days, most surely Ensign Wolseley would have added the magic letters V.C., to the numerous other distinctions he is entitled to bear.

An officer of the 80th Regiment, who, at the forcing of Myat-toon's position, received a severe wound in the arm, gives some interesting anecdotes of our hero at this time.

When Mr. Wolseley accompanied his regiment from Rangoon to take part in the operations against Myat-toon, a soldier, who was bathing with some comrades in the Irrawaddy, was carried away by the current. Seeing the man

* The Burmese War cost the Indian Government two millions of money, and the great sacrifice of life was a high price to pay even for the fertile province of Pegu. Between January, 1852, and May, 1853, 54 officers and 1,353 European soldiers, and 2,000 Sepoys died from the effects of climate and disease alone, exclusive of the large number who fell in action during the military operations. The military and naval forces engaged in Burmah received a medal and six months' batta, together with some prize-money, which was not distributed until ten years later.

in imminent danger of drowning, young Wolseley plunged into the stream, which ran with great velocity, but, notwithstanding all his exertions, the unfortunate soldier perished.

In the severe fighting on the 19th of March, Ensign Wolseley, says his brother officer, seeing his men hang back, headed the advance-guard, which consisted of only 3 or 4 men; it was then that he fell into the pit as mentioned in the preceding chapter, and to this circumstance he doubtless owed his preservation from death. After Wolseley made his retreat under a hot fire, and returned to his regiment, his brother officer was severely wounded in the arm; and Wolseley bound up the wound, and attended him when, owing to the heat of the sun and loss of blood, he became faint. When Wolseley, in company with Taylor, headed the second storming-party, and received his severe wound in the leg, the officer in question, who had lent him the only shirt he had besides the one on his back, mentally ejaculated, 'There goes my change of linen!' for he never expected to see any more of either his friend or his garment, a loss almost equally to be deplored in a campaign when an officer's kit consisted of little more than the towel and bit of soap considered sufficient by Sir Charles Napier.

Wolseley and his friend, with the other wounded, remained all night in the stockade, and, on the following morning, were put into a canoe and escorted down the river to a place of safety. The sailors prematurely set fire to the stockade, and Sir John Cheape and others narrowly escaped death. It was owing to his remembrance of this circumstance that our hero, during his Ashantee campaign, issued an order that no stockades or other entrenchments were to be fired before instructions had been given by himself, or some other responsible authority.

As it was apparent, on Ensign Wolseley's arrival at Rangoon, that his wound was of so serious a nature as to render his return home necessary, in May he embarked for England in the *Lady Joceyln*, steamer. The voyage home was performed without any noteworthy incident, beyond the circumstance that, during the four months of the passage, he suffered greatly from his wound, and was only convalescent and out of danger shortly before his arrival in England. Though his absence from his native land had been brief, it had been eventful, and on being released from a long period of confinement and suffering, and treading once more the turf of old England, his feelings were not inaptly described in Wordsworth's lines:—

> ' 'Tis joy enough and pride
> For one hour's perfect bliss, to tread the grass
> Of England once again !'

In the autumn of 1853, Ensign Wolseley proceeded to Dublin to stay with his family, and, on having sufficiently recovered his health, went to Paris, accompanied by a brother officer. He did not rejoin his old regiment, but was posted to a lieutenancy, without purchase, in the 90th Light Infantry, with which his name and fame are identified, although the officers of the 80th have cause to remember with pride that he made his *début* in the arena of arms in their regiment.

CHAPTER II.

THE CRIMEAN WAR.

The Crimean War.—Captain Wolseley proceeds to Sebastopol.—Work in the Trenches.—The Bombardment of the 9th to the 17th of April.—The Attack on the Quarries.—Gallant Services of Captain Wolseley.—The Assault of the 18th of June.—The Third, Fourth, and Fifth Bombardments of Sebastopol.—The Affair of the 30th of August.—Captain Wolseley is severely Wounded.—Service in the Quartermaster-General's Department.—Return to England.

THE winter of 1853 was a momentous period. Already were audible the distant mutterings of the storm brewing on the Turkish frontier, which was destined soon to break over Europe, and deluge a remote corner of the Continent with the blood of the bravest of three great Powers.

It was the eve of the Crimean War, a memorable contest in which was broken the spell of a forty years' peace, and which was destined to be the precursor of an era of conflict, which there is too much reason to fear has not yet been closed. Within the quarter of a century since passed, how many and vast have been the changes that have occurred and how stupendous the conflicts we have witnessed! An Empire has been founded, and a petty Kingdom has risen to the rank of a great Power; our ally of Crimean days, whose boast it was that Europe could only be at peace when she was satisfied, has expelled from her soil the dynasty of her mightiest soldier, and, after having drunk at the hands of her ancient foe of the bitter cup of defeat, spoliation and dismemberment, which she undertook, 'with a light heart,' to force upon her neighbour, has risen Phœnix-like from her ashes, under the ægis of the same form of government which produced a Hoche and a Dumouriez to lead her armies to victory.

The combined British and French Expedition sailed from Varna on the 3rd of September, 1854, and landed, without meeting any opposition, at Old Fort, near Eupatoria, on the 14th of that month. The troops at this time numbered 58,000 men, of whom 25,000 were English. The latter were under the orders of Lord Raglan, a tried veteran who had won the good opinion of his former chief, Wellington; and our Allies were commanded by Marshal St. Arnaud, who, dying soon after the Alma, gave place to General Canrobert. The fleet of war-ships and transports formed the most mighty Armada the world had seen; but, on the element where Briton and Gaul had so often fiercely contended, there was none to oppose them, and the laurels won by our sailors were gained on shore in the trenches before Sebastopol, or at the bombardments of Kertch and Kinburn.

On the 19th of September, the Allied Army quitted their encampment at Kalamita Bay, and, after a weary march, bivouacked on the right bank of the Bulganak. That night many brave men slept their last sleep, for, ere the morrow's sun had set, was fought and won the victory of the Alma. Six days later Balaklava surrendered after the memorable and much-discussed flank march, and the siege of Sebastopol was undertaken.

On the 10th of October, the first parallel, about 1,000 yards in extent, was traced at a distance of 1,350 yards from the Russian works; and on the 17th of October, the whole of the French and English batteries, the latter mounting 73 guns and mortars, assisted by the fleet, commenced to bombard the Russian works. At this time the Malakhoff had been reduced to a ruin, and the Redan was completely silenced, but unfortunately, although the troops were told off to storm, the attempt was not made. With wonderful energy and resource, the Russians repaired and strengthened their works, and, in a few days, possessed an artillery fully double that of the Allies.

On the 25th of October was fought the Battle of Balaklava, and, on the 5th of November took place the desperate struggle at Inkerman, the 'soldiers' battle' as it was called.

As it was now apparent that the siege would be prolonged, probably throughout the winter, preparations were made to withstand the onslaught of enemies far more dreaded than the Muscovite. Cold, the bitter cold of an almost Arctic winter, attacked the soldier without, while disease, the result of privation, gnawed at his vitals.

After the Battle of Inkerman, Lord Raglan made urgent requests for reinforcements to fill up the gaps caused by that sanguinary struggle and the demands of the siege. At this time that gallant soldier and ex-Governor-General of India, Viscount Hardinge, was Commander-in-Chief, and his Lordship had determined very wisely to abolish an exemption enjoyed by Light Infantry Regiments and the Rifle Brigade, by which they were relieved from service in the East. The 52nd and 43rd had gone out to India, and the 90th were warned for service there in the following year. However, Lord Raglan's demand for every soldier that could be spared, shook the expressed determination of the Horse Guards' Chief that the 90th should go nowhere, not even to the Crimea, until they had first served in India; and, yielding to the inevitable, that regiment, then quartered in Dublin, was ordered to embark forthwith for the seat of war. Lieutenant Wolseley was so disgusted by the prohibitory order regarding service in the Crimea, that he and a brother officer, Captain Barnston, had made all arrangements to exchange into a corps before Sebastopol, when the orders arrived for immediate embarkation. He describes how they were at church when the Colonel received telegraphic news of Inkerman, accompanied by the peremptory orders of the Field-Marshal Commanding-in-Chief. And so our hero, who had by this time quite recovered from his wound, was again placed in a position to win that distinction for which every soldier sighs.

The regiment sailed from Dublin on the 19th of November, 1854, and, landing at Balaklava on the 4th of December, immediately proceeded to the front. The first object that greeted Wolseley's eyes as he stepped out of the boat on to the inhospitable shores of the Crimea, was a firelock which lay half in and half out of the water. Lifting it up, he found it marked 'G Company,' and identified it as one of the Minié rifles that lately belonged to his own company. In those days when 'Brown Bess,' with her well-known proclivity of 'shooting round corners,' was the arm with which the British soldier was marshalled for battle, only a small portion, about twenty men of each company, were supplied with the Minié rifles; and, as the demand for these weapons during the Crimean War was greater than the supply, the 90th gave up their rifles, and placed their trust once more in 'Brown Bess.' Probably this arose from their being destined for India, where, we suppose, our experiences during the Afghan War had failed to teach the authorities how infinitely superior was the native 'juzail' to that antiquated, but, in the eyes of martinets of the old school, infallible weapon. The 90th, accordingly, landed at Balaklava armed with the musket, and, on the following day, marched down to the trenches.

The mismanagement which was so conspicuous in almost every military department, was apparent at this early stage of the Crimean experiences of the 90th Regiment.

The distance from Balaklava, the base of operations, to

the camps by way of the Col de Balaklava—which was the road we were forced to adopt in preference to the Woronzoff Road, after the Russians occupied the Turkish redoubts on the 25th of October—was about nine miles, and, until the construction of a tramway, the road was quite unformed, and without any metalling. The traffic was stated to be equal to that along Piccadilly, but yet to form and macadamize such a road, the working-party consisted at first of 400, and subsequently only of 150 sickly Turks, some of them too weak even to dig, and none working more than four hours a day. Besides the difficulty of procuring labour, the road itself passed through a rich alluvial soil, while the stones, which were only procurable about three-quarters of a mile distant, had to be carried by manual labour, the transport being insufficient to supply the troops with provisions. Such was the road along which the 90th Regiment marched when proceeding to the front, and such their first experience of service before Sebastopol.

Their arrival, and that of other reinforcements, must have been hailed with joy by the troops investing this fortress, if that could be called an investment in which the enemy were in a position to receive reinforcements, while almost surrounding the position of the Allies and blockading the base of supplies at Balaklava.* Before the landing of these reinforcements, the French Army mustered 39,450 men, while the British, who held an extent of ground, including the right and left attacks, of nine miles, numbered about 22,369 effectives, there being no less than 10,090 sick on the 30th of November, 1854. When we contrast the numerical inferiority of the Allies with the strength of the Russians, we cannot but be filled with admiration at the constancy and courage that animated every man, from Can-

* In the last days of December, the Russians withdrew from the valley of the Tchernaya, and abandoned the old Turkish redoubts, concentrating their troops in Sebastopol.

ARRIVAL BEFORE SEBASTOPOL.

robert and Raglan to the drummer and private in the ranks. Prince Menschikoff had under his orders, after the arrival of the 4th Corps d'Armée and other reinforcements, an army of 82,000 men, and though, according to what Fluellen would call 'the true disciplines of the wars,' the investing force should be double or treble that of the besieged, the latter was more numerous, and possessed a more powerful artillery.

The 90th arrived in the lines before Sebastopol on the 5th of December, and, on the following morning, went down to the trenches. In those days staff officers did not come up to the standard now exacted at Sandhurst, and Wolseley recounts how when his regiment was ordered to the front, no staff officer appeared to show them the way to the trenches. However, they managed to find their way down, and proceeding to the foremost rifle-pits, four or five companies, including Wolseley's, at once became engaged with the enemy, who opposed their rifles to the antiquated British musket. Presently the Russians opened fire with shot and shell, when the order came for the 90th to cease firing.

The first serious fighting that took place after our hero's arrival before Sebastopol, was on the night of the 11th of December, when the Russians made sorties against both the English and the French positions, and, again, on the 20th of December against the English lines.

Since his arrival before Sebastopol, Lieutenant Wolseley had been employed with his regiment in the trenches, but he was soon selected for the post of Acting-Engineer, the number of officers of the Royal Engineers being unequal to the severe work entailed upon them by the protracted siege. He was posted, accordingly, to the right attack on the 30th of December, and did duty for the first time as Assistant-Engineer on the 4th of January, 1855. On that day he was employed in 'Gordon's Battery,' and the working-party, consisting of only 31 men and 28 Sappers, 'finished laying two platforms, relaid the sleepers of a third, and cleared out the drains in the third parallel.'*

On the 1st of January, 1855, the effective of the British army, according to returns furnished at the time to Lord Raglan, numbered only 1,045 officers and 21,973 men. The French army, meanwhile, had received considerable reinforcements, and mustered at the same date about 67,000 of all arms. Their arrangements were also further advanced than ours. Their batteries were armed, their trenches had approached to within 180 yards of the Flagstaff Bastion, and they expected soon to be in readiness to assault Sebastopol in conjunction with their Allies. On our side, however, the insufficient number of workmen had retarded the construction of the defensive and offensive works, and the engineering operations were greatly hindered for want of such essentials as timber for the platforms and magazines, which could not be removed from Balaklava, where it was stored, owing to the limited supply of transport.

Throughout the siege the Engineers had to carry on their duties under the greatest difficulties, and generally without obtaining that support which was essential to the success of their operations. Irrespective of the inclemency of the weather, and the rocky nature of the soil, which rendered the construction of siege-works a task of great labour, the Engineers had to make up for their numerical paucity by increased exertions. The term of duty for Engineer officers was never less than twelve, and sometimes even twenty-four hours; and, after returning from the trenches, they had to write the report of the day's proceedings. Although skilled labour was in great demand for the construction of wharves,

* By the courtesy of General Browne when Deputy Adjutant-General at the Horse Guards, we have been enabled to make extracts from the original reports of the Engineer officers of the right attack throughout the siege, including those of Lord Wolseley.

hospitals, and storehouses at Balaklava, also for the road to the front, and the hutting of the troops and horses, as well as to carry on the siege and defensive works, yet the total effective force of Engineers on the 1st of January was only 28 officers and 395 non-commissioned officers and men.

Between New Year's Day and the 13th of January the weather was very unfavourable. At times the snow-storms and heavy drifts rendered it necessary to suspend the works entirely, and on the 13th of January the frost set in with so much severity that it was difficult to make any impression ou the ground even with a pickaxe. The snow lay on the plain from twelve to eighteen inches in depth, and the drifts were in some places dangerous. Owing to the disappearance of all fuel, even roots were eagerly grubbed up by the starving soldiers, and sold at a high price. The appearance of the camp was cold, dreary, and miserable; and no blazing fires could be seen to cheer the men or dry their clothes on their return from the trenches or other fatigue duty.

Owing to this great scarcity of wood, the sufferings of the troops on the exposed plateau of Sebastopol were much aggravated; and when a large supply of charcoal arrived at Balaklava, as no means of transport was available other than by manual labour, the Turks employed in the trenches were withdrawn from the Engineers, and the siege-works in consequence suffered.

During the latter half of January the British attacks had been so feebly guarded, owing to sickness, that, according to the official report, 'the covering party for the entire right attack, upwards of a mile in extent, never had exceeded, during this period of the siege, 350 men, and, on the night of the 21st of January, it mustered only 290 men. The guards for the other attacks were equally small.' According to Sir John Jones, the eminent Engineer officer of the Peninsular

War, 'the guard of the trenches ought never to be less than three-fourths of the garrison,' which mustered between 36,000 and 40,000 men. Such were the adverse circumstances under which this unparalleled siege was prosecuted! Fortunately the Russians were deficient in enterprise.

The guard being so small, it often happened that all repairs of importance had to be performed by the Sappers alone;[*] but when, on the 21st January, a French Division relieved the Light and Second Divisions from the guard of the extreme right flank, more adequate parties were furnished for the protection of the batteries and the assistance of the Engineers.

The duty in the trenches[†] was also very severe; and the enemy, by frequent sorties during the night, kept the troops on duty constantly on the alert.

Lieutenant Wolseley, whose talent for sketching and for topographical studies was well known, prepared for General Harry Jones, R.E., who assumed charge of the Engineering Department on the 8th January, a plan of the position of Inkerman, including the trenches. It was required to be done in water-colours; but so intense was the cold that the water froze on his brush, and he had to use charcoal to melt the ice and keep the water from freezing. He succeeded in completing the survey, and preparing the plan to the complete satisfaction of the General.

At this period the weather was very severe and unfavourable for siege operations, so that little progress could be made. The trenches were knee-deep in snow, which, when a shower of rain came on, was converted into liquid mud,

---

[*] Between the 16th and the 21st of January, the number of workmen in the right attack never exceeded 39. According to M. de Bazancourt's 'L'Expédition de la Crimée': 'The French employed daily 4,000 men on the works, and sometimes the number exceeded 6,000.

[†] In the month of January, Wolseley was on day duty in the trenches, on the 4th, 14th, and 24th; and on night duty on the 7th, 10th, 16th, 20th, and 27th.

THE STORY OF HIS PROMOTION. 31

employing the men in clearing it out from the trenches, or cutting drains as outlets for the water.

At this time occurred a singular circumstance in connection with Lieutenant Wolseley's promotion to a captaincy. He was gazetted to his company in December, 1854; but fourteen days after, the authorities, considering him too young—he was exactly twenty-one and a half years of age—cancelled the promotion they themselves had authorized. Considering this as a slur cast upon him, Wolseley at once wrote expressing his intention to resign his commission unless he was immediately reinstated; and, fortunately for his country, the order was rescinded. Some time afterwards Captain Wolseley learned the true cause of this extraordinary freak of the authorities; and it was this. The father of an officer of the 77th went to the Horse Guards and asked why his son, who was older than Captain Wolseley, had not been promoted to his company? The answer the anxious parent received was, that his son was too young, and that Captain Wolseley's promotion was an exception to the rule, *because he rose from the ranks*. Subsequently finding out the blunder they had committed, and that Wolseley had *not* risen from the ranks, the said authorities cancelled his promotion, only to reinstate him as before mentioned, and so ended this 'Comedy of Errors.'

The night of the 11th February was very stormy, and so inclement was the weather that no work was done in the left attack. Captain Wolseley,* who was in sole charge of a party of men in his (the right) attack, was busily employed, but on applying to the field officer on duty for a

---

* The day duty was generally from eight or nine a.m. to four or six p.m.; and the night duty from seven p.m. to four a.m. During the month of February, Captain Wolseley was on duty in the trenches—day, 7th, 15th, 22nd; night, 3rd, 11th, 18th. The working-party on this night, the 7th of February, which may be considered of an average strength, was constituted as follows: Line, first relief, 134 men; second relief, 140 men. Sappers, 4 brigades, or 32 men. Turks, 52 men.

larger number of men, his request was refused on the ground of the inclemency of the weather. On the 13th February, Captain H. C. Owen, R.E., arrived from England, and was appointed to duty with the right attack. On the first occasion of his proceeding to the trenches, which was in company with Captain Wolseley, the gallant officer proposed that they should proceed at once to trace out a new battery, the work then in hand. Wolseley vainly tried to dissuade him, as it was still light and the attempt might draw the enemy's fire upon them. However, Captain Owen was full of ardour, and Wolseley was not the man to throw cold water on any adventure, however risky; so they set to work. But, speedily, the Russians opened fire from all the surrounding rifle-pits; two men were killed, and Wolseley's coat was pierced by a ball. So the work was postponed till nightfall, when it was successfully accomplished.

On the 15th February, when Captain Wolseley was on duty with Captain Craigie, R.E., the weather being more favourable, the working-parties were increased to 400 men, and 48 Sappers; and on the 18th and 22nd, when an almost equal number were employed, the work in the trenches progressed rapidly. On their part the Russians were not idle in their works facing the right attack.

Early in March, upwards of 3,000 yards of parallel and approach had been made in the right attack; and, in the left, upwards of 4,200 yards. All this had been done on very rocky ground, with the enemy's works only 600 yards distant at the nearest point.

Captain Craigie, the Engineer officer in charge of the trenches on the 13th of March, who had never once been absent from his post, was killed in a somewhat singular manner. Captain Wolseley, on relieving him, asked if anything particular was going on. 'No,' said Craigie, 'matters are much as usual.' And so, bidding each other 'good-night,'

INCIDENTS OF DUTY IN THE TRENCHES. 33

they parted, he to return to his quarters, and Wolseley to take charge of the trenches. At this time an Artillery duel was in progress, but the Russian practice was wild, and their shells mostly burst short, causing the officers and men much diversion. They were in the middle of their merriment, when a sergeant arrived with the intelligence that Captain Craigie was killed. He was several hundred yards in rear of the batteries, and was in the act of giving a light to a Sapper from his pipe, when one of these erratic shells killed him instantly.

On the morning of the 17th of March,* when Captain Wolseley, accompanied by Captain King, R.E., went on duty, it was discovered that the enemy had formed new rifle-pits in front of the French on our right, which enfiladed the British new right advance. As it was impossible to employ the working-party† of 150 men, application was made to the officers commanding the Royal Artillery and Naval Brigade batteries, to open fire on these pits. The former fired only a few shots, but the sailors made such good practice with their eight-inch guns, that they knocked over the parapet, and sent the occupants flying out of the pits. A good day's work was then performed, under the directions of Captains Wolseley and King.

The Russians‡ continued to receive reinforcements, while their supply of guns was practically inexhaustible; their fire on the right attack during the latter part of March, was officially described as 'very heavy,' and among the casualties was Major J. W. Gordon, second in command of the siege

* Captain Wolseley was on duty during this month; day duty, 10th and 17th; night duty, 13th, 19th, and 30th.
† The total number of men employed in the trenches at this time, was 2,100, from which were furnished the working-parties, as well as the guards necessary for the defence of the batteries and parallels.
‡ The Russian infantry in Sebastopol, in April, numbered 36,600. There were besides, near the town, 35,400; at Eupatoria, 34,600; and in other parts 13,000. Total in the Crimea, including 15,000 cavalry, and 8,000 artillery, 142,600 men.

3

operations, who was severely wounded on the night of the 22nd, when the Russians made a determined sortie, not inaptly styled 'Inkerman on a small scale,' but were repulsed. During the early part of April, the Engineers were very busy preparing for the bombardment, which had been decided on by the Allied Commanders. On the 3rd, when Captain Wolseley was on duty, the enemy kept up a heavy fire, one of the casualties being Captain Bainbrigge, R.E., who was killed by the explosion of a shell. At this time, Captains Stanton and Armit, R.E., were respectively in charge of the right and left attacks, Major Chapman being in command of the whole, under Major-General Jones, who notified, in General Orders of the 4th of April, his 'great satisfaction with the manner in which the works were executed, reflecting great credit upon them, and the other Assistant-Engineers employed under them.'

On the morning of the 9th of April, the whole of the Allied Artillery opened fire. The British batteries were now armed with 20 thirteen-inch, and 16 ten-inch mortars, and 87 guns, giving a total of 123 pieces of ordnance—of which 49 were manned by the Naval Brigade, and 74 by the Royal Artillery. The French, on their part, opened fire with 303 pieces on the left, and 50 on the right.

The morning of the 9th of April broke in thick fog and drizzling rain, but shortly before half-past five, the mist partially rolled away, permitting the outlines of the Redan and Malakhoff to be seen. Exactly an hour later, the first gun was fired from the British batteries, and, in a few seconds, the whole of both attacks, with the exception of one battery, were in action; shortly afterwards the French opened fire, and the south side of Sebastopol, from the sea to Inkerman, was encircled in what Prince Gortschakoff well called a *feu d'enfer*. The Russians appeared to be taken by surprise, but about six o'clock their batteries began to reply;

though at no time of the day was their fire heavy or effective. The continuous rain and bad weather made the work very laborious, some of the platforms being under water and all very slippery. At dusk the fire on both sides ceased, with the exception of an occasional shell from the mortars. On the following day all our batteries opened fire at daylight, the Russians replying with spirit. Though the fire of the Mamelon was checked, and that of the Malakhoff Tower slackened, our fire made no material impression upon the Redan and Garden Batteries, by which alone it was answered. Much damage was done to the embrasures, magazines, and traverses of the British by the enemy's fire, and the Sappers behaved very well in repairing the embrasures, and even reconstructing them, under fire.

Lieutenant Graves, R.E.,[*] who, with Captains Owen, R.E., and Wolseley, was on duty, was wounded, and Wolseley himself had a narrow escape. The Russian fire had been very heavy, and the Artillery officers reported an embrasure as unserviceable. This, of course, it was the duty of the Engineer officers to repair; but from the proximity and precision of fire of the Russian batteries, it was a service of extreme hazard, for directly a man showed himself above the parapet, he became a mark for the Russian gunners. However, Graves and Wolseley, with two or three Sappers, set to work to repair an embrasure, and while they were building up one cheek with gabions, a round shot from the enemy carried away the other cheek, to which Wolseley had his back turned, killing a Sapper. At the time he was holding on to a handspike, prizing up one sandbag to put another under it, and it was, in racing parlance, 'a near thing' for him; indeed, he received a slight wound from the *débris* scattered by the round shot, though he did not report himself as wounded, it

[*] This gallant young officer was killed by a rifle bullet, on the 18th of June, in the assault on the Redan.

being a point of honour among the Engineers not to leave their post until disabled.

On the night of the 12th, Wolseley was again on duty, when much was done in effecting repairs, laying platforms, and other necessary work. Though our batteries had kept up a hot fire all day, little permanent effect was visible; and, so inexhaustible were the Russian resources, that fresh guns opened fire from embrasures whose guns had been dismounted or silenced. When Wolseley was next on duty, the night of the 15th of April, the enemy was very active, and Lieutenant-Colonel Tylden, R.E., in charge of the right attack, reported: 'Captain Wolseley, Assistant-Engineer, who was in charge of the working-party in the advanced trenches, retired the party from the most advanced part between twelve and one, finding it impossible to keep the men at work under the fire the enemy poured in.' Our loss on this occasion was heavy, being 3 officers killed, and 1 officer and 20 rank and file wounded.

The following incident, which happened on this night, is one of many such during the siege: Captain Wolseley was with Captain E. Stanton, R.E.,* who was sitting behind the Engineer park giving orders to two Sappers standing at attention before him. Suddenly a round shot took one man's head off, and drove his jaw-bone into the other man's face, to which it adhered, bespattering the party with blood. Men got into the way of considering these incidents as almost commonplace, and scarcely noteworthy, but, though such horrors bred a feeling of indifference to danger and death, few could lay claim to the possession of such imperturbable *sang-froid* as Captain W. Peel, R.N., of Her Majesty's ship *Diamond*, then serving on shore in the Naval Brigade. Wolseley, who saw much of Peel and his sailors, confesses that he never saw any man so indifferent in the

* Now General Sir Edward Stanton, K.C.M.G., C.B.

presence of seemingly *certain* death as this gallant sailor, and gives the following instance, among others, of this characteristic. He was walking one day during the bombardment with Captain Peel, in rear of the line of batteries, when a thirteen-inch shell, hurtling through the air, lit on the entrance of a magazine and crushed it in. Just for a passing second, Wolseley stood still, paralyzed as it were, while he waited for the whole party to be blown to atoms, a fate which seemed imminent. But Peel's undaunted heart quailed not even for that infinitesimal portion of time, and he dashed into the magazine, full as it was of powder, without a moment's hesitation or a thought of danger. A second later and Wolseley was by his side, and they were engaged pulling down the sand-bags, which guarded the entrance and were all on fire, and soon the magazine was built up again.

The subject of this memoir has, however, a more modest opinion of his courage than other people who know him well, and have seen him under fire. A distinguished General officer of Engineers, who served in the trenches with Captain Wolseley, perhaps on more occasions than any other man, and therefore had more ample opportunities of observing his bearing under the most trying circumstances, declared to us that he considered him 'the bravest man he ever knew.' He also mentioned that he was noted for always turning his face towards an approaching Russian shell; and, on being interrogated as to his reason for doing so, replied, that in the event of his being killed it could not be said of him that he turned his back on the enemy, or fell while running away from a shell. Such little traits as these give the clue to a man's character.

After eight days' incessant firing, the second bombardment ceased on the 17th of April, without any decisive result having been achieved, and though the Mamelon and

Malakhoff suffered considerably, the guns destroyed, or silenced, by day were replaced at night. On our side, 26 pieces of ordnance were disabled, and our expenditure of ammunition amounted to 47,854 rounds, of which upwards of 15,000 were shell.*

On the 19th of April, the 77th Regiment, led by Colonel Egerton, carried, by assault, the rifle-pits in advance of the right attack, when Colonel Egerton, 1 officer, and 10 men were killed, and 6 officers and 50 men were wounded. On the 18th of May, Lord Raglan, accompanied by General Jones and General de la Marmora, in command of the newly-arrived Piedmontese Division of 17,000 men, inspected the works of the left attack; and, on the 18th, when Captain Wolseley was on duty,† those of the right attack. On the following day, General Canrobert resigned the command of the French army to General Pelissier.

On the 6th of June, the third bombardment took place, when the English batteries mounted 154 mortars and guns. Of these, there were in the right attack 55 pieces, 22 of which were manned by the Naval Brigade; and 99 in the left attack, of which 36 were worked by the sailors. The whole fire of the right of the right attack was to be directed on the Mamelon and the Malakhoff, whilst the left of the right, and the left attack engaged the Redan and Barrack Battery. The Russian works stood out in bold relief under a cloudless sky, offering a strong contrast to the dismal circumstances of the last bombardment. The enemy replied vigorously at first, but about half-past four

---

* During the bombardment the Artillery lost 5 killed and 86 wounded; and the Naval Brigade, which suffered more severely, owing to their practice of not retiring behind the parapet after firing, lost 2 officers and 24 men killed, and 6 officers and 92 wounded.

† During this month, Captain Wolseley was on duty : day, 1st, 5th, 14th, and 18th ; night, 25th, 28th, and 31st. On the three last occasions he was the only Engineer officer with the working-parties, which numbered 150 men, and 20 Sappers.

the Mamelon and Malakhoff were almost silenced, and at dusk, when our fire, except from the mortars, ceased, the Russian works showed unmistakable evidences of the severe handling they had undergone. Our batteries reopened on the 7th, and on that evening was delivered the memorable assault on the Quarries by our troops, and that on the Mamelon by our Allies.

All that day a heavy cannonade was kept up ; but, at six o'clock, when the French and English assaulting columns were formed in the trenches, it burst forth with renewed intensity, the fire, for the hour that it lasted, being the heaviest during the siege.* The Russians had massed men on the Redan, evidently anticipating an assault, and so tremendous was the fire directed on that work, that 'the shells could be seen plunging and cutting gaps in the ranks, blowing the bodies of their victims into the air.'

At half-past six the French captured the Mamelon, and the 'Ouvrages Blancs,' which had been rendered almost untenable by the fire from our batteries, but, advancing towards the Malakhoff, were driven back. The Mamelon was now retaken by the enemy, but, after a renewed fire from the British batteries, once more changed hands.

A few minutes after the French had attacked the Mamelon, the British columns advanced on the Quarries and the Russian trench leading to the Karabelnaia Ravine. The column consisted of detachments of the Light and Second Divisions, who were supported at night by the 62nd Regiment. The command of these troops was entrusted to General Shirley, of the 88th, who was acting general officer of the trenches; and Lieutenant-Colonel Campbell, of Wolseley's regiment, the 90th, led the storming-party, and remained in the Quarries all night in command of the

* During the day the Royal Artillery had 47 killed and wounded, and the sailors 40 ; being the heaviest loss on one day during the siege.

troops. On the Engineer officers of the right attack, however, devolved, according to custom, the honourable and deadly duty of 'showing the way' to the storming column, and also of forming the lodgment after the enemy's works were won, and the communication from the parallel in our occupation, a trying and perilous task, as it had to be completed in the open and under the enemy's fire. Colonel Tylden, R.E., advised as to the attack and distribution of the troops, but the Engineer officers, who actually accompanied the assaulting columns, were Captains Browne, R.E.,* and Wolseley; and Lieutenants Elphinstone, R.E.,† Lowry, R.E., and Anderson, 96th Regiment. Already one officer of the corps, Captain Dawson, R.E., who had been in charge of the engineering duties during the day, had fallen, but he was not destined to be the only Engineer officer sacrificed on the altar of duty in the memorable struggle of the 7th of June.

The Quarries were carried with a rush, though the Russians made three desperate attempts to retake them‡ during the night, and again soon after daylight on the following morning, and it was in resisting these repeated efforts on the part of the enemy that the army sustained its chief loss. Among the officers who thus fell was Lieutenant Lowry, R.E., who was killed by a round shot whilst gallantly cheering on the men. Notwithstanding the frequency of the endeavours of the Russians to regain possession of the Quarries, and the interruptions to which these attacks gave rise, the Engineers made a lodgment of gabions and barrels, and also established the communication with their advanced sap, which, says Lord Raglan, 'redounds to the

---

* Now Lieut.-General J. F. M. Browne, C.B. On the 24th of August this officer was severely wounded in the shoulder by a rifle-bullet.

† Now Colonel Sir Howard Elphinstone, V.C., K.C.B., C.M.G.

‡ The Engineer officer in charge of the right attack says: 'The enemy actually expelled us three times and removed some of our gabions, which were immediately retaken.'

credit of Colonel Tylden, and that of the officers and men employed as the working-party; and I cannot,' adds the Field-Marshal, 'miss the opportunity to express my approbation of the conduct of the Sappers throughout the operations.'

Captain Browne, who was the senior Engineer officer accompanying the assaulting column, after passing a high encomium on the gallant young Lowry, proceeds : ' I beg to report most favourably on the conduct of Lieutenant Elphinstone, R.E., and of Captain Wolseley, 90th Regiment, Assistant-Engineer, who was employed in forming the lodgment and communication. Lieutenant Anderson, 96th Regiment, Assistant-Engineer, was unfortunately wounded in the leg early in the evening.' But the highest honour a soldier can receive, next to the approval of his country and his sovereign, was in reserve for Captain Wolseley, who was specially mentioned in the despatch of the Field-Marshal Commanding-in-Chief, as one of the officers 'who distinguished themselves on this occasion.'

The casualties on the 7th of June were proportionately heavy as the result attained was glorious. 10 officers and 117 rank and file were killed, and 36 officers and 486 men were wounded, besides 18 missing. Of the 6 Engineer officers engaged during the 6th and 7th of June, 2 were killed and 1 was wounded.

Captain Wolseley's personal share in the dangers and glories of this memorable day was arduous, and no officer was exposed for an equal length of time, or to a similar extent, to the perils incident to a bombardment and an assault. The cause of his having this double share of duty, entailing a corresponding increase of fatigue and exposure, we will now detail, as well as his experiences in the assault of the Quarries. For twenty-four hours before the time named for the attack on the Russian works, all the officers detailed for service were kept off duty, so as to be fresh for the arduous work in store for them. Among them, of course, was Wolseley; but in the morning Captain Dawson, who had gone on duty for the first time that day, was killed by a round shot, and he was ordered to take his place. Wolseley was, therefore, all day hard at work as the only Engineer officer of the right attack; and the bombardment was in full progress, requiring all his energies, besides entailing that great mental wear which is incidental to the performance of duties under such a terrific fire as raged on that day. When evening came, and the hour fixed for the assault arrived, most men would have had enough of it, but not so Wolseley; and though he had never quitted the trenches, when the hour struck—big with the fate of so many gallant hearts throbbing with eager expectancy, while they waited for the signal to quit the protection of their batteries to run the gauntlet of the open space ploughed by the death-dealing shells and bullets—Captain Wolseley took his place with the small band of Engineer officers, whose perilous duty it was to accompany the assaulting column.

There were two communications to be made—one between the parallel on the right and the Quarries, which he was directed to carry out; and the second direct between the Quarries and the parallel in rear, under the direction of Lieutenant Lowry. The difficulty of doing much towards effecting the lodgment and communications was enhanced by the fact that of the 800 men detailed as a working-party, only 250 were actually available, the remainder being engaged with the enemy. And so it was throughout this unparalleled siege; the British army was expected to perform, and, as a matter of history, *did* actually perform, duties that required the exertions of a force at least treble their numbers. It was a *dictum* of Nelson's that a British sailor was equal to three Frenchmen, and the saying certainly holds good of the relative value of the British soldier and his Russian foeman.

Wolseley began working the lateral communication too soon, and the enemy's fire was so hot that the party was driven back with loss. Just then he was sent to take the place of poor Lowry, and proceeded to make the direct communication on the open,* between 'Egerton's rifle-pits' and the captured works. While so engaged, he lost one-third of his working-party, and on the three occasions when the enemy expelled our soldiers from the Quarries, only in turn to be themselves driven out, he entered the Quarries with the victorious column. Not often has more desperate hand-to-hand fighting taken place than on that eventful night, and Wolseley's *penchant* for such work was amply gratified. That the position was retained in the end was perfectly marvellous, considering the persistent attacks made by the Russians with overwhelming numbers. Between these assaults he busied himself with building up, on the reverse side of the Quarries, a little parapet composed of anything he could lay his hands on, among the chief ingredients being the bodies of the fallen, friends or foes indiscriminately, the latter thus affording in death the welcome protection they would have denied while living.

Just before daybreak Wolseley saw a dense column of Russians, 'so long that he could not see the end of it,' issue from out of their works with the object of making a final dash to recover the lost Quarries; and had they known the real position of affairs they might have accomplished their purpose, temporarily at least. Our soldiers were so overcome with fatigue by the night's fighting and hard work,

* Gunner and Driver Thomas Arthur received the Victoria Cross for ' carrying barrels of infantry ammunition for the 7th Fusiliers several times during the evening across the open.' On this very 'open,' Captain Wolseley and the other Engineer officers and Sappers were engaged throughout the night.

that it was in vain the officers made the utmost efforts to rouse them from their sleep to resist the enemy. British officers have seldom failed to do their duty under the most trying circumstances, and they did not belie this characteristic of the race on this occasion. Finding their efforts useless, the officers, to the number of 20, with some few non-commissioned officers and men, certainly not more than 60, opened fire, the former with their pistols, on the advancing column; at the same time the bugler sounded, and the little band shouted and cheered to their utmost capacity. Never did the famous British cheer stand in such good stead to British throats as on this occasion. The Russian soldiers, remembering the bloody repulses they had already suffered, first wavered, and finally refused to advance. Wolseley saw the officers by turns imploring and threatening them, but all in vain; they could not be induced to proceed, and the British officers redoubling their efforts, the Russians gave up the task as hopeless and retired, and so ended their last effort to regain the Quarries. But it is the opinion of officers present, that had the Russians shown any enterprise they might have easily overcome the only opposition that awaited them, as there was no force in the Quarries capable of an effective resistance.

After his indefatigable exertions both by word of mouth and example, Captain Wolseley completely lost his voice, and could not speak above a low whisper; and when he was relieved in the morning, so overpowered was he with the exertions of the past twenty-four hours, and the strain upon his faculties, that he fell down from fatigue outside the Quarries, and lay there among a number of dead bodies, himself having the appearance of one numbered with the dead. So thought an officer of his regiment, who, passing by, found his friend lying on a heap of slain covered with blood. Though he had not reported himself wounded,

Wolseley had been hit on the thigh by a bullet from a canister-shot, which tore his trousers, and caused considerable loss of blood. He received this wound just as he got outside the parapet on his way to the Quarries to relieve Lieutenant Lowry. His friend of the 90th roused him with much difficulty, and assisted him to the camp at the Middle Ravine, a distance, allowing for the zigzag road, of over two miles. The kind Samaritan had almost to carry our hero, who was so fatigued that he fell down many times, and had to be roused up again, just as a man might who was intoxicated. It must have been a relief to them both, as it was a cause of thankfulness to Wolseley, when they met Major (now General) Maxwell, who dismounted and lent him his horse, on which, with assistance, he rode the remainder of the way, often nearly tumbling off with fatigue. His position was all the more trying, as he had completely lost his voice, so that when he mustered up sufficient strength to speak he was totally inaudible. And so concluded what Wolseley himself emphatically declares was 'the hardest day's work he ever did in his life.'

'It may be said,' writes Major-General Sir Harry Jones, 'that until the 7th June, when the Quarries, Mamelon, and "Ouvrages Blancs" had been captured and lodgments made in them, the Allies had scarcely gained an advantage over the enemy since October, 1854, a period of seven months.' By the capture of these works the besiegers were placed in a more favourable position for carrying on ulterior operations, while every man in the Allied Armies was inspired with increased spirit and energy, for they regarded these important successes as only the prelude to the fall of the great stronghold that had so long defied their utmost efforts, and attributed them chiefly to the substitution of Pelissier, emphatically a fighting general, for the more easy-going Canrobert. Considering the great strength of the enemy, it is surprising the want of energy they displayed. Their numerical superiority rendered it necessary to be prepared with strong reserves to repel an assault on the trenches by a powerful column; but to do this effectually would have been a task of great difficulty, there being no cover for troops in the immediate rear of the trenches, while the distance to the nearest camp was too great to afford any hope that a body of men could arrive in time to render immediate support. As this circumstance necessitated a stronger guard than is usual at an ordinary siege, the Engineers were unable to obtain the complement of men necessary to carry on the required works.

After the success of the 7th June, Lord Raglan and General Pelissier determined to press on the siege with redoubled energy, and preparations were made for a fourth bombardment, and the assault of the enemy's works extending from the Redan to Careening Bay. Two days after the capture of the Quarries Captain Wolseley was again on duty, accompanied by Lieutenant Darrah, R.E. The Russian fire during the day had been very heavy, and our loss was 3 officers and 7 rank and file killed, and 38 officers and men wounded, a severe loss for what might be called an 'off day.'*

A good many casualties were also caused on the 12th, when Captain Wolseley was on duty, 'by shells from a 2-gun

* Captain Wolseley says in his report, the original of which is lying before us: 'I had a special working-party of 400 men, 50 of whom, with half brigade of Sappers, repaired the embrasures in the 21-gun battery; 100 men, with a brigade of Sappers, revetted all the embrasures in Nos. 9, 12, and 14 Batteries; 50 men, with half brigade of Sappers, were employed mending and placing in a fighting condition the old third parallel and left advance; the remaining 200 men, with a brigade of Sappers, were engaged in the Quarries and the communication to them. They completed a rifle-screen overlooking the Woronzoff Ravine on our left. At two a.m., the battery parties were relieved by 150 men from the guard of the trenches, and the Quarry party by 50 men. All the batteries were placed in admirable repair, and our new lodgment considerably strengthened. The Russians were found to be working outside the proper right of the Redan.'

battery under the Garden batteries, which likewise annoyed the parties in the Quarries during the forenoon,' so that they had to be withdrawn. 'In the afternoon,' continues his report, 'some of the enemy's riflemen climbed up among the rocks on the opposite side of the Woronzoff Ravine under the advanced trenches of the left attack, and caused us some annoyance.' The working-parties of 400 men, besides Sappers, employed on the night of the 14th of June, 'worked well, but were annoyed by shells from the Garden batteries, and grape and canister from the salient gun in the Redan, which caused about ten casualties. The enemy were heard working through the night inside the Redan.' During this time, while our Engineers worked hard preparing for the attack, which it was hoped and anticipated would decide the fate of Sebastopol, the Russians were also busied strengthening the Redan, large parties of troops being seen bringing up gabions and pieces of timber. Between the 14th and 18th of June, our Engineers were employed improving the lodgment in the Quarries.

At daylight on the morning of the 17th of June, the British batteries[*] opened fire for the fourth general bombardment of the defences of Sebastopol, the fleet co-operating against the sea defences.

Our efforts were chiefly directed against the Redan and its flanking works, although the British gunners afforded powerful aid with the mortars of the right attack against the Malakhoff Tower. But though the Redan presented a shattered appearance it was only temporarily silenced, for at night fresh guns were mounted wherever they were disabled by our fire during the day. In the evening Captain Wolseley, accompanied by Lieutenants Graves and Murray, both of whom fell in the assault on the Redan on the follow-

[*] In the right attack were mounted 62 pieces of ordnance; and in the left attack 104.

ing day, went on duty with a working-party of 400 men and 12 Sappers.*

A heavy fire was kept up on the works from the mortars during the night of the 17th, and at daylight all the guns joined in the bombardment. The assault was fixed for the 18th of June, a singular choice, for though the anniversary of Waterloo is a day the memories of which must always exercise an inspiriting effect on British soldiers, the influence must be correspondingly depressing, not to say exasperating, to our Allies when acting in concert with us.

Before three a.m. Lord Raglan was at the signal post, accompanied by the headquarter staff, Generals Jones and Dacres, commanding the Engineers and Artillery; Colonel Warde, commanding Siege Train; and Captain Lushington, R.N., commanding Naval Brigade. Captain Wolseley was also there, having charge of the third parallel of batteries, in which Lord Raglan and staff were assembled. From this position he witnessed one of the most gallant attempts to carry an enemy's works, and at the same time one of the most sanguinary repulses of which we have any record in the annals of war.

No sooner had the three assaulting columns shown themselves beyond the trenches than they were assailed by a murderous fire of grape and musketry, such as Lord Raglan declared he had never witnessed before.

Both the British and French columns of attack were

* The responsibility of the engineering duties, even upon an 'off day,' devolving upon a young officer in his twenty-second year, may be gathered from Wolseley's report of the day's work: '140 men and 2 Sappers, with Major Campbell of the 46th Regiment, were employed carrying materials; 120 men with Lieutenant Graves, 100 men and 2 Sappers with Lieutenant Murray. All these parties were employed carrying materials to the places assigned for them; 20 men and 4 Sappers revetting embrasures in 21-gun battery; 20 men and 4 Sappers revetting embrasures in Nos. 9, 13, and 14 Batteries. These parties worked until two o'clock a.m., after which none were employed. There were three considerable fires in the town in the rear of the Flagstaff Battery. The enemy were working all night at the Redan, and seemed to be strengthening the abattis in its front.'

THE ASSAULT OF THE 18th OF JUNE.

driven back, our casualties being 21 officers, including Major-General Sir John Campbell, and Colonels Shadforth and Yea, and 244 men, killed; and 72 officers, including Major-General Sir William Eyre, Colonels (now Sir Daniel) Lysons, Johnson, Gwilt, and Cobbe, Captain Peel, R.N., and Mr. Midshipman Wood (now Sir Evelyn Wood), and 1,097 men wounded. The Russian loss was 16 officers and 783 men killed, and 152 officers and 4,826 men wounded.

The Engineers suffered heavily on this occasion. Three officers, Captain Jesse and Lieutenants Graves and Murray, were killed; and Major-General Jones, Major Bourchier (Brigade Major), and Colonel Tylden, Director of the right attack, were wounded; the latter officer was shot through both legs and died from the effects of the wounds. Captain Wolseley was near General Jones when he received his wound. He was standing at the time in rear of Lord Raglan, with whom General Jones was in conversation, when the latter, whose head was over the parapet, received a bullet-wound in the temple, which, with his white hair, was all dabbled with blood. Almost at the same time another officer received a severe wound. Wolseley was in conversation with Captains Beresford and Browne of the 88th, when a round shot carried off the arm of the latter, covering a new jacket Wolseley had put on that morning with blood. Captain Browne jumped up from the ground, and actually did not know of the loss he had experienced. To Wolseley's hurried question, 'What's the matter?' he replied, 'Nothing.' So exposed was the position occupied by Lord Raglan, that officers and soldiers, as they passed, cried out to his staff, 'If you want Lord Raglan to be killed, you'll let him stop there.'

The disastrous failure of the 18th of June told severely on the already failing health of Lord Raglan, and he expired on the 28th of June, four days after the death of General

Estcourt, his Adjutant-General. Thus, one by one, all the chief actors in this tremendous drama, had been removed—Nicholas, Menschikoff, St. Arnaud, and finally, Raglan, all were gone.

Lord Raglan was succeeded in the command by Lieutenant-General Simpson, his Chief of the Staff, although there was present with the army Sir Colin Campbell, a soldier who had served with distinction in almost every war in which our troops had been engaged from the battle of Corunna to Chillianwallah. But the 'seniority' system, which was the curse of our army, placing in the highest commands officers whose sole claim to lead our soldiers rested on the accident of birth, or service forty years before in the Peninsula, prevailed at this critical emergency.

After the assault of the 18th June, Captain Wolseley[*] and the other Engineer officers were employed in effecting the necessary repairs to the parapets and platforms consequent upon the damage they had sustained.

The enemy, on their side, guided by the genius of Todleben, were busily employed in strengthening their works, while large convoys were seen daily entering the town from the north, bringing in supplies and munitions to any extent. As the siege progressed, the place increased in strength, and never, perhaps, was an investment carried on under such disadvantages; but still the determination of the allied commanders to prosecute the enterprise to a successful conclusion never faltered, and, like Cato, their cry was 'Delenda est Carthago.'

During the month of July, the efforts of the Engineers were directed towards working up to the enemy's entrenchments, though, situated as they were between the two attacks of the French, and exposed to heavy artillery fire on both

---

[*] During the month of June he was on duty as follows: day duty, 4th, 7th, 12th, 21st, and 28th; night duty, 7th, 9th, 14th, 17th, 23rd, and 26th.

flanks, also from the Garden, Malakhoff, and intervening batteries, including that of the Redan, but little progress could be made in their attack.

Captain Wolseley was on duty on the 1st of July,[*] each relief of the working-party numbering 400 men and 24 Sappers, and the works were carried on under a heavy fire, the enemy shelling the Quarries and the new fourth parallel. On the 8th of July, when he was on night duty in the trenches, the working-party numbered 950 men, besides 20 Sappers; on this occasion, Lieutenant Gerald Graham,[†] of the Engineers, was severely wounded. He says in his report, the original of which is lying before me : 'Lieutenant Graham having been, unfortunately, struck in the face with some stones from a round shot, and, consequently, forced to leave his party on the left advanced sap, the officer of the 62nd Regiment, who commanded the party, withdrew his men, telling the Sapper then in charge, that he considered it too dangerous for linesmen. The enemy kept up a continual fire of shell and grape, and then a number of light balls, which greatly interrupted our work."

Wolseley and his coadjutors in the right attack completed Battery No. 18, for six mortars, and commenced No. 19. They also converted, for the occupation of our troops, the Russian trench nearest the third parallel, a work of great labour, many parts being of rock, and requiring the addition of earth to form a parapet ; and extended the right of the advanced works in front of the Quarries, to form a junction with this trench, which now became a fourth parallel, a perilous and difficult task, owing to the numerous light balls, which burnt nearly half-an-hour. Traverses were thrown up in the Quarries to protect the working-parties and guard of

---

[*] During this month Captain Wolseley was on day duty 1st, 6th, 12th, 15th, and 22nd ; night duty, 3rd, 8th, 15th, 19th, and 22nd.
[†] This officer, as Major-General Graham, commanded a brigade in Egypt, under Sir Garnet Wolseley.

the trenches, from the fire of the Garden batteries and Bastion du Mât. The casualties were heavy, owing to the proximity of the British works to the Redan, from which the enemy maintained a vertical fire from mortars, and discharges of grape and grenades. As this cannonade continued day and night, causing great loss to our troops, and hindering the prosecution of the engineering works, all our batteries that bore upon the Redan opened fire on the 10th of July, which had the desired effect.

The Engineers now being more free from annoyance, extended the fifth parallel as far as the small Quarry, and ran out a sap from its left. The works were pushed on with the utmost alacrity, and at no time of the siege were the Engineer officers harder worked, Wolseley being the only one on duty, on the 12th of July, to direct the two reliefs of the working-party, each of which numbered 400 men, with 24 Sappers. In conjunction with Major Stanton and Lieutenant Somerville, he was on continuous duty for twenty-four hours on the 15th of July. During the afternoon, the enemy opened a very heavy, well-directed fire on the right of the fifth parallel, and the working-party was obliged to be partially withdrawn. Most of the damage was, however, made good during the night; but the labour was very great in consequence of the men having to carry the earth some distance, and there were several casualties from grape and case-shot fired from the left of the Redan.

The night of the 19th, when Wolseley was again on duty, passed off more quietly, and the working-parties were enabled to do a fair average of work. The parapets and batteries were put in a thorough state of repair during the latter part of July, and the platforms for the guns were removed to batteries more in advance, while new communications were made from the third parallel and the Quarries to Battery No. 19. At this time, orders were issued by

ILLNESS OF WOLSELEY.

General Simpson that the night-guard in the trenches of the left attack was to be increased to 1,400 men, and in the right attack to 2,400, under a General of the day, and three field officers. Of this number 600 were to work, if required by the Engineer officers, from four to eight a.m., when they were to return to camp, if they could be spared; the remainder were to furnish working-parties during the day, There was also to be a special working-party of 400 men, independently of the guard, who were to return to camp at daybreak.

On the 22nd of July, Captain Wolseley was again on duty for twenty-four hours.* There were no less than 1,050 men at work in the trenches under the orders of the Engineer officers, besides 52 Sappers and 16 carpenters, and the work was very heavy. During the day, the right attack kept up a fire on the Redan for some hours with mortars, and a shell from the enemy, falling among a heap of carcases in the new batteries of the right attack, ignited about fifty of them, and the gabions being very dry, they also were set on fire; but the flames were extinguished by earth being shovelled over them. During the night also there was hot work, and Wolseley's exertions, under constant fire from grape and shell, were too much even for his constitution. He had been suffering for some time from dysentery, but with that devotion to duty which had characterized him since he joined the besieging force in December of the previous year, he battled against his ailment, and could not be induced to go on the sick list. This arduous and prolonged duty of twenty-four hours, however, incapacitated him for further exertion, and the medical authorities directed

---

* The officer commanding the Royal Engineers in his remarks on the progress of the siege, says : 'The young officers of Engineers, and of the Sappers lately joined from England, suffer very much from the heat. They soon fall ill with fever. This makes the duty in the trenches very severe upon those who are able to bear the fatigue.'

his removal to Balaklava, thence to proceed on board ship for a period of a fortnight at least, or until the restoration of his health had been established. But Wolseley could not be persuaded to remain beyond a week, and returned to duty not much better than when he quitted the trenches.

Captain Wolseley was in charge of the trenches, with a working-party of 400 men and 20 Sappers, on the night of the 16th of August, and on the following morning, when the fifth bombardment of Sebastopol commenced. He says : ' The enemy appeared to be working at, and in the neighbourhood of the 6-gun battery to their left of the Karabelnaia Ravine. Their vertical fire was heavier than usual, as they fired salvoes from three mortars on the left flank of the Redan. Upon a signal of three mortar shells from No. 13 Battery, fire was opened this morning at daybreak from all our batteries.' During the night there were 39 casualties in the right attack. At this time the British batteries mounted 186 pieces of ordnance, of which 77 were in the right attack.

On the morning of the 19th, the Redan being much damaged, and the Malakhoff almost silent, orders were issued to cease firing.*

During the 21st of August, Captain Wolseley was on duty with two reliefs of 300 men each, besides a strong body of Sappers and carpenters, the latter being engaged in making platforms and placing frames for magazines. The men worked well and much progress was made, though under a brisk fire from the enemy. A sap was commenced from the fifth parallel in advance upon the capital† of the Redan. Fifty-eight yards were executed without interruption from the enemy, and during the night of the 23rd, Wolseley managed to execute about fourteen more yards,

---

* During the forty-eight hours of the bombardment, the British batteries expended 26,270 rounds of ammunition, the total weight being 81 tons.
† The capital is the centre line which divides a bastion into two equal parts.

PREPARATIONS FOR THE ASSAULT. 55

but under a heavy fire from the Redan. In consequence of their proximity to this work, there were 52 casualties among his men on this day. Captain Wolseley was on duty in the trenches, with a working-party of 800 men from five a.m. to seven p.m. on the 27th of August, when, under orders from General Simpson, a heavy fire was opened by the batteries of both attacks—77 in the right and 120 in the left—on the salient angle of the Redan. Of the effect of this fire, Wolseley says in his report : 'The salient of the Redan was considerably injured towards the evening by our fire. The enemy's fire during the day was heavier than usual, and they kept up a continual fire upon the several working-parties.'

Preparations for the final assault were pushed forward with much energy, and the Engineer staff were worked to the utmost, making up by their goodwill and indomitable perseverance for their numerical inferiority. The time since the repulse of the 18th of June had been utilized by the Allies, and an incredible amount of work had been performed. The French had established themselves close to the crest of the counterscarp of the Malakhoff, the key of the position, and scarcely less difficult was the task our troops performed in their advance against the Redan.

During the month of August, the Russians, rendered desperate by the sight of the iron ring which was growing in strength day by day, made repeated efforts to break through. Frequent sorties were made all through the month, and the fighting in that confined and blood-stained arena became fast and furious. The genius of a second Homer—'whose verses,' says Bacon, 'have a slide and easiness more than the verses of other poets'—would be worthily taxed in describing the heroic deeds of our gallant soldiers and sailors and their Allies. Failing the pen of 'the blind old bard of Scio's rocky isle,' we will, in homely prose, depict an event in the life of our hero who, like Achilles in his ardour for the fight, was '*impiger, iracundus, inexorabilis, acer.*'

On the night of the 30th August, an event occurred in Wolseley's life which, at length, after his many narrow escapes, incapacitated him from taking part in the closing scene of the struggle in which he had been so long engaged. At eight p.m., Wolseley, accompanied by Lieutenant Dumaresq, R.E., proceeded on duty, and had charge of the advanced flying sap, which he was directed to carry on as far towards the Redan as the time at his disposal before daylight, and the endurance of his working-party of 400 men and 20 Sappers, would permit. The work progressed as satisfactorily as could be expected, but there was very little earth, and most of the gabions had to be filled with rubble and stone as substitutes. However, he managed to place sixty gabions when the moon rose, and her unwelcome light put a stop to all further proceedings for that night, when, taking advantage of this enforced period of idleness, he proceeded to make a sketch of the ground in order to give his successor an idea of the topography, so that he might carry on the work in hand. Wolseley was thus engaged, when suddenly the Russians made a sortie, and he found himself surrounded by the uncouth visages and strange forms of the soldiery of the Czar, who looked more formidable by the pale and uncertain moonlight. The sortie was made under circumstances and at an hour to call for the exercise of that promptitude and presence of mind which the great Napoleon once described as 'two o'clock in the morning courage,' and said he rarely found even among the bravest of his soldiers.

This serious state of affairs had arisen through the neglect of the field-officer in command, who could not be induced to cover the working-party properly, notwithstanding the repeated representations of Captain Wolseley, who begged

SORTIE BY THE RUSSIANS.

him to take a rifle-pit that was annoying his men, and showed how it might be done with most advantage. However, this officer would not do as he was requested, and as the Russians kept firing volleys from it all night, Wolseley's men had to work lying down. As a further consequence, the front was not protected by sentries, so that a sortie or surprise of some sort was just what might have been anticipated. As we have seen, there was a sortie, and the surprise was complete, but Wolseley was equal to the occasion.

The working-party, finding themselves surrounded, cast down their tools or arms and bolted to a man. In vain the officers did all they could to stop the stampede. Wolseley seized by the belt one man who was in the act of flying, but was instantly knocked down by another fellow who took this irregular method of releasing his comrade. On recovering his feet, Wolseley found there was nothing between himself and the Russians but the gabions, which they were pulling down with all celerity. Looking about him with the intent of rallying his men, he found that he was alone; all had fled, the officers, recognising the futility of resistance without their men, being the last to retire. Another moment's hesitation on Wolseley's part and it would have been too late for him to secure his own safety, and he had barely time to spring over the work and run back to the nearest parallel about 150 yards in rear. British soldiers do not often, or for any length of time, forget themselves; and the same men who, taken by surprise, had just fled in panic from the face of their enemies, rallied in a few minutes, and, led by their officers, drove the Russians pell-mell out of the advanced sap.*

* The following is the official narrative of this affair: 'At about half-past twelve a.m., a party of the enemy made an attack on the advance up the little ravine from the fifth parallel. The working-party retired in great confusion, in spite of repeated attempts on Captain Wolseley's part to rally them, and the Russians threw down about fifty gabions into the trench; they then retreated, keeping up a fire of musketry, which caused consider-

The field-officer whose negligence had caused this unfortunate business, now asked Captain Wolseley, 'What was to be done?'

'I will do nothing,' replied Wolseley, 'until you have carried the rifle-pit I requested you to take before.'

A gallant officer, Captain Pechell, of the 77th, who was killed two nights later, was standing by, and, hearing this colloquy, said, 'I will take the rifle-pit.' And this he did with a small party of his own men, who carried it with a rush.

The Russians had not only pulled up some of the gabions, which had been filled at such great cost of time and labour, but they had rolled others down the hill; Wolseley, therefore, taking with him a strong party of men, recovered most of these gabions, and was engaged in the task of putting up and refilling them when he received his wound. He was at the end of the sap talking to two Sappers, who were assisting him to fill with stones one of the gabions; one hand was stretched back, and the other was resting on a spike of the gabion, when a round shot dashed into the middle of the group. He had just time to call 'Look out!' when down went both the Sappers, while he felt himself hurled to the ground with resistless force. The round shot had struck the gabion, which was full of stones, and, scattering its

---

able loss. The guns also from the batteries below the Malakhoff opened, and caused numerous casualties by stones. Amongst the wounded, I regret to say, was Captain Wolseley, who was severely cut in the face and leg by stones. The guard of the trenches was very strong in the fifth parallel, and there were abundance of men near the entrance to the sap; but the attack was so sudden, that unless the working-party themselves repulsed the enemy, the mischief done to the trench could not be prevented. Captain Wolseley had placed about fifty gabions, and was proceeding to fill them, when the attack took place, all of which, and a considerable quantity besides, were overturned into the trench by the enemy. No more work was done there, on account of the precision of the artillery-fire from the Malakhoff batteries, and also the incessant fire of musketry, as the enemy only retired about 200 yards down the ravine. The casualties among the working-party were very great, amounting to 12 out of 65, and these in a very short space of time.'

contents with terrific violence, instantaneously killed the poor fellows by his side, the head of one man being taken off, while the other was disembowelled. As for himself, he lay senseless until a sergeant of Sappers picked him up, and, after a time, he rallied sufficiently to avail himself of the assistance of this man and of Prince Victor Hohenlohe,[*] of the Naval Brigade, who, coming up, helped him to walk towards the doctor's hut in the trenches. He just managed to totter so far, and was laid down outside the hut in a semi-unconscious state.

Prince Victor called the attention of the surgeon to his newly arrived patient, and the reply was, after a hasty glance, for he was too busy just then to examine him, 'He's a dead un.' This roused up the wounded officer, who, though half-unconscious, seemed to regard the remark in the light of a reflection; and turning himself as he lay there all smothered in blood, he made answer, 'I am worth a good many dead men yet.'

This remark caused the doctor, who fancied from his appearance that his injuries were mortal, to turn his attention to Captain Wolseley, and from the nature of the wounds, and the shock to the system their number and extent would have caused in most cases, it seemed as if the surgeon had only been a little premature in his rough and ready diagnosis. Wolseley's head and body presented a shocking appearance. His features were not distinguishable as those of a human being, while blood flowed from innumerable wounds caused by the stones with which he had been struck. Sharp fragments were embedded all over his face, and his left cheek had been almost cut completely away. The doctor fancied, after probing the wound, that his jawbone was shattered;

[*] When Prince Victor again met Sir Garnet at a public dinner, after his return from the Gold Coast, he reminded him of the circumstances of their last meeting.

but Wolseley made him pull out the substance in his mouth, when a large stone came away. The surgeon then lifted up and stitched the cheek. Both his eyes were completely closed, and the injury to one of them was so serious that the sight has been permanently lost. Not a square inch of his face but what was battered and cut about, while his body was wounded all over, just as if he had been peppered with small-shot. He had received also a severe wound on his right leg, so that both limbs had now been injured, the wound in the left thigh, received in Burmah, rendering him slightly lame.

For many years afterwards the wound on the shin, received on this 30th of August, caused him much suffering; and, when on duty in Canada, nearly ten years after the event, he was under the necessity of returning to England for medical advice regarding the bone, which was exfoliating. Considering the extent of his wounds, Wolseley's recovery must be chiefly attributed to his wonderful constitution, and, in a scarcely less degree, to his strong vitality and buoyant courage.

After the surgeon had dressed his wounds, Captain Wolseley was placed on a stretcher, and carried by four soldiers to St. George's Monastery, situated on the sea-coast not far from Balaklava, and there he passed some weeks, the sight of both eyes being too much injured to subject them to the light. While he was pent up in this gloomy cell, meditating on the sad prospect of being totally blind for the remainder of his days, news arrived of the fall of Sebastopol. The great Russian stronghold, which had for so many weary months defied the utmost efforts of two Great Powers, was at length carried by assault on the 8th of September, and Captain Wolseley had the additional mortification of feeling that all his devotion and suffering had not received the reward he most coveted

WOLSELEY AND THE ROYAL ENGINEERS. 61

—that of participating in the storm of the Russian stronghold.*

The Siege of Sebastopol stands in many respects without example in the annals of war. The Russian works extended for nearly fifteen miles, while the besiegers' trenches were no less than fifty-two miles in length, and comprised 109 batteries, armed with 806 pieces. The expenditure of ammunition during the siege, during the 327 days the batteries were open, amounted to about one and a half million rounds. The Russians opposed to the Allies an army numerically superior, intrenched behind formidable defences, mounting no less than 1,100 cannon, and protected by the guns of their fleet.

Immediately on learning the news of the fall of Sebastopol, Captain Wolseley resigned his post of Assistant-Engineer, and his name was removed from the list from the 7th of November. He had been ordered to England for the recovery of his health, and to seek the best medical advice for his eyes, the sight of both of which it was at first feared was permanently lost.

Sir Harry Jones, in a confidential Memorandum to the Secretary of State for War, brought to his lordship's notice the names of the officers whom he recommended for promotion, among them being that of Captain Wolseley. Throughout the siege the duties of the trenches fell with great severity on the Engineer officers, of whom the General said he 'could not speak too highly in praise of the zeal and intelligence they displayed;' day and night they were constantly under fire in the most advanced positions, directing the working-parties, and it is surprising that any of those,

---

* Our loss on the 8th of September was 29 officers, and 356 men killed ; 124 officers and 1,762 men wounded ; and 175 missing. The French lost 145 officers and 1,489 men killed ; 254 officers and 4,259 men wounded ; and 10 officers and 1,400 men missing.

who, like Wolseley, served continuously for many months, escaped with their lives.

The total number of non-commissioned officers and men of the Royal Engineers employed throughout the siege, amounted to only 935; of these 218 were killed or died, and 119 became non-effective from various causes, leaving 598 in the Crimea on the 9th of September. During the same time, 69 officers of the Royal Engineers, and 19 other officers, acting as Assistant-Engineers, served with the corps; of the former, 18 were killed or died (exclusive of Lieutenant H. G. Teesdale, who died of wounds received at the Alma), and 14 were wounded, while 2 Assistant-Engineers were killed, and 6 wounded.*

During the nine months Captain Wolseley served uninterruptedly before Sebastopol (with the exception of a week's sick leave at Balaklava), he was, perhaps, as often on duty in the trenches as any officer in the British Army; while as one of the Engineer officers of the right attack, he was in the post of the greatest danger, as evinced by the fact that of the 14 officers killed at the siege, 12 belonged to the right attack, or were killed when doing duty there.† The preceding pages show the nature of the duty performed by Captain Wolseley during the siege. In the dreary winter of 1854-55, he, in common with every officer and man, suffered from hunger and cold; but, though for weeks his diet was an insufficient allowance of unwholesome biscuit and still more unwholesome water, he cheerfully performed his tour of duty in the trenches, and faced the Russian fire and the biting cold of an Arctic winter, which proved fatal to so many gallant

* The total loss of the British Army in the Crimea was 243 officers and 4,531 killed and died of wounds; 577 officers and 10,800 men wounded; and 13 officers and 491 men missing. The Naval Brigade, out of 135 officers and 4,334 men engaged, lost 5 officers and 95 men killed; and 38 officers and 437 men wounded.

† The reason is obvious why the mortality in the right attack was greater than in the left. The right attack was on the slope of the Redan, while a ravine intervened between the Russian batteries and the left attack.

officers and men. While the army was perishing from want and cold in the trenches, ship after ship arrived at Balaklava, stowed with boots too small for use, and greatcoats that would not button: and when officers, even at headquarters, were fain to be thankful for mouldy biscuits, preserved meats and vegetables were rotting on the quays of Balaklava. Routine and red-tapeism reigned supreme, and the world wondered at the astounding display of mismanagement in every department of our complicated military machine. The one satisfactory feature was the valour and patience of our officers and soldiers, who doggedly fought on, and never murmured when affairs looked their blackest.

It was a point of honour among the Engineer officers and Sappers to bear up against sickness, and hold out as long as they could stand on their legs; and Wolseley, though he frequently suffered from illness and overwork, with the exception of a brief interval in July, remained at his post until severe wounds incapacitated him for further duty. Speaking of the officers and men of the Royal Engineers, he has expressed an opinion that 'he never saw men work like them,' and considers their conduct in this unparalleled siege as 'beyond all praise.'

Captain Wolseley was wounded severely on the 30th of August, and slightly on the 10th of April, and 7th of June. On the 15th of February his coat was pierced by a ball; on the 10th of April a round shot struck the embrasure at which he was working, and cut his trousers; and on the 7th of June a ball passed through his forage-cap from the peak to the back, knocking it off his head. It may be said, without exaggeration, that he bore a charmed life; for, at the termination of the siege, of three messes of four members each to which he had belonged, he was the only officer remaining in the Crimea, all the others being either killed or forced to leave through wounds.

Captain Wolseley was about to return to England for the recovery of his health, when he was offered an appointment in the Quartermaster-General's Department, which he resolved to accept. There was a great improvement in the sight of one of his eyes, though, as he told us, he has never recovered the sight of the other—as Wordsworth's naval showman says of Nelson:

> 'One eye he had, which, bright as ten,
> Burn'd like a fire among his men.'

He was employed on the Quartermaster-General's staff, in conjunction with two officers of the 90th Light Infantry, Major Barnston (who died of wounds received at the Relief of Lucknow, and of whom Wolseley speaks as 'the best officer he ever knew'), and Captain Crealock, whose gallantry on the disastrous 8th of September, and in the China Campaign of 1860, and skill as an accomplished artist, have made his name famous. Captain Wolseley and Major Barnston were attached, for surveying duties, to a French army of 20,000 men and a small force of English cavalry, which had taken up a position in the valley of the Belbec, menacing the left flank of the Russians, who, after the fall of the south side of Sebastopol, occupied a line extending from the Star Fort to the extreme left on the Mackenzie Heights. At this time the Allies had, in the Crimea, an army of about 210,000 men, of which the British portion numbered, on the 16th of October, 56,000,[*] of whom only 4,500 were ineffective through wounds or sickness.

---

[*] This total was composed of 14 regiments of Cavalry, about 5,000 sabres; 52 battalions of Infantry, about 33,000 bayonets; and 14 batteries of Artillery, and 9 companies of Sappers, about 9,000 men. The remaining 9,000 were made up of non-combatants, as Land Transport, Army Works, and Medical Staff. This was exclusive of the Turkish Contingent of 20,000 men. There were in the United Kingdom only 7 regiments of Cavalry, exclusive of the Household Brigade, and 8 regiments of Infantry, besides 5 in the Mediterranean.

THE LAST DAYS IN THE CRIMEA.

While employed with the French *corps d'armée* in the valley of the Belbec on surveying duties, Captain Wolseley had many narrow escapes from capture. Every morning, he and Major Barnston would leave the French camp, either alone, or escorted by a few troopers, and many a hot chase they had when the Russians, annoyed at seeing British officers reconnoitring and sketching close up to their advanced posts, sent some of their hardest-riding Cossacks in pursuit. When the French force fell back, and it became too cold for surveying, Wolseley was appointed Deputy Assistant-Quartermaster-General to the Light Division, then under the command of Lord William Paulet.

Captain Wolseley remained in the Crimea until the conclusion of peace with Russia, when he assisted Colonel Hallowell, at Balaklava, in despatching homewards the troops of his division, a great portion of the army embarking at Kasatch Bay, near Kamiesch, where the fleet lay. On 5th of July, 1856, Marshal Pelissier, with his staff, sailed from Kamiesch; and, on the 12th of July, Sir William Codrington, commanding the British Army, having made over the Dockyard of Sebastopol, and Port of Balaklava, to the officer in command of the Russian troops, embarked on board H.M.S. *Algiers*. After the departure of all the regiments, Captain Wolseley embarked for England, being one of the last men to quit the land where he had done and suffered so much in his country's service.

CHAPTER III.

THE INDIAN MUTINY.

Captain Wolseley proceeds on Service to India.—Wrecked at Banca.—Arrival at Calcutta—Proceeds up-Country.—In Action near Cawnpore.—March to Alumbagh.—The Relief of Lucknow.—Wolseley storms the Mess-house.—Occupies the Motee Mahul, and effects Communication with the Residency of Lucknow.—The Defence of Alumbagh.—Campaigning in Oude.—Actions at Baree and Nawabgunge.—Service on the Nepaul Frontier.

ON his return from the Crimea, Captain Wolseley* rejoined the 90th Regiment, then stationed at Aldershot, but was soon after employed in reporting on a new system of visual telegraphy. For this purpose he came up to London, in order that he might acquire a knowledge of the system from the German Professor, who sought, but unsuccessfully, to introduce it into our army. On his return to Aldershot, he was attached to the staff of Lord William Paulet, then commanding a brigade at the camp, as 'galloper,' or extra aide-de-camp, without, however, the extra pay.

In the beginning of February, 1857, the 90th, being one of the regiments under orders to proceed to India, was sent for a few months to Portsmouth to enjoy the pleasures and relaxation of a garrison town, to which it had certainly earned

---

* Notwithstanding that he had been specially mentioned in despatches by Lord Raglan, and recommended for promotion by Sir Harry Jones, K.C.B., Wolseley did not receive the brevet-majority to which he might have been considered entitled for his meritorious services at the siege of Sebastopol. The French Emperor nominated him a Knight of the Legion of Honour, and the Sultan conferred on him the Fifth Class of the Medjidie.

WOLSELEY IS ORDERED TO THE EAST. 67

a title after its sufferings in the Crimea. The regiment, however, had only been a few days at that famous seaport, when orders were received for it to proceed to India at a week's notice. But the authorities at the War Office altered their determination, and a reprieve of a week was allowed; finally, the officers, who had all been hastily recalled from leave, were given to understand that *positively* the regiment would not embark for foreign service until June, the usual period for the despatch of Indian reliefs, so that the troops might land in the cool season.

But a British soldier, who may be called upon at any moment to defend the most distant dependency of an empire 'upon which the sun never sets,' can never, even for a few months, consider his destination 'finally' settled, while the War Office twenty years ago—there is more consideration for officers and men nowadays—habitually hated finality in making up its mind to anything, and cared little for the expense and inconvenience it caused to officers who drew the munificent pay of a grateful country. The present afforded a notable instance of this lordly disregard of other people's comfort; for about three weeks after all had been settled, the regiment received orders to hold itself in readiness to proceed forthwith to China.

At this time the 90th was commanded by Colonel Campbell, an officer whose brilliant defence of the Quarries on the night of the 7th of June—when our troops, acting alone and without the assistance of our Allies, achieved almost the only striking success throughout the siege—gained him the well-merited honours of the Bath. The regiment now mustered a thousand bayonets, and it was a goodly sight to witness the 90th on parade, as smart a corps as any in Her Majesty's service. Captain Wolseley's company, like all the others, numbered 100 non-commissioned officers and men, and he had three subalterns, Lieutenants Herford and Carter, and

Ensign Haig. Of the entire strength of the regiment, 700 men, with head-quarters, embarked in the *Himalaya*, under command of Colonel Campbell, C.B.; and Major Barnston, with the three remaining companies, under Captains Wosleley, Guise, and Irby, sailed in the *Transit*, whose history, from her cradle to her grave, bore a singular resemblance to that of another trooper, the ill-fated *Megæra*.*

Besides 300 men of the 90th, the *Transit* embarked for Hong Kong a detachment of the 59th Regiment and 200 men of the Medical Staff Corps, a body recently organized for furnishing military hospitals with attendants. The whole force was under the command of Lieut.-Colonel Stephenson, who had been appointed Assistant Adjutant-General to the China Expedition, then fitting out under the command of the late Major-General Hon. T. Ashburnham, C.B. The troubles of the *Transit* commenced before she had lost sight of land. Directly after quitting Spithead, a dense fog came on, when Commander Chambers, her captain, brought-to in the Solent. On weighing anchor the following day, he found the ship making water so fast that he had to run back to Spithead, flying the ensign 'Union down,' as a signal of distress. The *Transit* managed to creep into Portsmouth Harbour, and, discharging the troops into a hulk, hauled off to the dockyard, nearly sinking before she could be pumped

---

* Lieutenant (now retired Captain) J. S. A. Herford, in his work, 'Stirring Times under Canvas,' describes the ship in the following terms: 'The *Transit* had always been an unfortunate ship. Bought, if not literally on the stocks, yet in an unfinished state, from a private company, she was completed by the Royal Navy authorities, by which ingenious plan, whenever anything afterwards went wrong, the original builders and the finishers were able to shift the blame on each other. She was continually breaking down in her various voyages to and from the Crimea with troops. Those who were so unfortunate as to be embarked in her knew well enough that something was certain to happen in the course of the voyage. Yet the authorities had still a firm belief in her merits; so, putting a new pair of engines in her, they determined to send troops in her a short way—only to China! The new engines were smaller, but more powerful, than the last had been, and, to steady the ship and keep her together, two large iron beams, running fore and aft, were added. To these beams we probably, at a later period, owed our lives.'

out and docked. It was then discovered that she had knocked a hole in her bottom, which was probably occasioned by her settling on her anchor at low water when in a tideway. On the necessary repairs being effected, the *Transit*, having re-shipped the troops and the guns and military stores which formed her cargo, once more proceeded on her long voyage. But it was only to encounter further ill-luck. A strong gale came on in the 'chops of the Channel,' and the rigging having been loosely set up, the masts swayed about to such an extent that the captain made all preparations to cut them away. The gale moderating, the *Transit* put into Corunna, where Captain Wolseley and the other officers proceeded ashore, and visited the grave of one of England's bravest and best soldiers, Sir John Moore. The rigging having been set up, the *Transit* proceeded once more to sea; but on arriving at the Cape, on May the 28th, it was discovered that she had sprung a leak near her sternpost; however, on examination by a diver, it was pronounced as of no consequence, and so the *Transit* proceeded on her long flight across the Indian Ocean, her donkey-engine working the whole time to keep the leak under. When near St. Paul's, the island on which the *Megæra*, of evil memory, left her bones, the *Transit* encountered a hurricane, and it seemed as if the ship was to add another to those mysteries of the deep which are every now and then chronicled in the public papers.

Wolseley described her condition to us: 'For three days and three nights the cyclone lasted. All our sails were carried away, and the mainyard went to pieces. An enormous leak showed itself; some plates were supposed to have burst, so that the water poured in like a sluice. We had on board the *Transit* nearly 900 souls, and it was as much as all hands could do, by constant pumping, to keep her afloat.' But Providence destined the gallant hearts on board the *Transit* to fight their country's battles in a great crisis, and the gale moderated when matters looked so serious that it only seemed a question of how many hours they could keep afloat the worn-out hull in which 'the authorities' had so perversely sent them to the other side of the world. By dint of hard pumping the leak was kept under, and the ship, having passed through the Straits of Sunda, headed north for Singapore, when officers and men began to count the days before they might expect to sight the rich and varied foliage amid which that city is embosomed. Soon they were steaming rapidly through the Straits of Banca, whose well-wooded shores and sandy coves excited their admiration, as we remember it did ours when cruising in those seas. But their acquaintance was destined to be not altogether of a pleasurable tinge, and our hero, like everyone who has been much at sea, learnt the truth of the saying of Juvenal, that on that unstable element a man is at all times removed from death 'by four fingers' breadth or seven at most.' At ten o'clock on the morning of the 10th of July, as the *Transit* was passing through the Straits, the Island of Banca being on the starboard hand and Sumatra on the port side, and the sea as smooth as a mill-pond, the crazy old ship suddenly crashed on a coral reef, on which she remained immovable. Then it was seen what discipline could effect among men whose lives were not passed, like sailors, amid the perils incidental to a nautical profession, but who suddenly found themselves confronted by a novel danger.

'The majority of the troops,' says Captain Herford, 'were on the main-deck at the mess-tables. On feeling the first shock they naturally rose *en masse*, and were about to rush on deck, when Major Barnston, who was quietly writing in his cabin, appeared before them, and lifting his hand, said in his usual undisturbed voice, ' It's all right, men ; stay where you are !" These few words, coming from an officer who inspired confidence and was generally beloved, acted like magic. The men, like so many children, obeyed and sat down.'

The ship's company, meanwhile, lowered the boats, and it was found, on taking soundings, that there was not less than nine fathoms all round. In the meantime the ship began to settle by the stern, and there was great danger of her sliding off the rock and sinking in the deep water alongside, when a lamentable loss of life must have ensued. The engine-room was soon full of water, which rushed in with great velocity. While the soldiers were busy bringing up on deck the provisions and arms, the sailors lowered the remaining boats, and prepared them for the reception of the troops, who were landed on a reef distant about a mile and a half, as it was considered desirable to remove all hands from the wreck with the utmost despatch, the Island of Banca being about two miles farther away. When this had been completed, the crew first proceeded to the mainland with what provisions they could save, and, having deposited these on the sandy beach, returned to the reef, which was now nearly submerged by the advancing tide, and removed the soldiers to the neighbouring shore. Here large fires had been lit, and, as a fine stream of water was close at hand, the gallant light-hearted fellows of both services were soon making themselves merry over biscuit and water, thankful that they had escaped with their lives.

Captain Wolseley lost everything he possessed in the world except the clothes on his back, for strict orders had been issued by Captain Chambers that nothing was to be passed into the boats except provisions, so that officers and men saved only their arms, each man taking with him also four rounds of ammunition. This was the first time Wolseley had suffered this misfortune, one of the most trying of the chances of active service; but it was not destined to be the last, for, not many months later, when the rebels defeated General Windham and burned Cawnpore, he and his brother officers lost the second kit they had provided themselves with in Calcutta: among his losses at Cawnpore were his Legion of Honour and Crimean Medal, which were afterwards found on the body of a dead 'Pandy.' Again, during his absence from England, on his Ashantee Campaign, Wolseley had the misfortune to lose all his furniture and goods, which he had warehoused in the Pantechnicon, in the great fire which, in a few hours, reduced to ashes that vast building and its costly contents.

On the following morning, when it was found that the bows of the *Transit* were still visible above water, an attempt was made to secure some baggage and necessaries, but the salvage from the wreck was inconsiderable and almost valueless.

The spot on which the shipwrecked crew and passengers of the *Transit* had landed was not without a certain historical interest for soldiers and sailors, as, on examination, there were found among the trees and brushwood the remains of ditches and embankments, indicating that it was at this spot the British constructed a fort during the Expedition to Java, in 1811. The Island of Banca is under the protection of the Dutch, whose settlement at Minto was some eight miles distant. To this place Captain Chambers, on the morning after the disaster, sent the cutter to ask for assistance; when the Governor immediately despatched one gunboat to Singapore to advise the authorities there, and another to protect the wreck from the depredations of the natives, who had commenced seizing all they could pick up. As all the fresh provisions and live stock had been lost, the shipwrecked people had to subsist on salt meat and biscuits; a fare which was varied by the flesh of baboons, which they shot, and made into a nutritious, if not very palatable, soup. The natives also drove a good business in the sale of pine-apples, yams, bread, eggs, and poultry, though the supply was limited, and the price demanded so great as to be almost prohibitory. With such eatables, and sheltered by the sails of the *Transit*, which were spread between the trees, officers and men passed a not unpleasant Robinson Crusoe sort of life for eight days ; and just when the sense of novelty had worn off, and this mode of existence began to pall, Her Majesty's gunboat *Dove* arrived from Singapore, and brought some startling news, that altered the destination of the 90th Regiment, and opened a new chapter in the adventurous career of Captain Wolseley.

This was the announcement that the Bengal Native Army was in full mutiny, and had inaugurated the movement by the destruction of Meerut and the seizure of Delhi, while massacres were perpetrated throughout the land, coupled with an urgent demand for the aid of every European soldier to uphold the banner of British supremacy and withstand the mighty uprising to 'drive the British leopard into the sea,' as Napoleon would have styled it. Already the headquarters of the regiment, which had sailed in the *Himalaya*, had been despatched to Calcutta, and, at once proceeding up-country, formed part of the reinforcements brought up by Sir James Outram, when that most distinguished of Indian Generals, fresh from his Persian triumphs, marched to join Havelock, then battling against tremendous odds.

Two days after the arrival of the *Dove*, H.M.S. *Actæon*, Captain Bates, steamed up to Banca, and embarked the three companies of the 90th, which, on arriving at Singapore, on the 23rd of July, were quartered in some large roomy huts about three miles outside that picturesque-looking town, whose situation on one of the chief highways of commerce, surely marks it out for a great future. On the 29th, H.M.S.

Shannon, Captain William Peel, with Lord Elgin on board, arrived from Hong Kong, and on the following day she and H.M.S. *Pearl*, Captain Sotheby, embarked the 90th for Calcutta, Captain Wolseley's company sailing in the latter ship.

The arrival of these reinforcements was most opportune. Delhi had not yet been captured, and Lucknow was closely besieged by the enemy, while every day brought fresh news of rebellion, and the air was thick with rumours of disaster. Men's hearts failed them for fear, and Fort William itself presented the aspect of a fortress in an enemy's country.

On the morning after their arrival at Calcutta, the detachment proceeded in a river steamer to Chinsurah, and here they remained for some weeks, during which the soldiers received a new outfit, and exchanged their arms, which had been damaged, for more serviceable weapons. The officers ordered new outfits in Calcutta, and Captain Wolseley expended £100 in restoring his lost kit; but though they sent in their claims for compensation for lost baggage, which, according to the War Office Regulations, would be immediately honoured, three years elapsed before the expenses they had incurred were refunded.

At length, all the arrangements for the transport of the detachments being complete, on the 29th of August, Captain Wolseley's company left Chinsurah by rail for the long journey up-country. The first halting-place was Raneegunge, about 112 miles from Calcutta, and as the rail went no further, the company started in bullock 'gharees' for Benares. The detachment marched by companies, each 'bullock-train' accommodating 80 men, and each 'gharee' either 6 men, or 2 officers with their baggage, while one-third of the men, with an officer, as a guard, proceeded on foot. The average pace was about two miles an hour, and the bullocks were changed every ten miles; thus the company marched until, on the following morning, a halt was made for some hours at the staging bungalow. As time was of importance, and they were occasionally delayed by the rivers, which were swelled by the heavy monsoon rains, forced marches had sometimes to be made during the heat of the day, which, at first, was found to be very trying to unacclimatized soldiers.

After passing Dehree, burnt bungalows and devastated villages afforded signs that they were approaching the scene of operations, and, on the 10th of September, Captain Wolseley and his company crossed the Ganges in a paddle-boat worked by manual, or rather pedal, labour, and proceeded to a palace of the Rajah of Benares, situated about three miles from that city, which had been prepared for their reception. The Holy City of the Hindoos was, at this time, the hot-bed of sedition. Earthworks, mounted with guns, commanded the town, and it was intimated to the inhabitants that any overt act of rebellion would be the signal for the destruction of their chief temple.

On the following day the company started from Benares, again by bullock-dâk, and, after two days' marching, recrossed the Ganges, and entered the fort of Allahabad, which, situated at the junction of that sacred river with the Jumna, is a place of the greatest strategical importance, though, like Delhi and other arsenals in Upper India, at the time of the Mutiny it was denuded of white troops by the insane policy that dictated our military dispositions.

Proceeding by forced marches through Futtehpore, Captain Wolseley arrived, about the 27th of September, at Cawnpore—whose very name arouses sad memories in the minds of everyone who was in India in that terrible year, 1857. Formerly one of the largest and finest military stations in India, Cawnpore now presented a desolate appearance. On every side were burnt cantonments and bungalows, and Wolseley passed the entrenchment defended with such desperate tenacity by Sir Hugh Wheeler and his handful of British troops, and the small low-roofed row of houses in which was consummated the butchery of the helpless women and children, and the neighbouring well in which their still palpitating corpses were cast by the orders of the monster, Nana Sahib. All these sights were viewed by the officers and men of the 90th, and aroused in them, as in every regiment, which on arriving up-country had visited in succession these harrowing scenes, feelings of hate and revenge, which found ample vent at the Relief and Siege of Lucknow in the following November and March.

In October, Captain Wolseley had his first brush with the Pandies. A report reached Cawnpore that the insurgents were mustering in force at Sheo Rajpore, some miles from Bhitoor, the residence of Nana Sahib. At midnight, on the 17th of October, Brigadier Wilson,* of the 64th Regiment, taking with him a field battery, a few Native horse and 650 bayonets—made up of detachments of the Madras Fusiliers and the 64th and 90th Regiments—carrying four days' provisions, moved off rapidly towards Bhitoor. It was the time of the Native Festival of the Dewalee, or Feast of Lamps, and hopes were expressed of inflicting a severe blow on the rebels. The force proceeded all night, the infantry being mounted on elephants and camels; at daybreak they dismounted, and marching briskly, approached Bhitoor early in the morning. On the way they learned that the enemy occupied a grove of trees half a mile in front, with 2 guns, a 9-pounder and a 24-pounder, in position. The British column was marching along a hard 'pucka' † road, when, the enemy beginning to open fire, Brigadier Wilson deployed his force. Wolseley's company—which,

---

* This gallant officer fell on the 27th of November, when the Gwalior troops attacked General Windham in his entrenchments at Cawnpore.

† *Pucka* is a word of very general use and many significations in Hindostanee; here it denotes 'permanent,' as opposed to *cutcha*, raw or new.

with the detachment of Native cavalry, formed the advanced guard—was marching in column of sections, when the round shot and shell began to fly down the road pretty freely. One shot passed through his files, and, bursting in front of the other companies of the 90th, which were in rear and in the act of deploying, killed and wounded seven men. The cavalry thereupon turned and bolted, charging through Wolseley's company. He now quickly threw his men into skirmishing order, and Major Barnston proposed to the Brigadier that he should advance upon the guns—for, like most soldiers who had served at Sebastopol, and had been daily under shell-fire, he had not that dread of attacking guns which generally characterizes inexperienced soldiers. But Wilson, though personally as gallant a soldier as any in Her Majesty's service, feared to incur the responsibility of the act, and, though Wolseley was already advancing on the guns, countermanded the attack, and halting his force, brought up his battery and opened fire on the enemy. This occupied some time, as the guns were drawn by bullocks, and before he had fired many rounds the enemy had limbered up and made off with their guns, leaving behind only two waggons and three country carts with ammunition.

The 19th of October was occupied in destroying Bhitoor, the troops bivouacking that night in Nana Sahib's compound, and the 'bawachee,' or cook, of Wolseley's mess used for fuel the legs of the Nana's billiard-tables. On the following day the column returned to Cawnpore, having first destroyed Sheo Rajpore.

At this time, though Delhi had fallen, and a portion of the army—which, at the time of the assault, numbered 10,000 effectives—was free for ulterior operations, the position of affairs at Lucknow was still most critical. On the 25th of September, General Havelock and Sir James Outram had effected the relief of the Residency; but little had been accomplished beyond increasing the strength of the garrison, and occupying the Furreed Buksh and Chuttur Munzil Palaces, and other buildings. The entire British force in Lucknow only numbered 3,000 effectives, and the rebel hordes were swelled to some 70,000 fighting men.

On the day preceding his entry into Lucknow, Havelock left at Alumbagh all his baggage and some 130 sick and wounded, under a guard of 400 men, with some guns. On the 3rd of October, a convoy of provisions from Cawnpore was thrown into Alumbagh, and, on the 11th, orders were issued that 500 men, under Major Barnston, including the detachment of the 90th, with 4 guns, was to march to Alumbagh with supplies. As they were to return in a few days, the column was ordered to leave behind at Cawnpore all their *impedimenta*, with which, however, neither Captain Wolseley nor any of his brother officers were destined to be encumbered any farther.

Accordingly, on the 21st of October, 300 waggons, laden with stores, and eight camels, were sent across the river; and, early in the ensuing morning the column crossed over the bridge of boats, and after a march of a few miles, halted under some trees, no tents being taken for the same reason that the baggage was left behind. At midnight, Major Barnston started again, and marched till eight in the morning. On the second day he learnt that the rebels, 700 strong, with 2 guns, intended to dispute the passage of the river Sye, at the Bunnee Bridge, the centre arch of which they had undermined. Having made his dispositions, Major Barnston advanced his small force, Captain Guise's company forming the advanced guard; 'but,' writes Captain Herford, 'Wolseley, who followed, told Guise that he must let him go in and take one of the guns.'

However, the gallant officers were disappointed of their game this time, for on reaching the Sye it was found that a

A SKIRMISH NEAR ALUMBAGH.

battery had indeed been built, but the birds were flown! Nothing remained but to cross the river without the excitement of performing the operation under fire, and this was a work of much difficulty and requiring considerable time. It took eight hours of hard work before the long train, which covered nearly two miles of ground, was transported across the river and pulled up the steep bank on to the road on the opposite side. Proceeding three-quarters of a mile farther on, the force halted under a 'tope' of trees: Alumbagh was only about eight miles distant, and the small column marched on the following morning, Captain Wolseley's company forming the rear-guard, which was destined to be the post of honour. The force had just cleared two topes, and debouched on a large plain, when the enemy opened fire upon the rear-guard. The road along which they marched was a 'pucka' road, and extended through the centre of a vast plain forming a dead level, and admirably adapted for the operations of cavalry. The enemy's horse galloped up in a threatening attitude, but Wolseley received them with a volley, and they hung back. Some desultory fighting then ensued, and the Enfield proved its efficiency at long ranges. Major Barnston ordered the centre column to fall back and assist Wolseley's company; this was done, and the enemy, after a show of resistance, retreated, deserting two stockades they had constructed. Soon after, the long convoy was passed in safety into Alumbagh.

Alumbagh ('Garden of the World,' as it means in Persian) stands almost three miles due south of Lucknow, and had been a favourite residence of one of the Queens of Oude. At this time it consisted of a walled enclosure 500 yards square, having turreted buildings at the four corners, in each of which were mounted 2 guns. Its defences were further strengthened by an abattis of felled trees and a trench, and the walls were loopholed, while a 32-pounder at the principal entrance commanded the road; but the place was incapable of resisting artillery, had the rebels possessed sufficient enterprise to attack it. From the turrets of the building in the centre, were visible the domes and minarets of Lucknow, as well as the Residency, to the beleaguered garrison of which the maintenance of this post proved of essential benefit, as it was the means of securing their communications with Cawnpore. One set of 'kossids' carried correspondence, worded in French, but written in the Greek character, from the Residency—a work of the greatest difficulty and danger, and which only very large bribes could induce natives to undertake—and another set performed the comparatively safe task of conveying messages thence to Cawnpore.

Major Barnston had received orders to return to Cawnpore three days after his arrival at Alumbagh; but Colonel McIntyre, commanding at that post, requiring the aid of the column to defend the post, obtained leave for them to remain with him. The enemy had planted heavy guns within range of the enclosure, and greatly annoyed the garrison, who, though anxious to sally out and capture or spike the cannon, were not permitted to quit the walls, except on foraging expeditions for the supply of the immense herd of camels and elephants.

So passed a short period of inactivity, until the 30th of October, when Brigadier-General (the late Sir) Hope Grant crossed the Ganges, with some 4,000 men. On the 4th of November the road to Cawnpore being open, all the waggons, with the camels, elephants, and other animals, which were in a half-starved state, were sent thither from Alumbagh, while the convoy of provisions escorted by Grant was thrown into the place. On the 9th, a semaphore communication was opened with the Lucknow Residency from the roof of the building in the centre of Alumbagh, and the first use to which it was put was to announce the arrival, on the following day, of Mr. Kavanagh, who, disguised as a native, had brought a message from Outram to Sir Colin Campbell. It was a most gallant deed, and Kavanagh received the Victoria Cross, was admitted into the Covenanted Service, and awarded a grant of £2,000.

On the 12th of November, Sir Colin Campbell arrived at Alumbagh with some additional troops, and, on the following afternoon, the detachment of the 90th received the welcome order to march out of Alumbagh, and join the 4th Brigade camping outside, under the command of Brigadier Hon. Adrian Hope, of the 93rd Highlanders. The brigade was composed of the 53rd and the 93rd, and a battalion of about 600 men, made up of companies of the 90th, 84th, and Madras Fusiliers, under the command of Major Barnston.

The Alumbagh garrison was relieved by the 75th Regiment, which had seen much hard fighting and suffered heavily at Delhi. The Commander-in-Chief had under his command, for the proposed operations for the relief of the Residency, only some 4,550 men and 32 guns.

On the 14th of November, about nine a.m., the British army started on its momentous mission of effecting the final relief of our countrymen, the 4th Brigade bringing up the rear of the main column. The Dilkhoosha and Martinière were carried with small loss, and the latter was occupied by the 90th. Wolseley, on ascending to the roof, had presented to him for the first time a fine view of the superb Eastern city spread at his feet.

A little later, the 90th were directed to encamp in a tope in rear of a mud wall, behind which the rebels had taken up a position, and the men were about to dine, when a heavy musketry-fire denoted that the rebels were making an attempt, in great force, to retake the position. The battalion were at once hurried off to support the 93rd Highlanders, who were out skirmishing to their left, and, forming line, advanced to where two heavy guns of the *Shannon* Brigade, under Captain Peel, were pounding away at the enemy. Wolseley, profiting by the halt, was snatching the luxury of a 'tub,' when he was summoned to the front. Hastily dressing himself, he turned out with his company, and came up just as Peel began firing. As he passed between the guns the charge in one of them exploded, owing to the vent not being 'served,' and carried off the head of a sailor. Bullets began to fly about plentifully, and a brass shell rolled down and exploded quite close to Wolseley; round shot were also fired from guns posted over the canal, and the 90th received orders to advance and take them. On reaching the canal, however, it was found that the rebels had dammed it at this point, and, instead of being only ankle-deep, the water came up to a man's shoulders. It was now getting dark, and as Sir Colin determined to bivouac on the banks of the canal for the night, Captain Wolseley received orders to 'picket' his company on the spot, the rest of the force retiring. Sentries were placed on the canal bank, and Wolseley enjoined silence, as they were so close to the rebel sentries posted on the opposite side, in front of Banks' house, that their conversation could be heard. So passed the night, which was dark and cold, for though the sun was overpoweringly hot during the day, the temperature fell very considerably after nightfall. All the following day, during which the troops remained stationary, waiting for a fresh supply of ammunition, Major Barnston's battalion was on picket, retiring a few yards into a hollow, while musketry-fire raged over their heads. At length, after being on continuous duty for thirty-six hours, Wolseley was relieved, and he and his men enjoyed a night's rest.

On the following morning (16th of November) the Commander-in-Chief, having left all his baggage at Dilkhoosha,

A WARM DAY'S WORK. 83

crossed the canal and resumed operations. At ten o'clock, he rode up to Major Barnston, and calling the officers of his battalion together, told them that when fired at in the streets it was best not to stop and return the fire, but to fix bayonets and rush on. It was decided that Barnston's battalion was to have the honour of being the first of the main body; but, subsequently, this was changed, and Brigadier Hope arranged that they were to follow the 93rd, the 53rd forming the advance-guard. At twelve o'clock the battalion started, and crossing the canal, made a detour to the right; soon they were in the thick of the firing, but Barnston pressed on, and reached some houses on the edge of an open space, across which ran a road, now commanded by the guns of the rebels. Captain Wolseley was directed to double across this open, a run of about 300 yards, and occupy some ruined houses on the other side. This he did amid a shower of shot and bullets. After keeping up a musketry duel from behind the remains of some walls scarcely breast-high, Wolseley advanced with the intention of driving out the enemy.

Marching rapidly along a narrow lane, his company led into the town. The enemy retired, keeping up a hot fusillade, and as they gave ground the guns were brought forward, Wolseley, with a party of his men, himself assisting in dragging them to the front, through the sand which lay ankle-deep. At this time the enemy's fire was so hot, that, as he said, 'the bullets hopped off the tires of the guns like peas off a drum.' How any man of the score or so of his company who assisted him escaped with their lives, was marvellous. Among those who particularly distinguished themselves were Sergeant Newman (now Quartermaster of the 90th), and another of Wolseley's sergeants, who, though wounded by a musket-ball, which carried away his upper lip, and passed clean through his face, refused to leave, and remained till the close of the action.

Wolseley was now ordered to protect the flank of Captain Blunt's troop of Horse Artillery, which came into action in brilliant style. While the rest of Major Barnston's battalion advanced towards the Secundrabagh, he pushed past that enclosure, and leaving it untaken in the rear, advanced to a line of huts. Here he remained for the rest of the day, protecting the flank of the forces engaged in taking the Shah Nujeef, and fighting from house to house. That night Wolseley's company bivouacked outside the Secundrabagh. Thus he had his share of the hard fighting that rendered this day the most memorable during the operations connected with the Relief.

When he retired in the evening with his company, and joined the rest of the battalion, he was grieved to learn that his friend and brother officer, Major Barnston, had been severely wounded in the thigh. Like so many others who were wounded, he ultimately sank under the effects of the climate, though he spoke cheerfully of his recovery to the last.

Meanwhile Sir Colin Campbell had been conducting the main operations of the army with signal success. The enemy had fortified the Secundrabagh—a garden 120 yards square, surrounded by a high wall of solid masonry, which had been carefully loopholed. The artillery having effected a breach, the 93rd Highlanders and 4th Sikhs stormed the enclosure, and the rebels, mostly Sepoys of the regular service, were slaughtered like rats in a barn. In the evening, when the bayonet had completed its fatal work, the men were employed in burying the dead in two large pits. Captain Wolseley, who was engaged on this unpleasant task, mentions as a singular coincidence, that when counting the corpses, as they were flung into the pits, it was found that they numbered 1857—the date of the year; this number was exclusive of others who were killed outside when seeking to make their escape.

WOLSELEY STORMS THE MESS-HOUSE.

From the Secundrabagh, Sir Colin proceeded against the Shah Nujeef, a tomb of one of the kings of Oude, and here ensued the sternest struggle of the Relief. Lieutenant Wynne and Ensign Powell, of the 90th, were wounded, and it was while bringing up the remainder of his battalion that Major Barnston received his death-wound from a shell. Peel now battered the place with his heavy guns, after which the 93rd stormed it. On the morning of the 17th operations were resumed, and the services of Captain Wolseley during the day were of so marked a character, that he had the coveted honour of seeing his name specially mentioned in the Commander-in-Chief's despatch. This was in connection with the attack on the 32nd Mess-house,* formerly known as the Khoorsheyd Munzil ('Happy Palace'), a building of considerable size, defended by a ditch and loopholed wall.

During the morning of the 17th, Sir Colin was engaged in pressing back the enemy, and about noon Captain Peel brought up his guns, and kept up a heavy fire on the Mess-house. After the building had been battered for about three hours, Sir Colin determined to storm, and sent for Captain Wolseley, whom he had known by repute in the Crimea. The Commander-in-Chief, addressing him, said that he had selected him to command the storming-party, and that he would be supported by a company of Sikhs and the detachment of his regiment, which was led by Captain Guise, the officer next in seniority to Major Barnston. On Wolseley's expressing his extreme gratification at being selected for this honourable task, Sir Colin described the work as being sur-

* The late Mr. Martin Gubbins, at this time Financial Commissioner of Lucknow, in his 'Mutinies in Oude,' describes the Mess-house in the following terms: 'Its structure is massive; all the windows on the ground-floor are furnished with strong iron gratings, and it is surrounded by a moat, passable only at the two entrances, of which the principal immediately faces us. All those windows are bricked-up inside the iron grating for three parts of their height, and the masonry is most carefully loopholed.'

rounded by a ditch, about twelve feet broad and scarped with masonry, and beyond that a loopholed mud wall; there were also drawbridges, but he did not know whether they were down. His instructions were that, in the event of the drawbridges being up, and his not being able to effect an entrance, he was to leave his men under cover and return and report to him.*

Wolseley left the Chief, and proceeded to carry out his instructions. Captain Peel, who was battering the Messhouse with his heavy guns, was requested to cease firing; but just as Wolseley gave the order, 'Double,' to his men, Peel characteristically turned to Sir Colin Campbell, and asked leave just to give 'one more broadside.' The favour granted, Wolseley amid a hot fire from the neighbouring buildings, outstripping his men with the fierce energy that distinguished him in the assault of Myat-toon's position, ran over the intervening space; arrived under the garden wall, he halted to get breath, and then clambered over it. Inside the garden he found many matchlockmen, who fired at him, but, though the bullets flew about him, he ran on unscathed and entered the Mess-house without opposition. As he gained the drawbridge, which was down, he called to the bugler to sound the advance, to show that he had done the work entrusted to him, and then bounded up the steps to the roof of the building, on which he† planted the British flag. The enemy opened fire from every gun they could

---

* We have been assured by an officer of the 90th, who accompanied Wolseley on this occasion, that the Commander-in-Chief promised him the Victoria Cross before he dismissed him from his presence. While on this subject of the Victoria Cross, we may mention that, during the Crimean War, the late Sir W. Gordon, of 'Gordon's Battery,' recommended Captain Wolseley for the distinction, for his conspicuous gallantry on the 7th of June, and again on the 30th of August, on the occasion of his receiving his wound.

† By a singular coincidence he was accompanied by Lieutenant F. Roberts, of the Bengal Artillery, Deputy Assistant Quartermaster-General, an officer who has since acquired a world-wide renown by his remarkable achievements in Afghanistan,

bring to bear on the Mess-house, and so heavy was the fire that twice the flag was struck down, only to be replaced, (and, finally, he had to retire with men under cover.)*

At this time Captain Irby came up with his company of the 90th, and Wolseley directed him to take some houses to the left, while he proceeded to attack those to the right, the fire being heavy from both directions. Irby succeeded in occupying the Tara Kothie,† or observatory, without meeting with any opposition, though during the latter part of the day he had hard work in holding the position.

And now one more task remained—the occupation of the Motee Mahul Palace,‡ situated on the banks of the Goomtee, the last post which separated the besieged and their deliverers. While Irby held the Tara Kothie, Wolseley proceeded to the attack of the Motee Mahul, and the success

* Mr. Gubbins, who, in company with General Havelock, witnessed this exploit from their post of observation, the roof of the Chuttur Munzil Palace, thus graphically describes it: 'It is now three o'clock, and if the enemy have any men concealed in that massive pile, the Mess-house, we shall soon see, for the red-coats are approaching; they are moving down in regular order along the road leading from the Shah Nujeef, and now are lost to view. Presently a part of them are seen advancing in skirmishing order. They have reached the enclosing wall; they are over it, through the shrubbery, and now the leading officer enters at the door which we have been watching; and while a larger body follow, rushing at a double up the building, he reappears upon the roof, and presently a British ensign floats on the right-hand tower of the Khoorsheyd Munzil. It is Captain Wolseley, of the 90th, who has placed it there.

'The building was indeed, as we supposed, abandoned, but the fire is so heavy from the Tara Kotee and adjacent buildings that it is no easy work that our noble fellows have to do. See! the ensign is struck down, and now it is again raised and fixed more firmly than before. But again a shot strikes it down, and probably the staff is damaged, for they have taken it down through the garden to that group of officers—probably Sir Colin himself and staff—whose caps are visible inside the enclosing compound wall. To the right, this wall is lined by the captors of the Mess-house, and a heavy fire of musketry, with occasional shot and shell, is directed from the Kaiser Bagh upon them; and now they cross the wall, enter the Tara Kotee enclosure, charge up its main avenue, and are hid from us by the trees.'

† Tara means 'stars,' and Kothie, 'pucka,' or permanent building.

‡ This Motee Mahul ('Pearl of Palaces'), like similar edifices, is enclosed within a high wall, and is one of the most spacious and graceful buildings of its kind in Lucknow. Here the King of Oude was wont to regale his European guests.

he achieved with only his company forms one of the most extraordinary episodes of the war. Quitting the garden of the Mess-house, he ran the gauntlet across the road under a heavy fire, but, on arriving at the Motee Mahul, found that the gateway was built up and loopholed. He was met by a volley, but proceeded with his company to subdue the enemy's fire, and at length, by dint of hard fighting, won the loopholes, though with the loss of many of his brave fellows. He now sent back an officer with a few men, to bring up crowbars and pickaxes to force the newly-made brickwork of the gateway. This was a service of some danger, as the road was still swept by musketry and canister. In the meantime, Wolseley kept his company as much under cover as possible. Soon the men were seen returning with the tools, and Private Andrews, a gallant fellow who had been Wolseley's servant in the Crimea, ran out from under shelter to show his comrades the way across. No sooner, however, had he darted into the street, than he was shot through the body from one of the loopholes. Wolseley had a particular regard for this fine fellow, and, though he was lying out in the street within five or six yards of the loophole from whence he had been shot, sprang out and bore him back in his arms. As he was carrying Andrews, a Pandy took deliberate aim at the officer, but the bullet passed through the body of the soldier.*

At this time, while Wolseley was busy with his men in knocking a hole in the wall of the Motee Mahul, the late Mr. Kavanagh, V.C., arrived on the scene and offered to guide

* Andrews, we may observe, still lives, and, for his services and wounds, enjoys the magnificent pension of eightpence per diem. Like the greater portion of the 90th, of Crimean and Indian Mutiny days, he was a cockney, as the regiment recruited largely in the metropolis; and, in the opinion of Wolseley, your Londoner is peculiarly adapted for light infantry work, by reason of his superior intelligence and general smartness. This incident of the rescue of Andrews formed the subject of a painting, which was exhibited in the Royal Academy Exhibition of 1881.

him to a place where an entrance could be effected. Wolseley gladly closed with the proposal, and, leaving injunctions with his subalterns to get on as fast as they could with the work in hand, accompanied Kavanagh on his perilous mission. Proceeding down the street about one hundred yards with the 'whish' of a rifle-bullet occasionally ringing in their ears, they passed through broken walls, and gardens, and deserted courts, but their endeavours to find an entrance into the palace were unsuccessful. After an absence of about ten minutes, during which Kavanagh found that all the entrances he knew of were built up, they returned, and arrived just as Ensign Haig was wriggling through an aperture knocked in the wall.

Soon the hole was sufficiently enlarged for Wolseley and all his men to make their way into a courtyard of the Motee Mahul, whence, proceeding into the palace, they drove the enemy from room to room, and from yard to yard, firing and receiving their fire as the fight progressed towards the river, on the banks of which the palace was built. At length they drove them all out of this great agglomeration of buildings, and, closely following the fugitives, forced them into the Goomtee, where a number of them were shot as they tried to swim across.*

Having cleared the Motee Mahul, Wolseley proceeded with his company, which nobly responded to the calls made upon them by their chief, to force his way into the Residency itself. Now it so happened that the 90th, which, under the command of Colonel Purnell, the successor of the lamented Colonel Campbell, formed a portion of the Lucknow garrison, held the most advanced post in the Residency; and, just at this time, a company of the regi-

* Kavanagh says of Wolseley, in his work, 'How I Won the Victoria Cross': 'Captain Wolseley, who delighted in dash and danger, fell upon the enemy as they tried to escape, and in half an hour he was seen on the top of the inner buildings, waving the British banner.'

ment made a sortie, so that, strange to relate, the first of the relieved and their deliverers to join hands were the officers and men of the gallant 90th Light Infantry! It was a singular coincidence, and '*terque, quaterque beatus,*' to borrow a Virgilian phrase, was Captain Wolseley, in being the undoubted claimant to the distinction of first effecting a junction with the heroic garrison of the Lucknow Residency.

And now the three noble chiefs, Campbell, Outram, and Havelock, at length met, and there was presented the group delineated by the artist, Mr. Barker, in his great painting of the ' Relief of Lucknow.'*

Fortune had certainly smiled on Wolseley. It was so at the Quarries, when he participated in almost the only successful assault of the English army, and now, on this memorable occasion, the 'fickle jade' again favoured her favourite child; on his part, the young soldier eagerly seized each opportunity for winning her favours as it was presented to him, and, by his judgment and impetuous valour, justified the choice.

All was now gratulation and hand-shaking; and the British soldiers and sailors of the relieving force eagerly greeted their comrades and the women and children they had dared so many perils to rescue from the clutches of the rebellious Sepoys surrounding them. The detachment of the 90th, which lately had Major Barnston for its leader, welcomed their comrades, who, embarking in the *Himalaya*, had marched up-country with Sir James Outram, and earned for the regiment immortal renown by their bearing throughout those trying days in September, when Havelock forced

---

* The engraving of this painting, with the heads of Hope Grant, Mansfield, Napier, Inglis, Greathed, Peel, Adrian Hope, Alison, Little, David Russell, Hope Johnstone, Norman, Anson, Hodson, Probyn, Watson, Kavanagh, and other gallant soldiers, is well known to old Indians. The painting itself fetched, on the 24th of April, 1875, at the Manley Hall Sale, £1,018.

his way through the heart of Lucknow with only 2,600 men. Wolseley now learnt, with sincere regret, of the death of Colonel Campbell, who had expired of his wound only four days before, and also of other friends and gallant soldiers of humbler rank. The loss sustained by the relieving army, which only numbered 4,550 men, between the 14th and 25th of November, was 10 officers and 112 men killed, and 35 officers (of whom 3 died) and 379 rank and file wounded.

It will be allowed that Wolseley had good reason to anticipate the congratulations and thanks of the Commander-in-Chief for his conduct, but what was his astonishment on learning from his Brigadier, the Hon. Adrian Hope, that Sir Colin was furious with him for having exceeded the letter of instructions, in that when he was only ordered to take the Mess-house, he actually, of his own motion, had driven the enemy out of the Motee Mahul! The Brigadier advised him to keep out of the way, as the Chief was asking for him, and he never saw a man more enraged in his life.

Captain Wolseley's company passed the night of the 17th of November* in the Shah Nujeef, where the Commander-in-Chief and his staff had taken up their quarters; the

* Wolseley's adventures on this 17th November did not end when he effected a junction with Captain Tinling's company of his regiment. Being desirous of showing in a practical form his regard for his old comrades, he had brought with him some tobacco, which he distributed among the officers and men of this company, to whom it was a real godsend. But there was still one desideratum which was requisite to make the gallant fellows happy, and that was—rum. This also their thoughtful comrade had not forgotten, but the liquor, being bulky, had been left behind at the place from which he had started in the morning, when proceeding to storm the Mess-house. It was now between six and eight in the evening, and getting dark; but Wolseley, though his exertions had been of a sufficiently arduous character to tire most men, started off on his charitable errand, with four or five men, who volunteered to accompany him. At length, having secured the rum, he slung it on a pole between two men, and commenced his return march. It was pitch-dark as he passed through the Mess-house gardens, and suddenly, as he was proceeding along, himself leading the way, he heard a scream. Turning round, he found that one of the pole-bearers had been run through the body by a Pandy, who was prowling about the grounds, and whom he had himself just passed. In the dark Wolseley lost his way,

building was commanded by the enemy, who still occupied the Kaiser Bagh, from which they kept up a cannonade, but the British soldiers slept the sleep of the weary, having learned to disregard such interruptions provided they were not too personal.

After the warning he had received from his Brigadier, Wolseley, on the following morning, kept out of the way of the 'Lord Sahib;' but Sir Colin espied him, and calling to him, began to administer a severe 'wigging.' He commenced by asking him what he meant by exceeding his instructions; that he had ordered him to take the Messhouse, and how dared he attack the Motee Mahul? He then told him that he was very angry with him on the previous night; indeed, he did not think he was ever so much incensed against any man in his life, and it was lucky for him that he could not be found. The ire of the old Chief now began to cool, and his tone became half jocular. He invited Wolseley by a gesticulation to pace up and down with him, and, after warning him against the heinousness of exceeding instructions, the veteran, who could not but admire gallantry, such as he himself had displayed through-

---

and it was some hours before he gained the garden of the Furreed Buksh, where he was told his brother officers were assembled, in a summer-house in the centre of the grounds. Proceeding there, he put his head in and glanced round the room, where he saw a number of men sitting at a table in the centre, but he did not recognise any of them. As he was going away, one of the number, Captain (now Sir Harry) Goodricke, called out: 'Why, that's Wolseley.' He turned, and then recognised his old messmates, who were so altered by privation and constant duty that, at first, he actually did not know them.

An amusing circumstance happened during the night. Wolseley heard Lieutenant Carter raging and swearing at some one, and, on inquiring the exciting cause of his subaltern's wrath, learned that, in the dark, some 'beastly nigger' had attempted to place one of the legs of a charpoy, or light wooden bedstead, on his stomach. Lieutenant Carter naturally resented this indignity, but the language in which he couched his protest was far from parliamentary, or complimentary to the native in question. After a laugh at this slight *contretemps* the officers went to sleep. On awaking in the morning, Carter's consternation may be imagined when he discovered that the 'beastly nigger' of the previous night was none other than His Excellency the Commander-in-Chief, the lord of many legions.

out his fifty years' service, ended by congratulating him on the courage and ability he had displayed, and expressed his intention to recommend him for promotion.

Sir Colin Campbell having resolved to withdraw from Lucknow, contrary to the advice of both Outram and Havelock, the 90th and other regiments were engaged in making a direct road from that portion of the Residency where the ladies and children had been confined, to the ground occupied by the relieving force. In order to effect this, walls and houses were broken down, and all open spaces between Martin's House and the Motee Mahul and Secundrabagh were screened from fire by means of shutters, doors, and anything that came to hand. In the evening, after being thus engaged all day, Wolseley's company and the remainder of the detachment were sent back, and placed on picket on the side of the road close to the Shah Nujeef. On the 19th commenced the withdrawal to Dilkhoosha of the ladies and children, who numbered about 500, and sick and wounded 1,500 more.

The 90th pickets had received orders to wait till the garrison had passed out, and cover the retreat as far as Secundrabagh, a duty which the detachment performed with perfect order and regularity. At midnight of the 22nd, leaving all lights still burning, Outram's soldiers marched silently out of the post they had so long defended, being followed by Hope's Brigade, which had been quartered in the Motee Mahul, the 90th bringing up the rear, while the sullen boom of the cannon told that the enemy, unaware of what had happened, were still firing into the position which was now unoccupied. On arriving at Secundrabagh, the army continued its movement of retreat in the same order towards Dilkhoosha, which was reached at half-past three in the morning. At noon of the 23rd of November, the detachment drew up in line opposite the Martinière, and the non-effectives, baggage, and ammunition, forming an immense convoy, were passed through it.*

Early in the morning of the 24th of November, the detachment paraded, and Sir Colin's General Order of the previous day, complimenting the relieving army, was read to the men; and then, as they were about to rejoin the headquarters of the regiment, under the command of Colonel Purnell, Brigadier Hope rode up, and addressed the officers and men on leaving his brigade. This the gallant Brigadier did in a graceful, manly speech, which was responded to by three hearty cheers. The 90th was attached to Outram's Division, which it was decided should remain at Alumbagh. The object of this occupation was threefold, viz., to avoid the appearance of having abandoned Oude; to keep the insurgents around Lucknow in check; and to secure a point on which our advance for the re-conquest of Oude might be made.

The entire army halted at Alumbagh on the 26th of November, and, on the following day, the Commander-in-Chief commenced his march for Cawnpore with General Grant's Division, and the whole of the sick and wounded, and Lucknow refugees.

Sir James Outram took up a position about 1,500 yards from Alumbagh on the vast plain which, smooth as a billiard table, extends without a break to the Bunnee Bridge. The Alumbagh enclosure was one of his outposts, as were also the neighbouring villages, which were all fortified; and, at these posts, strongly occupied by our troops, desultory fighting took place almost daily. The division—which

* Captain Wolseley was witness to a curious and suggestive scene that happened on this night. Captain Magennis, of the 90th, was in charge of some State prisoners of high rank, including the King of Oude's brother. As they passed, Wolseley, whose company was the last picket in the direction of Lucknow, heard Magennis ask a sergeant where was his prisoner. 'Oh, sir, he wouldn't come on, and so I just shot him,' replied the non-commissioned officer, who seemed to think it the most natural, as it was the easiest, way of curing a fit of obstinacy.

numbered only 4,400 men of all arms, inclusive of those at Bunnee—consisted of Her Majesty's 5th, 78th, 84th, and 90th Regiments, and Captain Brasyer's Ferozepore Regiment of Sikhs, 800 strong, the whole being organized into two brigades, under Colonels Hamilton (78th) and Stisted (64th). The artillery, under the command of Major Vincent Eyre, included the batteries of Captain Maude (Royal Artillery), and Captain Olpherts (Bengal Artillery), and many guns of position, forming a total of about forty pieces. The cavalry consisted of Major Robertson's battalion of Military Train, which now acted as light horse, and some of the 12th Native Irregulars, the whole numbering not more than 250 sabres. But any deficiency of numbers was made up by the gallantry of these veteran soldiers, the remarkable capacity of the staff and other officers, and, more than aught else, by the *prestige* attaching to the name of the Commander, to which, doubtless, was due the fact that a force of little more than 4,000 men was able successfully to defend an open position against the attacks of 100,000 rebels, of whom half were trained soldiers—for this was the number of armed men Outram, on one occasion, assured Wolseley were assembled in Lucknow and its neighbourhood, according to reliable information he had received.

Outram did not think it beneath his dignity to seek to make his soldiers regard him with personal affection, as well as with that respect which he inspired in the minds of everyone who came within his influence; rarely indeed has any character afforded such an admixture of dignity and amiability, of heroism and gentleness, of a high and noble ambition and a yet loftier and purer self-sacrifice, of which his whole life afforded many memorable instances.* Every

* Such high authorities as Lord Napier of Magdala, Lord Wolseley, and the late Sir Vincent Eyre, are agreed as to Outram's distinction as a general. Lord Napier once said of him : ' Of all those whose names are borne in the annals of the history of India, or enshrined in the hearts of its people, there

officer and man of the 90th loved the General, who, in return, showed his appreciation of their regard by numerous acts of kindness and thoughtfulness. Among such traits, Wolseley mentions that he would, when visiting the Alumbagh or other outposts, read out to the officer in command any intelligence he had received from Cawnpore or Calcutta in a sufficiently loud tone of voice for the men about to hear the news.

Almost daily there was fighting at the outposts near Alumbagh, but the enemy shrank from continuous and determined attacks in full force on the standing camp, and there was no rebel leader of sufficient enterprise to attempt to repeat the tactics of Cawnpore. The camp had Alumbagh in front, the small fort of Jellalabad to the right front, some villages to the left front, and outposts at villages on the right and left rear; a strong detachment also was at Bunnee Bridge, about eight miles on the road to Cawnpore, under command of Colonel Fisher.

Wolseley had not been long at Alumbagh when he was sent for a week to do outpost duty at the old fort of Jellalabad, which was decidedly the pleasantest post in the position, some ten miles in circumference, which Sir James Outram undertook to defend with his small division.

In the middle of December, a convoy arrived from Cawnpore, and then Wolseley and his brother officers who sailed in the *Transit*, learned that the kit which they had deposited there had all been burnt by the Gwalior mutineers, who first defeated General Windham—'Redan Windham,' as he was called—and then besieged him in his intrenchments.

---

is none more noble, none more worthy of love, admiration, and gratitude than Sir James Outram.' Sir Garnet Wolseley declared to the writer that Outram was 'the finest soldier he ever served under;' and Sir V. Eyre said, 'As a commander in the field, he possessed a rare and most valuable combination of pluck and caution, and he knew exactly the time for bringing each quality into play.'

ACTION OF THE 22nd DECEMBER.

Thus, for the second time, Wolseley was a heavy loser by the chances of war.

On the 20th of December, information was brought to Sir James Outram by his spies, that the rebels intended surrounding his position, with the object of cutting off his supplies and intercepting his communications with Bunnee. He accordingly determined to anticipate them and strike a blow, and, at 2.30 a.m., on the 22nd of December, a column of 1,000 men and 2 guns marched out under his personal command to attack the enemy, who had left a space of about half a mile intervening between their position and the gardens skirting the canal and the Dilkhoosha. Outram, seeing his advantage, resolved to take them by surprise, and cut off their retreat from Lucknow.

It was cold and rather dark when Captain Wolseley proceeded with his regiment, which formed the right column of the attacking force. Favoured by a heavy mist, Outram was enabled to approach quite close to the left flank of the enemy, whose cavalry vedettes challenged, and then, firing their carbines, galloped off to the main body. Outram gave the order to deploy, and with a loud hurrah the right column, under the command of Colonel Purnell, of the 90th, charged the enemy in line, and, in spite of a heavy fire of grape and musketry, carried the position with a rush. The left column, under Colonel Guy, of the 5th Fusiliers, was equally successful, and soon the rebels were in full retreat across the plain, pursued by the cavalry, until they found refuge in a village, from which they opened a heavy fire of grape and musketry. Olpherts now came into action with his guns, and speedily dislodged the enemy, who, changing their line of retreat, endeavoured to reach the city by the Dilkhoosha. The Military Train, detached to make a flank movement, followed them up so rapidly that they dispersed their cavalry, and captured their 4 guns. Outram's arrangements were rewarded with the success they merited; the surprise had been complete, and in the village were found the children and women cooking their *chupatties*, or oatcakes. The houses were fired after the non-combatants were driven away, and the column returned, the men carrying vegetables and dragging or leading away all the live stock they could lay their hands on, such as goats, sheep, and bullocks. As they were moving off, a large body of the enemy advanced towards the burning village, but finding that they were too late to be of assistance, halted and retraced their steps to Lucknow. Before noon Outram had returned to his camp, having taught the Natives a severe lesson regarding the danger of attempting to interfere with his communications.

On the following day, Captain Wolseley proceeded to Cawnpore, with his company, to escort supplies. The journey occupied three days, the force marching about fifteen miles a day. The first night the escort halted at Bunnee, up to which point there was desultory fighting with the enemy. The second night they halted at Busserutgunge, a walled village with a high road running through the centre. On arriving at Cawnpore, Wolseley learnt with deep sorrow the death of his friend, Major Barnston, who had been wounded five weeks before. The escort returned immediately to Alumbagh with the convoy, and, on New Year's Day, there were athletic sports, Sir James Outram and the officers subscribing liberally for prizes for the men.

On the 12th of January, 1858, the rebels made a most determined assault on the British position. As on the previous occasion, he had received information from his spies that the enemy would attack, and made the necessary dispositions. At daybreak the troops breakfasted, and were held in readiness for immediate service. About sunrise large masses of the enemy, calculated by Outram to amount 'at the lowest estimate to 30,000 men,' were seen on the left front, and they gradually surrounded the whole front and flanks of the position, a distance of at least six miles. As soon as their movements were sufficiently developed, Outram marched his small army, decreased by the absence on convoy duty of 530 men and 4 guns, in two brigades, the right mustering 713 Europeans, and the left, with which was Wolseley's company, 733 bayonets, with 100 of Brasyer's Sikhs. Fighting commenced all along the line about half-past eight a.m., and it was not until four p.m. that the enemy, who suffered very considerably from the fire of the guns, finally withdrew, and returned to Lucknow or to their original positions in the gardens and villages in front of the British camp.

Again, only four days later, the rebels made a determined attempt to overwhelm the small band of Englishmen, whom it must have been most galling to them to see entrenched within a few miles of the great stronghold of rebeldom.

Captain Wolseley was on picket at the left-front village, on the morning of the 16th of January, when the enemy were seen advancing in great numbers. They made repeated attempts throughout the day to carry the village, but were driven back with severe loss. After dark they assembled in great strength, and, about eight o'clock, 'screwing their courage to the sticking-place,' advanced to attack the village to the inspiriting calls of many bugles, sounding the 'assembly,' the 'advance,' and the 'double.' They were distinctly heard encouraging one another with 'Chelow-bhye !' (Go on quick, brother !), and other exclamations by which the 'mild Hindoo' is wont to prompt his neighbour to deeds of gallantry, and keep up his own failing heart. They occupied a 'tope' of trees to the left of the village, and advanced into the open ; but the guns and infantry reserved their fire. At length, when they had approached to within seventy yards of the position, they were met by discharges of grape from the battery, and a volley from Wolseley's company. Still they hesitated, thus giving time to reload to their opponents, whom they might have annihilated had they mustered only sufficient pluck to charge at this critical moment when only 100 British bayonets intervened between them and the revenge they thirsted for. That hesitancy of a moment was fatal. A second volley of grape and rifle-bullets swept through their ranks, when they broke and fled in the utmost confusion, carrying away, according to custom, most of their killed and wounded. 'After they had retired,' says Lieutenant Herford, 'we wandered over the ground near the topes, and found a few dead bodies, some pools of blood, and heaps of shoes, which had been kicked off, lying about everywhere.'

The enemies from whose attacks the gallant Alumbagh garrison most suffered at this time were *ennui* and dust. The former was irksome, after the excitement of long marches and hard campaigning; but the latter was unbearable, and caused the greatest discomfort, almost amounting to positive misery. The dust, which lay some six inches deep, was blown in great clouds and eddies, which swept over the plain, searching out every chink and crevice of the flimsy tents, and filled the mouth and eyes and entered into the composition of every dish.

Nothing of importance occurred until the 21st of February, when the enemy made the long-threatened 'grand attack,' which was not only carefully designed, but was so well matured that had they evinced determination, the Alumbagh garrison would have been hard pressed. The Moulvie, Mansoob Ali, and the Begum, Huzrut Mahul, wife of the ex-King of Oude, agreed to set aside their differences for that day; and the Oude local troops and the regulars entered heart and soul into the matter. The plan was to surround the British camp, and make simultaneous assaults from five or six dif-

FINAL ROUT OF THE REBELS. 101

ferent points, while demonstrations against the intermediate portions of the wide-extended *enceinte* were to prevent a concentration of Outram's troops, and at the same time distract his attention and embarrass his defensive operations. But Outram was not the man to wait quietly on the defensive.

He moved out with cavalry and guns, and attacking with spirit, put them to the rout. Meantime some sharp fighting took place at Alumbagh, where Wolseley was stationed. A few shots struck the centre building, and at seven a.m. the enemy came on at all points, lining every shrub and tree where they could get cover. But they were deficient in spirit, and dispersed under the musketry-fire and discharges of grape. The rebel commanders confessed to the Durbar that their losses were between 400 and 500; but their intentions were praiseworthy and their preparations complete, for Outram's spies reported that they had scaling-ladders all ready for storming Alumbagh.

Sir James Outram went out with some cavalry and guns on the 24th of February, and again, on the following day, proceeded beyond Jellalabad, when he encountered and defeated the enemy, who had come out under the leadership of the Begum. During the night the rebels attacked all along the British front and left flank where Wolseley's company was posted, and were bold enough to fire grape from the 'tope' of trees on the left-front picket, where the fighting took place on the 16th of January. They, however, soon retreated; and this was the last time the Alumbagh force, as such, received molestation from the enemy.

In the meantime, Sir Colin Campbell had been organizing his 'grand army'[*] for the reconquest of Lucknow and Oude,

---

[*] On the 2nd of March the effective force consisted of: Artillery, 1,613 officers and men; Engineers, 2,002; Cavalry, 3,613; Infantry, 11,940; Total, 19,771. On the 5th of March it was joined by General Franks' Division, numbering 5,893 men, the Goorkha portion of which, 3,000 bayonets, joined the Nepaul Maharajah when he arrived before Lucknow with his division, 9,000 strong.

and on learning that Rose's and Whitlock's columns were well on their march towards Jhansi, he pushed his troops across the Ganges, and arrived at Buntara, about four miles from Alumbagh, on the 1st of March. On the following morning Sir Colin Campbell moved up from Buntara to Dilkhoosha with General Lugard's Division and the cavalry, commanded by Brigadier-General Hope Grant, who had been carrying on operations against the rebels in Oude during the month of February. In the meantime, Jellalabad had been formed into a commissariat depôt on the largest scale, there being attached to the advancing army no less than 16,000 camels, a siege-train park covering a square of 400 yards, with 12,000 oxen, and a following of 60,000 non-combatants.

Since the Commander-in-Chief had evacuated Lucknow, taking with him the women and children of the Residency, the rebels had fortified the city with no little care and skill. Behind the canal they had thrown up earthworks, while the Martinière, Secundrabagh, Shah Nujeef, Mess-house, and Motee Mahul were fortified; the Kaiser Bagh also was a perfect citadel, and the streets and houses had been loopholed.

Between the 3rd and 4th of March the Third Division, under General Walpole, came up to Alumbagh, and, at the same time, Sir James Outram was directed to take command of the division, which the Commander-in-Chief had determined to detach across the Goomtee, to operate on Lucknow from that side. And so the 90th was parted from the General, under whom they had served for many months in the defence of Alumbagh.* Even after the seve-

* The garrison of Jellalabad, in Afghanistan, gained the title of 'illustrious' from Lord Ellenborough for their gallant defence of a position protected by walls and bastions. Though the Afghans are a fiercer race than the natives of India, yet the 37th Bengal Native Infantry (which mutinied in 1857) repeatedly encountered and defeated them; and Akbar Khan, in his great effort against the Jellalabad garrison, on the 7th of April, 1842, only

THE ADVANCE ON LUCKNOW. 103

rance of the connection that had been cemented on the battle-field and the bivouac, the good General showed that he did not forget the gallant fellows who had fought and bled under him, for he used regularly to send the 90th a liberal supply of newspapers and periodicals for the use of the men.

On the afternoon of the 6th of March, the 90th left their old camping-ground at Alumbagh, and started to join the Commander-in-Chief at Dilkhoosha. The night was very dark, and the road bad, and, being encumbered with baggage and ammunition, it was not until the morning, after a march of nearly twelve hours, that they reached the camping-ground marked out for them in rear of the artillery park. Scarcely had they arrived, and were counting upon breakfast and a little rest, than they received fresh orders to move again, as it was decided that the 90th should be brigaded with the 42nd, 93rd, and 4th Punjaub Rifles, forming the 4th Brigade of the 2nd, or General Lugard's, Division, under the command of their old Brigadier, the Hon. Adrian Hope. On the following day, the whole regiment was sent on picket about five p.m., with orders to line some of the walls surrounding the Dilkhoosha Park.

---

mustered 6,000 men to his standard, while Outram's force was assailed by 30,000, including some of the finest regiments of the Sepoy army, and experienced artillerymen. Sir Vincent Eyre, in a letter addressed some years ago to the author, then employed on a memoir of Sir James Outram, says: 'Outram's prolonged occupation of Alumbagh plain, comprising a frontage of two miles and a circuit of seven, with a small army of occupation never exceeding 3,500 men, within cannon-range of Lucknow, to hold in check an enemy mustering 100,000 strong within the walls, was a masterpiece of cautious warfare, to which justice has never yet been done, because his precarious position there, in obedience to Sir Colin Campbell's commands, has never up to this moment been properly understood.' Lord Napier of Magdala also said: 'No achievement in the events of 1857 surpassed in skill and resolution the maintenance of the position of Alumbagh with a mere handful of troops against overwhelming numbers, well supplied with artillery. There were no walls or ramparts, merely an open camp, protected by a few well-selected intrenched outposts, and a scanty line of bayonets, ever ready, day and night, to repel attack.' The Alumbagh force and its heroic chief have never had justice rendered to them for their defence of this position.

During the morning of the 9th of March a heavy artillery fire was maintained on the Martinière, and General Lugard received instructions to carry the position. The Commander-in-Chief's orders specified that 'the men employed in the attack will use nothing but the bayonet. They are absolutely forbidden to fire a shot till the position is won.' At two o'clock the 42nd Highlanders and 4th Sikhs stormed the Martinière, with slight loss, the 90th, which acted in support, only losing one man from a discharge of grape. The regiment passed the night of the 9th in the Martinière, and on the following day was divided into detachments, which were placed on picket in different places. Captain Wolseley was employed with his company (the I Company) covering the pontoon bridge which had been thrown across the Goomtee just beyond the enemy's first line of works.

Early on the morning of the 11th, Wolseley's company, with two others of his regiment, was directed to cover some Horse Artillery guns engaged in the open. While thus employed a round shot carried away the end of an elephant's trunk, when the poor beast, frantic with rage and pain, came rushing down through the skirmishers. After this service, Wolseley proceeded on picket in the open space in front of the Secundrabagh,* where he remained all night.

On Sunday morning, the 14th of March, Kaiser Bagh, the chief stronghold of Lucknow, was won. Wolseley's and the two other detached companies of the 90th and the 53rd, having been relieved by the 97th, were ordered to proceed to the Kaiser Bagh in support. Passing up loopholed streets, round by batteries, the guns of which still threatened them, and over a bridge of loose planks, past burn-

* While under the enemy's fire, Wolseley was attracted by a curious-looking projectile which dropped near him. Taking it up, he found that it was a large cut-glass knob, which the native gunners, being hard pushed for round shot, had doubtless broken off from one of the magnificent chandeliers of the Kaiser Bagh. This singular projectile he presented to Sir Hope Grant, by whom it was used as a letter-weight.

ing timber, they reached the enclosure of the Kaiser Bagh, where they found that the remainder of the 90th Regiment were already established, they having rushed in by one entry while the Sikhs and 10th Foot effected an entrance by another. The scene that presented itself to Captain Wolseley's eyes within the building, or rather collection of palaces, courts, and gardens, which for magnificence and costliness of fittings enjoyed a reputation that was not belied by the reality, baffles description.

The Kaiser Bagh was given up to plunder, and there ensued a scene of vandalism and wilful destruction paralleled in those pages of Gibbon wherein he describes the sack of Ctesiphon, in the year 627, by the Saracenic hordes led by the ruthless Caliph Omar. Sikh and Briton vied with each other, as with clubbed muskets they shivered to fragments the costly glass chandeliers, battered to pieces the statues and gilt furniture, and strewed the floor with the mirrors they could not remove. Filled with the wanton spirit of mischief they broke into atoms on the floor 'large boxes of japanned work containing literally thousands of cups and vessels of jade, of crystal, and of china.' Entering the library, they tore into fragments the books, and lit their pipes with the illuminated MSS. and coloured miniatures, while boxes, swords, and pistols were shattered to pieces for the jewels with which they were inlaid. In some instances men sold for a few rupees, priceless jewels, believed to be worthless on account of their size and bad setting; and one case is recorded of a soldier who, for £10, parted with some jewels which were resold for £7,500. Officers in many instances were seized with the desire to grow rich, though Wolseley was among the number of those who could contemplate the loot with Platonic indifference, and he did not appropriate a gold mohur, or any article whatever. His men secured their fair share of plunder, and one officer, who had a bundle of thirty Cashmere shawls, gave him, unsolicited, one of great value; however, he did not long retain the gift, for while sleeping on it that night, he hurried out on the occasion of an alarm, and upon his return the shawl had been appropriated. On the following day, the men of his company presented him with two large silver bowls; but he was equally unfortunate with these mementoes, for one night some thieves stole from the head of his bed the box in which they were deposited.

After the capture of the Kaiser Bagh, Captain Wolseley's company rejoined the headquarters of the regiment, which was operating in the immediate neighbourhood. During the day, the Mess-house, Tara Kothie, Motee Mahul, and the Chuttur Munzil were rapidly occupied by our troops, which occasionally met with opposition. The 90th assisted in driving the enemy out of these strongly fortified positions, and on the 16th was relieved by the 97th, when the regiment returned to camp near the Dilkhoosha.*

After the capture of Lucknow, Sir Hope Grant was placed in command of a division, called the 'Lucknow Field Force;' and, on the 1st of April, the 90th, which was to form part of the force, struck their tents at Dilkhoosha, and marched into the city. They were quartered in a palace called Zoor-Buksh, near the Kaiser Bagh. But Wolseley's good fortune in always sharing in whatever fighting was in progress, again favoured him, and he did not for any length of time occupy his new quarters. A vacancy occurring on Sir Hope Grant's Staff, by the return to England on sick-leave of Lieutenant (now Major-General Sir Frederick) Roberts, V.C., Colonel the Hon. William Pakenham (now the Earl of Longford), an excellent officer, who succeeded

---

* The losses of Sir Colin Campbell's army between the 2nd and 21st of March inclusive, were 16 officers and 111 of all ranks killed, 51 officers and 545 wounded, and 13 missing.

General Estcourt as Adjutant-General in the Crimea, and held the same office for the royal troops in Bengal, recommended Captain Wolseley, with whose services he was familiar, for employment. Wolseley was, accordingly, appointed to the charge of the Quartermaster-General's Department of the Oude Division. It was a curious coincidence that thus, for the second time, brought into connection these two distinguished and representative officers, whose deeds form a proud page in the history of the British army.

Wolseley had not been many days in his new post, when, on the 11th of April, he accompanied Sir Hope Grant in an expedition, or *dour*, to Baree, a village twenty-five miles from Lucknow, on the Seetapore road, where Mansoob Ali, known as 'the Fyzabad Moulvie,' who had displayed great ability and energy in the defence of Lucknow, had taken up a position with a strong body of rebels.

On the 13th of April, the column, 3,000 men of all arms, came up with the enemy, some 6,000 infantry and 1,000 cavalry, who had taken up a strong position on the banks of a stream, having hills on either side. As the General had received intelligence of the close proximity of the rebels, Captain Wolseley,[*] as Quartermaster-General of the force, proceeded to reconnoitre their position, taking with him a guide and an escort of Native cavalry.

It was three o'clock in the morning when he started, the rest of the troops following soon after. About daybreak he suddenly came upon the enemy's cavalry, which, led by the redoubtable Moulvie in person, was seen charging down the

[*] On Wolseley devolved the task of learning the roads, marking out the camping ground, and securing the services of guides. The following was the method he adopted for acquiring trustworthy guides. In the evening he would send out a chuprassie, or one of the Native police, to the next village. The first four men he encountered in it were asked if they knew the way to such and such a place ; if they answered in the affirmative, they were immediately seized and brought into camp. When the march was over they were dismissed ; but woe to them if they misled the column !

road. Wolseley, who at this time was in advance with only five troopers, galloped back to the advanced guard, consisting of a squadron of the 7th Hussars, a detachment of Wales' Punjaub Horse, 2 guns, and about 150 infantry, the whole under Colonel Hagart. There was barely time to unlimber the guns, and fire a round of grape into the enemy, before the rebel horsemen were down upon them. Wolseley had to draw his sword, and a sharp hand-to-hand affair ensued. The enemy's cavalry charged the guns, but were repulsed, and an attempt by the rebel horse to capture the baggage was also repelled.

Wolseley was hard at work all day, which was a busy one for all arms of the small force, and very trying, owing to the excessive heat; and he met with an accident which caused him considerable inconvenience and pain. While jumping over banks carrying orders, and seeing to the disposition of the force, his sword tilted up, and struck his elbow-joint, inducing the formation of a large abscess, which caused him much suffering, though he refused to lay up, and continued his duties with his arm in a sling.

The column visited various places, and, on the 23rd of April, returned to Lucknow. On his arrival there Wolseley was gratified to learn that he had been gazetted Brevet-Major for his distinguished services during the Mutiny.

Sir Hope Grant now received orders from Lord Clyde to make a *dour* to disperse a large rebel force. Leaving Lucknow on the 27th of April, the column visited Poorwah, Parthan, Dhoundhea Keira, and other places, and at eleven p.m., on the 11th of May, proceeded on its march to Nuggur, over a broken country. On the following day—after a killing march of seven miles in the blazing sun, over ploughed fields, standing crops, and brushwood, when many men suffered from sunstroke—Sir Hope arrived about five o'clock at Sirsee, where he was informed the rebel leaders, Bene

Madhoo and Shewrutten Singh, had assembled an army of 15,000 infantry, 1,600 cavalry, and 11 guns.

On his arrival at Sirsee, he found the enemy had taken up a strong position along a nullah, with a jungle, containing the village and fort of Towrie, in their rear. The rebels opened fire about five o'clock, but, forming his column with the cavalry and Horse Artillery covering his right flank, he attacked with his infantry, under Brigadier (now Sir Alfred) Horsford, with such vigour that they gave way, and were driven into the jungle, leaving 2 guns in the hands of the victors. Owing to their superior numbers, the enemy at one time almost surrounded the small British force, but they were defeated with considerable loss, Shewrutten Singh, the rebel talookdar who held the neighbouring lands, being among the killed.

On the following morning, 13th of May, the column returned to Nuggur, and, proceeding by easy marches, encamped near the Martinière on the 21st of May. This *dour* was attended with serious loss to our troops, for out of less than 3,500 men, 32 died of sunstroke and 500 were sick, being nearly one-sixth of the entire force.* But Sir Hope was not disposed to allow even the hot weather that had set in with unusual intensity to deter him from resuming active operations, and learning that the enemy, under Bene Madhoo, were threatening the Cawnpore road, he marched on the 25th of May. Jessenda and Poorwah were visited, but hearing that the enemy was in force at Nawabgunge Bara-Bankee,† a village on the Fyzabad road, about eighteen

---

* Of this number the 90th lost 4 men, and 75 went into hospital. Since the regiment left England, early in the preceding year, 13 officers had been killed and 5 had died. In the Crimea the 90th lost 21 officers and 307 non-commissioned officers and men, killed, wounded, and missing. This was exclusive of the large number who died from the effects of disease in hospital.

† The 'big' Nawabgunge, so called to distinguish it from the Nawabgunge on the Cawnpore road.

miles from Lucknow, Sir Hope, at eleven p.m. on the 12th of June, marched across country with great rapidity, in order to accomplish the distance of twelve miles in the darkness, and save his men from the fearful effects of a forced march in the hot sun. Major Wolseley had a busy time making the necessary inquiries regarding the route, procuring guides, and seeing to the other arrangements of his department.

The enemy, who numbered 16,000 men, had taken up a strong position on a large plateau, surrounded on three sides by a stream, which was crossed by a stone bridge at a little distance from the town, on the fourth side being a jungle. The General's object was to turn their right, and to interpose between them and the jungle. The forced march across country was made with the loss of several men from heat apoplexy, and the stone bridge was reached about half an hour before daybreak.

After a short rest, the troops fell in at daylight, and having crossed the stream, Sir Hope advanced against the centre of the position. Though the enemy had been surprised by the celerity of the attack, they opened fire, and tried to surround the force, but were repulsed by Johnson's guns, supported by the Bays, while their attack on the right rear was met by the 3rd Battalion Rifle Brigade and Hodson's Horse, which had just crossed the stream. A severe struggle ensued, and the enemy stood their ground well, but were driven back, the Rifles attacking with the bayonet, and Hodson's Horse charging over broken ground in gallant style. Meanwhile Mackinnon's battery and the 7th Hussars were hotly engaged to the front, and, supported by the remainder of the Rifle Brigade, under Colonel Glyn, drove the enemy with serious loss from their position on the left. At this time a body of Ghazees displayed the most desperate courage; after sustaining the fire of Carleton's battery, they withstood two charges of the 7th Hussars, led by Sir William

THE ACTION OF NAWABGUNGE.

Russell, and left 125 dead round 2 guns they defended. During the action Brigadier Horsford attacked the enemy on the extreme left and captured 2 guns.

The action lasted three hours, and the troops were thoroughly exhausted, having been under arms from ten p.m. on the previous night, to nine a.m. on the morning of the 13th, when the enemy finally quitted the field of battle, on which they left 600 dead and 9 guns. The British loss in killed and wounded was 67; and, in addition, 33 men died from sunstroke, and 250 went into hospital.

In his despatch the General, who had before specially mentioned the services of Major Wolseley during the action at Baree, again highly commended him. After the battle Major Wolseley surveyed the ground, and drew a plan which was sent to the Commander-in-Chief. Indeed, at Baree, and after every action throughout the campaign in Oude, of which province there were no maps in existence, Wolseley executed plans, which were forwarded to head-quarters, and were of essential use to Lord Clyde when he went over the same ground.*

After gaining this important success, which had a marked moral effect upon the rebels, greatly dispiriting them and their leaders, the column encamped on the large sandy plain in rear of the village of Nawabgunge, where they erected huts with straw-thatched roofs.

---

* Wolseley was in the habit of keeping a journal of all the marches and movements, which were posted up daily, the book being stowed away in a large pocket on his person. In this journal he entered the hours of march-ing and halting, and minute details of the towns and villages, their inhabit-ants and capabilities. These particulars were transferred to a weekly report, which was sent to the Quartermaster-General of the Army; but it was so injured by damp while kept in store, that some years after, upon his apply-ing to the Quartermaster-General in Oude, portions of the writing were found to be obliterated; what could be deciphered was copied out, at his request, and sent to England, but unfortunately it was destroyed, with the rest of his papers and effects, at the fire at the Pantechnicon. Wolseley also kept a private journal of his Indian experiences, but this he unluckily lost in China.

Sir Hope Grant's energy was untiring, and, thanks to a strong constitution and spare habit of body, he, in common with Major Wolseley, appeared to be exempt from the evil effects of campaigning during the four monsoon months. While his forces melted away under the fervent heat, and the members of his personal and divisional staff, one after another, suffered from its effects—the gallant Anson, his aide-de-camp, being ill with dysentery, and Hamilton, his Assistant Adjutant-General, dying while proceeding to Calcutta on his way to England—the veteran General knew not what it was to have a day's illness, an immunity also enjoyed by Wolseley, whom wounds and exposure to Arctic cold and torrid heat appeared to have hardened to the point necessary for a soldier whose fortune it was to fight his country's battles in the four quarters of the globe.

On the 21st of July Sir Hope Grant marched to Fyzabad, to the assistance of Maun Singh, a powerful chief, who, after being one of the mainsprings of the rebellion, had deserted a failing cause, and was besieged by a large body of the enemy at Shahgunge. But the rebels dispersed, and Sir Hope pushed on to Ajudia, four miles lower down on the Gogra, where his guns opened fire on a portion of the fugitives as they were crossing the river. On the 9th of August, the General having returned to Fyzabad, despatched Brigadier Horsford towards Sultanpore to follow up the rebels; but learning that they mustered 20,000 men, with 15 guns, he proceeded to his assistance with the main body of his troops, and after an irksome march across cultivated fields and through marshes, in which the guns sank to the axle, joined the Brigadier on the 22nd August.

The Engineers having constructed a raft from some small boats and canoes, the General crossed the greater part of his force over the Goomtee, between the 25th and 27th of August, an operation which was skilfully performed in the face of the enemy, who, led by Bene Madhoo, opened fire with their guns posted on high ground on the opposite bank. At three a.m. on the 29th of August, Sir Hope, after repulsing an attack on the previous night, moved on the enemy, who, however, evacuated the position they had taken up.

The General entrusted all the arrangements for the passage of the river, which, owing to the heavy rains, was greatly swollen, to Major Wolseley, who had no rest for two nights and one day, while superintending the transport of the little army. The manner in which the difficult operation of crossing a swiftly-flowing and broad stream (the Goomtee at Sultanpore being 400 feet wide) was accomplished, in the face of a strong rebel army, with a powerful artillery, and with only three rafts made from dinghies, was creditable to Major Wolseley, 'who,' says Sir Hope Grant, 'as Deputy Assistant-Quartermaster-General, had the superintendence of the arrangements for crossing the river, and who performed them to my perfect satisfaction.'

The country was now tolerably clear, and the force remained at Sultanpore, further operations against the rebels being deferred until the cold weather in October. The interval was employed in throwing a bridge across the Goomtee, in which Wolseley gave his advice and assistance to the Engineer officers. Sir Hope Grant marched on the 11th of October with a small column towards Tanda, but returned to Sultanpore on the 23rd, proceeding thence again to Kandoo Nuddee, where 4,000 of the enemy were posted with several guns. But the rebels fled on the approach of the British force; and a few days later the column returned to Sultanpore.

The Lucknow Field Force was not allowed a lengthy period of repose, and, on the 3rd of November, Sir Hope marched to Amethie to operate against the rebel Rajah, in conjunction with Lord Clyde; and, accompanied by Major Wolseley and his staff, reconnoitred the fort, which he found to be of great strength and extent. However, the Rajah surrendered on the following day, and Sir Hope proceeded to Purseedapore on the 11th of November, and, on the following morning, took possession of the strong fort of Shunkerpore, belonging to Bene Madhoo, whom he had defeated at Nawabgunge. Under instructions from Lord Clyde, Sir Hope proceeded to Fyzabad, on the Gogra, which he crossed before daylight on the 27th of November, and, under fire of his heavy guns, carried the enemy's position. The cavalry and field-artillery went in pursuit, and six guns were captured and brought into camp.

On the 3rd of December, the column, which had returned to Nawabgunge, marched in the direction of Bunkussia, and, whilst proceeding to reconnoitre, suddenly came upon the main body of the Gondah Rajah's troops, about 4,000 men. The enemy opened fire from 3 guns, upon which Sir Hope advanced and drove them through the jungle, a distance of two miles, capturing 2 guns. On the 7th the column reached Bunkussia, the principal fort of the Gondah Rajah, which was destroyed, after which Sir Hope crossed the Raptee, and visited Bulrampore and Toolsepore. In order to prevent the enemy escaping to the Goruckpore district, he marched to Dulhurree, close to the Nepaul frontier, and then proceeded to Pushuroa. Disposing two small columns, under Brigadiers Rowcroft and Taylor, to cut off the escape of Bala Rao, who, with a force of 6,000 men and 15 guns, had retreated to near Kundakote, he moved forward to attack the rebel chief on the 4th of January, 1859. The enemy were, however, so thoroughly disheartened by the continuous defeats they had sustained, that neither Bene Madhoo, Bala Rao, nor any other of their

END OF THE OUDE CAMPAIGN.

leaders (the Fyzabad Moulvie, the most able of them, having fallen) could succeed in bringing their men to face our troops, and they fled, leaving 15 guns in the hands of the victors. After this they dispersed, most of them making their way into Nepaul.

Sir Hope Grant, accompanied by Major Wolseley, marched to Fyzabad, whence he proceeded by boat to Amorha, on the opposite side of the Gogra. Here he received information that 4,000 of the enemy had taken up a position near Bunkussia, and another party of 1,800 had made for the Gogra. The General, determined to give no rest to the rebels, who were moving from Nepaul into the Terai, divided his forces, sending one portion by Rampore Thana to scour the jungles, himself following in their track along the banks of the Gogra, while a third column was despatched into the jungle about Bunkussia. At midnight of the 20th of May, he marched from Burgudwa, and arrived soon after sunrise at the jungle covering the entrance to the Jerwah Pass. Here he received information that the Nana and Bala Rao, with 2,000 men and 2 guns, were at the mouth of the Pass, and Mummoo Khan, with 500 followers, a little to the west, on the same ground where he had inflicted a severe defeat on Bala Rao on the 4th of January.

Sir Hope, having ordered the cavalry and artillery to encamp, sent Colonel Brasyer with his Sikhs against Mummoo Khan, who, however, dispersed on his approach, and himself moved with the 7th Punjaubees into the Pass. The enemy occupied the spurs of the mountain stretching into the jungle on either side of the Pass, from the gorge of which their two guns opened fire. One company of the Punjaubees, led by Wolseley, Biddulph, and Wilmot, three officers of the divisional staff, climbed the hill to the left and drove the enemy before them, and the remainder of the regiment cleared the ridge on the right and captured the guns, but owing to the troops having marched twenty miles, they were not able to overtake the retreating enemy.

Thus ended almost the last conflict of this great and memorable struggle, which had lasted two years, as it was on Sunday, the 10th of May, 1857, that the 3rd Bengal Cavalry mutinied at Meerut. As the last band of the rebels, deprived of their only remaining guns, was now driven beyond the Nepaul frontier, the General, leaving some small columns to meet any attempt on their part to break through, proceeded to Lucknow on the 4th of June, and, with his staff, took up his residence in the Dilkhoosha.

In the distribution of honours on the conclusion of the Mutiny, Wolseley received the brevet of Lieutenant-Colonel. He was young to have attained so high a rank, for it was on the twenty-sixth anniversary of his birth, that, in company with his chief, he entered Lucknow, and, for a brief period, enjoyed the 'blessings of peace.' He was now employed in laying out the new cantonments, those formerly in use by our troops having been utterly destroyed by the rebels. Henceforth it was decided that Europeans should form a large proportion of the garrison of this important city, and his experience in quartering troops was of essential service when this question of the new cantonments came up for consideration.

Wolseley had only been established some five mouths in his comfortable quarters in the fine old palace near Lucknow, when he was once more offered a position on the staff of an army about to take the field, and, action being to him as the breath of life, he gladly accepted the proposal.

Early in October, Sir Hope Grant was nominated to the command of the troops about to proceed, in conjunction with a French army, to the north of China, to bring to terms the Imperial Government. Sir Hope Grant was desirous of appointing Colonel Wolseley to the head of the

Quartermaster-General's Department, but Lord Clyde nominated the late Colonel Kenneth McKenzie, a most able and distinguished officer, and Wolseley went as Deputy Assistant-Quartermaster-General in charge of the Topographical Department.

Had it not been for the sudden outbreak of the Indian Mutiny, Wolseley would have been serving during the past two years in China, to which country he found himself once more under orders. And what an eventful period in the history of this country, and of her great Asiatic dependency, as well as in his own life, had been those two years just concluded!

India has ever afforded the grandest field for the display of those talents and qualities which have rendered this country the Rome of modern history. In India, whether in war or statesmanship, the Anglo-Saxon race has appeared to the greatest advantage. This may in part be due to the superiority over natives which we share with all European nations; but we do not think we shall be guilty of self-laudation, if we chiefly attribute it to that peculiarity of the Anglo-Saxon race, by which resistance and difficulties only increase the determination to succeed. It is morally certain that no other Power save England could have retained her hold of India during the year 1857, with a military force which, at the time of the outbreak, only numbered 38,000 soldiers in the three Presidencies. To use Canning's phrase, 'India is fertile in heroes;' and probably at no previous period of our history have the attributes which peculiarly distinguish our countrymen and countrywomen received a more striking illustration. Our women were heroines, and our incomparable rank and file nobly did their duty; while as for the officers throughout the long-drawn hardships, the dramatic episodes, and the glorious triumphs of the Indian Mutiny, we cannot do better than repeat the saying of that great leader who may be regarded as the type, as he was the greatest representative, of the class. 'Brave,' would the great Duke of Wellington impatiently say, when anyone spoke in commendatory terms of the courage of British officers, 'of course they are; all Englishmen are brave; but it is the spirit of the gentleman that makes a British officer.'

Those who were privileged to take part in those glorious feats of arms, the Siege and Storm of Delhi and the Defence and Relief of Lucknow, may be congratulated in having been actors in some of those historic scenes, the record of which will never fade from the page of history.

CHAPTER IV.

THE CHINA WAR.

The Occupation of Chusan.—The Disembarkation at Peh-tang.—The Action at Sinho.—The Capture of the Taku Forts.—The Advance on Pekin.—Narrow Escape of Colonel Wolseley from Capture.—The Looting of the Summer Palace and Surrender of Pekin.—Colonel Wolseley's Visit to Japan and Mission to Nankin.—Return to England.

COLONEL WOLSELEY accompanied Sir Hope Grant to Calcutta, and, with the other members of his staff, sailed on the 26th of February, 1860, in the *Fiery Cross*, one of Jardine's steamers, which cast anchor at Hong-Kong on the 13th of March. As the transports arrived from England, India, and the Cape of Good Hope, the troops were disembarked and encamped at Kowloon, opposite Hong-Kong, which Colonel Wolseley surveyed, the other officers of the department, under Colonel Kenneth McKenzie, being engaged in arranging for the reception of the British troops. In a very short time, the required space was converted from a rocky waste into a neat camp, with tents and lines for the horses.

The first step was the joint occupation, by the British and French forces, of the island of Chusan, which was accordingly undertaken under instructions from the Home Government, who, in this, followed the precedent of the war of 1840-42, though Colonel Wolseley has expressed his opinion that the step was of little use, either from a military or political point of view.* The expedition rendezvoused off King-tang, opposite the town of Chin-hai, at the mouth of the Ning-po, and, on the 21st of April, dropped anchor in the noble harbour of Ting-hai, the capital of Chusan, which immediately capitulated. On the following day, the naval and military commanders, with their staffs and a small guard, landed and made an inspection of the town and its vicinity, at which Wolseley, being in charge of the Quartermaster-General's Department, was present with the General.

One thousand soldiers only were landed, there being great difficulty in finding accommodation in the various yamuns, or official residences, and 300 Marines were placed in the Custom-house and adjoining buildings. Wolseley took over the requisite buildings from the native officials, and made the necessary arrangements, in conjunction with the French staff-officer, for the quartering of the garrison. He returned with Sir Hope Grant to the *Grenada*, on the evening of the 23rd of April, and, on the following morning, the steamer proceeded to Poo-too, an island lying to the eastward of the Chusan group, which, it was considered, might be suitable for a military sanatorium. Wolseley proceeded on shore with the General, and visited the temples and monasteries, of which this sacred city alone consists. In the evening the party returned to the *Grenada*, which then sailed for Hong-Kong.

One of the chief difficulties that had to be encountered in the organization of the army destined to proceed to the north of China, was that of transport; but at length, in May, every preparation being completed, some sailing transports left Hong-Kong for the seat of war, with a portion of the infantry, and the main body followed on the 8th of June.

* See Colonel Wolseley's interesting work 'Narrative of the War with China, in 1860,' which was written daily while the operations were in progress.

The British army, of which the Divisional Commanders were Sir Robert Napier and Sir John Michel, Brigadier Pattle being in command of the cavalry, numbered about 14,000 men, and that of the French, under General Montauban, which mustered at Shanghai, about 7,000. The fleet, under Admiral Sir James Hope, consisted of 70 ships of war, including gunboats, and the hired transports numbered 120 sail.

On the 16th of June, the *Grenada*, in which Colonel Wolseley had embarked with the Commander-in-Chief, and some troopships, proceeded to sea, and put in at Shanghai, where, at the earnest entreaty of the European residents and Chinese authorities, some troops were landed to protect the town against the rebels, better known as Taipings, who, for the past eight years, had desolated the country. Three days after quitting Shanghai, the *Grenada* cast anchor off the town of Wei-hei-wei, on the western shore of the Gulf of Pechili, the transports, with the greater portion of the troops, having already arrived at Talien-wan, on the eastern side. Wolseley and other officers landed at Wei-hei-wei, and visited the town, which is of considerable extent. On the following morning he explored the neighbouring country, but its capabilities for supplying water were unpromising in the extreme.

According to the plan of operations agreed upon between the allied commanders, the French were to rendezvous at Chefoo,* in the province of Shantung, and the British at Talien-wan.

Sir Hope Grant, with his staff, remained on board the *Grenada*, in Victoria Bay, whence a small steamer daily went

* Chefoo and Talien-wan were fixed upon as the respective bases of operations of the French and English armies, because it was known that along the coast near Takoo the ice in winter prevented all approach for several months; but there was deep water at these places, which were free from ice all the year round. Colonel Wolseley visited Chefoo, and was pleased with the order and regularity of the French camp near that town.

the round of the great bay or harbour, carrying orders to the various encampments.

Lord Elgin arrived at Talien-wan on the 9th of July, in the Indian Navy steam-frigate *Feroze*, and, after many conferences, it was decided by Sir Hope Grant and General Montauban, that both armies should sail for Peh-tang on the 26th of July. Accordingly, on that day, the vast armada, presenting a grand spectacle, weighed anchor, and started with a fair wind for the general rendezvous, twenty miles south of the Peiho; and in the evening the French fleet of 33 sail hove in sight, passing round the Meatow Islands. On Saturday, the 28th of July, the entire Expedition was assembled at the appointed rendezvous, and, on Monday, weighed and stood in for the mouth of the Peiho river.

A memorandum was issued by the Quartermaster-General for the guidance of the officers superintending the disembarkation of the troops, and, on the 1st of August, the Indian Navy troopship *Coromandel*, having on board Sir James Hope and Sir Hope Grant, with his staff, including Colonel Wolseley, led the way, followed by the gunboats, with their decks crowded with men, each towing six launches, full of troops. The French flotilla also put off at the same time.

Soon after two o'clock, the gunboats anchored about 2,000 yards from the famous Taku forts, situated about three miles from the mouth of the river, the passage of which they command.

It was decided by Generals Grant and Montauban that a reconnoissance should be made in the direction of a causeway running towards Taku, and 400 men, drawn equally from the English and French armies, were landed on a soft, sticky, mud flat, through which, for nearly a mile, the men floundered and struggled before reaching a hard patch of ground. 'Nearly every man,' says Mr. Bowlby, the *Times* correspondent, 'was disembarrassed of his lower integuments, and one gallant brigadier led on his men with no other garment than his shirt.' The Tartars now retreated along the causeway, and the rest of the force was disembarked by five o'clock. 'Never,' says Mr. Bowlby, 'did more hopeless prospect greet an army. Mud and water everywhere, and "not a drop to drink." Pools of brackish water were scattered about here and there, but perfectly undrinkable, and not a well or spring could be found. They were on an island cut off from the causeway by a deep ditch forty feet wide, through which the tide flowed. In plunged the brigades, and sank middle deep in the vilest and most stinking slush; but the men struggled gallantly on, and in a few seconds the whole force was on the road.'

The bridge and gate of the town were occupied, but the greater portion of the troops rested for the night on the causeway, and Colonel Wolseley and a large party halted on the hard ground, cut off from it by a deep ditch. They were all in a plight calculated to try the temper of Mark Tapley himself, for not only were they destitute of water, every man having long before consumed the pint he carried in his water-bottle, but they were cold and wet, and had to lie on the damp ground. It is under such circumstances that the real nature of a man reveals itself. As Wolseley says: 'The noble-hearted come to the front, at once ready to help others, and being themselves generous and jolly, make the best of untoward events; whilst the selfish man stands out in his true colours, whining and pining like an ill-tempered child, a picture of misery himself, and likely to make others so, by his captious ill-humour. We were a large party of people, odds and ends of all sorts, including some who, in the dark, could not make their way any farther to the front. All were horribly thirsty. To go back to the boats for water, through the slush, was really a fatiguing journey; but the task had to be accomplished, and never did the weary traveller in an arid desert hail a spring with greater joy than we all did our Judge-Advocate-General's return with a small barrel of water, after his trip there. Subsequently the invaluable Coolie corps* made their appearance with breakers of a like nature, which supplied everyone.'

But Wolseley, in his published work, omits to mention that he accompanied Major Wilmot on his errand of mercy —for such it really was, as many of the men were so fatigued and overcome by thirst, that their tongues were hanging out of their mouths—and on their return from their long tramp through the mud, laden with the precious liquid, the gallant officers were cheered heartily by their comrades.

The night was as unpleasant a one as Colonel Wolseley ever spent, even bearing in mind his Crimean and Indian bivouacs. He had, of course, no bedding, and it was impossible to lie down on the wet mud with any hope of obtaining rest. So he walked about and shivered through the night without closing his eyes. In the morning the town was occupied, but 'looting' was strictly prohibited, and any men found indulging in the unlawful pursuit were instantly tied up and flogged on the spot.

Our men landed with three days' provisions, but after the fourth day supplies of food and water were regularly issued to them. The French arrangements not being so complete or successful, our gallant allies had exciting sport in chasing and killing all the pigs they could lay hands on, not even disdaining to regale themselves on such deceased porkers as they found in ditches; indeed, for the first week they seemed to subsist on little else. Our military system also appeared in favourable contrast to that of our allies, as regards strictness of discipline and employment of the troops, for

* The Coolie corps, organized and led by Major Temple, of the Indian army, consisted of 2,500 Chinamen, recruited at Canton and Hong-Kong.

while their officers and men were sauntering about the town with their hands in their pockets, our men, of all ranks and arms of the service, were busily employed constructing wooden wharves and piers, and improving the principal thoroughfares for the passage of guns.

The Allied Generals having decided on a reconnoissance in force of the enemy's position, on the 3rd of August a strong column, consisting of 1,000 French and as many English, under the command of General Collineau, moved out along the raised causeway leading towards the Taku Forts. Colonel Wolseley was selected by Sir Hope Grant to accompany the force, and indeed throughout this war, so highly did the General estimate his services, that whenever he decided to undertake some duty requiring tact or capacity, he would always inquire, 'Where's Wolseley? Send him.' And Wolseley, ever ready to undertake any charge entailing responsibility, would respond to the call with cheerful alacrity. His duties as the officer in charge of the topographical survey of a country totally unknown, naturally required his presence in the van of the army, and whether there, or sweeping round the flanks with a handful of Native cavalry for an escort, he carried his life in his hand and narrowly escaped capture, which would have involved torture or death at the hands of the barbarous enemy. On one occasion the fate that befell another lamented officer of his department, Captain Brabazon, would have been his, but for an accidental circumstance, or rather should we say, having regard to the services he was spared to render to his country, by the interposition of that Divinity which, says Hamlet, 'shapes our ends, roughhew them how we may.'

The Allied force started at four a.m., and, after a march of about four miles, came upon the main body of the enemy, who were waiting just beyond a bridge, about half a mile farther on. As soon as the French, who led the advance, had passed the bridge, the enemy opened fire, and a large body of Tartar cavalry threatened the flanks of the allies, when General Collineau opened fire with two guns, and, having forced them back, advanced, the French on the right, and the English on the left, towards a large intrenchment about a mile distant. The force now halted, and Brigadier Sutton sent Colonel Wolseley to Sir Hope Grant to apprise him of the state of affairs, and request reinforcements if the enemy's position was to be forced. Wolseley galloped back, and, having given the necessary information, returned with 2 guns, and the Allied Generals immediately followed with a reinforcement, but the reconnoitring party was already on the return march to Pehtang, and the day's proceedings ended somewhat abortively, the Tartars, in their ignorance of the object sought to be attained, claiming a victory, and sending flaming reports to Pekin of their having forced the white soldiers to retreat.

On the 9th of August, Colonel Wolseley was selected to command a second reconnoitring party, consisting of 200 cavalry and 100 infantry, and Sir Hope gave him positive instructions, before starting, on no account to bring on an engagement. Proceeding along the causeway for two miles, he placed his infantry in position in a ruined farmhouse, usually held by a cavalry picket of the enemy, while he moved off to reconnoitre with the cavalry, whose exposed flank was thus protected. Leaving the causeway to his left, Wolseley made a long circuit, until he approached within a mile of the enemy's works on the Peiho, and, having surveyed the whole of the enemy's position, and the line on their flank by which the advance was to be made, and having further ascertained that the country in that direction was practicable for all arms, and abounded in pools of fresh water, he returned without having exchanged a shot with the enemy. Immediately on his arrival in camp, Wolseley made a report of the survey he had completed, and having that night executed a plan, he had copies struck off from a steel plate of the size of a sheet of foolscap, and by an early hour on the following morning these copies were in the hands of every staff officer of both armies.

On Sunday, the 12th of August, the Allied Army began its march towards the Taku Forts, and everyone was in high spirits at leaving that detestable place with its inodorous smells. It was arranged that the 2nd, or Sir Robert Napier's, Division, should move out along the track reconnoitred on the 9th, guided by Wolseley, who had laid down the route by which the division, when attacking in flank, should march so as to avoid the swamps and quicksands which abounded on both sides of the causeway, and yet at the same time keep intact the communications with the main body. Sir Robert Napier was directed to turn the left of the enemy's position, whilst the 1st Division and the French, advancing along the causeway, should attack the enemy's works in front. As the ground on the right was admirably adapted for the operations of cavalry, the whole of that arm was attached to Napier's Division. At four a.m. the march began through slush and mud, which was terribly heavy for the artillery horses. After advancing for three miles from the causeway, Napier opened fire on the enemy with 15 guns, and he expressed his admiration of the unflinching fortitude with which the Tartar cavalry stood the iron hail at 450 yards' range. A portion of them charged our cavalry, but were met half-way, and utterly routed by the Sikh horse, led by those gallant *sabreurs*, Fane and Probyn, supported by a squadron of the 1st Dragoon Guards.

In the meantime, the 1st Division and the French, moving along the causeway leading from Pehtang towards the enemy's intrenched camp before the village of Sinho, deployed within 1,400 yards of these works, and, after a brief artillery fire, the whole army advanced and occupied the place.

Throughout this China War, our allies, notwithstanding their gallantry, did not show to advantage, which was chiefly due to the incapacity of General Cousin de Montauban, who was a gasconading, self-opiniated man, without a particle of military talent. At no time throughout the campaign did the French Division muster more than 4,000 effectives, while we had in China a well-appointed army numbering 19,000 men, of whom 14,000 were at the seat of war. Thus the co-operation of the French was quite unnecessary; but Lord Palmerston, sacrificing military considerations to the political requirements involved in the maintenance of the *entente cordiale*, accepted the proffered assistance of the Emperor Napoleon. The campaign had not been inaugurated many days before Montauban gave evidence of his military incompetence, which went so far in assisting to wreck his country in the memorable days preceding the catastrophe of Sedan.*

From the Allied position, distant about two miles and a half, was visible the large intrenchment around the village of Tangku, having a long narrow causeway, with ditches, leading from Sinho towards it.

Notwithstanding Sir Hope Grant's refusal to advance upon the enemy's position until bridges had been thrown across the canals which separated the roadway and village from the open, firm ground to the south of the causeway, Montauban sallied out with his division; but after two hours

---

* Wolseley was in the heart of the American Continent, conducting his Red River Expedition, in the autumn of the memorable year 1870, when he received intelligence that the Count de Palikao had been nominated Minister-at-War, thus receiving charge of the destinies of his country at a most momentous crisis. Turning to his officers, he exclaimed : ' Then it is all over for poor France !'

CAPTURE OF TANGKU. 129

spent in a purposeless cannonading, returned to Sinho, *re infectâ*.

On the following day Colonel Wolseley made a reconnaissance up the banks of the Peiho, which resulted in showing that the enemy had retired to the southern bank of the river, with the exception of the troops garrisoning the forts.

On the morning of the 14th, the First Division, with all the artillery, having their right flank resting on the Peiho, advanced to attack the enemy's intrenchments. Our allies, having taken up a position on our left, their left flank resting upon the Tangku causeway, the whole line of artillery, consisting of 12 French and 24 British guns, opened fire, under which the infantry advanced and entered the enemy's intrenchments. About 45 guns, of various calibre, between four and twenty-four pounders, of which 16 were brass and the remainder iron, fell into the hands of the victors.

Colonel Wolseley accompanied the Commander-in-Chief in his reconnaissance towards the Taku Forts, but not much information was gained, as the enemy opened fire on the escort.

Sir Hope Grant now busied himself in perfecting his arrangements for the attack on these formidable works; heavy guns and ammunition were brought to the front, and ten days' provisions collected at Sinho.

The question of the attack on the Taku Forts was one upon which the British and French Commanders-in-Chief were divided. Sir Hope Grant, who was strongly supported in his views by Sir Robert Napier, proposed to operate against the northern fort, which enfiladed those on the southern bank, and was the key to the position; but General Montauban was loud in favour of crossing the river and assaulting the southern forts. However, finding his colleague determined to abide by his own judgment, Montauban made a formal protest, and then acted in loyal concert with the British

General. During the halt at Tangku, the Engineers had been busy constructing a road towards the forts, also bridges or causeways over the canals, and batteries, which were armed during the night of the 20th with 16 guns and 3 mortars. At daybreak on the following morning, 23 pieces of ordnance, including 4 of the French, opened fire on the forts, which replied with spirit.

The British force detailed for the assault was drawn from Sir Robert Napier's Division, and numbered 2,500 men.* The French assaulting column, numbering 1,000 men, was under the command of General Collineau.

About six o'clock a tremendous explosion took place in the nearest fort; half an hour later, a second explosion occurred in the larger northern fort, and, by seven o'clock, most of the enemy's guns had been dismounted. The field-guns were advanced to within 500 yards of the fort, and the fire of the works having been silenced, a breach was commenced near the gate, and the storming-party advanced to within thirty yards, keeping up a hot fire, the French infantry being on the right, and the English on the left. Under a heavy musketry-fire from the enemy, who quitted their cover on the troops forming up for the assault, our men advanced straight to their front towards the gate of the fort, the French advancing by the right and approaching the angle of the work resting on the river's bank. It very soon became apparent that our engineering arrangements had been faulty, for, instead of using a number of light ladders, or a small plank bridge resting on wheels, on which to cross the wet ditch, a pontoon bridge had been taken, and a round

---

* The assaulting column consisted of a wing of the 44th, under Colonel MacMahon, and a wing of the 67th, under Colonel Thomas, the other wings of these regiments acting as supports; the Royal Marines, under Colonel Gascoigne, and a detachment of the same corps carrying a pontoon bridge for crossing the wet ditches, under Colonel Travers; and a company of Royal Engineers under Major Graham, V.C.

shot, passing through one of the metal pontoons of which it was constructed, rendered it unserviceable.

The French, with great dash, escaladed the walls, and almost simultaneously our men forced their way through the breach in single file, the foremost being Ensign Chaplin, of the 67th, who planted the colours on the top of the parapet, and Lieutenants Rogers (44th), Lenon and Burslem (67th).

In seeking to lay down the pontoon bridge, 15 Sappers were almost instantaneously placed *hors de combat*, and, by an unlucky round shot, the bridge was rendered useless. Wolseley was with the advance party at the time, and used his utmost endeavours to withdraw the bolt by which the damaged portion was fastened to the superstructure; this, however, was a work of extreme difficulty, as owing to a portion of the bridge being in the water, a great strain was brought to bear on the bolt, which could not be withdrawn. Wolseley recounts some instances of gallantry that attracted his attention, which was always interested in observing the exhibition of that greatest of military virtues in others. While our men were endeavouring to cross the ditches, he was standing by Major Graham, V.C.*—an old comrade in the trenches before Sebastopol—who, being almost the only mounted officer, offered an easy mark to the Chinese matchlockmen. So deafening was the uproar of great guns and small arms at this time, that Wolseley, having some remark to communicate to Graham, placed his hand on that officer's thigh to draw his attention. 'Don't put your hand there,' exclaimed Major Graham, wincing under the torture, 'there is a jingal-ball lodged in my leg.' It was the first notice he had taken of his wound.

Colonel Mann, commanding the Royal Engineers, was one of the first to cross the two ditches, and Major (the

* Now Major-General Sir Gerald Graham, who commanded a brigade in the Egyptian Expedition under Lord Wolseley.

late Colonel) Hon. A. Anson, A.D.C., on reaching the other side, which was covered with pointed bamboo stakes, proceeded to swarm up a pole, to the summit of which the rope drawing up the drawbridge was made fast. The daring act attracted the fire of the enemy's marksmen, but the gallant officer, nothing daunted, hacked away with his sword, until he cut the rope, when down fell the drawbridge with a great clang. It was so shattered by shot that it seemed scarcely capable of sustaining any weight, but our men managed to cross a few at a time.

The scene presented in the interior of the captured work evinced the determination with which the garrison had held the place, and among the dead, who were estimated to number about 2,000, was a General and the officer commanding the northern forts.

The losses incurred by the Allies in achieving this really brilliant triumph were moderate, considering the strength of the defences they had stormed. Our loss was 17 killed and 161 wounded, of whom 22 were officers. The French had about 130 casualties.

Without loss of time, preparations were commenced to attack the large northern fort, distant exactly 1,000 yards, which had a raised causeway running towards it, with wet ditches on either side. Colonel Wolseley proceeded, with a small escort, under a heavy fire, to reconnoitre the ground to the north of the causeway, and, slowly advancing his party in skirmishing order towards the space, ascertained its fitness for the purposes required. But the Chinese had no heart for further resistance, and as the Allied troops advanced towards the north fort, the garrison, numbering 2,000 men, surrendered at discretion. A little later the enemy evacuated the southern works, and in the evening Mr. (now Sir Harry) Parkes received the unconditional surrender of the whole country on the banks of the Peiho as far as Tientsin. The day closed with a tremendous storm of wind and rain, and soon the roads by which the troops had advanced were quite submerged. The camp was flooded, and, under such depressing influences, Wolseley rode back a distance of five miles, to find the interior of his tent a pond, with every article therein floating about as if another flood had covered the face of the earth. Thus, without light or fire to dry the wet clothes on his back, and after a frugal supper of biscuit and brandy-and-water, he turned in, ruminating, doubtless, on the changes and chances of a soldier's life.

The first phase of the war was completed by the capture of the famous Taku Forts, which, though taken by our sailors in 1858, had, in the following year, successfully resisted a naval force, under Admiral Sir James Hope, when conveying the British Minister to Pekin, for the purpose of exchanging the ratification of the treaty concluded at Tientsin, in June, 1858. Our Government now determined that the violated treaty should be ratified at Pekin, as this would imply a sense of defeat and humiliation which the Imperial Government, skilled as it is in sophisms, could not argue away in the lying proclamations it was in the habit of addressing to its many millions of subjects.

Sir James Hope pushed on to Tientsin on the 23rd of August, and, so demoralized were the enemy, that the forts at that place were occupied without a shot being fired. Two days later Lord Elgin and Sir Hope Grant followed with the troops, leaving a garrison at Taku and Sinho. Eight days were wasted at Tientsin in negotiations with unaccredited envoys, and at length it was decided to commence the march towards Tungchow. But there were difficulties to be overcome; the road between Tientsin and Pekin was little known, as also the capabilities of the country to furnish supplies for the large number of soldiers, non-combatants, and animals. It was Colonel Wolseley's duty to collect information on these points, and the Topographical Department, of which he had been in charge from the outset of the campaign, was, at this time, reorganized, his assistants being Lieutenant Harrison, R.E., who had served at Alumbagh and Lucknow, and Mr. Robert Swinhoe, Interpreter in the British Consular Service, who had hitherto been acting in that capacity on Sir Robert Napier's staff.

Owing to the difficulty as to supplies, it was arranged that the two armies should advance by detachments. Brigadier Reeves started on the 8th of September, with his brigade, and, on the following day, Lord Elgin and Sir Hope Grant, and Wolseley with his assistants, quitted Tientsin.

The French troops, about 3,000, left Tientsin on the 10th of September, and Sir John Michel marched with the remainder of the First Division on the 12th, Sir Robert Napier remaining behind with the Second Division to garrison the place. On their arrival at Yangtsun, the headquarters camp remained immovable, owing to the flight of the drivers with the mules and ponies.* Parties were sent

* During the night of the 10th all the Chinese drivers of the carts of Lord Elgin's and Sir Hope Grant's establishments had decamped, taking with them the whole of their mules and ponies. Wolseley alone retained his drivers, and that he did so was owing to an amusing circumstance. While riding out of Tientsin, he was conversing with the Ressaldar, or native commissioned officer, in command of his escort, and told him to impress upon his men that unless he and they looked sharply after the native drivers and prevented them from deserting, they would be left behind, and could not participate in the capture of Pekin. The native officer and his sowars took the hint, and on the following morning there was not a driver in the camp, except his own, who had all been tied together by their tails, and then made fast to the tent-pole! Thereafter this was done every night, and Wolseley arrived at Pekin with the carts and drivers and ponies he had started with, the only officer who did so. 'The small camp of our department,' says Mr. Swinhoe, 'consisted of one Indian tent and two bell-tents. The Chinese servants and carters generally built huts of mats and millet-stalks, and the two native servants were accommodated with a *tente d'abri*. Besides our three horses, picketed in a row, there were six luggage ponies belonging to the carts, and the carts themselves, and in the group hard by, the eleven Sikh troopers detailed to us as guard, with their tents and horses. The whole made quite a conspicuous little group to the observation of passers-by.'

out into the country to try and recover the lost animals, or procure others, but without success, and, at length, as no other means of transport were available, several junks were seized, into which the greater portion of the stores and luggage was stowed.

Colonel Wolseley commenced his surveying duties immediately upon quitting Tientsin; he himself, accompanied by the interpreter, proceeded along the road, Lieutenant Harrison taking the course of the Peiho for his part of the survey. The country on either side of the Peiho, which is fenced in with artificial dykes, is one vast level plain, covered, as far as the eye could reach, with crops of maize and millet; and were it not for occasional brick-kilns and watch-towers, an accurate survey of the road would have been most arduous. As it was, Colonel Wolseley, in order to insure accuracy, paced the road, and afterwards compared the distances so noted with the revolutions of the perambulator. On their first day's march to Pookow, about twelve and a half miles from Tientsin, several distant large villages were passed, the names of which may be found in the survey maps of the road to Pekin executed by Colonel Wolseley and Lieutenant Harrison. On the 11th he proceeded on to Yangtsun, on the 12th to Nantsai, and on the 13th to Ho-se-woo, where he was engaged upon the survey of the river, and his assistant worked on the road. As this town appeared to be a good half-way station between Tientsin and Pekin, being about forty miles distant from each, a hospital and a depôt were established here.

At a meeting held at Tungchow between Messrs. Wade and Parkes and some Imperial Commissioners, it was decided that the Allied army should march to within a mile and a half of Chang-kia-wan, whence Lord Elgin, with an escort of 1,000 men, was to proceed to Tungchow, and, after signing the Convention, to the capital for the purpose of ratifying the 1858 Treaty. On the 17th of September, the British force, with 1,000 French, marched to Matow, a distance of twelve miles, and Wolseley resumed his survey of the road, but encountered great difficulty in procuring information, as the native villagers fled on the approach of their invaders, and had to be chased and run down by the Sikh escort. The following day, the 18th of September, was destined to be a memorable one in the history of the campaign, and before the sun went down, convincing proofs were afforded —though, indeed, none were required save to enlighten the understanding and open the eyes of the diplomatists*—that the Chinese Government and its Commissioners were acting with their wonted duplicity and treachery.

The army marched at daylight on the 18th of September; but Wolseley remained behind during the forenoon, having obtained permission from Sir Hope Grant, on the previous night, to halt at Matow, and continue the survey of the road, promising, on its completion, to join him at Changkia-wan. After being busy for some hours, he was sitting in his tent, when Captain Gunter, of the King's Dragoon Guards, galloped up, calling out to him to be on his guard. 'The General,' he said, 'had sent him with orders to move up the rear-guard, which had charge of the baggage, with all despatch, as there was a large body of cavalry ahead.' Soon after Wolseley, who had betaken himself to the raised road, saw puffs of smoke in the air,

---

* Speaking of the simplicity displayed by the representatives of our Foreign Office, Wolseley observes: 'Military men are far less confiding than civilians in dealing with uncivilized nations. The little experience that I have had goes to prove that the latter are far more rash and less liable to take the precautions which ordinary military knowledge would indicate as necessary. How often have I known civilians, accompanying an army, scoff at the caution of general officers, forgetting altogether that any commander who fails to provide against every possible mistake, or probable contingency, is deeply culpable. By the strange contrariety of human nature, it is generally these irresponsible gentlemen who are first loudest in their abuse of officers who fail in anything through rashness, or want of caution.

denoting the firing of shells, and clouds of dust, such as are caused by cavalry charges. The thought flashed across him of the precarious position in which he and his party were placed, as in that open plain their white tents were visible a long way, and would doubtless draw upon them the observation of some of the Tartar cavalry, which was even now clearly carrying out the tactics of surrounding the Allied army, which Sang-ko-lin-sin was always able to adopt, by reason of his numerical superiority. With the utmost despatch, he caused the tents to be struck and packed, himself and his officers assisting, and in a few minutes the party were on their way to join the army.

Wolseley says that he never spent a more anxious time in his life than while making that march of four miles. It was not that he feared for himself and his mounted followers, but his soldier-servant and the corporal of Engineers were on foot, and he could not desert them in the event of an attack by the Tartar horse. He had made up his mind to throw himself and his men in the first house they passed on the road, and defend themselves to the last extremity with the guns and pistols they could muster. But, at length, he began to breathe more freely as he approached a village containing the baggage in charge of a strong rear-guard; and, in a few minutes, he had the satisfaction of seeing in safety, not only the *personnel* of his detachment, but also all the results of his surveys, which had cost him so much labour, and were almost equally precious to him. To show how critical was the position of the party, and how near they were sharing the sad fate that overtook some of our countrymen, who were tortured to death by the savage foe, it may be mentioned that a large force of Tartar cavalry had actually passed between them and the rear-guard, and crossed the river less than half an hour before their arrival. Leaving his baggage along with the rest, Colonel Wolseley's party galloped along the road, turned off to the left along the bank of the Seau-ho ('Little River'), and proceeded to the spot where Sir Hope Grant was resting under the shade of some trees.

He now learnt that the Allies had encountered, and driven from their position, a Chinese army of about 20,000 men, which barred their progress towards Tungchow, and captured 74 guns, with but slight loss. But the elation consequent upon this great success was dimmed by the consideration that the enemy had in their hands many of our countrymen, and fears were entertained for their safety, which proved but too well founded. Captain Brabazon, Lieutenant Anderson, Messrs. Bowlby and De Norman, and many of the sowars and Frenchmen, died a cruel death, which Wolseley was near sharing, as Sir Hope Grant had sent for him to accompany Mr. Loch, of the Embassy, to proceed to Tungchow, to bring back the party there, and it was in consequence of his absence in the rear, completing the survey of the road, that Captain Brabazon was directed to proceed in his place.

On the 20th of September, Colonel Wolseley rode back to Matow, and having completed the survey of the road between that village and Chang-kia-wan, returned in time to move out with the Allied army, which, at daybreak on the following morning, marched to engage the enemy, who were drawn up about two miles distant from the town.

Colonel Wolseley attended Sir Hope Grant during the day, and, with the rest of the staff, had a narrow escape of falling into the hands of the enemy. He says: 'When we had marched a mile, we found ourselves in presence of a large army, their cavalry stretching away to the right as far as we could see, and endeavouring to turn our left flank; their infantry strongly posted in the numerous clumps of trees and enclosures which lay between us and the canal.

As soon as we came within range, they opened fire upon us from hundreds of jingals and small field-pieces, to which our allies replied with their rifled cannon. Sir Hope Grant rode forward towards the French for the purpose of examining the position, and having advanced beyond our line of skirmishers, rode almost in amongst the Tartars, mistaking them for the French. Upon turning back to rejoin our troops, the Tartar cavalry, seeing him and his numerous staff cantering away from them, evidently thought it was some of our cavalry running away, and at once gave pursuit with loud yells. Stirling's guns, however, opened heavily upon them when they were about 250 yards from our line, saluting them well with canister, which sent them to the right-about as briskly as they had advanced.' Soon after the Tartar cavalry tried to outflank the Allies, upon which our cavalry charged them; and, says Wolseley, 'riding over ponies and men, knocked both down like so many ninepins.'

Sir Hope Grant now moved in pursuit to the left, and captured several camps, with tents standing, which were all burnt. The enemy having disappeared from the front and flank, he retired towards the wooden bridge over the Yuliang-ho Canal.

The French had meanwhile captured all the camps which lay near the Pa-le-cheaou* Bridge, over which they drove the enemy at the point of the bayonet, with great slaughter. Here General Paou, commanding the Tartar cavalry, received his mortal wound. Towards evening, the French encamped close to the canal upon the British right. Sir Hope Grant, though within sight of Pekin, was unable to push his advantage and compel the surrender of the capital, as, relying upon the assurances of the diplomatists, he had

* General Montauban took his title of Count de Palikao from this bridge, which means '8 le bridge,' so called because it is 8 le, or 2¾ miles, along the paved road from Tung-chow.

left his siege-guns at Tientsin. However, Sir Robert Napier, to whom he had sent word after the action of the 18th, advanced by forced marches, and arrived on the 24th of September. Five days later the siege-guns came into camp, and, by the 3rd of October, all the available troops from the rear had arrived.

During the halt, Colonel Wolseley was very busy surveying the country between Chang-kia-wan and Pekin, and also reconnoitring about the capital and obtaining information from the villagers as to the movements of Sang-ko-lin-sin's army, which was reported to be in position to the north of the city. Proceeding almost daily with a small party of cavalry as an escort, he, and other staff officers, advanced occasionally within a few hundred yards of the walls of Pekin.

On the 3rd of October, the camp at Pa-le-cheaou was broken up, and the British force, 6,000 strong, crossed the canal by the bridge of boats prepared for the purpose, and encamped on the paved road leading to Pekin. Two days later, the French having received the reinforcements for which they had been waiting, the combined army, numbering about 10,000 combatants, carrying three days' cooked rations, and without tents, advanced in lines of contiguous columns. After a march of between four and five miles, our army bivouacked. Colonel Wolseley located himself and assistants in an old broken-down homestead, the sole occupant of which was a deaf and imbecile old woman; and, ere 'the early village cock had twice done salutation to the morn,' was only too glad to be astir and quit his squalid quarters. The Allied armies now advanced, the English moving on the right into some abandoned intrenchments, and thence advancing upon the main road leading to the An-ting gate of the city, where Sir Hope Grant halted for the night.

Meanwhile the French Division, accompanied by the British cavalry, arrived about sunset at the central gate of the Summer Palace, which is distant about six miles in a north-westerly direction from Pekin.

At daybreak on the following morning, the 7th of October, Sir Hope Grant, in order to apprise our cavalry and the French of his whereabouts, fired 2 guns, and directed Colonel Wolseley to proceed with an escort of two squadrons of cavalry, and ascertain their position. Wolseley took the road towards the Summer Palace, and proceeded nearly due west for about a mile. He adopted the course familiar to fox-hunters at home, and took 'casts' in order to come on the track of the French. At length he sighted, in the distance, a sowar, who was on duty as a cavalry vedette. Wolseley rode towards him, but the man, mistaking the escort for the enemy, put spurs to his horse, and, notwithstanding that Wolseley shouted to him to stop, the fellow rode at full speed, and so the chase continued for a distance of two miles. Following the fugitive, Wolseley entered the parks and gardens of the Summer Palace—known as Yuen-ming-yuen, or, 'Round and Brilliant Garden'—which is enclosed by high granite walls. General Montauban had fixed his camp in a fine grove of trees near the grand entrance; and Wolseley, after communicating with him and Brigadier Pattle, rode back to headquarters to report, escorted by two sowars.

About noon, Lord Elgin and Sir Hope Grant, guided by Colonel Wolseley, who had just time before starting to snatch a hasty breakfast, rode over to Yuen-ming-yuen, for the purpose of conferring with General Montauban. On arrival, the Generals with their staffs proceeded into the palace. It was a curious sight that met Wolseley's eyes as he entered the palace, which for two hundred years had been the most cherished abode of the dynasty of the Emperor

Hien-fung, who, among other titles, arrogated to himself those of 'the Sacred Son of Heaven,' and 'the Governor and Tranquillizer of the Universe.'

The grand entrance opened into a paved courtyard, crossing which, the party of 'barbarians' entered the Hall of Audience, at the upper end of which, opposite the door, was the Imperial throne. The chamber was highly coloured and gilt, and the floor was of polished marble; an immense picture, representing the surrounding palaces and gardens, covered the upper portion of one wall, and the rosewood throne, surrounded by an open-work balustrade, was a fine piece of workmanship. Around the apartment were handsomely-carved sideboards and tables, on which were arranged enamel and china vases, porcelain bowls, and large French clocks. Passing through the gardens, the party of British and French officers entered the suite of private rooms occupied by the Emperor, which were filled with the rarest and choicest articles of *vertu* of native and European manufacture. When Wolseley entered, everything was *in statu quo* as when the Emperor fled. 'His small cap, decorated with the character of longevity embroidered upon it, lay upon his bed; his pipe and tobacco-pouch were upon a small table close by. In all the adjoining rooms were immense wardrobes filled with silks, satins, and fur coats. Cloaks covered with the richest golden needlework, mandarin dresses edged with ermine and sable, and marked with the representations of the five-clawed dragons, showing that they were intended for royalty, were stored in presses. The cushions upon the chairs and sofas were covered with the finest yellow satin, embroidered over with figures of dragons and flowers. Yellow is the Imperial colour, and none but those of royal birth are permitted to wear clothes made of it. Jade-stone is of all precious articles the most highly prized in China, some of it fetching immense prices. For centuries past the

THE LOOT OF THE SUMMER PALACE. 143

finest pieces have been purchased by the Emperors, and stored up in Yuen-ming-yuen. In some rooms large chests were filled with cups, vases, plates, etc., made of jade-stone.'

The private apartments of the Emperor were surrounded by those of his wives, retainers, eunuchs, and servants; these, in addition to the buildings, each stored with different articles of use or luxury, made up a vast group of some fifteen or twenty pavilions. One was full of furs, another of silks, another of drawings, a series of 4,000, illustrating the whole history of China, which, during the sack, the soldiers, ignorant of their value, trod underfoot, and used as firing, so that scarce 200 were saved. Then there was the Carriage Palace, in which were found two howitzers and two magnificent coaches, presented by Lord Amherst to the Emperor Taou-Kwang, in 1818, but which had never been used; also Lord Macartney's presents to the 'Brother of the Sun and Moon,' during his embassy in 1793; and, lastly, in his Majesty's private room, was found Lord Elgin's Treaty of 1858, in its envelope.

Passing to the rear of the buildings, Wolseley took a brief survey of the park, enclosed by a wall some twelve miles in circumference. The walks and paths seemed endless, and led over marble bridges, canals, and fish-ponds, upon some of which were mimic fleets of war-junks armed with brass cannon, which afforded amusement to the Emperor.

A Mixed Commission was nominated to divide the booty between the soldiers of the two armies; but the French managed to secure more than their rightful share by looting.*

---

* 'If the reader will imagine,' says Wolseley, 'some 3,000 men let loose into a city composed only of Museums and Wardour Streets, he may have some faint idea of what Yuen-ming-yuen looked like after it had been about twenty hours in the possession of the French. Officers and men seemed to have been seized with a temporary insanity; in body and soul they were

On the 11th of October, a sale was held of the booty, which realized 123,000 dollars (about £24,000 sterling), a sum which enabled each soldier to receive seventeen dollars (£3 10s.), and the officers, who were divided into three classes, and received one-third of the whole, were paid in like proportion. But Sir Hope Grant declined to take his share, throwing it into the common fund, an example which was followed by the Generals of Division.

Wolseley returned with Sir Hope Grant to the British camp before the Teh-shun gate, and on the 9th the French, having burnt the Emperor's private residence to the ground, quitted Yuen-ming-yuen and encamped to the British left, opposite the An-ting gate of Pekin. On the following day the Allied commanders drew up and forwarded a summons to the Prince of Kung, demanding the surrender of the An-ting gate by noon of the 13th of October, failing which the city should be bombarded. A reconnaissance was made of the northern face of the city defences, during which Wolseley, and other officers of the staff, rode up to the edge of the ditch, and a position was settled for the breaching batteries, about 600 yards to the east of the An-ting gate.

On the night of the 12th all arrangements for opening fire at noon of the following day were completed, and the batteries were unmasked; when at the last moment the resolution of Prince Kung gave way. The Allied troops marched in, and soon the Union Jack and Tricolour were flying side by side on the walls of the chief city of the most populous kingdom of the world.

A few days after the occupation of Pekin, Colonel Wolseley, while engaged on a survey of the west wall,

---

absorbed in one pursuit, which was plunder, plunder. I stood by while one of the regiments was supposed to be parading; but although their "fall-in" was sounded over and over again, I do not believe there was an average of ten men a company present.'

accompanied by his interpreter, Mr. Swinhoe, and an escort of cavalry, encountered a party of Chinamen with five carts. On examination, he found that each cart contained a coffin, with the body of one of our countrymen who had been captured on the 18th of September, and died of the cruel treatment to which they had been subjected. The bodies were interred with befitting ceremony in the Russian cemetery, which General Ignatieff, the Russian Ambassador, placed at the disposal of the British Commander.

Lord Elgin demanded as compensation the payment of 300,000 taels, about £100,000, which was paid on the 22nd October, and in expiation of the foul crime his lordship directed the destruction of the Palace of Yuen-ming-yuen, which was acccordingly carried into effect by Sir John Michel's Division. Colonel Wolseley was present during the 18th and 19th October, while the work of destruction was in progress, and took the opportunity of inspecting the country around the palaces, and that lying between them and the neighbouring hills. He was among the last to quit the heap of smouldering ashes that alone remained to mark the site of the palace in which for centuries the Emperors of the Mantchoo, or Ta-tsing, dynasty received the embassies of some of the most powerful nations on earth.

The ratification and signature of the Treaty of Tientsin took place on the 24th of October, Colonel Wolseley, in consequence of rumours of treachery, having on the preceding evening proceeded into the city and made a careful inspection of the Hall of Ceremonies, one of the six Imperial Boards, the scene of the meeting.

Colonel Wolseley now proceeded to Tungchow, to superintend the transport, by boat, from thence to Tientsin, of the sick and heavy stores. During his stay before Pekin, by great diligence, and with the assistance of Lieutenant Harrison, he had managed to make surveys of the country around the capital, with the exception of the south side, which was too distant from the camp to enable him to reconnoitre there with a suitable force and return on the same day. In all other directions, however, the localities were closely examined, and the beautifully executed maps he prepared are, doubtless, to be found in the Quartermaster-General's Department at the Horse Guards. In his history of the campaign, where his own name nowhere appears, he states that the maps were prepared 'under the superintendence of Colonel Mackenzie;' and merely adds: 'All the information that could be obtained was collected, so that in the event of any future operations being required in those regions, our work will be much simplified.' The good work he had done did not, however, escape the notice of those most competent to judge, and whose favourable opinion would be therefore all the more highly appreciated. The Commanding General bestowed high praise upon him, and frequently mentioned him in despatches.

On the 7th of November, the Second Division quitted Pekin, Sir Hope Grant and the First Division marching on the following day. Quitting Tungchow, the army proceeded to Tientsin, where a garrison was left under Brigadier Staveley. The embarkation was commenced about the middle of November—the cavalry proceeding on to Taku, where they embarked—and completed by the end of the month, and very hard work it was for the officers of the Quartermaster-General's Department and the gunboats, which day and night were busy, amid very severe weather, conveying the troops to the fleet. But the arduous duty was performed with exemplary regularity, and without a hitch or accident of any kind, though not a day too soon, for, on the 25th of November, the mouth of the Peiho was completely frozen over near the ctiy, and Colonel Wolseley and other officers walked across the river.

Wolseley accompanied Sir Hope Grant to Shanghai, where they, and twelve other officers, hired a steamer, and made a pleasure-trip to Japan, every important port of which interesting country they visited. On their arrival at Yokohama, the party rode to Yeddo, a distance of nine miles, and stayed at the British Embassy; and, finally, having obtained the permission of the Japanese Government, proceeded on their return voyage—this being only the second steamer to make her appearance in those waters—through the famous Inland Sea, the beautiful scenery of which has been described by Oliphant and other writers.

With the departure of Sir Hope Grant for England, the China War of 1860 was 'as a tale that was told.'* As this campaign was one of the shortest, so it was one of the most ably conducted this country had hitherto waged. The more recent Abyssinian, Ashantee and Egyptian Expeditions have accustomed us to short and sharp campaigns, crowned with brilliant success, for which we are indebted to the genius of the commanders who led British soldiers across the mountain passes of Abyssinia and the forests and deserts of the Gold Coast and Egypt; but the Chinese War of 1860 is not without its lessons, and though not so romantic in its incidents, or watched with such eager expectancy by the British public, as were those memorable Expeditions, Sir Hope Grant scarcely received adequate praise or reward for the great success he achieved. The storm of the Taku Forts was a gallant feat, and the advance upon and occupation of the populous Chinese capital—the Kamballi of Marco Polo, around which hung a halo of romance as the place whence Kublai Khan issued his decrees to the ambassadors of dependent nations—was a daring act for so small a force to

* The army engaged in this war received a medal, and those present at the storm of the Taku Forts and the capture of Pekin were awarded two clasps. The thanks of both Houses of Parliament were voted to Sir Hope Grant and those who had served under his command.

execute. The distance traversed was limited in comparison with that over which Sir Robert Napier and Sir Garnet Wolseley advanced in 1868 and 1874, and there were no natural obstacles to overcome, but the country might have been made impracticable had Sang-ko-lin-sin adopted the tactics of Napoleon in 1812, while the population was enormous, though happily unwarlike. The loss in all these campaigns whether in the field of battle or on the march, was very small, and the operations were conducted with extraordinary rapidity and a masterly adaptation of means to ends. Not only is the conduct of these 'little wars' fraught with weighty lessons to students of the art military, but, in each case, the incidents were full of interest to all Englishmen, and the *dénouement* was replete with tragic effect and grandeur. The treacherous murder of our countrymen by Hien-fung, the wholesale massacres of Theodore, and the sanguinary orgies of Koffee Kalcalli, received a fitting expiation in the destruction, by the purifying agency of fire, of the Summer Palace, with its priceless contents, of Magdala, left a blackened rock, and of Coomassie, with its Golgotha of decaying corpses.

In the month of January, 1861, Colonel Wolseley was directed to proceed to Nankin, accompanied by an interpreter, on a semi-diplomatic, semi-military mission, with the object of reporting to the military authorities upon the position and prospects of the Taipings,* who had now been

* The Taiping cause at that time was taken up by a small clique in England, who appeared to think that, as these people were nominally Christians, they were justified, in their iconoclastic zeal, in committing wholesale murder and rapine. The real facts of the case were misrepresented, from interested motives, by some of the merchants, and from bigoted zeal by certain of the Protestant missionaries, who regarded these rebels with favour because they expressed a determination to extirpate idolatry, whether heathen or Popish, from the face of the land. But their religion was a mixture of blasphemy and barbarity, the chief head, 'Tien-wan,' being a prophet who lived at Nankin, in seclusion with his 300 female domestics and 68 wives, in a state of the most grovelling sensuality, until he died by his own hand, some four years later. All who opposed the new religionists were put to the sword, and entire provinces were desolated, the

eleven years in arms; and also of notifying to the rebel king our treaty with the Imperial Government, by which the Yang-tze-Kiang was opened to foreign trade, and that our merchants intended to send vessels up to Hankow immediately, and our Government proposed establishing Consulates there, and at Hu-Kau, and Ching-Kiang-foo. At Nankin he was accommodated in a palace belonging to the Chung-wan, or 'Faithful King,' one of the eleven Taiping Chiefs, and received daily a supply of fowl, eggs, and other eatables, for which no money was required, it being the avowed intention of the leaders to abolish the use of coin, and reduce society to the patriarchal state; actually, on Wolseley's offering money to the wretched starving coolies who carried his wearing apparel, they refused to accept it if anyone was present, from dread of the executioner's sword.

All communications between him and the Taiping authorities were carried on through Tsan-wan, the cousin of Tien-wan (the 'Heavenly King'), with whom he had great influence. Wolseley used to stroll about the city unquestioned, visiting all that was worth seeing, including the famous 'Porcelain Tower,' the old tombs of the Ming dynasty, and the extensive field-works surrounding the walls, thrown up by the Imperialists during their siege of the city, extending over several years. The only annoyance he suffered was caused by the crowds of idlers who followed him about, much as a London mob tracks the footsteps of any Eastern visitor, whose peculiarity of dress attracts the eye of the cockney *gamin*. But in China the *hoi polloi*,

---

rebel soldiers pillaging the cities they conquered, and recruiting their armies by pressing into their service all males capable of bearing arms. Colonel Wolseley says that, knowing the imbecility and corruption of the Imperial Government, he went to Nankin strongly prejudiced in favour of the Taipings, but he came away enlightened as to the real character of this mock Christianity.

though perhaps not more personal in their remarks, are certainly less complimentary, and the opprobrious epithet of 'fan-qui' (foreign devil) was applied to Wolseley more audibly than was at all agreeable.

'Crowds of men and women,' he writes, 'came daily to see us; all were most good-humoured, and took considerable pleasure in examining our clothes, and watching us eat. One evening a great procession carrying lanterns visited us.'

Wolseley visited a new palace built by Tien-wan—which was levelled to the ground by the Imperialists in 1864—in order to witness the ceremonies attendant upon the promulgation of a royal edict, and one which he saw was worded in the most blasphemous language, the name of Tien-wan being coupled with the Trinity, as he was declared to be the brother and equal of Christ.

During Wolseley's stay at Nankin, the *Yang-tse*, a fine steamer belonging to Messrs. Dent and Co., arrived there on its way to Hankow, and Admiral Hope's squadron not having yet appeared so far up the Yang-tze-Kiang, he gladly availed himself of an invitation to proceed thither from a member of the firm, who happened to be on board. On the 28th of February, 1861, he quitted the city of Nankin, and, after a pleasant trip up the Yang-tse-Kiang, which he describes in detail in his Journal, arrived at Hankow at four p.m. on the 5th of March.

Wolseley was received with the utmost consideration by the Viceroy, Kwang-wan, and, on the occasion of his making a state visit, was attended by the Commandant and a 'three-button Mandarin,' who escorted him in his state barge. A triumphal arch, covered with flags and coloured cloth, was erected in his honour, and a vast crowd lined the river-front of the city, along which he was carried in a sedan-chair, all anxious to catch a glimpse of the 'foreign devil,' and only

HIS REPORT ON THE TAIPINGS.   151

kept in order by the police, who freely used their whips of twisted thongs. Colonel Wolseley quitted Hankow on the 10th of March, and reached Shanghai on the evening of the 16th, when he bade adieu to the hospitable owner of the *Yang-tse*, having greatly enjoyed his trip.

When quitting Shanghai for his mission to Nankin, Wolseley had been furnished with merely verbal instructions to gain all the information practicable of the position and prospects of the Taipings, considered from a military point of view. The conclusion he arrived at from a close survey of their resources, was most unfavourable to their eventual success. In the opinions he formed he was not, however, supported by British officials, who, it might be thought, from their long residence in the country, and intimacy with the people and their language, would have arrived at juster conclusions. Thus, Consul Meadows, in a despatch to Lord John Russell, dated 19th of February in this year, took a favourable view of the rebel power, stating : ' I entirely deny that the Taipings have no regular government, and have no claim to be considered a political power ;' and also expressed an opinion that to subjugate the Taipings it would require on the part of the power which had just humiliated the Imperial Government, and defeated and dispersed its armies, 'a large fleet of steamers and some 20,000 troops operating in three or four armies in the country under their authority, extending 800 or 900 miles from north to south, and 1,000 or 1,100 east and west.' Colonel Wolseley, in his Report, took a far different view of the strength of the Taipings, which turned out to be but weakness when, with native troops alone, Colonel Gordon, in his brief campaign of three months, completely shattered this power, which, to the consular mind, appeared so formidable a military organization.

From Shanghai, Colonel Wolseley proceeded to Hong-

Kong, whence he embarked, the last of the headquarter staff to leave the country, in one of the steamers of the Peninsular and Oriental Company, and landed in England in May, 1861, after an absence of something over four years.

During that brief space in Wolseley's military career, incidents had been crowded sufficient to make a lifetime eventful. This country had emerged triumphant from one of the most tremendous struggles in which she has been engaged since, in the words of Thomas Campbell, Europe

> 'Taught her proud barks the winding way to shape,
> And braved the stormy spirit of the Cape.'

She had also humbled to the dust the pride and military power of the most populous, and one of the most ancient, empires in the world. By these achievements England had regained her pride of place, for though her position as one of the Great Powers can never be disputed, as long as she wields the sceptre of the seas, her prestige and military status had received a severe shock by the events of the Crimean War.

During those four years, also, Wolseley had frequently found himself face to face with Death in many of the varied forms 'the lean abhorred monster' assumes in his battle with life. He had encountered him amid the terrors of the storm and shipwreck, when it seemed as if the sea was to engulph the 'twice five hundred iron men,' who had embarked in the ill-fated *Transit*. He had met him in the battlefield, and when struggling through the narrow streets of Lucknow with matchlockmen aiming at him from 'tower and turret and bartizan;' and he had wrestled with him in the form the Destroyer assumes, when he is in his fellest mood—that of the pestilence which, even in the hour of victory, dogs the footsteps of our armies in the East, and, in the shape of cholera or heat apoplexy, carries off his victims from among our bravest and most vigorous. From all these perils, by land and by sea, by battle, fire, and wreck, he had been preserved to land once more in his country, and we doubt not that on sighting the white cliffs of his native land, he offered up heartfelt thanks to the Providence that had watched over his safety during the past four eventful years.

On his arrival in England, Colonel Wolseley, who was promoted for his services to a substantive majority, got his long leave of eighteen months, and, after visiting his family, proceeded in the autumn of 1861 to Paris, where he employed his leisure in painting in oils and water-colours, for, like some other officers of the British army, he added to his professional acquirements the skill of an accomplished artist. Wolseley seemed, however,—like the 'stormy petrel' of the ocean—to be the harbinger of wars and rumours of wars, for, as on his return from Burmah, he had scarcely set foot on the soil of his native land, than he found her embroiled in a stupendous conflict with one of the most powerful empires of the world, in the vortex of which he was himself quickly drawn, so again, hardly had he landed from service in the East, than there was every indication that this country would be soon grappling in a life-and-death struggle with the greatest Republic of modern times.

CHAPTER V.

SERVICE IN CANADA.

The Trent Affair.—Colonel Wolseley embarks for Canada, and is employed on Transport Duty.—His Visit to the Headquarters of Generals Lee and Longstreet, and Impressions of the Confederate Armies.—Colonel Wolseley's Services during the Fenian Invasion in 1866.

In this politically hard-living age—when, within a decade, empires are founded and subverted, ancient despotisms humbled to the dust, and new republics given to the European system; when wars of the first magnitude are waged, resulting in battles and sieges, wherein hundreds of thousands of combatants are engaged—it has, perhaps, been forgotten that, in 1861, this country was on the verge of hostilities with the United States, then not long entered upon that 'War of Secession' which demonstrated the vast resources of the Great Republic and the warlike spirit which only slumbered within the breasts of her citizens, who, whether as Confederates or Federals, showed themselves no unworthy scions of the Anglo-Saxon stock.

In the winter of 1861 nothing looked more certain on the political horizon than the embroilment of this country in that momentous struggle, the issues of which would, in that event, have been far different from what history records. At that time the destinies of England were still wielded by the aged statesman, Lord Palmerston, who exhibited in this crisis all the warlike spirit and energy for which his name was almost a synonym, until the Danish business, when what Lord Derby called the 'meddle and muddle' policy of his Foreign Secretary, caused it to be associated with something like pusillanimity. *Stat magni nominis umbra* might have been written of his lordship after that *fiasco*.

The incident which nearly precipitated this country into war was that known as the '*Trent* Affair.' On the 8th of November, Commodore Wilkes, commanding the United States ship-of-war *San Jacinto*, boarded the British Mail Company's steamship *Trent*, on the high seas, and seized Messrs. Mason and Slidell, the Confederate Agents accredited to the Courts of London and Paris. Though the act was a clear violation of national rights and international law, Commodore Wilkes was raised to the height of popularity among the rowdy writers of the American press, who indulged in that species of 'tall' talk expressively known as 'spread-eagleism;' and even an eminent statesman like Everett, who had been Secretary of State to President Fillmore, and previously Minister in England, gave Wilkes' conduct the sanction of his approval.

England was seized with a patriotic mania, and the most pacific were fired with a determination to uphold the honour of the flag and avenge this outrage, if reparation were not promptly made by the surrender of the Confederate Envoys. But the American press and public were equally outspoken against the possibility of concession, and for some weeks a war seemed inevitable. Our Government displayed the utmost energy in the preparations they made to meet the contingency, and the country waited with feverish anxiety the reply to Lord Russell's ultimatum of the 30th of November, addressed to Lord Lyons, requiring 'the liberation of the four gentlemen and their delivery to your lordship in order that they may again be placed under British protection, and a suitable apology for the aggression which has been committed.' The dockyards resounded with the din of workmen fitting vessels for sea, troops were despatched to Canada with all possible despatch, and that colony, with the loyalty for which it has ever been remarkable, called out its militia and volunteers in readiness to defend its borders from aggression. Happily, however, wise counsels prevailed in the Lincoln Cabinet; it was seen by the American Government and people that John Bull was really in earnest this time and meant to fight; all the Governments of Europe were as one upon the merits of the question, and the cabinets of Paris, Berlin, and Vienna addressed weighty remonstrances to the Washington Government, recommending them to make the *amende* and release the prisoners; and, finally, after an irritating delay, a despatch, dated 26th of December, was received from Mr. Seward, who, after arguing the case at most immoderate length, stated that 'the four persons in question are now held in military custody at Fort Warren, in the State of Massachusetts. They will be cheerfully liberated. Your lordship will please indicate a time and place for receiving them.' This was done by placing them on board H.M.S. *Rinaldo*, Commander (now Admiral Sir William) Hewett, who was specially sent out to receive them; and they arrived at Southampton on the 29th of January, 1862, in the *La Plata*. But we are anticipating.

On the 17th of November, the day the news of the *Trent* outrage reached London, a Cabinet Council was held, and, on the following day, the War Office ordered the despatch of troops and stores, and Special Service officers were selected to prepare for the reception of the troops which were to be despatched in large swift steamers. Colonel McKenzie was appointed Quartermaster-General, and he immediately asked for the services of Colonel Wolseley, who at this time was on leave, hunting in the county Cork. He had just bought two horses, and had enjoyed one day's sport on each animal, when a telegram came from Colonel McKenzie offering him employment on active service as Assistant Quartermaster-General. Not many hours were suffered to elapse before the hunters were given away, and Wolseley was in London. Colonel McKenzie proposed to the War Office that he, and the other selected officers, should proceed to Canada by the next mail steamer; but, with singular obtuseness, it was directed that they should embark in the *Melbourne*, which was notorious during the China War, where she had been employed as a transport, for her slowness and a habit she had of breaking down. In vain Colonel McKenzie, who knew from experience the steamer's unseaworthy qualities, pointed out that the object for which the Special Service officers were proceeding to Canada, namely, to prepare for the reception of the troops under orders for that country, would be best attained by their embarking in a swift mail steamer. It was all to no purpose; and the influences which were paramount when valuable lives were embarked in the *Transit*, and, more recently, in the *Megæra*, again prevailed.

The *Melbourne* sailed on the 7th of December with a battery of artillery, 30,000 stand of arms, and about 900 tons of stores. Besides Colonels McKenzie and Wolseley, she had on board Colonel Lysons* (selected to organize the Canadian Militia), Captain Stoddart, R.E., and the late lamented Sir William Gordon, R.E., of 'Gordon's Battery,' a man of the true heroic mould, who proceeded in command

* The ground to be traversed by the troops proceeding to Quebec was familiar to Colonel (now Sir Daniel) Lysons, who, in 1843, when a young officer in the Royal Scots, on the occasion of the wreck at Cape Chat, near the mouth of the St. Lawrence, of the *Premier*, sailing transport, conveying his regiment from Canada, volunteered to proceed on snow-shoes to Quebec, a distance of 300 miles. This distance he actually accomplished by walking and travelling in carts, within six days. A ship was started off to the rescue immediately on his arrival, and was just in time to embark the troops before the river was frozen over. On the occasion of the wreck it was mainly by his gallantry and devotion that the lives of some hundreds of men, women, and children were saved.

of the troops. No sooner had the *Melbourne* sailed than she showed her unseaworthy qualities.

After a weary passage, the ship, according to orders, tried to get through the ice to Bic, on the St. Lawrence; but this being found wholly impracticable, she bore up, under stress of weather and want of coal, for Sydney, Cape Breton Island. The miseries of that passage had been paralleled before by Wolseley in his *Transit* experiences; but still it was a peculiarly hard fate that forced him and his shipmates to pass the Christmas Day of 1861, coiled up on tables and benches in the cuddy, while the 'green seas' washed at their sweet will under and over them, and the ship laboured heavily against the wintry gale. The *Melbourne* was thirty days performing a voyage which the *Persia*, carrying a portion of the reinforcements for whose reception they had been despatched to prepare, made in nearly one-third of that time. While at Sydney, a telegram arrived from Halifax, announcing the surrender of Messrs. Mason and Slidell, and that all chance of war was at an end. The *Melbourne* then proceeded to Halifax, where she found three transports which had disembarked their troops, the War Office having determined to send to Canada 10,000 men and 4 batteries of artillery.

From Halifax Colonel Wolseley and other officers proceeded, by a Cunard mail steamer, to Boston, on their voyage to Montreal. It was feared that the Boston people would be uncivil, and the officers were warned that the lower classes, in the excited state of public feeling, might even offer violence were they to display the British red coat in the streets. On their arrival, however, they found it was far otherwise; they were treated most respectfully while walking about during their afternoon's stay, looking at the lions of the city, and were regaled sumptuously by a private citizen. The same night they started for Canada; and, after

HIS DUTIES AS TRANSPORT OFFICER. 159

a cold journey during the depth of an inclement winter, arrived at Montreal on a Sunday. On the following morning Colonel Wolseley started off on a journey of 300 miles, down the river to Rivière du Loup, situated on the terminus of the Grand Trunk Railway, where the troops coming from St. John's, New Brunswick, including a battalion of the Scots Fusilier Guards and two batteries of artillery, which arrived out in the *Hibernian*, were transhipped from sleighs, or sleds, in which they had travelled, *viâ* Fredericton, to the railway, by which they proceeded to their destinations at Quebec, Montreal, Hamilton, Kingston, or Toronto. Colonel Wolseley was the only staff officer at Rivière du Loup, and had to make all the arrangements for the accommodation and passage of the troops, who, after sleeping one night at the village, continued their journey on the following morning.

During his stay at this cheerless little place, the troops passed through at the rate of nearly 200 men a day. It was his task to lodge, feed, and clothe them from the stores placed under his charge, and then to start them off on their long journey by rail. These duties were fulfilled without a hitch or a single accident; and of the large force that passed through his hands only one man deserted, although inducements were held out to them to forsake the flag of their country, and during the transit they passed close to the American frontier, at one place only a frozen river forming the boundary. In the middle of March, on the completion of his duties at Rivière du Loup, Wolseley returned to Montreal, the headquarters of the army in the Dominion, then under the command of Sir W. F. Williams (of Kars). Soon after these events Colonel McKenzie proceeded to England, and Wolseley acted for some months as Deputy Quartermaster-General, until relieved by Colonel Lysons.[*]

---

[*] This officer, soon after his first arrival in Canada for the purpose of organizing the Militia, had returned to England, upon the rejection by the

Colonel Wolseley went on leave in the latter part of August, 1862, but like many great actors, who, they say, on taking a holiday, may generally be found in the stalls of a theatre scrutinizing the performance of a brother artist, his strong professional proclivities induced him, instead of enjoying a little well-earned relaxation, to repair to the seat of war then raging in its fiercest intensity between the Federal and Confederate States. While living at Montreal with his friend, Inspector-General (now Sir William) Muir, Chief Medical Officer in Canada, they decided the question as to which of them should join the headquarters of the Northern, and which those of the Southern, army, with the view of comparing notes afterwards, by the familiar method of 'tossing up.' Wolseley 'won the toss,' and elected to proceed South, in order to seek instruction under that unequalled master of the art of war, General Robert Lee— 'unequalled,' we say advisedly, for it is Wolseley's opinion that in military genius Lee has had no superior since the great Napoleon, and he even places him above the great German Generals of the war of 1870. But to join a Confederate army in the field, or even to enter Richmond, was not only a most difficult, but an extremely hazardous adventure, for, even if he escaped the toils of the Northerners, and avoided being seized as a spy, the British Government highly reprobated such proceedings on the part of their officers, and the experiment was one that entailed the risk of his commission. However, considerations of danger were not likely to deter Wolseley from carrying out any scheme on which he had set his heart, so he proceeded to lay his plans, and procure letters of introduction to lead-

---

Opposition, led by the late Sir George Cartier, of the Government Militia Bill, a measure founded upon the scheme elaborated by Colonel Lyons at Quebec, and brought forward by the Ministry of Sir John Macdonald, who resigned upon failing to pass his Bill.

ing Southerners from sympathizers and correspondents. Having first proceeded to New York, he left that city for Baltimore on the 11th of September, and there made arrangements, in conjunction with his friends, for crossing the frontier by 'underground railway,' as the method by which communication was kept up between the North and Secessia was called.

Armed with letters of introduction, he prepared to follow in the footsteps of the adventurous messengers, who were wont to 'run the blockade of the Potomac,' when conveying information between Richmond and the Northern States. There was, however, a difficulty in his case, for his 'patois English,' as the Yankees called it, would inevitably betray his nationality, and all our countrymen were under a ban in the North, as 'rebel sympathizers.' Then there was the inevitable portmanteau of civilized life, without which an English gentleman, who has a regard for personal cleanliness and a change of linen, would not care to travel in country places where hotels are unknown, but which was not considered a necessity in a land where your 'free-born American' thinks himself amply provided with a few paper collars and a pocket-comb.

When preparing to leave Baltimore he met the Hon. Frank Lawley, a brother of Lord Wenlock's, at that time one of the *Times* correspondents in America, a clever and adventurous gentleman, and they agreed to run the blockade together. But in the first instance it was a matter of difficulty to reach the banks of the Potomac, whose broad stream, again, patrolled by numerous Federal gunboats, offered an almost impassable barrier to anyone seeking to cross over into Dixie's Land. Though the Federal gunboats patrolling the river were not as numerous as between July, 1863, when the battle of Gettysburg was fought, and April, 1865, at the close of the War, on the other hand, at this time, as Mr. Lawley observes, 'there was no such organization for running the blockade between Baltimore and Richmond as was established during 1863, and as was available for those rightly initiated into its mysteries until the spring of 1865.'

The Potomac, at the point of crossing, is rather an arm of the sea than a river, and varies between ten and thirteen miles in breadth, so that during the prevalence of south-east winds, its broad bosom is scarcely less agitated than the Atlantic outside the Capes of the Chesapeake. Mr. Lawley says: 'It was necessary for the boatmen connected with the Signal Service of the Confederate Government to be well acquainted with the moods of the mighty and dangerous river, in order to understand the seasons when it was safe for a row-boat with muffled oars to cross. In addition, the phase of the moon had to be closely watched, in order that a dark night might be selected. But even during the blackest night there were the Federal gunboats, which were at last no less thick upon the stream than policemen in the Strand between midnight and sunrise. Each of these boats was armed with a calcium or lime light, and if the slightest sound was heard at night upon the surface of the stream, a broad luminous ray of light was shot forth from the sentinel vessel, which illumined the river for a quarter of a mile, so that the head of a swimming otter was discernible.'

But before the Potomac could be crossed, the two Englishmen had to smuggle themselves from Baltimore to the northern bank, every road and path leading to which was patrolled by bodies of Federal troops. The start was made in a waggon and pair, driven by a trusty agent, who had been well paid for the trouble and risk. In this conveyance they contrived to slip from the country-house of one Secession sympathizer to another, and as bodies of patrolling cavalry and infantry had at that time regular beats, and fixed hours for traversing them, which were well known to the farmers in that part of Maryland, who were nearly all Secessionists, they managed to elude the patrols while proceeding from house to house. 'I travelled,' says Colonel Wolseley,* 'about thirty miles a day, until I reached the village from which I had arranged that my final start should be made, and where I was informed certain people, with whose names I had been furnished, would arrange all matters for me. For the first few nights of our journeyings we stopped at different gentlemen's houses, where we were entertained with patriarchal hospitality. It was interesting in some instances to hear the history of these homesteads; many of them had been built before the Declaration of Independence, and more than one was of brick imported from England. All the proprietors boasted of their English descent from good families, and seemed to attach far greater importance to blood and ancient pedigree than even we do.'

At length they arrived at a farm-house on the river, but had great difficulty in procuring a boat. After many disappointments, they were directed to a smuggler on the river, who had a craft of his own, in which he consented to take them over. 'We remained,' says Wolseley, 'for a night at his abode, sleeping in a garret destitute of windows, but abounding with rats which sadly disturbed my friend's rest; though I slept soundly, being accustomed to rough it in every part of the globe.' They were astir early, and embarked in the smuggler's boat. 'The creek,' says Wolseley, ' into which we had hoped to run on the Virginian shore, was about a couple of miles higher up than the point from which we started, but, unfortunately, a gunboat lay off the entrance to it, and there were two others at no very great distance. After due deliberation, it was determined

* See an article in *Blackwood's Magazine* for January, 1863, entitled 'A Month's Visit to the Confederate Headquarters, by an English Officer.' This is not the only article Colonel Wolseley has written in 'Old Ebony.'

that we should make for a spot about five miles higher up, and endeavour to get there by running close along the left bank of the river, so as not to attract attention, and, when clear of all gunboats, to push out into the centre of the stream, and then watch a favourable opportunity for steering into the desired haven. The tide being in our favour, we dropped slowly up on it, until about mid-day, when it turned, and, the wind dying away, we were obliged to make close in for shore and anchor.

'My friend and I had landed, and spent the day in an old ruined shed surrounded by reeds and rushes. Large steamers and gun-vessels of various sizes kept passing and re-passing all day; but none of them seemed to notice our little craft. On one occasion we saw a boat put off from one of the gunboats and come in our direction; but, instead of visiting us, its crew boarded a small cutter which lay becalmed in the centre of the river, and then returned to their own vessel. At sunset a slight breeze arose, before which we glided directly up the river. When we passed the mid-stream and approached near the Virginian shore, the owner of the boat became quite nervous, and began lamenting his fate in having to turn smuggler; but the hard times, he said, had left him no alternative, his farm having been destroyed by the Northern troops. He seemed to have a superstitious awe of gunboats, too; and told us he had heard that the officers on board of them possessed telescopes through which they could see distinctly for *miles* at night. Several steamers passed us when we were about two-thirds of the way over, but although the moon every now and then emerged brightly from behind the drifting clouds, we had got under the shade of the land, and managed so that she always shone upon our sails on the side away from the 'enemy.' We could hear the steamers for about twenty minutes before we caught sight of their light, and during that time the anxious face of the smuggler would have made a glorious study for an artist of the Rembrandt school. The cargo consisted of coffee and sugar, and, if safely landed, would be in itself a small fortune to the owner of the boat; that he should feel alarmed for its safety, therefore, was not surprising.

'As we approached the shore, the wind died away, so we were obliged to punt the little craft along; the men thus employed taking off their boots, lest they should make any noise in moving upon the deck. Now and then one of the gunboats, anchored off the neighbouring creek, would throw a light along the waters in all directions; once we all fancied that it was approaching nearer to us, and on another occasion we thought we heard the sound of oars, and as there was not a breath of wind to help us along, and punting is a slow process, we felt far from comfortable. Half-past ten found us safe in a little creek almost land-locked, so there was no danger of discovery there; and a run of about a mile and a half up it took us to the point of landing. After a dreary walk of about five miles over a forest road, we reached a small village, and, having spent a considerable time in knocking at the door of the house to which we had been directed, we at last succeeded in gaining admittance. The landlord was absent, being in concealment at a farmhouse in the neighbourhood; but his niece, a very nice girl, did the honours in his stead. She told us that the Yankees had made a descent upon the village, and carried off several of the inhabitants as prisoners to Washington. The place was suspected of containing smugglers, consequently the Federal troops frequently visited it in search of contraband goods.'

Mr. Lawley thus describes the passage across the Potomac, and an interview in the smuggler's cottage with a Federal officer commanding a patrol, which, but for the presence of mind displayed by our hero, must have proved fatal to the success of their undertaking, if not to their liberty:

'We succeeded, one evening at nightfall, in making our way to a cottage which looked down upon the broad and tranquil river. Its owner was a fisherman, who told us that his house was usually visited during the night by a patrol, and that it would be unsafe for us to sleep there; but he promised that, if we would return on the morrow at noon, he would have a friend named Hunt to meet us, with whom we might probably make a bargain. Meantime, we adjourned to a village some two or three miles distant, where, what between heat and insects, we passed an awful night. At noon we were again at our friend's house, and covenanted with a son of Hunt the fisherman, for twenty dollars a piece in gold, that his father's boat would take us on board that night at ten o'clock, in an adjoining creek, and would land us before daybreak on the Virginian shore. But the intervening afternoon brought with it fresh adventures. We were forbidden by our host to leave the house, because the telescopes of the Federals in the neighbouring gunboat were said to be constantly sweeping the shore, and would infallibly detect the presence of strangers in the little hut. Shortly after two o'clock we were horrified by the sight of a Federal officer, in the well-known blue uniform of the United States army, who was ascending on foot by a little path which led to the house from the river. In his hand he carried a revolver, and behind him followed 7 soldiers, who, with their leader, had just got out of a boat. The consternation of our host during the few seconds of suspense before the Federals reached the house, was pitiable in the extreme. There was scant time for consultation, and when the officer looked into the hut and descried Colonel Wolseley and myself, he seemed scarcely less disquieted than our host. Having in previous years shot canvas-backs and blue-wings on the Potomac, I stepped forward as spokesman, and asked the officer whether it would be possible for us to hire a boat, as I had often before done, with a view to doing some "gunning" on the river. The officer answered that no "gunning" was now permitted on the river. I then asked him how it would be possible for my companion and me to get back to Washington. Just as he was hesitating about his answer, Colonel Wolseley adroitly advanced, cigar-case in hand, and offered him a "regalia." That judiciously proffered cigar turned the balance in our favour. The officer answered that a steamboat would call the following morning about four o'clock at the neighbouring wharf, by which we might take passage to Washington. We parted the best friends, in spite of the whispered remonstrances of a sergeant, who probably thought our appearance suspicious, and remarked that we had no guns with us. Long before four o'clock of the following morning, Hunt and his two sons had landed us in Virginia. Colonel Wolseley and I had to lie down and conceal ourselves below the gunwale, and I remember how long the *trajet* seemed to us, as the fishing-boat tacked hither and thither while casting its nets, and approached uncomfortably near the Federal gunboat. After I had passed two or three months at Richmond, and become intimate with the officers of the Signal Service, I heard that poor Hunt had been subsequently caught in carrying passengers across the Potomac—that his boat had been seized, and himself sent to prison. But I have often thought how severely the Federal authorities, and especially Mr. Seward, would have blamed the young gentleman who thus allowed so distinguished a British officer as Colonel Wolseley to slip through his fingers.'

On landing in Virginia, Colonel Wolseley and his friend walked to the village of Dumfries; it was dark and the roads were bad, but they were light-hearted and contented at having crossed the dreaded Potomac and eluded the Federal cruisers. At Dumfries they procured a farmer's cart without springs, drawn by two mules, and in this comfortless conveyance, which jolted along over 'the very worst road' Wolseley had seen even in all his Indian and China experiences, they drove into Fredericksburg, crossing the Rappahannock River.

Early on the following morning they again started, and, taking the road leading under Mary's Heights, which, three months later, was the scene of one of the most sanguinary struggles of the war, reached Beaverdam Station, on the Virginia Central Railroad, in time for the afternoon train, which took them to Richmond. Wolseley says:

'All the carriages were crowded with passengers, of whom a large proportion were the sick and wounded coming from General Lee's army at Winchester. They had been all day on the railroad, and some of the poor fellows seemed quite worn out with fatigue. My friend and I stood on what is called the platform of the car, during the journey of two hours and a half, as the regular passenger-cars were full, and those containing the sick and wounded were anything but inviting, as men with legs and arms amputated, and whose pale, haggard faces assumed an expression of anguish at even the slightest jolting of the railway carriages, lay stretched across the seats. At every station where we stopped, a rush for water was made by the crowds of men carrying the canteens and calabashes of those whose disabled condition prevented them from assisting themselves. The filth and stench within those moving hospitals were intolerable, and, though well inured to the sight of human suffering, I never remember feeling so moved by it as during that short railway journey.

'Upon reaching Richmond we found a dense crowd on the platform, men and women searching for brothers, fathers, husbands, and lovers. A military guard, with fixed bayonets, was endeavouring to keep order and a clear passage for those on crutches, or limping along with the aid of a stick or the arm of some less severely wounded comrade.'

The two Englishmen drove off to the Spottiswood Hotel, but were informed that there was not even one room vacant. The same answer was given at the American; but at the Exchange they obtained a little double-bedded apartment up four flights of stairs. Congress was sitting, so the best apartments at most houses were engaged by the members of the Legislature, and wounded men occupied almost all the other available bedrooms. As Wolseley says, when black tea was selling at sixteen dollars a pound, and everything else, except bread and meat, was proportionately expensive, it may be readily imagined that the fare was far from good. Four dollars a day, however, for board and lodging, was not very exorbitant; but no wine or spirits was procurable at any hotel, the manufacture and sale of all intoxicating liquors having been prohibited by Government.

On this question of spirits as it concerns the health of soldiers on active service, Colonel Wolseley has always entertained opinions in consonance with those of Sir Wilfrid Lawson, and, though no teetotaler, has ever been averse from serving out spirits to troops in the field.* This view he has studiously carried out in the campaigns which he himself has conducted, and he attributes the health enjoyed

* He remarks: 'When the Confederate army was first enrolled, each man received a daily ration of spirits; but this practice has been long since discontinued, and, strange to say, without causing any discontent amongst the men—a practical refutation of the assertion that a certain amount of stimulants is absolutely necessary for soldiers, and that without it they cannot endure the fatigues of active service. For what army in modern times has made the long marches, day after day, that Jackson's corps of "foot cavalry," as they are facetiously called, have accomplished? Doubtless there are circumstances when an allowance of grog is very beneficial to health—such as bivouacking in swampy places and during heavy rains; but in ordinary cases, and in fine weather, I am convinced that men will go through as much continuous hard work without any stimulants whatever as with them.'

by the troops in the Red River and Ashantee Expeditions, in no small degree, to the fact of their abstention from spirituous liquors.*

Wolseley and his friends were received with open arms by the Southern leaders, and such letters of introduction as they had managed to retain, having previously sewn them up in their clothes, proved an 'open sesame' in society. They were received and hospitably entertained by the members of the Government, including Mr. Benjamin, Secretary of State for Foreign Affairs, and General Randolph, the Secretary at War, who was most obliging in furnishing them with passes to go wherever they pleased, and with letters to the various military authorities. The first Confederate officer who called upon them at their hotel, was the late General John B. Magruder, who, when in Canada, had made many friends among the British officers.

One can scarcely realize the intensity of the passionate fervour with which the gallant Southerners maintained the unequal conflict with their gigantic opponent. Whatever had been the original cause of the war, it was now, in the opinion of Lord Russell, 'a contest for dominion on the part of the North, and for independence on the part of the South,' a conclusion which the *Times* endorsed on the 19th of January, 1862, when it declared that the war was 'a purely political quarrel;' adding, 'that as the cause of Italy against Austria is the cause of freedom, so also the cause of the South gallantly defending itself against the cruel and desolating invasion of the North, is the cause of freedom.'†

---

* The same applies to the campaign in Egypt, where, under his instructions, only coffee and a double allowance of tea were served out to his troops, no spirits being allowed to either officers or men.

† Early in the struggle it was manifest that the Northern statesmen and Congress would sacrifice principle to retain the seceding States, for on the 3rd of March, 1861, after the formation into a Confederacy of the six States and the inauguration of Jefferson Davis, and on the day preceding the installation of Abraham Lincoln, President Buchanan and the Congress amended the Constitution in these terms: 'That no amendment shall be

At the time of Wolseley's arrival at Richmond, the Confederate army had just returned from the expedition into Maryland, after having fought, on the 17th of September, the sanguinary but indecisive battle of Antietam, or Sharpsburg; and he mentions as an interesting fact, that during a conversation with General Lee, he assured him that throughout the day he never had more than 35,000 men engaged; and with these he fought a drawn battle with McClellan's host of 90,000 men, General Stonewall Jackson being engaged in reducing Harper's Ferry with the remainder of the Confederate army which had crossed the Potomac. While at Richmond, Wolseley visited the scene of the seven days' desperate fighting which took place in its vicinity in the previous June, when, in his opinion, General Lee showed himself as consummate a master of the art of war as Napoleon himself. He says of these battle-fields: ' In some places the numerous graves and pits filled with dead bodies but slightly covered over, testified to the severity of the fighting there. The *débris* of all things pertaining to an army, which lay strewn about on the ground camped on by McClellan's troops, was immense. In many places the blackened embers of flour-barrels, clothing-cases, and com-

---

made to the Constitution which shall authorize or give Congress power to abolish or interfere within any State with the institutions thereof, including that of persons held to labour or servitude by the laws of the said State.' Cordially hating slavery as we do, whether in its worst form, as we have seen it on the east coast of Africa, or as a 'domestic institution,' as it appeared in the Southern States, we cannot but rejoice that it was crushed out once and for ever from the American Continent. Englishmen should remember, with humility and shame, that all the misery and bloodshed of this great Civil War was the *damnosa hereditas* bequeathed by our ancestors to our American colonies. Though slaves were first imported into America by the Spanish missionary, Las Casas (who was horrified by the cruelty with which the Aborigines were treated by the European settlers), it was in 1562, long before the settlement of Virginia, that Queen Elizabeth founded a company for its promotion, while Charles II. made grants of lands to the colonists in proportion to the number of their slaves. William III. gave further encouragement to slavery; and finally, in the reign of George II., free trade in slaves was declared.

missariat stores covered large spaces, showing the haste with which the general retreat was commenced, and the great quantity of stores which it had been found necessary to destroy. In some parts the very trunks of the trees were riddled through, huge pines being cut down by round shot, and great branches torn off by bursting shells.' His comments on the strategy of the rival commanders, as coming from a master of the art, and one who had studied the ground, are of great interest and no little value.

Before leaving Richmond, Colonel Wolseley and Mr. Lawley spent a day at Drury's Bluff (or Fort Darling, as it was called in the North), which was attacked by the *Monitor*, *Galena*, and some other Federal ironclad gunboats, when McClellan's army was on the peninsula. Captain Lee, formerly of the United States Navy (brother to General R. Lee, and father to General Fitzhugh Lee), was in command of the troops and position, and showed them round the works, pointing out all the new improvements in guns, carriages, and projectiles. Wolseley also inspected the *Richmond* (or *Merrimac*, No. 2), and was astonished at the success of the efforts of the Southerners in the art of shipbuilding and the manufacture of gunpowder and other munitions of war.

Having been furnished by the War Minister with letters of introduction to General Lee, and the necessary passes, Colonel Wolseley and his companion left Richmond by the Virginia Central Railroad, and reached Staunton in the evening. This place, owing to the war, was in a forlorn condition; no business was doing, and Wolseley searched in vain through a number of shops for such common domestic utensils as a teapot or kettle of any description. Being the railway terminus, and the commencement of the turnpike-road line of communication with the army, Staunton had become an *entrepôt* for stores, waggons, and ambulances, and most of the best houses had been converted into hospitals.

No other means of transport being available, they succeeded, with some difficulty, in getting permission to proceed in an ambulance cart, one of a train of thirteen going up to carry back sick and wounded men. It was four-wheeled, fitted with a tarpaulin hood, and drawn by two horses, the body of the cart being made to carry two men on stretchers, with room for another man beside the driver. Not more than five-and-twenty miles were made the first day, and a halt was called for the night in a field a few miles short of Harrisonburg. The night was cold, with a heavy dew, but they soon lighted good fires, and, squatting around them, made themselves tolerably comfortable. The waggon would only admit of two sleeping in it, so one of their party of three had to lie on the ground with his feet to the fire in correct bivouac fashion.

The following night the ambulance-train halted between Mount Jackson and Woodstock, and, on the third night, at Middletown, about thirteen miles from Winchester. It had been raining all day, and the prospect of a bivouac was far from agreeable, so Wolseley and his two companions—one a Southerner—shouldered their baggage and marched for the inn at the village. As usual, the place was crowded to excess, so, tired, wet, and hungry, two of his companions, one carrying a candle, sallied forth in search of a lodging for the night, while Wolseley mounted sentry over their traps. At length, an old woman consented to give them shelter, and was most kind and attentive.

On the fourth day after leaving Winchester* they arrived

---

* Wolseley remarks in his Journal: 'Every day during our journey to Winchester we passed batches of convalescents marching to join the army many of whom were totally unfit for any work, and also batches of sick and wounded going to the rear. It was an extremely painful sight to see such numbers of weakly men struggling slowly home, many of them without boots or shoes, and all indifferently clad; but posts were established every

at Staunton, and, having procured passes from the Provost-Marshal, without which no one could have passed the guards posted on all the roads, proceeded to General Lee's headquarters, which were close to the Martinsburg road, about six miles from Winchester. Colonel Wolseley and his friend presented their letter to the Adjutant-General, by whom they were introduced to the famous Commander-in-Chief of the Confederate forces, who received them with kindness and the stately courtesy for which he was remarkable. Of General Lee, and the impression he created in his mind, Wolseley says: 'He is a strongly-built man, about five feet eleven in height, and apparently not more than fifty years of age. His hair and beard are nearly white; but his dark-brown eyes still shine with all the brightness of youth, and beam with a most pleasing expression. Indeed, his whole face is kindly and benevolent in the highest degree. In manner, though sufficiently conversible, he is slightly reserved; but he is a person that, wherever seen, whether in a castle or a hovel, alone or in a crowd, must at once attract attention as being a splendid specimen of an English gentleman, with one of the most rarely handsome faces I ever saw. He had had a fall during the Maryland Expedition, from which he was not yet recovered, and which still crippled his right hand considerably. We sat with him for a long time in his tent, conversing upon a variety of topics, the state of

---

seventeen miles along the road, containing commissariat supplies for provisioning them. Into whatever camp you go, you are sure to see tents, carts, horses, and guns all marked with the " U. S." Officers have declared to me that they have seen whole regiments go into action with smooth-bore muskets and without great-coats, and known them in the evening to be well provided with everything—having changed their old muskets for rifles! The Northern prisoners we passed on the road were well clothed in the regular blue frock-coat and light-blue trousers, whilst their mounted guard wore every variety—jackets or coats, it seemed to matter little to them; and, indeed, many rode along in their shirt-sleeves, as gay and happy as if they were decked with gold and the richest trappings.' As General Lee said to Wolseley, when alluding to the ragged uniforms of his soldiers: 'There is one attitude in which I should never be ashamed for you to see my men—that is to say, when they fight.'

public affairs being of course the leading one. You have only to be in his society for a very brief period to be convinced that whatever he says may be implicitly relied upon, and that he is quite incapable of departing from the truth under any circumstances.'

Wolseley, who had seen so many French and British armies in the field, was greatly struck with the marked absence of all the 'pomp and circumstance of glorious war' at General Lee's headquarters. 'They consisted,' he says, 'of about seven or eight pole-tents, pitched with their backs to a stake fence, upon a piece of ground so rocky that it was unpleasant to ride over it—its only recommendation being a little stream of good water which flowed close by the General's tent. In front of the tents were some three or four wheeled waggons, drawn up without any regularity. No guard or sentries were to be seen in the vicinity, and no crowd of aides-de-camp loitering about. A large farm-house stands close by, which, in any other army, would have been the General's residence; but as no liberties are allowed to be taken with personal property in Lee's army, he is particular in setting a good example himself. His staff were crowded together two or three in a tent: none are allowed to carry more baggage than a small box each, and his own kit is but very little larger. Everyone who approaches him does so with marked respect, although there is none of that bowing and flourishing of forage-caps which occurs in the presence of European Generals; and whilst all honour him and place implicit faith in his courage and ability, those with whom he is most intimate feel for him the affection of sons to a father. Old General Scott was correct in saying that when Lee joined the Southern cause, it was worth as much as the accession of 20,000 men. Though his house on the Pamunky river was burnt to the ground, and his residence on the Arlington Heights not only gutted of its furniture, but even the very relics of George Washington were stolen from it and paraded in triumph in the saloons of New York and Boston, he neither evinced any bitterness of feeling, nor gave utterance to a single violent expression, but alluded to many of his former friends and companions amongst the Northerners in the kindest terms. He spoke as a man proud of the victories won by his country, and confident of ultimate success under the blessing of the Almighty, whom he glorified for past successes, and whose aid he invoked for all future operations. He regretted that his limited supply of tents and available accommodation would prevent him from putting us up, but he kindly placed at our disposal horses, or a two-horsed waggon, if we preferred it, to drive about in.'

Upon leaving General Lee, they drove to Bunker's Hill, six miles nearer Martinsburg, where that extraordinary man, General Stonewall Jackson, had his headquarters. With him they passed a most pleasant hour, and were agreeably surprised to find him very affable, having been led to expect that he was silent and almost morose. Wolseley's description of this noble soldier, whose loss, soon after, dealt an irreparable blow to the Confederate cause, is graphic and full of interest: 'Dressed in his grey uniform, he looks the hero that he is; and his thin compressed lips and calm glance, which meets yours unflinchingly, gave evidence of that firmness and decision of character for which he is so famous. He has a broad open forehead, from which the hair is well brushed back; a shapely nose, straight and long; thin colourless cheeks, with only a very small allowance of whisker; a cleanly shaven upper lip and chin; and a pair of fine greyish-blue eyes, rather sunken, with overhanging brows, which intensify the keenness of his gaze, but without imparting any fierceness to it. Such are the general characteristics of his face; and I have only to add, that a smile seems always lurking about his mouth when he speaks; and that though his voice partakes slightly of that harshness which Europeans unjustly attribute to *all* Americans, there is much unmistakable cordiality in his manner: and to us he talked most affectionately of England, and of his brief but enjoyable sojourn there. The religious element seems strongly developed in him; and though his conversation is perfectly free from all puritanical cant, it is evident that he is a man who never loses sight of the fact that there is an omnipresent Deity ever presiding over the minutest occurrences of life, as well as over the most important. Altogether, as one of his soldiers said to me when speaking of him, "he is a glorious fellow!" and, after I left him, I felt that I had at last solved a mystery and discovered why it was that he had accomplished such almost miraculous feats. With such a leader men would go anywhere, and face any amount of difficulties. For myself,' adds Wolseley, with the enthusiasm of a soldier, ' I believe that, inspired by the presence of such a man, I should be perfectly insensible to fatigue, and reckon on success as a moral certainty.'*

The army at Winchester was composed of two *corps d'armée* under the command of Generals Jackson and Longstreet, each consisting of four divisions. Wolseley was present whilst the latter officer inspected one of his divisions, and was highly pleased with the appearance of the men, and the manner in which they marched. He says: ' I remarked that, however slovenly the dress of the men of any

* Wolseley thus analyzes the nature of the different feelings with which these two remarkable soldiers inspired their devoted followers: 'Whilst Lee is regarded in the light of the infallible Jove, a man to be reverenced, Jackson is loved and adored with all that childlike and trustful affection which the ancients are said to have lavished upon the particular deity presiding over their affairs. The feeling of the soldiers for General Lee resembles that which Wellington's troops entertained for him—namely, a fixed and unshakable faith in all he did, and a calm confidence of victory when serving under him. But Jackson, like Napoleon, is idolized with that intense fervour which, consisting of mingled personal attachment and devoted loyalty, causes them to meet death for his sake, and bless him when dying.'

particular company might be, their rifles were invariably in good serviceable order. They marched, too, with an elastic tread, the pace being somewhat slower than that of our troops, and seemed vigorous and healthy. I have seen many armies file past in all the pomp of bright clothing and well-polished accoutrements; but I never saw one composed of finer men, or that looked more like *work*, than that portion of General Lee's army which I was fortunate enough to see inspected.'

Wolseley saw but little of the Confederate cavalry, as General Steuart had left for his raid into Pennsylvania the day he reached headquarters, and only returned a couple of days before he commenced his homeward journey. He remarked, however, 'that though their knowledge of drill is limited, all the men ride well, in which particular they present a striking contrast to the Northern cavalry, who can scarcely sit their horses, even when trotting.'

Colonel Wolseley had quitted New York for his trip 'down South' on the 11th of September, and had to report himself at Montreal on the expiration of his six weeks' leave. The short time at his disposal was the great drawback to the enjoyment of this visit to the headquarters of the Confederate army; but he made the most of it, and altogether he never passed a pleasanter time than when 'running the blockade,' with its attendant excitement, while, as an enthusiastic soldier, he considered himself amply repaid for any discomfort by his conversations with Robert Lee and Stonewall Jackson, whose deeds will live in song and story as long as high character, spotless patriotism, and brilliant military genius command the admiration of the human race.

After his return to Canada, Colonel Wolseley suffered greatly from the wound in the right leg he had received in the Crimea seven years before. His exertions on foot caused the wound to open afresh, and, under medical advice, he was constrained to proceed to England. Here he placed himself under the eminent surgeon, Sir William Fergusson. There was considerable exfoliation of the right shin-bone, and he did not begin to mend until after Sir William had cut out the part affected. Wolseley returned to Canada in the spring of 1863, and resumed his duties as Assistant Quartermaster-General, under Colonel Lysons.

In the autumn of 1865 the Fenians in the United States, by their threatening attitude, gave cause for anxiety to the Dominion Government, and Colonel (now General Sir) Patrick McDougall, who came out to the Dominion to organize the local forces, established a Camp of Instruction for cadets, in order to test the efficiency of the training imparted by the Canadian Military Schools. At his request, the services of Colonel Wolseley were placed at his disposal by Sir John Michel, commanding the forces, and he appointed him to command the first Camp of Instruction ever established in Canada. The place selected for this experiment was La Prairie, about nine miles distant from Montreal, on the opposite side of the river.

A general and regimental staff were placed under Wolseley's orders, and quartermasters and sergeant-majors were appointed permanently to battalions from among the discharged non-commissioned officers resident in Canada. The remaining battalion officers and non-commissioned officers were furnished by the cadets themselves in rotation, except that two cadets were named permanently as sergeants, and two as corporals to each company. The force was formed into three battalions. The cadets of the Toronto school, and the schools west of Toronto, numbering 366, were formed into the right battalion; the cadets of the Kingston school, and the English-speaking cadets of the Montreal and Quebec schools, 334, composed the centre battalion; and the cadets of French-Canadian origin composed the left battalion, 405 strong.

By utilizing the small barrack at La Prairie, Colonel Wolseley was enabled to place each battalion under canvas during two weeks, and in quarters one week.*

The late Sir James Lindsay, then commanding the Montreal Division, marched into La Prairie on the 4th of October, with the Montreal garrison of regular troops, and held two divisional field-days, when the Montreal garrison acted as one brigade, and the cadets, with a battery of Royal Artillery temporarily attached, formed a second brigade under Colonel Wolseley. The second field-day was held in the presence of Sir John Michel, and, says Colonel McDougall, 'I can fully corroborate Colonel Wolseley's opinion that the cadets compared most favourably with the regular troops, an opinion that was shared in and expressed by both Sir John Michel and the Major-General, and that they executed all the movements of a sham fight with the same precision and quickness.'

Wolseley performed his arduous duties during the three weeks the camp was established to the entire satisfaction of his superiors, and Colonel McDougall reported in the following terms: 'I desire to record as strongly as possible my sense of the ability and energy with which the immediate command of the camp was exercised by Colonel Wolseley, and to which is attributable a large share in the success of

* The cadets, among whom were three French-Canadian Members of Parliament, and one Upper Canadian Member, also Lord Aylmer, and several gentlemen holding the rank of Lieutenant-Colonel in the Sedentary Militia, and officers who had served in the Regular Army, fell into the usual routine of camp life with surprising readiness; and though their duties were precisely the same as those performed by soldiers of the Regular Army in camp, their demeanour throughout was beyond praise. Every cadet had an opportunity for showing his ability in drilling a squad or company, as well as for acting as captain and covering sergeant of a company in battalion; and the aptitude and knowledge they generally displayed was a matter of surprise to Colonels McDougall and Wolseley, and afforded a gratifying testimony to the value of the Military Schools which had been established in the Province.

the experiment. It was a charge requiring unusually delicate management; but in Colonel Wolseley's qualifications, tact is combined with firmness, and both with an intimate knowledge of his profession in an unusual degree.'

At length, after many 'scares,' on the night of the 31st of May, the Fenian leader, 'General' O'Neil, crossed the Niagara river with about 1,200 men, and, having captured Fort Erie, some three miles from Buffalo, advanced towards Ridgeway, where he threw up breastworks and awaited reinforcements.

On receipt of intelligence of this daring act the whole Dominion was thrown into a perfect fever of indignation and patriotic ardour. The call to arms was responded to by all classes, and had the necessity arisen, the whole Volunteer Militia force could have been collected in a few days. On the 31st of May, Colonel McDougall, Adjutant-General of Militia, received instructions to call out for actual service 14,000 Volunteers, and within twenty-four hours the companies were all ready, and many had moved to the stations assigned them. On the 2nd of June the whole of the Volunteer force, not already called out, was placed on actual service, and on the following day the Province had more than 20,000 men under arms. Notwithstanding that the season of the year entailed heavy sacrifices on those of the Volunteers who were business men, all joined with eagerness; and, 'experience has shown,' wrote the Adjutant-General, 'that, in the event of a regular invasion, 100,000 men, in addition to the Volunteer force, would eagerly come forward in forty-eight hours to aid in defending the country.'

When the news of the Fenian invasion arrived at Montreal, Colonel Wolseley, under orders from Sir John Michel, started thence for Toronto, and joined a column of regular troops, consisting of a battery of Artillery and the 16th and

47th Regiments, under the command of Colonel Lowry, of the 47th, which was about to start to attack the Fenians. The column arrived that night at the Suspension Bridge over the Niagara river; but on reaching Fort Erie, on the following day, they learnt that a fight had already taken place, with indecisive results, at Ridgeway.* Far different must it have been had the inexperienced commander of the Militia awaited the arrival of the regular troops under Colonel Lowry, or a second column under Colonel Peacock, which, unfortunately, had taken the wrong road.

Wolseley was sent on the following day to Stratford, a railway station near Georgian Bay, on Lake Huron, to take command of a brigade, consisting of a battery of Artillery, the 16th Regiment, and two battalions of Canadian Militia.

But there was no further attempt at invasion by the Fenians, and when Wolseley's brigade was broken up, he returned to Montreal. He had scarcely resumed his duties when, in the autumn of this year (1866), he was placed in command of a Camp of Observation, consisting of the 16th Regiment, two troops of Volunteer Cavalry, and three battalions of Militia, at Thorold, near St. Catherine's, on the Welland Canal, which the Fenians had expressed their intention to destroy. The large and wealthy city of Buffalo, on the American side, was at this time the centre of the Fenian military organization, and Wolseley had very responsible duties in watching the frontier between Fort Cockburn and the Niagara Falls. He remained at Thorold about a month, exercising his troops, and during this time

* At eight a.m. on the 2nd of June two battalions of Canadian Militia, the 'Hamilton' and 'Queen's Own' Volunteers, marching from Toronto, attacked the Fenians at Ridgeway, between Forts Cockburn and Erie; but, though there was no lack of enthusiasm and gallantry, the commander was inexperienced, and the ammunition failed. The Canadians got into some confusion, and were forced back, but again attacked the Fenians, and drove them back, many being killed and wounded on both sides. The Fenians now retreated across the river, when many of them were captured by an United States war-steamer.

nearly all the Militia of Upper Canada passed through his hands. Three battalions, of about 1,000 men each, were drilled a week at a time, and the work was arduous for Wolseley, who was in the saddle all day and every day.

On the approach of winter the camp was broken up, and he returned once again to Montreal; but, during the succeeding months, there were constant Fenian alarms, and the Generals and staff officers were kept on the *qui vive*. Indeed, in January, 1867, the alarm of threatened invasion was so great that field brigades were established in all the principal military centres, fully equipped, and in constant readiness to turn out should their services be required. Colonel Wolseley was sent to Toronto, where he organized the Toronto Brigade; but in April, 1867, when matters looked more settled, he proceeded to England, being relieved as Assistant Quartermaster-General by Sir Henry Havelock.

Wolseley's services in Canada had been so meritorious, and his claims for promotion were so generally acknowledged, that he was almost immediately nominated to succeed Colonel Lysons as head of the department in which he had acquired such vast experience in the Crimea, India, and China, irrespective of the special knowledge of its working gained in Canada during the past five years. Colonel Lysons' term of service expired in the autumn of 1867, and, in September, Wolseley returned to the Dominion as Deputy Quartermaster-General, being, as we were assured by his predecessor, the youngest officer who was ever nominated to fill that responsible post. He came home to England, on two months' private leave, in 1868, and during his stay occurred an important event in his life, his marriage with Miss Erskine, who accompanied him on his return to Canada.

In the following year was published his 'Soldier's Pocket

Book for Field Service,'* which is considered in the army a standard authority. This invaluable little work offers, in a handy form, as its name implies, information on every subject of a professional nature, and to every rank in the army, from the private who wants information how to keep his accoutrements clean or to cook a beafsteak, to the 'non-combatant' officer in search of a 'form' for indenting for stores, or the General in the field who seeks to solve some knotty point in military law, or in the manœuvring of the 'three arms.' It is, in short, a most trustworthy and indispensable *vade mecum*, and its value has been universally acknowledged. Much of the information embodied in its pages, with the brevity and conciseness of style becoming a soldier, is original; and the articles on Staff duties, such as reconnoitring, surveying, and other duties of an officer of the Quartermaster-General's Department, embody the results of the writer's own lengthened experience in what was, before the new organization at the Horse Guards, and the establishment of an Intelligence Department, the most important section of the Military Staff.

* The preface to the first edition of the 'Soldier's Pocket Book' was written in Canada, and dated 'Montreal, March, 1869.' A second edition of this work was issued in 1871, and a third and revised edition in 1875, and a fourth in 1882. Wolseley is also the author of a 'Field Pocket Book for the Auxiliary Forces,' a work of more recent date.

CHAPTER VI.

THE RED RIVER EXPEDITION.

The Red River Expedition.—The Organization of the Force, and Start for Thunder Bay.—The Road thence to the Shebandowan Lake.—Down the Lake, and across the ' Portages ' to Fort Frances.—Running the Rapids of the Winnipeg River to Fort Alexander.—The Arrival at Fort Garry.—Success of the Expedition.—Return of Sir Garnet Wolseley to England.

EARLY in 1870, the troubles on the Red River became of so pressing a nature that the Dominion Government, with the consent of the Home Colonial Office, determined on sending an expedition to restore the Queen's authority in that Settlement. The consensus of public opinion in the Colony pointed to Colonel Wolseley, who was exceedingly popular among all classes of the Canadians, and in an especial degree commanded the confidence of the Militia, as the fittest officer to lead a combined force of Regulars and Volunteers, and Major-General Hon. James Lindsay[*] accordingly nominated him to the command of the Red River Expedition.[†] After eighteen years' service, Colonel

---

[*] On the abolition of the divisional commands at Montreal and Toronto, and the withdrawal of all British troops from the Dominion to Halifax, General Lindsay had proceeded to England, and at this time held the post of Inspector-General of Reserve Forces at the Horse Guards, only returning to Canada to organize and despatch the Red River Force, and to make the necessary arrangements for handing over to the Dominion authorities the Government military buildings and *matériel* of war.

[†] In writing this portion of the Memoir we are indebted to the following sources : The late Captain Huyshe's ' The Red River Expedition ;' to a ' Narrative ' published in *Blackwood's Magazine*, written by Sir Garnet Wolseley himself; to the private journal of Mr. M. B. Irvine, C.B., C.M.G., in charge of the Control Department of the Expedition ; to that officer's official ' Report on the Red River Expedition of 1870 ;' to Colonel Wol-

Wolseley found himself entrusted with supreme command, thus, at length, being afforded the opportunity of achieving distinction for which, as an ambitious soldier, confident in his own capacity for independent command, he had long been sighing.

The Red River Territory, the inhabited portion of which, called the Red River Settlement, now forms a portion of the province of Manitoba, is a large tract lying nearly in the centre of British North America, and receives its name from the Red River. Fort Garry—which is situated close to Winnipeg, the capital, on the left bank of the Red River, where it is joined by the Assiniboine—is only sixty miles from the United States frontier, and therefore is easily accessible to citizens of the Republic desirous of fomenting troubles, or to disloyal British subjects. Owing to its geographical position, the Settlement is completely isolated from the outside world, as the nearest railway station in Canada is 900 miles distant, as 'the crow flies,' and the railway system of the United States is also some hundreds of miles to the southward.* The inhabited portion, or Settlement, is merely the strip lying along the banks of the Red River, and of its affluent, the Assiniboine; its population at the beginning of 1870, exclusive of Indians, numbered about 15,000 souls, a large proportion of whom were French 'half-breeds,' as the descendants of European fathers and Indian mothers are called.

The Red River Territory had long been under the rule of

---

seley's 'Correspondence relative to the recent Expedition to the Red River Settlement, with Journal of Operations'—both these latter being in the Blue Book presented to the Houses of Parliament. Also to a Lecture delivered by Captain Huyshe at the Royal United Service Institution, on the 20th of January, 1871 (which appears in No. 62, Vol. XV., of the Journal), the first part of which, treating of the origin of the expedition and organization of the force, was written by Colonel Wolseley.

* This was written nine years ago, since which vast changes have occurred in these regions.

THE DIFFICULTY ON THE RED RIVER. 187

the Hudson's Bay Company, which, in 1670, had received a charter from Charles II., granting them sovereign rights over a vast extent of country, the geographical limits of which were not clearly defined. After many years of fruitless negotiations between Canada and this great trading community, a three-cornered arrangement was arrived at, England acting as a sort of go-between, by which the vast territories, officially known as Rupert's Land, together with all territorial rights, were first transferred, on paper, to this country, and then made over, by royal proclamation, to the Confederation of the North American Provinces, which paid to the Hudson's Bay Company the sum of £300,000, the transfer to take effect from the 1st of December, 1869. It appears that in these negotiations the people of the Red River Settlement were consulted by neither the Canadian statesmen nor the directors of the Hudson's Bay Company sitting in London. They, and the French half-breeds in particular, naturally resented such cavalier treatment, and when, in 1869, the Canadian Government sent thither a surveying party, some eighteen half-breeds, under Louis Riel, compelled them to quit the country.

The Dominion Government nominated to the post of Lieutenant-Governor Mr. W. McDougall; but the people refused to acknowledge him, and, on the 24th of November, Riel took possession of Fort Garry, and assumed the Presidency of the so-called 'Republic of the North-West.' The Canadian Government then sent Mr. Donald Smith to Fort Garry as Special Commissioner, but his mission proved abortive. Riel now conducted himself with great violence, and, on the 4th of March, executed, after a sham court-martial, a man named Thomas Scott, who formed one of a party of loyal English and Scotch half-breeds, who had attempted to effect the release of some sixty British subjects illegally confined in Fort Garry. Scott's execution aroused a feeling of intense indignation throughout Canada.

In the meantime, Colonel Wolseley had prepared an able Report, in which he entered into minute details regarding the composition, equipment, and organization of the force, as well as its victualling, clothing, and transport. Equally important with the question of the organization of the Expeditionary Force, was the question of its leader ; and when it was announced that Colonel Wolseley was to command, there was a chorus of approval from the Canadian public and press, and it was universally felt that the success of the expedition was already assured. It was decided that the force was to consist of 1,200 men, and that the Home Government should bear one-fourth of the charges. The Dominion Government were to raise two battalions of Militia, each of which, as in the case of the 60th Rifles, was to consist of seven companies of 50 men each, with the object of making them more handy for boat service, with 3 officers per company.

On the 4th of May, 1870, Colonel Wolseley left Montreal for Toronto to organize the column. Thence he proceeded to Collingwood, on the shores of Lake Huron, 94 miles distant from Toronto, accompanied by Mr. S. J. Dawson, the able executive officer of the Public Works Department, whose services had been placed at Colonel Wolseley's disposal by the Canadian Government.

Almost insuperable were the difficulties involved in transporting a large armed force, with all the *matériel* of war, a distance of 600 miles, through rivers and lakes, and over no less than 47 'portages'—a word applied to the breaks in the navigation between two lakes, or between a river and a lake —across which everything had to be 'portaged,' or carried on men's backs, a necessity which caused a most serious addition to the labours of the route, as the portages varied

THE ROUTE TO FORT GARRY.

in length from 20 yards to 1½ mile. Of the entire distance of 600 miles, 48 only—that from Thunder Bay to Lake Shebandowan—was by land transport, over a road only partially constructed by Mr. Dawson. From Lake Shebandowan to Lake of the Woods was a distance of 310 miles by rivers and lakes, with about 17 portages, and from thence to Fort Garry was only about 100 miles in a straight line by land; but, says Wolseley, 'there was only a road made for about 60 miles of that distance, the unmade portion being laid out over most difficult swamps. If, therefore, the troops could not advance by that route, as was subsequently found to be the case, the only other way of reaching Manitoba was *viâ* the Winnipeg River, the navigation of which was known to be so difficult and dangerous that none but experienced guides ever attempted it. There were about 30 portages in the extra 160 miles thus added to the total length of the distance to be traversed.'

The distance to Fort Garry might thus have been shortened by 160 miles, had it been possible to adopt the former route, which struck off towards the fort from the north-west angle of the Lake of the Woods; but the wisdom of Wolseley's adopting the route by Lake Winnipeg was amply proved when, on his arrival at Fort Garry, Colonel Bolton, whom he sent to inspect the direct road to the Lake of the Woods, reported that the last 33 miles had not yet been cut, and that there were such heavy morasses and thick woods, that only a small body of men could get through.* Considering all the enormous obstacles to the transport of stores and

* There was a second route to Fort Garry, employed by the Hudson's Bay Company, who landed at York Factory in Hudson Bay, and ascended the Nelson River to Lake Winnipeg. This had been made use of in the conveyance of small bodies of troops, which, on two occasions, under Colonel Crofton and Major Seton, had been quartered at Fort Garry. But these had never exceeded a few hundred men, and the whole resources of the Hudson's Bay Company had been placed at their disposal. Again, the sea off York Factory is only free from ice about six weeks in the year, and the navigation of the Arctic Ocean is both difficult and dangerous.

warlike *matériel*, Colonel Wolseley exhibited throughout the expedition a patience, energy, and forethought that stamp him as a true leader of men. Often during the long and weary march the spirits of his officers and men were seriously affected by the difficulties of the route; more than once it was anticipated by all that the expedition would have to be abandoned; but, as we were told by an officer who accompanied Colonel Wolseley, and had the best opportunity of daily judging of his temper and intentions throughout the expedition, he alone never once lost heart, but was always cheerful and confident, and bent on pushing on.

The country between Lake Superior and Red River was known to be a wilderness of poor timber, lakes, rivers, and rocks, and to be uninhabited except by wandering tribes of Chippewa Indians. From Collingwood, on Lake Huron, to Thunder Bay, on Lake Superior,* whence this long journey of 600 miles was to commence, was a further distance of 534 miles, the communication being through a broad channel called St. Mary's River, about 50 miles in length, which forms the boundary between the American State of Michigan and British territory. There is a canal on the American side, by which some rapids in the river can be avoided, but the American authorities at first refused to allow the troops and stores to pass through the canal. Everything had to be landed on the Canadian side of the rapids, transported by land across a three-mile 'portage,' and re-embarked again at the upper end on board a second steamer. Subsequently, this unfriendly order was withdrawn, and a free passage was allowed to all articles not contraband of war.

Colonel R. J. Fielden, of the 60th Rifles, second in command of the expedition, was, meanwhile, engaged in raising and organizing two battalions of Canadian Militia.

* The great lake system of America extends 1,085 miles in length from Kingston on Lake Ontario to Fort William on Lake Superior, covering an area of 80,000 square miles, or more than the superficies of Great Britain.

THE PERSONNEL OF THE EXPEDITION. 191

The force* consisted of—1st battalion 60th Rifles, 26 officers and 350 men, under Colonel Fielden; 1st, or Ontario, Militia, 28 officers and 350 men, under Lieut.-Colonel Jarvis; 2nd, or Quebec, Militia, 28 officers and 350 men, under Lieut.-Colonel Casault. Lieutenant Alleyne, R.A., and 19 men, with 4 7-pounder bronze mountain guns; Lieutenant Heneage, R.A., and 19 men; Army Service Corps, 12 men, and Army Hospital Corps, 8 men. The total of all ranks was 1,214, with about 400 *voyageurs*, and 100 teamsters. The *voyageurs* were collected by Mr. Dawson, but a large portion of them were found to be utterly ignorant of the management of boats; about 100 of the number were Irroquois Indians, from villages near Montreal, who were fully capable of navigating boats in rapid water, and indeed without their services the expedition could not have been conducted. Two hundred boats were specially constructed under the directions of Mr. Dawson, and were on an average from 25 to 32 feet long, from 6 to 7 broad, with a draught, when loaded, of 20 to 30 inches, and a carrying capacity of from 2½ to 4 tons. Their crews, as subsequently arranged, consisted of from 8 to 9 officers and soldiers, and 2 *voyageurs*. The boats were fitted with masts and sails, in addition to oars, and with arm-chests for the rifles of the men and officers,† who were armed with breech-loading carbines in lieu of swords. In addition to this 'Boat Transport Corps' was the Land Transport

* The staff officers of the force were: Captain Huyshe, Rifle Brigade, and Lieut. F. C. Denison, Militia, orderly officers; Lieut.-Colonel Bolton, R.A., Deputy Assistant-Adjutant-General, and Major McLeod, of the Militia, his assistant. Lieut.-Colonel J. C. McNeill, V.C., 48th Regiment, Military Secretary of the Governor-General, was, at his request, attached to the staff. Surgeon-Major Young, M.D., was principal medical officer, with a staff of four assistant-surgeons. The chief control officer was Assistant-Controller M. B. Irvine, a member of a Canadian family, assisted by 6 commissaries, and 3 officers of the lately dissolved Royal Canadian Rifles, and 1 from the Militia, who were attached for transport duties.

† The luggage of officers, without distinction of rank, was restricted to 90 lb., including cooking utensils, bedding, etc., which were carried in two waterproof bags.

Corps, for the carriage of boats and stores from Thunder Bay to Lake Shebandowan, which consisted of 150 horses, 100 teamsters, a number of waggons and carts, and about 36 draughtsmen.

A multiplicity of articles had to be supplied for the comfort of the men, such as waterproof kit-bags, mocassins, cases of mosquito oil, and veils of fine black netting to protect the face and head from the attacks of flies. The utmost care and forethought were expended in the organization of the little force, which required multitudinous details for the different species of transport—by railway, steamer, land-carriage, and boats. Colonel Wolseley looked to everything himself, considering no detail too small to engage his time and attention.

Between the 6th and 12th of May he was busily engaged at Toronto in organizing the expedition, selecting horses, and completing the two battalions of Militia. General Lindsay furnished Colonel Wolseley with instructions for his guidance, in which, however, 'the detail of the arrangements for an advance of the force and transport of stores' were left to his discretion; and, on the 14th of May, when everything was ready for the start, Wolseley issued his 'Standing Orders for the Red River Expeditionary Force,' a lengthy and able paper, drawn up under thirty-four heads, which completely and fully met every requirement as it arose during the long march of 600 miles.

At noon of the same day two companies of the Ontario Rifles left Toronto for the Sault St. Marie, under Colonel Bolton, to complete the road across the portage, and get the stores re-shipped on Lake Superior. Owing to telegraphic information from Ottawa respecting Fenian intentions to annoy the expeditionary force, Colonel Wolseley, on the 16th, sent two more companies of the Ontario Rifles to join Colonel Bolton's camp, and it is certain that had he not thus early taken steps to frustrate the purposes of those doughty warriors, who soon afterwards made a raid on the Huntingdon Border, an effort would have been made to destroy the stores accumulated at the Sault, which, had it been successful, would have probably deferred the enterprise for another year. On the 21st of May, Colonel Wolseley, accompanied by his staff, with a company of the 60th Rifles, quitted Toronto amid the hearty good wishes of all classes of the community; the headquarters and four more companies of the Rifles followed the same day, and the expedition was now fairly started.

The *Chicora*, with Colonel Wolseley on board, having landed the troops and military equipment at the Sault St. Marie, and steamed over to the American side to pass through the canal, again re-embarked the soldiers and Colonel Wolseley at the upper end of the rapids, and, steaming across the broad bosom of Lake Superior, anchored, on the 25th of May, in Thunder Bay, off the end of the road leading to Lake Shebandowan. On its shores, at the mouth of the Kaministiquia River, is the Hudson's Bay Company's post of Fort William, and, about four miles farther on, was a small clearing with a few wooden huts and tents, which marked the first stage of the march to Fort Garry. The scenery was calculated to have a most depressing effect on the spirits of officers and men, as a great forest fire had recently raged over the country, destroying all vegetation, and leaving only the tall, gaunt, and blackened trunks of the huge trees to greet the eyes of visitors to this desolate shore.

Colonel Wolseley immediately landed, and gave to the spot the name of 'Prince Arthur's Landing,' in honour of his Royal Highness, who was then serving in Canada with his regiment, the Rifle Brigade. The troops and camp equipment were disembarked by means of a large 'scow,' and by ten p.m. the work was completed, an earnest of what was to follow.

The following anecdote, illustrative of Wolseley's readiness of resource and unvarying cheerfulness and *bonhomie*, was told us by one of the heads of departments. On disembarking, it was found that in the hurry of re-embarking the military stores on the Lake Superior side of the Sault St. Marie portage, though the tents and camp equipage belonging to the 60th Rifles and Headquarter Staff had been brought, all the tent-poles had been left behind. The chief Control officer had expected an explosion of ill-humour at the oversight; but, on reporting the circumstance to Colonel Wolseley with some trepidation, he was met with a hearty laugh, and the query, 'You have not forgotten the axes too?' Receiving a reply in the negative, he promptly added, pointing to the primeval forest around the landing-place, 'Then you can help yourself to as many tent-poles as you require.' This cheery way of regarding a simple omission had the best possible effect among the officers and men, and encouraged them to exert themselves and merit the confidence of a chief who only encountered difficulties to overcome them.

Wolseley's experience as an old campaigner was of essential service in a way that would never have entered into the philosophy of a general officer of the Horse-Guards type. His domestic arrangements, as regards kit and cooking utensils, were identical with those of the other officers of the force, and thus it happened that to Lieutenant Riddell, of the 60th Rifles, was relegated the duty of cooking the dinner of the Commander. This young officer had no personal knowledge of the most important of all the arts, so that when he came to cook a piece of pork, all his efforts ended in failure. The fire had gone out, and the subaltern was abusing the pork for not boiling, when a *deus ex machinâ*, in the person of the Chief, made his appearance. Equally at home making the pot boil, or planning and executing an arduous military expedition, Wolseley set to work, and, says Riddell, 'he showed me, in the scientific manner of an old campaigner, how to dig a trench in the ground, and with stones and sticks to construct a fender over it, on which to place my cooking utensils; and the result was, that when dinner-time approached a hard tough mass of over-boiled meat was fished out of the pot, with the assistance of a forked stick, and served up with tea and biscuit, as the midday repast of the officers.' Later on, fresh bread and meat were issued daily, officers and men having the same rations; and the salt pork, which was sent out from England, was husbanded for the line of march where live cattle could not be had.

Encouraged by the example of a leader who could turn his hand to anything, officers and men cheerfully set to work the day after their arrival, clearing roads, establishing the depôt for supplies, a hospital for the sick, and a redoubt to repel an attack from the Fenians, who had openly expressed their intention to destroy the depôt when the troops had set out on their long march for Fort Garry.

Early on the morning following his arrival at Thunder Bay, Colonel Wolseley, accompanied by Mr. Russell, the engineer employed during the spring upon the construction of the road to the Shebandowan Lake, started off on horseback to inspect its condition. He returned at noon of the following day, having ridden and inspected the road as far as it was practicable for teams, some thirty-one miles out of the forty-four intended to be constructed, a footpath only being designed for the remaining four miles. But there still remained thirteen miles of road to be made to the lake, over a hilly and thickly wooded country, a business involving considerable time and trouble. When at Ottawa, in the month of April, Colonel Wolseley had been positively assured that the road would be open for traffic by the 25th of May, and on this assurance his calculations had been based.

Again, on Monday, 6th of June, he started at half-past four a.m., to make a second inspection of the road as far as its limit at the Oskondagee Creek, some thirty-nine miles. He says, 'It poured with rain all Monday, Tuesday, and yesterday, up to about four o'clock p.m. At the present moment the road may be said to end at the Oskondagee Creek, seventy-five feet wide, which is still unbridged. For the last eight or nine miles before reaching that creek the road is only a track, and is impassable for loaded waggons in wet weather. My horse was tired out in going over it at a walk.' Colonel Wolseley camped for the night on the bank of the Oskondagee Creek, which is the third of the three rivers that had to be bridged between Thunder Bay and Shebandowan, the others being the Kaministiquia, twenty-two miles from the camp, and the Matawan, twenty-seven miles.

On Tuesday, the 7th, he crossed the creek on a temporary raft, and walked to a hill which commanded a view of the line of march. The scene was not reassuring, and Wolseley describes the track a mile beyond the creek as 'execrable.' He immediately had a strong gang of men turned on it, and Colonel McNeill,* who proceeded a week later to inspect the road, reported that rather more than four miles had been cleared of timber, and a rough waggon-road formed; the remaining four miles to the lake had not been touched. He reported also that owing to the recent heavy rains there were places one and two miles in extent that would be impassable for horse transport for a week or ten days at least.

* Now Sir John McNeill, Equerry to the Queen, who served under Sir Garnet Wolseley in Ashantee, and in Egypt on the staff of the Duke of Connaught.

Added to this, the carts provided were found to be useless for carrying supplies, and owing to the state of the roads the horses could only drag loads of 1,000 pounds in each waggon. Matters looked very gloomy for the success of the expedition, and those best qualified to judge laughed at the idea of reaching Fort Garry, so as to return before the winter set in. Under these adverse circumstances, Colonel Wolseley preserved his equanimity, and spoke confidently of ultimate success.

Directly after his first inspection of the road on the 26th of May, on finding its condition and the progress made so unsatisfactory, he turned his attention to another mode of transport. On questioning Mr. Dawson on the feasibility of passing boats up the Kaministiquia* and Matawan Rivers, so as to relieve the land transport, that gentleman did not think the proposal practicable; but Mr. MacIntyre, the Hudson's Bay Company's officer at Fort William, thought otherwise, and placed his *voyageurs* and guides at the commander's disposal. Wolseley accordingly selected Captain Young, of the 60th Rifles, an officer of energy and resource, to make the attempt with thirty-four men and six boats. Captain Young left the camp early on the 4th of June, and, his boats having been towed to Fort William, began to pull up the Kaministiquia River, which falls into Thunder Bay at that point. They poled and tracked along the river, or marched by the side while the Indians took the boats up the Rapids, or carried them across the portages, until, on the 8th of June, he met Colonel Wolseley, who, after riding over the road as far as Oskondagee Creek, descended the rapids of the Kaministiquia River in a canoe, in order to see what progress he had made. Wolseley was delighted to find that his project to relieve the land transport was feasible,

---

* This Indian word means, according to Sir John Richardson, 'the river that runs far about.'

and, having directed Captain Young to proceed up to the Kaministiquia Bridge—a structure 320 feet long and 18 broad, supported on eight arches—and continue the route by boats as far as Matawan Bridge, he proceeded on his journey to the camp by the river route.

After crossing four more portages, Captain Young arrived at Kaministiquia Bridge on the 10th of June, and, on the 12th, reached Matawan Bridge, with his men and stores in perfect condition, thus conclusively proving, notwithstanding the predictions of 'experienced' persons, that the water route was practicable, and that the word 'impossible' was unknown in the vocabulary of the gallant Commander of the Red River Expedition. Colonel Wolseley determined to send the whole of his boats by this route, and to devote his land transport to supplies, and Mr. Dawson acceded to this arrangement.

In the meanwhile the troops continued to arrive at Thunder Bay. Two companies of the 60th Rifles were employed at Kaministiquia and Matawan Bridges, forming depôts for stores, and the remainder of the force were busily occupied turning Prince Arthur's Landing into a miniature Balaclava, without its chaotic confusion. As the work progressed, more detachments of troops were sent from Thunder Bay, those in advance proceeding towards Lake Shebandowan. By the 19th of June there were thirty-five days' rations for 1,500 men in depôt, either at Kaministiquia or Matawan Bridges, and Colonel Wolseley reported: 'When I have 100, or even 80 boats on the lake, and provisions for 1,500 men for sixty days there, I shall move off by detachments. I am still in hopes of being able to leave Fort Frances for Fort Garry on the 1st of August.'

On the 3rd of June, Wolseley despatched to the Matawan Bridge the first four boats mounted on platforms set on the wheels of waggons. On reaching the river the boats were launched and moored—a wise precaution, which secured them against the ravages of a fire which swept over the country, destroying all the stores and huts. The weather at this time was wretched in the extreme, and officers and men worked daily in their wet clothes. Notwithstanding this, and the hardships they endured, the health of the camp was most satisfactory, a result due, doubtless, to Colonel Wolseley having strictly prohibited the use of spirits, which was an unknown luxury in the camp, save in the form of 'medical comforts.'

On the 21st of June, he rode over the whole road, three miles in advance of the Oskondagee Creek, returning at ten a.m. on the 23rd, having ridden that morning from the Matawan Bridge, a distance of twenty-seven miles. He says in his report, he found the road between the Matawan and Oskondagee, at many places, 'even in fine weather, practically impassable for waggons;' and that 'no horse transport in the world could stand having to get over such places, as the horses would be knocked up in a few days.' On his arrival he directed Mr. Dawson to employ all his men to cut a branch road of one mile from the main road to the river, at a point about four miles from the Matawan Bridge, and settled the arrangements for the transport of stores as follows: By horse teams from the camp to the Matawan Bridge, a structure 216 feet long, supported on five piers; thence by boats two miles further along the road to a point named Young's Landing, where the river leaves the road; thence by ox teams to Calderon's Landing, for a distance of two miles up the road, and one mile along a branch road then being cut to the river; thence up the river to Oskondagee Creek by boats; thence to the Dam Site, a distance of five miles, by ox teams; and finally, thence up the river to McNeill's Bay on the Shebandowan Lake, in flat-bottomed boats, a path for the troops being cut through the woods for this last four miles. The obstacles to be overcome, even in this preliminary portion of the route, seemed insurmountable; but Wolseley was confident and cheerful, and, though it was not till the first week in July that the branch road to Calderon's Landing and the road to the Dam Site were fit for traffic, he would reply to all queries of when the start would be made: 'As soon as I have 150 boats and two months' provisions at the lake.'

On the 29th of June, General Lindsay arrived at Prince Arthur's Landing; and, on the following day, accompanied by Colonels Wolseley and McNeill, he rode over the whole road as far as the Dam Site, and thence proceeded to the Shebandowan Lake in a canoe, arriving at camp in the evening of the 3rd of July, by the Kaministiquia River. At daylight on the same day, under Colonel Wolseley's orders, the headquarters of the 60th Rifles, under Colonel Feilden, marched from Matawan; and, on the following day, the Ontario Rifles quitted the camp for the Kaministiquia Bridge.

Another even more welcome visitor at Prince Arthur's Landing than General Lindsay was Mrs. Wolseley, who unexpectedly arrived in one of the transport steamers, returning to Toronto after a brief visit of a few days.

Before finally quitting the camp for the front, Colonel Wolseley drew up, in French and English, a 'Proclamation to the loyal inhabitants of Manitoba,' which he entrusted for delivery to Mr. Donald Smith, who had arrived at Fort William on his way to succeed Mr. McTavish as Governor of the Hudson's Bay Company's posts. He also sent copies of this Proclamation,* which was dated the '30th of June,'

* In this document he said: 'Our mission is one of peace, and the sole object of the expedition is to secure Her Majesty's sovereign authority. The force which I have the honour of commanding will enter your province, representing no party, either in religion or politics, and will afford equal protection to the lives and property of all races and all creeds. The strictest order and discipline will be maintained, and private property will be care-

to the Protestant and Roman Catholic Bishops, and to the Hudson's Bay Company's officer at Fort Garry, and letters requesting them to take measures for pushing on the road from Fort Garry to the Lake of the Woods, although it was well known that it could not be completed in time for the use of the troops. This *ruse de guerre* of Colonel Wolseley's succeeded admirably, for on his arrival at Fort Frances he learned that Riel had placed armed men on the look-out in the neighbourhood of the spot where he thought the disembarkation on the shores of the Lake of the Woods would take place.

While at Thunder Bay Colonel Wolseley had an opportunity of being introduced, for the first time, to the Red Indian of Fenimore Cooper's novels, and very different he found him from the ideal limned by that picturesque, but untrustworthy, writer. The party consisted of ' Black Stone,' a Chippewa, or Ojibbeway chief, two of his tribe, and a squaw—ugly, dirty, half-naked savages, who came ostensibly to express their loyalty to the 'great mother,' but in reality to get what they could, and report what was going on to their tribe. Indeed, 'Black Stone's' sole claim to the picturesqueness of garb, with which we are accustomed to accredit the creations of the novelist, lay in his having 'tied round his head a mink-skin, from which at the back stood up a row of eagle's feathers, with here and there an ermine-tail hanging from them,' while the influences on his condition of advancing civilization were only discernible in the fact that he boasted the possession of a piece of soap, with which he was seen furtively smoothing his hair, previous to being ushered into the presence of the Chief of the 'pale-faces.'

---

fully protected. All supplies furnished by the inhabitants to the troops will be duly paid for. Should anyone consider himself injured by any individual attached to the force, his grievance shall be promptly inquired into. All loyal people are earnestly invited to aid me in carrying out the above-mentioned objects.'

Colonel Wolseley received the Indians with great politeness, and reassured them as to his intentions regarding their lands, and they took their departure, thoroughly satisfied with their reception and the presents they had received.

On the 5th of July, Colonel Wolseley moved his headquarters to the Matawan, which in the Indian tongue means 'fork.' Starting at five a.m., he rode the distance of twenty-seven miles, and, procuring a fresh horse at the bridge, went up the road a further five miles, as far as the end of 'Brown's Lane,' where the branch road meets the river. The weather was simply frightful, the rain pouring all day in cataracts; but he cared nothing for this, and, on the following morning, as appears by his Journal, was again in the saddle, 'showing the working-party of the 60th Rifles where they were to work;' and in the afternoon 'rode off again to Brown's Lane to see Captain Young off with the three boats to the Oskondagee.' Thus daily he personally saw to the work of making the roads passable for waggons, and it progressed rapidly under his superintendence. The 60th Rifles moved to Calderon's Landing, at the end of Brown's Lane, on the 8th of July, and for the nonce the gallant fellows were turned into labourers. The costume of officers and men did not belie the novel character thus assumed. The only garments worn by all ranks of one of Her Majesty's crack regiments were a flannel shirt, with breast-pocket for handkerchief, and uniform trousers, with Canadian mocassins and a felt helmet. What would Sir George Brown and others of 'the old school' have said on learning 'that the officers, who have been going up and down the river with boats, all wear the sleeves of their shirts tucked up, and their arms are as black as negroes; some have their shirts open, with their breasts exposed. At night we all wear red or blue nightcaps?'

The road to the Oskondagee Creek was still almost impassable, and 'for a few miles was nothing but a track through the woods.' 'The teams that took in the ammunition,' says Mr. Irvine, in his Journal, 'have returned with others along this road, with ninety shoes off sixty horses. The teamsters state it was all the horses could do to drag the empty waggons, the bed of the waggon being constantly in the mud, and the horses up to their bellies.'

For the past few days, owing to over-exertion, and being constantly all day in wet clothes, Colonel Wolseley was very unwell, suffering much from diarrhœa; but still, at four a.m. on this 14th of July, he finally quitted his camp at the Matawan Bridge, and rode to the camp at McNeill's Bay. On the following evening he walked down to the wharf to superintend the despatch of the first detachment of troops in the boats on the Shebandowan Lake. Discarding the yet unfinished road for the transport of stores, he had for some time been employing the Irroquois Indians in taking up boats and stores from Ward's Landing to McNeill's Bay, a distance of three miles, having no less than six rapids.*

The night of the 15th of July was signalised by a storm of thunder, lightning, and rain of exceptional severity, even after their experience of twenty-three days' rain since the 1st of June; and the only accident that happened during the expedition, and one that was nearly proving fatal to the commander, occurred on this night. In the middle of the storm, a tree close to where Colonel Wolseley was sleeping, fell and crushed a boat. The tempest, which raged over the whole of Canada, was most destructive, great numbers of men and cattle being killed.

* Infinite trouble and delay had been caused by the uselessness of most of the so-called *voyageurs*, some of whom had been picked up indiscriminately from the streets of Toronto, and had never seen either a canoe or a rapid. To guard against the force being encumbered by these loafers, Colonel Wolseley, on the 14th of July, addressed a letter to Mr. Dawson, directing that none but skilled *voyageurs* would be permitted to embark on the boats. He says: 'Only two classes of men can be allowed in the boats, viz., the soldiers constituting the Red River Force and the skilled *voyageurs* capable of managing boats and of instructing the soldiers how to do so.'

The morning of the 16th of July broke bright and clear, and when Colonel Wolseley arrived at McNeill's Bay at five in the evening, it seemed hopeless to expect the fulfilment of his determination, expressed long before, that the start *must* be made on that day. Mr. Dawson, ill-assisted, had done all that lay in the power of one man; the Irroquois Indians and the soldiers had worked indefatigably, overcoming the difficulties of the road and transport and fitting out the boats with their gear; but still much remained to be done. Wolseley, however, was resolved to be as good as his word, even if the men had to work till midnight, and, by half-past eight p.m., the first three brigades of boats, seventeen in all, containing two companies of the 60th Rifles, under Captains Young and Ward, also the detachments of Royal Artillery* and Royal Engineers, the whole commanded by Colonel Feilden, were ready moored in the bay. As they moved off on their long journey of 560 miles, the *avant garde* of the Red River Force, the waters of that silent and sequestered American lake resounded with rounds of hearty British cheers, which were caught up and echoed back no less warmly by their comrades, who watched the dip of the oars until the shades of evening hid from their sight the quick-retreating flotilla.

It must have been a proud and happy moment for the Commander when, turning from the wharf, after the last sound of oars had died away in the distance, he walked to his tent; and the extreme beauty of the evening, doubtless, appeared to his sanguine mind a happy augury for the success of the undertaking on which he had embarked. One present gave expression to a pleasant *bon mot*, when, in the words of the opening stanza of Virgil's famous epic, he exclaimed, '*Arma virumque cano*,' which he rendered by a *very* free translation into 'arms, men, and canoes.'

---

* Two guns were taken with this expedition, the other two being left in the redoubt at Thunder Bay.

THE START ON LAKE SHEBANDOWAN. 205

The whole force was divided into twenty-one brigades, which were distinguished by the letters of the alphabet, the brigades consisting of six boats, each of which carried, besides the necessary stores, about nine officers and men, and two *voyageurs*. Of the total number of 150 boats, 31, constructed in Quebec, were 'carvel-built,' 16 being rigged with 'sprits,' and the others with lug-sails; the remaining 119 boats were 'clinker-built.'* All were fitted with two masts, and six oars were generally used. The boats and *voyageurs* not required for the conveyance of troops were employed in forwarding a reserve of supplies to Fort Frances, at the head of Rainy Lake. The brigades of boats—lettered from A to X, omitting J, U, and W— followed each other daily in quick succession, the 60th Rifles first, then the Ontario Rifles, and lastly the Quebec Rifles.

On the 1st of August the last brigade had left; and, on the 3rd, Colonel McNeill, who had remained to superintend the embarkation, quitted the bay called after him. On this day the leading brigades had reached Bare Portage, 150 miles ahead, the others being scattered along the intermediate space; but as arrangements had been made for communicating and sending either backwards or forwards, and as Colonel Wolseley himself proceeded in a canoe well manned by Indians, going from one detachment to another, as he considered necessary, all were well in hand, and under his control for concentration at any time, should circumstances have required it.†

---

* A boat is said to be 'clinker-built' when the planks overlap each other, and 'carvel-built' when the planks are all flush and smooth, the edges being laid close to each other, and caulked to render them water-tight. The latter were found to be stronger and more serviceable.

† Few guides were forthcoming, but the officers commanding the boat brigades had been furnished with maps, which, however, were far from accurate. The boat with the Army Hospital and Army Staff Corps, under Mr. Mellish, carried also the equipment of a field-hospital, consisting of bell-tents for 36 men, a field-bakery for Fort Frances, and medical comforts

The old Hudson's Bay canoe route was by Dog Lake, but the new route, discovered by Mr. Dawson, which was that now adopted, passed through Lakes Shebandowan and Kashaboiwe; then crossed, by one of the lowest passes, the 'Height of Land'—as is termed the watershed which, rising gradually from Lake Superior to a height of nearly 1,000 feet, forms the line whence the streams diverge to the west and north, or to the east—and, turning westward into Lac-des-Mille-Lacs, there joined the old canoe route, which it followed for the remainder of the way to the Red River.

On Saturday, the 23rd of July, Colonel Wolseley, accompanied by Mr. Irvine, his soldier-servant and eight *voyageurs* —six Irroquois and two French Canadians—making eleven in all, quitted the camp at Ward's Landing in a bark canoe; and, on its being equipped at McNeill's Bay for the voyage, started at half-past four the same afternoon, having first seen off two brigades of the Ontario Militia. The weather was remarkably beautiful, and the light bark canoe quickly sped over the nine miles that intervened between the point of departure and the first camping-ground on the north shore of the lake. The camp equipment consisted of a small tent for the officers, and a bell-tent for the men; and the first camp was pitched just as it was growing dusk.

At 3.30 a.m. on the following morning the small camp was astir, and, an hour later, after a frugal repast of hot tea, pork, and biscuits—the Commander throughout the expedition having the same rations as the private soldier—the party embarked, arriving a little before eight at the first

---

and stores. In addition to the minimum of sixty days' rations per man, provisions sufficient to last the force until the 30th of September were carried in the boats. The fresh-meat supply, which had been served out hitherto, was, of course, discontinued; but Colonel Wolseley arranged with Mr. Dawson to send on to Fort Frances, by the 15th of September, 20,000 rations complete.

THE FIRST PORTAGE.

portage, the Kashaboiwe, where they found a block of four brigades, which gave an earnest of what might be expected in crossing the remaining portages. This one was a very stiff one, nearly 1,500 yards in length, and the labour of transporting the boats, stores, camp equipment, ammunition, and sixty days' provisions carried by the force, was excessive.*

A little after eleven Colonel Wolseley was in his canoe, paddling up the Kashaboiwe Lake, about nine miles in length, and, before two, reached the head of the lake, which is studded with beautifully-wooded islands. Between it and the Lac-des-Mille-Lacs lies the high land forming the watershed between Hudson's Bay and the Gulf of St. Lawrence, Lac-des-Mille-Lacs discharging its waters into the former, and the Kashaboiwe Lake into the latter. The intervening space between these two lakes is about two and a half miles wide, and Wolseley made one portage of about 1,900 yards, by going up a small shallow creek, which, however, was so

* The following was the method adopted of crossing these portages: 'On the arrival at the portages,' says Wolseley, 'the boats were at once drawn into the shore as close as possible, and unloaded, the stores belonging to each boat being put into a separate pile. These were covered over with tarpaulins, if the time was too late for work; or if—as was always the case with the leading detachment, consisting of three brigades—the road over the portage had to be opened out, and rollers for the boat laid down upon it. At other times the men began to carry over the stores without delay, piling them in heaps, one for each boat, at the end of the road. After a little practice most of the soldiers soon learned to use the common portage-strap, their officers setting them the example by themselves carrying heavy loads with it. As soon as all the stores were conveyed across the portage, the boats were hauled ashore and dragged over, their keels resting on small trees felled across the path to act as rollers. The labour involved by hauling a heavy boat up a very steep incline, to a height of about 100 feet, is no child's play. In each boat there was a strong painter and a towing-line, by means of which and the leather portage-strap, a sort of man-harness was formed when required, so that forty or fifty men could haul together. Say the portage was a mile long (some were more), and that each man had to make ten trips across it before all the stores of his brigade were got over, he would have walked nineteen miles during the operation, being heavily laden for ten miles of them. At some portages considerable engineering ingenuity was required; small streams had to be bridged and marshy spots to be corduroyed over. By the time our men returned many of them were expert axemen, and all were more or less skilled in the craft of the *voyageur* and American woodsman.'

choked up with reeds, that all the men had to get out of the boats into the water and pull them through. A paddle of about half a mile brought the party to the camping-ground for the night on the north shore of the Lac-des-Mille-Lacs, a fine sheet of water about thirty miles long and six to ten miles broad, and studded with innumerable islets, through which even the guides have difficulty in steering their way, so that often it is necessary to have recourse to the compass.

Early on the 25th of July, the canoe was under weigh, and, at one o'clock, the 'Baril' portage, 350 yards long, was reached, the distance from the 'Height of Land' portage being twenty miles, though owing to Wolseley having lost his way—as did all the boats, that of the correspondent of the *Toronto Globe* for two days—the actual distance traversed was far greater.

After a vain search that afternoon, on the Baril Lake, nine miles in length, for the Brulé portage, they landed at the south-western extremity of that lake. On the following day they found the portage, which is 500 yards long, and while the provisions and stores were being carried across, the boats were taken, for half the distance, through a little creek that runs between Lakes Baril and Windegoostigon (an Indian name meaning 'a series of lakes'), which Wolseley reached by proceeding along a narrow winding stream, through a series of small lakes connected by rapids and creeks, fringed with cedar and spruce, and covered with white and golden-hued lilies, forming an enchanting scene of secluded loveliness.

That afternoon they arrived at the 'French' portage, two miles in length, over steep and rocky hills that would have occupied the brigade three or four days to traverse; but fortunately the river, though long and winding, was found to be navigable, with the exception of some falls, round which the leading detachment of the 60th Rifles had cut a new portage, 440 yards long, and very steep and rocky. Colonel Wolseley sent his canoe by the stream, which from the portage to the 'French Lake' is quite twelve miles in length, and walked two miles over the old path.

On the following day, they passed down a winding river, about two miles in length, thick with reeds and water-lilies, which led into Kaogassikok, or Pickerel Lake, some thirteen miles long by two to four broad, at the western extremity of which is the 'Pine' portage, where they encamped. As the portage was difficult to find, Colonel Wolseley, on the following morning, returned in the canoe a considerable distance to 'blaze' the trees at every point, in order to show the way to the brigades in rear; and we have been informed by a companion that the gallant Commander was noted for the judgment he displayed, while passing the islands, in selecting the trees to be blazed, and the dexterity with which he would spring out of the canoe and wield his hand-hatchet, leaving a mark in a prominent place that was discernible a long way astern.

After crossing the Pine portage, 550 yards long, Wolseley sailed over Doré Lake, about a mile across, to the 'Deux Rivières' portage, where they found at work the three leading brigades under Colonel Feilden. This was a very stiff portage, some 750 yards long, but Ignace—the 'boss,' or leader, of the Irroquois, a splendid specimen of the Red Indian, who had accompanied Sir George Simpson and Dr. Rae in their Arctic explorations, and whose services throughout the Expedition were beyond all praise—with ten of his men, by five p.m., had made an excellent road, in one place crossing a ravine, by cutting down and laying lengthwise some huge pines, over which skids were placed on notches, thus enabling the boats to be transported with ease.*

* 'In the centre of the portage,' says Lieutenant Riddell, 'was a high rock up which a ladder of felled trees had been constructed, and at the sides steps were cut for the men to carry their loads up. Had one of the

Wolseley proceeded ahead some distance, and then returned and blazed the way, which was very tortuous and not easy to find, being in one part rocky and shallow, and in another, passing through a marshy creek, overgrown with rushes and lilies.

The route, on the following day, was very intricate, owing to the numerous long bays, but Colonel Wolseley blazed trees at every point and turn. They sailed through Sturgeon Lake, which is about sixteen miles long, and, passing through Tanner's Lake—which empties itself into Lake La Croix, through Sturgeon River, about eighteen miles in length—soon reached the four heavy rapids, 'about which,' says Colonel Wolseley, 'we had heard such a gloomy account at Ottawa from those who professed to know them well. At the first we disembarked the men, when the boats were taken down by the Irroquois. At the second rapid, cargoes as well as men had to be taken out and portaged over a distance of 100 yards, the boats being then run safely down by the Irroquois. The third and fourth rapids were run with men and cargoes in the boats, the Irroquois steering the boats.' Colonel Wolseley left these men at the rapids to navigate the boats of the succeeding brigades, and nailed up a notice at the first rapid, directing all commanding officers to halt until Ignace arrived, and to act precisely as he should direct them.* At six o'clock the

---

ropes snapped when hauling the boats up this ladder, the men at work would, doubtless, have received very severe injuries, and the boat been broken to a certainty.'

* In going over these rapids, four Indians generally rowed or paddled, while two others, with large-sized paddles, steered, one in the bow, the post of honour, and the other in the stern. 'With a rush,' says Riddell, 'and pulled as hard as the strong arms at work were capable of, the boats entered the rapids. The slightest mistake on the part of the steersman, and they would have been smashed to pieces on the huge rocks that we passed nearer than was pleasant. Everyone worked as for his life; and the wild cries of the Indians as they shouted directions to each other made those looking on from the shore feel certain some accident was going to happen; but the cheers and laughter of the crews, as the boats were pulled into smooth water at the foot of the rapids, soon dispelled the illusion.'

headquarters encamped below Portage de l'Isle, the last of the rapids.

The following day they crossed Tanner's Lake, at the outlet of which are Tanner's Rapids, where everything had to be portaged a distance of 175 yards, and reached Island portage, which is about eighty yards across. As the party was strong in Indians, all hands set to work and soon made the road and laid down the skids for the succeeding brigades of boats.

On the 31st of July they followed the course from the south-west extremity of Lac-la-Croix in a southerly direction for six miles, into Lake Loon, then west, and then north into Lake Namekan, where it joined the old canoe route again, thus avoiding all the dangerous rapids; there were, however, three portages, aggregating 634 yards. After the gig and canoe were passed over the rapids, the party encamped for the night. On the following day Colonel Wolseley reached Bare portage, which consists really of two portages, divided by a small pond, and all hands set to work to make the road over them. On the arrival of the leading brigades of boats, Wolseley started on his voyage up the 'Rainy' Lake, a fair stretch of water, fifty miles in length, by about thirty to forty miles in breadth, and encamped at eight p.m. The following day, owing to a gale, they were compelled to encamp on an island at the head of Rainy Lake, but the whole flotilla was under weigh at four on the morning of the 4th of August, and descending the Rainy River* for three miles, soon reached Fort Frances,

* At the entrance to Rainy River Wolseley was hailed by a canoe, in which was Lieutenant (now Lieut.-Colonel) Butler, 69th Regiment, who had arrived at Fort Frances that morning from Fort Garry. He had been sent on a special mission from Canada by General Lindsay; and, after visiting the towns on the south shore of Lake Superior, to learn what prospect there was of the threateaed Fenian irruption on the communications of the expedition, and passing through St. Paul's in Minnesota, he proceeded to the lower fort, near Fort Garry, where he received a visit from Riel. On quitting the Settlement, on the 24th of July, he went up the Winnipeg River, and

'the half-way house' to Fort Garry, the sight of which was hailed with joy by every man in the force. During the nineteen days that had elapsed since the first detachment quitted McNeill's Bay, they had traversed 200 miles, having taken their boats and stores over seventeen portages, at all of which they had made good, practicable roads.

Fort Frances is not a military work, as its name would imply, but a collection of wooden one-storied houses, standing on the right bank of the Rainy River, immediately below the falls, which are twenty-two feet high.

Two days after his arrival Colonel Wolseley gave a formal interview, or 'pow-wow,' to 'Crooked Neck,' the principal chief of a large body of Chippewa Indians, who had assembled to see what they could get out of the 'pale-faces,' and about a dozen of his principal followers. 'Crooked Neck' made a very long speech, to which Wolseley replied in brief terms to the effect that he was sorry he had no provisions to give away, as he had only sufficient for his own men, but that next year Government would send him presents for helping them through. The ceremony concluded, as it had begun, with hand-shaking all round, and they were dismissed with a small present of flour and pork. Colonel Wolseley also gave an interview to another great chief, who presented a grotesque appearance, with his painted face and parti-coloured raiment somewhat similar to those worn by negro melodists.

While at Fort Frances, Wolseley received letters from Henry Price, the chief of the Salteux, or 'Swampy,' Indians, full of loyalty, and breathing hatred towards Riel and his party; and from the Protestant bishop, and others, expressing ardent longings for his arrival, as affairs at the

---

brought much valuable information concerning the position of affairs at Fort Garry, which Riel openly declared the Expeditionary Force would never reach.

THE START FROM FORT FRANCES.

Settlement were 'in a serious and threatening state.' During his stay at Fort Frances, he took advantage of the arrival of the brigades to weed out the many useless *voyageurs*, who were sent back to Canada.

At daylight, on the 10th of August, Colonel Wolseley, after despatching the brigades, as they arrived in succession, up to K Brigade, including the whole of the 60th Rifles (the I Brigade of the Ontario Militia being left to garrison Fort Frances), started in his birch canoe, carrying fourteen days' provisions, for Fort Alexander, the route to which lay through Rainy River, seventy-five miles long; Lake of the Woods, seventy-two miles; and the River Winnipeg, a further distance of 163 miles.

He was accompanied, as before, by Mr. Irvine and his servant, with eight Indians, the gig keeping company, with his two orderly officers and a crew of four soldiers and two Indians. As they pushed off below the falls, near Fort Frances, 'we were,' says Wolseley, 'twisted round for some time in every direction, by the numerous whirlpools formed by the falling of such a great body of water into a circular basin, where it acquired a rotary motion. At one moment the boat was going at the rate of about nine miles an hour, the next it was perfectly stationary, having stopped without any shock, but as suddenly as if it had struck a rock. In some instances minutes elapsed ere the utmost exertion at the oar, the whole crew pulling their best, could impart the least motion to the boat. Then after some moments of hard pulling, every muscle being strained to the utmost, the boat was released so suddenly that it bounded forward as a spring would which had been kept back by a rope that had suddenly snapped.' The Rainy River, which forms the frontier between British North America and the United States, runs a distance of seventy miles from Fort Frances to its *embouchure* into the Lake of the Woods, its breadth varying from 300 to 400 yards. The navigation is unbroken except at two rapids, the 'Manitou' and 'Longsault,' thirty-two and thirty-nine miles from Fort Frances; and its banks are well-wooded, with vistas of glade and forest.

The evening being fine and the moon nearly full, Colonel Wolseley, instead of camping at night, determined to try the plan adopted by the *employés* of the Hudson's Bay Company, of lashing the canoe and gig together, and drifting down the river, all hands turning in, except one man in each boat to steer and keep watch. It was pleasant enough, though the limited space cramped the legs, until the rain began to fall, accompanied by a strong westerly wind, and as the boats could make no progress and the night was dark 'as a wolf's mouth,' he decided to run them ashore. A miserable and sleepless night was passed by the occupants of the canoe, who cowered, as best they could, under their waterproofs; and at dawn, dripping with wet and stiff with cold, they were glad to get out of their boat. After some hot tea the party were under weigh, and made a stop for breakfast about two miles from the mouth of Rainy River, at a small trading-post of the Hudson's Bay Company, called 'Hungry Hall,' from the number of men who had, from time to time, nearly died from starvation while quartered there, though it has since received the less ill-omened name of Fort Louisa.

Just before his arrival here, Colonel Wolseley met a small canoe, containing three Indians, who brought letters from Rat portage, announcing the arrival there of six boats purchased by the loyal Protestant laity and clergy of the Red River Settlement of all sects, to help the expedition down the Winnipeg River. The bearers of the letters were at once utilized as guides, and handed over to the K Brigade which came up at that moment. Favoured by a fair breeze, which filled their sails, the canoe and gig soon passed along the marshy banks on both sides of the mouth of the Rainy

A LOST DAY. 215

River, from which the wild duck rose in numbers, into the Lake of the Woods,* from the north-west angle of which lay the direct road to Fort Garry, 115 miles 'as the crow flies,' but only eighty of which was passable for carts, the remainder of the road lying through swamps. Soon they encountered the full force of the gale that was blowing, and some heavy seas that broke over the boats drove them, soon after midday, to take shelter on an island, which they named 'Detention Island.'

The gale continued all that night and the following day; but at eight p.m., the wind having lulled, the K Brigade started, and soon after a canoe arrived bringing mails with Toronto papers to the 29th of July, and London papers of the 15th July, containing the startling intelligence of the outbreak of war between France and Prussia. During the evening two of the large Red River boats arrived under Mr. Sinclair, bringing letters from Colonel Feilden from Rat portage, at the entrance to the Winnipeg River, and from Bishop Macrae, urging the necessity of at once despatching two guns and 100 men to Red River. Colonel Wolseley had been chafing all day at his enforced idleness, but to every proposal to proceed the Indians had assured him that the high sea on the lake would inevitably break the frail bark canoe to pieces. He could, however, brook delay no longer, so started in the gig in company with Captain Huyshe. Having no guide, they steered by the stars, and after three hours' hard pulling, made an island at one a.m., on which they bivouacked for the night. Only four hours was allowed for repose, and the gig was then under weigh steering N.N.W. To the eastward lay a group of islands, through which an opening to escape the rough sea was looked for in vain; and to the westward stretched an unbroken expanse of water,

* Lake of the Woods is about seventy-two miles long and nearly as many broad, and is divided by clusters of islands into three distinct lakes.

with no land in sight. The whole of that day was passed in threading an interminable labyrinth of islands, Colonel Wolseley taking up his station in the bows of the boat, and steering by compass, with the aid of Mr. Dawson's very inaccurate chart. The usual halts were made for breakfast and dinner, and when it was too dark to see, the party bivouacked on an island. At four o'clock on the following morning Colonel Wolseley was afloat again, hoping soon to reach the Rat portage, which he calculated was only about ten miles distant. He steered north, but found himself in a *cul de sac;* then east, then west, trying every opening amongst the innumerable islands, in the vain hope of making the mouth of the Winnipeg River. It certainly was a very awkward position for the Commander of the Expedition; but at length, after wandering about hopelessly in the labyrinth of islets and passages, at half-past three an Indian encampment was sighted.

A present of a little tea and biscuit induced the father of the family to embark in his canoe and act as guide, and at eight p.m. on the 14th of August, after only one halt for breakfast, the party in the gig arrived at Rat portage, faint with hunger and fatigue. Here they learned that the canoe and two Red River boats had arrived from Detention Island early that morning, and that the four remaining Red River boats, in charge of the Rev. Mr. Gardiner, Presbyterian minister, had gone on with the leading brigades, to help them down the dangerous rapids of the Winnipeg River, which could not have been traversed without accident but for these boats and their skilled crews.

Rat portage, at the head of the Lake of the Woods, where there is a Hudson's Bay Company's post, consists of three portages, the Winnipeg River, which is here some three miles broad, finding its way down to the lower level by three distinct waterfalls. The first is not much used. The second,

THE DESCENT OF THE WINNIPEG.

close to it, is 300 yards long, and, as it is chiefly used for canoes, Colonel Wolseley passed over it. The third and regular portage, which is three miles to the south of the post, is 130 yards long, and as it is generally used for the Company's boats, the brigades passed over it.

Colonel Wolseley remained at Rat portage during the 15th of August, arranging for guides to be sent back to Fort Frances to conduct the remaining brigades across the Lake of the Woods, and also sent Lieutenant Butler, in a light canoe, to Fort Alexander, at the mouth of the Winnipeg River, to engage guides and send them up to Islington Mission, where the most dangerous part of the river begins. At sunset Colonel McNeill arrived in a canoe, having been only twelve days coming from Shebandowan Lake, and reported all well with the brigades in the rear, which he had passed in succession, having quitted McNeill's Bay two days after the despatch of the X Brigade. The mails for Canada being made up and despatched on the 16th of August, Colonel Wolseley, accompanied by Colonel McNeill's canoe, and the gig with the two orderly officers, quitted Rat portage to make the descent of the Winnipeg River.*

Favoured by a fair breeze, the first ten miles, including 'Les Dalles' Rapids, were run without any difficulty, and tents were pitched for the night about twenty miles from the Rat portage. The fine weather they had enjoyed since their departure from Lake Shebandowan here deserted them; the night was rainy, with a cold raw fog, and the start on the following morning was made amid rain and a blustering head-wind, but, by dint of hard work at the oars,

* During its tortuous course of 163 miles, the Winnipeg River descends 350 feet by a succession of noble cataracts and rapids, which present scenery of a singularly wild and picturesque character, and, at places, the river expands into large lakes, full of rocky islands, and bounded by precipitous cliffs.

they quickly ran the intervening distance until the rapids, called 'Grand Décharge,' were reached. Here the stores were portaged, and the boats run down the rapids, with four men rowing and the two Indians steering.

They now passed, in succession, Yellow Mud portage, 110 yards long; a fall of six feet, which was run; Pine portage, 240 yards long, very steep and slippery, which took them an hour to cross; and, a little farther on, Cave Rapids, which were run. At three they passed Islington Mission, an oasis in the sterile rocky scenery around, with its fields of yellow corn and green pasturage, and, at 6.35, the little flotilla reached De l'Isle Rapids, which were shot with full cargoes, though great excitement was caused as the plunge was taken, the dexterous Indians guiding the canoe with consummate skill amid the surging waters and boiling eddies that appeared as if they would engulf the frail craft. The party halted at the foot of the rapids for the night, during which the rain came down with steady persistency, and they were all glad to be off before five a.m., with rain and a bleak cold wind as travelling companions. At noon they reached the 'Chute à Jacquot,' about twenty miles below Islington Mission, a very pretty fall in a series of terraces, where they met two Hudson's Bay boats, carrying supplies for the Company—enormous craft so strongly built that when shooting rapids they are proof against the effects of a bump on a rock. The half-breeds working them had their families with them, and lived chiefly on 'pemican,' or buffalo meat and fat, dried and then beaten together into a mass, and pressed into bags made of buffalo-skin.

Having portaged the canoes and gig, with their cargoes, the party had dinner at the far end of the portage, which is 150 yards across, and made their next halt at 'Trois Pointes des Bois,' which consists of three portages close together, round three very picturesque falls; the portages were 306,

110, and sixty yards long respectively. Eight miles further on lie 'Slave Falls,' and in a bay, 400 yards to the right, is the portage, 750 yards across, where the skids were laid for the boats. The canoe portage is round a jutting ledge of rock quite close to the falls, and very dangerous except for skilled boatmen well acquainted with the locality. Colonel Wolseley's Irroquois took his canoe by this portage, though Colonel McNeill's Chippewas, more fearful or prudent, as also the gig and all the boats, proceeded to the regular portage, some 500 yards above.

Wolseley narrates in graphic terms his sensations on an occasion when his coolness in the presence of danger was put to almost as severe a test as any he encountered during his adventurous career. He says: 'No length of time, nor any amount of future adventures, can erase from my mind the arrival at the Slave Falls. I was in a birch canoe manned by Irroquois, one of whom acted as guide. The regular portage for boats was several hundred yards from the falls, and lay in a slack-water bay, reached without any danger as long as the boats kept tolerably well in towards the bank on that side. Our astonishment was great at finding the guide take the canoe out into mid-stream, where the current ran at an exciting pace, becoming swifter at every yard, until at last, as we approached the vicinity of the falls, it was palpably evident we were descending a steeply inclined plane. Consoling ourselves at first with the reflection that the guide knew best what he was about, we sat motionless, but, let us confess it, awe-stricken, as we swept into the narrow gully at the end of which the great noisy roar of falling waters, and the columns of spray that curled up like clouds into the air, announced the position of the fall. We were close to the brink. We appeared to have reached that point which exists in most falls, whence the water seems to begin its run preparatory to a good jump over into the abyss below; and we knew, from having watched many great cataracts for hours, that it was a bourne from whence there was no return. Quick as lightning the idea flashed across us that the Indians had made a mistake, and that everything was over for us in this world. In that infinitesimal fraction of time a glimpse of the countenance of the sturdy bowman rather confirmed this idea, his teeth appeared set, and there was an unusual look in his eye. All creations of our own heated fancy; for in another second the canoe's head swept in towards the rocks, and was turned nose up stream in tolerably slack water, two of the paddlers jumping out and holding it firmly there. All our poetical fancies were rudely dispersed by a cheer and chorus of laughter from the Irroquois crew. The breaking of a paddle in the hands of either bowman or steersman would have been fatal at that critical moment when we turned sharply into the bank, the stern being allowed to swing round in the heavy stream, and by so doing aid in driving the bow inwards. Nothing could have saved us if such an accident had occurred; yet there were these Indians chuckling over the danger they had just escaped by the exertion of their greatest skill and of their utmost muscular power. They had needlessly and willingly encountered it, for they could have gained the shore about 100 yards higher up with comparative ease, and then lowered their canoes through the slack-water pools in the rocks along the side, to the place they had only reached with extreme danger. There was no use in arguing with them on the subject; they had confidence in themselves, and gloried in any danger which they felt certain of overcoming.' It is not at all improbable, however, that the Indians had a purpose in paddling so perilously near the brink of these dangerous falls, and that it was done to test the courage of the young Commander, whom every man among the 'pale-faces' obeyed and trusted so implicitly; and truly the ingenuity of man could not have devised a more crucial test. To sit calmly in the stern-sheets of a canoe, which, carried away in the mighty vortex of a current running like a sluice, was hurrying over a chasm to, apparently, certain and immediate destruction, and neither by word nor gesture to express a sign of fear, was an ordeal of the most trying character. But it was triumphantly endured, and if the Irroquois watched the countenance of the British leader in order to note a change in its habitual expression, they looked in vain, and he preserved the stoicism of a Red Indian at the stake.

That night they encamped below the falls, and on the following day the gig and canoes passed the Barrière portage, the Otter Falls, and the Sept portages. These last are a succession of seven heavy falls, and rapids, with sunken rocks and whirlpools, nearly three miles long, at each of which they had to go through the task of unloading, portaging, and reloading, thus causing excessive labour to the soldiers with the heavy boats.

Colonel Wolseley was astir soon after three on the following morning, raising the camp, as was his wont throughout the expedition, by the cry of 'Fort Garry!' shouted in cheery tones at the top of his voice. When they started, an hour later, the prospect before them was of a still more arduous day's work, as Colonel Wolseley expressed his determination to reach Fort Alexander on the 20th of August, and it was known that nothing would turn him from his purpose, when, as President Lincoln used to say, he 'put his foot down.' Crossing Lac de Bonnet, they passed Galais du Bonnet portage, 145 yards long; the Second Bonnet, 100 yards long; the Grand Bonnet, one of the largest portages on the route, upwards of 1,300 yards in length, and the Petit Bonnet. At one o'clock they were at White Mud portage, 280 yards long; and an hour later reached the two Silver Falls portage, respectively 200 and thirty yards in length. The falls are described as most magnificent, the volume of water over the cascades being enormous, and the scenery being, according to Wolseley, 'the finest on the river.' Embarking again, a further pull of five miles, with two or three difficult rapids, brought them to Pine portage, the last on the route to Fort Garry, which is about 350 yards across. For the last time they embarked; and, pulling over the reach of eight miles, broken by two easily-run rapids, arrived, at 6.35 on the 20th of August, at Fort Alexander, situated about two miles from the mouth of the Winnipeg, whose rapids they had run and portages surmounted without the loss of a single boat—a feat, having regard to the dangers of its falls, eddies, currents, and sunken rocks, which cannot be contemplated without admiration at the skilful management of the crews and forethought of the leader.

When expatiating on the dangers of the Winnipeg River, the experienced crews of the Hudson's Bay boats had stated that it would take twenty days to get to Fort Alexander, but the distance was accomplished by British soldiers in exactly half that time. Whereas before the expedition, says Wolseley, 'we found a general conviction stamped upon the minds of every one of every class that we met, that the British soldier was a fine brave fellow, who, as a fighting-man, was equal to two of any other nation, but utterly useless for any other purpose, such as carrying loads, performing heavy bodily labour, or enduring great physical fatigue, we now bear a very different reputation in those parts, and have left behind us a character for every manly virtue.'

Colonel Wolseley was received at Fort Alexander by Mr. Donald Smith, the Governor of the Hudson's Bay Company, and the soldiers who had preceded him gathered round the top of the steps leading to the fort, and gave their leader

THE RUN ACROSS LAKE WINNIPEG. 223

three ringing cheers. 'There was not a sick man,' he says, 'amongst those collected at Fort Alexander; all looked the picture of health and of soldier-like bearing. Up to the 20th of August it had rained upon thirteen days in that month. The work had been incessant from daylight until dark, but no murmur was heard.'

Sunday was a day of well-earned rest. Divine service was held, at which the troops attended, though the beneficial effect was rather marred by an unconscionably long sermon, which drew from one of the men, who were assembled under arms in the open air and greatly felt the heat, the irreverent remark, that 'it was worse than a long portage.' At three p.m. on the following day the advance was sounded, and away down the Winnipeg River, with a fair wind, sailed the flotilla of about fifty boats. Colonel Wolseley now quitted the canoe in which he had journeyed from Shebandowan Lake, and led the van, accompanied by Mr. Donald Smith, in one of the large Red River boats.

On arrival at the mouth of the Winnipeg River, the flotilla stood out into Lake Winnipeg,* and proceeded to Elk Island, twenty miles from Fort Alexander, where the boats were drawn up on a fine sandy beach. 'Fort Garry' was sounded at 3.30 on the following morning, and, thanks to a favouring breeze and fine weather, the flotilla set sail, presenting an imposing appearance as they sped—

'Through seas where sail was never spread before.'

A quick run was made across the southern portion of Lake Winnipeg, to the mouth of the Red River; and, before three, the flotilla was sailing up the centre of the three channels by which it flows into Lake Winnipeg. Colonel Wolseley sent his canoe ahead, with orders to keep a sharp

* Lake Winnipeg has an area of 9,000 square miles, and measures 264 miles, by an average width of 35. The name signifies, in the Chippewa tongue, 'dirty water.'

look-out, and report anything unusual or suspicious; and he himself led the boats, which followed in two lines immediately astern of Colonel Feilden. At sunset the force encamped on the right bank of the river, about eleven miles below the Stone Fort (or Lower Fort Garry), and just opposite the lodges of the Swampy Indians, whose chief, Henry Prince, and a few of the tribe, in their full dress of feathers and paint, paid a visit of ceremony to the British Commander. After the usual compliments they were dismissed with Colonel Wolseley's hearty thanks for their loyalty, accompanied by a substantial present of pork and flour, and every precaution was adopted to prevent the news of the arrival of the flotilla from spreading.

It rained all that night, and the *réveillé* sounded at 3.30, when the men started after the usual cup of hot tea. The flotilla continued its course up the river in the same order as on the preceding day, and received a welcome from all classes, the men cheering, the women waving their handkerchiefs, and the bells of the churches, which are Protestant below Fort Garry, ringing out a merry peal, while the Indians turned out of their camps, and gave vent to their joy by discharging their firearms. At eight o'clock the flotilla reached Stone Fort, a square enclosure with large circular bastions at each angle. No reliable information could be obtained of Riel, though it was anticipated that he would resist if he could get his followers to fight. The boats were lightened of all superfluous stores; and as Colonel Wolseley was anxious to get to Fort Garry, if possible, before dark, only a day's rations were taken. It was necessary to advance with caution, and Captain Wallace's company of the 60th was detached as an advance-guard and flanking-party on the left bank of the river, which is here sprinkled with white houses and neat farms. That officer received orders to keep his main body on the

THE ADVANCE ON FORT GARRY.

road about a quarter of a mile in front of the boats, with connecting files to the river's bank, and an advance-party of one section of his company about 500 yards further ahead; two signal-men, with flags, to facilitate communication with the boats, were also furnished to him. The distance between the two forts being twenty-two miles by road, the company was mounted on ponies and in country carts, and had orders to stop all persons on their way up the river, but not to interfere with those going down the stream. Lieutenant Butler was also detached on horseback up the right bank, which is mostly covered with willows, with orders to patrol along the road a little ahead of the boats, and to show himself at intervals. The adoption of these precautions was attended with perfect success, as it was found that, as the troops advanced, the actual appearance of the boats was the first intimation the people had of the arrival of the expedition; and it was afterwards ascertained that Riel was kept so completely in the dark as to the proximity of the British force, that though he, in company with O'Donoghue, rode out late that night towards the British pickets, for the purpose of verifying the rumours that had come to his ears, he returned without having ascertained any certain information.

Colonel Wolseley, embarking in the gig, led the flotilla; the boats, with the 2 seven-pounders mounted in the bows, proceeded in the same order as before, and everything and everybody was in readiness to give Riel a warm reception in the event of his disputing the passage of the river. The flotilla, without much difficulty, poled and tracked up the Grand Rapids, which were child's play after those of the Winnipeg River; but as it was found impossible to reach Fort Garry that night, the camp was pitched on the left bank, about six miles below the fort by road, and eight or nine by the river. Outlying pickets were thrown out on both sides of the river, and a chain of sentries posted, to cut off all communication between the fort and the settlements in rear of the force. It rained hard all night, with a strong breeze from the north-west, and it was wretched work turning out on the following morning. 'As we bent over our fires at daybreak,' says Wolseley, 'trying to get warmth for our bodies, and sufficient heat to boil the kettles, a more miserable-looking lot of objects it would be impossible to imagine. Everyone was wet through; we were cold and hungry; our very enemies would have pitied our plight.'

The heavy rain having rendered the road ankle-deep in black mud, Colonel Wolseley was obliged to abandon his intention of marching on the fort, and before six a.m., amid a torrent of rain, the troops, having struck their tents and breakfasted, embarked in their boats. Captain Wallace's company, which had been on picket all night, again continued its march along the road on the flank, which in places was a sheet of water, through which the men had to wade. About eight o'clock the troops were disembarked at Point Douglas, about two miles from the fort by land. The soldiers, forming up in open column of companies, plodded on cheerfully through the sea of mud, with the rain beating in their faces. Colonel Wolseley and his staff mounted some ponies brought by the country people. The 60th Rifles led, throwing out skirmishers about 400 yards in advance of the column; then came the artillery, with the 2 guns limbered on to carts, followed by the Engineers, with a company of Rifles as rear-guard. In this formation the column, led by Wolseley and accompanied by a few loyal inhabitants on horseback, who were useful as scouts and guides, marched over the prairie in rear of the village of Winnipeg, and advanced on the fort. At this point, messengers who had been sent the previous night to

Winnipeg, arrived with the assurance that Riel and his gang were still inside the fort, and meant to fight. The spirits of the men immediately rose at this announcement, and, as they briskly approached the fort, all the appearances pointed to the same conclusion : no flag was flying from the flag-staff, the gate commanding the village and prairie was closed, and there was a gun in position over the gateway, and others in the embrasures bearing upon them. Not a soul appeared to be stirring, and everything looked as if a surprise was intended. The excitement increased momentarily as the skirmishers quickened their pace.

Colonel Wolseley now sent Colonel McNeill and Lieutenant Denison round the fort to ascertain the state of affairs, and presently they returned with the intelligence that the southern gate was wide open, and the fort appeared to be evacuated. The disappointment among all ranks was keen and outspoken, for they had given Riel credit, after all his bravado, for sufficient courage to try a passage of arms with them, and to be thus deprived of the opportunity of gaining a little honour at his expense was 'very hard lines' on men who, since the 21st of May, when Colonel Wolseley and the advanced guard of the expedition quitted Toronto, had sailed, and marched, and tugged at the oars, and laboured over forty-seven portages, for a distance of 1,200 miles. However, the *éclat* that would have surrounded the expedition had Riel caused the expenditure of some powder, with its concomitant of death and wounds, was denied to the troops, and so thus was won a bloodless victory, but one which, nevertheless, having regard to the difficulties overcome, must ever be regarded as shedding an additional lustre on the name of the British soldier.

Amid a continual downpour, the troops entered by the southern gate, when the fort was found to be empty of its late defenders — Riel, Lepine, and O'Donoghue having ridden off only a quarter of an hour before.* Some field-guns, mounted on the bastions and over the gateway in the fort, were now taken outside, the troops formed up in line near them, the Union Jack was hoisted under a royal salute, and three hearty cheers were given for the Queen, caught up by the people who flocked to the spot, the soldiers finishing by 'one cheer more' for their Commander, under whose leadership this great success had been achieved.

Thus, on Wednesday, the 24th of August, the British flag once move waved over Fort Garry, *within twenty-four hours of the time specified by Colonel Wolseley when he undertook the conduct of the expedition.* Four years later he displayed similar military punctuality in keeping his engagements, when, *to the day he designated before leaving Cape Coast*, his victorious army formed up in the main street of Coomassie, to give three cheers for Her Majesty. It certainly is a novel feature in warfare, and one that deserves to be specially recorded, that in two expeditions, undertaken under circumstances that seemed, in a peculiar degree, to defy the exigencies of time, a General should months beforehand point to the day in the almanack on which he would be at his goal, and fulfil his engagement in spite of all the difficulties of time, transport, weather, the accidents that await all human undertakings, and the physical obstacles

---

* These three ringleaders made their escape to Pembina, in United States territory. In 1873 Riel was elected by acclamation a Member for Provencher in the Dominion House of Commons, and at the General Election was re-elected by a majority of three to one. There was great excitement at Ottawa when, on the 30th of March, 1874, he went to the clerk's office, took the oath, and signed the Parliamentary roll, but then disappeared. A true bill was found against him on the charge of murder, and a warrant of outlawry was issued by the Queen's Bench, Manitoba, on the 15th of October, 1874, and the Government of Ontario offered a reward of 5,000 dollars for his apprehension. His 'Adjutant-General,' Lepine, who presided over the mock court-martial that tried and sentenced to death the loyal Canadian, Thomas Scott, and commanded the shooting-party, was brought to trial at Winnipeg, and condemned to death on the 10th of October, 1874, but the capital sentence was commuted by Lord Dufferin.

encountered in traversing regions untrod before by any but travellers.*

As the men were in a miserable plight from the drenching rain, accommodation was found for all in the buildings inside the fort. So hurried had been the flight of 'President' Riel, who refused to credit the approach of the troops until he actually saw them marching round the village, that the breakfast-table was laid, and the late Dictator of the Red River and his Ministers had only half partaken of the viands that more honest men were destined to enjoy.

Colonel Wolseley was only too glad that Riel had fled, as his capture would have complicated matters in the state of Canadian Parliamentary parties; no attempt was, therefore, made to pursue and arrest the fugitives, though they might easily have been captured. Indeed many of the inhabitants offered voluntarily to capture Riel and his associates, if he would only authorize them to do so; but to all these applicants the same answer was made, 'Go to a magistrate for a warrant, and when obtained, Mr. Smith will provide the means for execution.' Wolseley had not been invested by the Canadian Government with civil authority, and though the most influential of the inhabitants requested him to assume the reins of power, with equal good sense and moderation he declined to do so; but, pending the arrival of the new Lieutenant-Governor, Mr. Archibald, handed over the conduct of civil affairs to Mr. Donald Smith, who, as Governor of the Hudson's Bay Company, was the legal representative of the Government until the advent of his successor. No arrests were made by the military, and the three or four prisoners who were detained when the troops marched into the fort, were released during the day, there being no warrant out against them, and no sworn

* Since the above was written, as will appear further on in this narrative, the subject of this memoir was equally punctual in his engagements in the campaigns against Secocoeni and Arabi.

information. In fact no proper constables could be procured to execute warrants, and Colonel Wolseley, who acted throughout these somewhat difficult and unfamiliar circumstances with marked good sense and discretion, positively refused to allow his soldiers to be converted into policemen.

The position of affairs in the interval between the 22nd of August, and the arrival of Mr. Archibald on the 2nd of September, was one requiring delicate management, as the reaction from the state of fear in which the settlers had lived for the preceding ten months, to one of perfect security, turned the heads of many of them, and there was some trouble in keeping them in proper restraint; also, though the rebel leaders had disappeared, many of their adherents had merely retired to their homes, and loud dissatisfaction was expressed by the loyally disposed at these rebels being allowed to remain at large. Colonel Wolseley took every precaution to keep the peace, by patrolling Winnipeg and the neighbourhood of the fort with armed parties of his soldiers, but though he could have easily maintained order by proclaiming military law, he considered it essential, for political reasons, to keep the military element in the background, and make it appear that law and order were maintained as in other Canadian provinces. The difficulty of this task may be appreciated, when it is remembered that all the former machinery of government had disappeared, and even the few magistrates who remained were either afraid or disinclined to act. There was no law officer of any description, so that in reality the revival of public confidence was due to the moral effect produced by the presence of the troops, and by the consciousness that they would be used at any moment, if necessary, for the suppression of disturbance and the maintenance of order.

Mr. Smith entertained Colonel Wolseley and the headquarter staff during their stay in Fort Garry right hospitably, and, after their long abstinence, they all thoroughly enjoyed the fine old port provided by the Hudson's Bay Company for their Governor, with the exception of the Commander, who touched not one drop. When starting on this expedition, Wolseley had laid it down as his rule of conduct to set an example of abstinence to his men : acting upon views he had for years strongly entertained, as to the positive injury to health caused by dram-drinking, even in moderation, he would permit no liquor of any sort—except a small quantity of brandy in each brigade of boats, as 'medical comforts,' under the charge of the commanding officer—to form part of the commissariat department. But he sanctioned a liberal allowance of tea, which was freely taken by officers and men twice and thrice a day, and though they were constantly wet to the skin, and had to perform the hardest work in damp clothes, the medical returns were almost blank, and crime and any serious cases of sickness were alike unknown in the force. So scrupulously did Colonel Wolseley set the example of abstemiousness to his men, that when, on the return journey from Fort Garry, it was proposed to him that a bottle of whisky he had taken in his canoe as 'medical comforts,' should be broached when starting on Lake Shebandowan, he replied, 'No, I have promised it to Kane'—his soldier servant of the 60th Rifles—and to Kane it was ultimately handed over unopened, after performing a journey of 2,400 miles.

On his arrival at Fort Garry,* the newly installed Governor

* Fort Garry, called also 'the Upper Fort,' is a rectangular edifice, crowded with buildings, having an area of 200 by 85 yards. The original fort, which was built about the year 1840, and was 100 yards in length, is surrounded by a stone wall 10 feet high, with circular bastions pierced for guns. Ten years later, when a detachment of the 6th Regiment was quartered here, it was doubled in size, and surrounded by a wooden palisading on a stone foundation. The fort stands at the angle formed by the junction

placed at Colonel Wolseley's disposal the best and most roomy apartment as a sleeping chamber; and when Mr. Irvine, his companion in the tent during the hard times of the long march, was proceeding to put up for the night as usual, Wolseley, with the feelings of comradeship of a true soldier, would not listen to this, but made his *compagnon de voyage* share his good luck, and place his mattress in a corner of the room. Such small traits give the clue to the character of a man, and, in our opinion, are not too trivial to be chronicled by a biographer.

On the 28th of August, Colonel Wolseley issued an order* recounting the labours imposed on the troops, and thanking them for their 'unparalleled exertions' in surmounting them. What these were, were recognised by a competent judge— Mr. Archibald, the new Lieutenant-Governor of Manitoba, who wrote to Colonel Wolseley: 'I can judge of the work

---

of the Assiniboine and Red Rivers, and is 100 yards distant from the former. The village of Winnipeg, about half a mile distant, was, in 1870, a collection of some fifty houses, forming one wide street.

* In this order he said: 'You have endured excessive fatigue in the performance of a service that, for its arduous nature, can bear comparison with any previous military expedition. In coming here from Prince Arthur's Landing you have traversed a distance of upwards of 600 miles. Your labours began with road-making and the construction of defensive works; then followed the arduous duty of taking the boats up a height of 800 feet, along 50 miles of river full of rapids, and where portages were numerous. From the time you left Shebandowan Lake until Fort Garry was reached, your labour at the oar has been incessant from daybreak to dark every day. Forty-seven portages were got over, entailing the unparalleled exertion of carrying the boats, guns, ammunition, stores, and provisions over a total distance of upwards of seven miles. It may be said that the whole journey has been made through a wilderness, where, as there were no supplies of any sort whatever to be had, everything had to be taken with you in the boats. I have throughout viewed with pleasure the manner in which officers have vied with their men in carrying heavy loads. It has rained upon forty-five days out of ninety-four that have passed since we landed at Thunder Bay, and upon many occasions every man has been wet through for days together. There has not been the slightest murmur of discontent heard from anyone. It may be confidently asserted that no force has ever had to endure more continuous labour, and it may be as truthfully said that no men on service have ever been better behaved, or more cheerful under the trials arising from exposure to inclement weather, excessive fatigue, and to the annoyance caused by flies.'

THE RETURN TO CANADA.

you have had to do all the better from having seen for myself the physical obstacles that had to be met and overcome —obstacles which, I assure you, exceed anything I could have imagined. It is impossible not to feel that the men who have triumphed over such difficulties must not only have themselves worked well, but also have been well led; and I should not be doing justice to my own feelings if I were not, on my arrival here, to repeat the expressions of admiration extorted from me as I passed along in view of the difficulties you had to meet, and which you have so triumphantly surmounted.'

On the following day, the Regular troops, being relieved by the Ontario Militia, commenced to leave for Canada by the Winnipeg River, Captain Buller's[*] company of the 60th Rifles, guided by Mr. Monkman, proceeding by the road to the north-west angle of Lake of the Woods, where they were to exchange for boats the pack-horses that had formed their means of transport. By the 3rd of September all the Regulars had left Fort Garry on their return to Canada.

Mr. Archibald was duly installed as Lieutenant-Governor of Manitoba on the 6th of September, and on the 10th Colonel Wolseley started by the road between Fort Garry and Lake of the Woods. The Militia regiments remained in the territory; the Ontario Rifles in Fort Garry, where the two guns were also left; and the Quebec Rifles at the Stone Fort.

The troops performed in safety the return journey to Prince Arthur's Landing, which was very arduous, as the rapids of the Winnipeg had to be laboriously 'poled' and 'tracked,' instead of 'run.' As they arrived at Thunder

[*] Now Sir Redvers Buller, V.C., K.C.M.G., C.B., who served under his old chief in Ashantee and Egypt, and is acknowledged to be one of the best officers in the army. During the Zulu War he and Sir Evelyn Wood, another of those so unworthily stigmatized as the 'Ashantee Ring,' confessedly came out as the heroes in a war that was the grave of so many reputations.

Bay, they embarked for Collingwood, whence they proceeded by train to Toronto and Montreal, where the last detachment arrived on the 14th of October. General Lindsay was enabled to report to the War Office, that 'with the exception of one man left at Fort Garry, with inflammation of the lungs, the Regular force returned to Canada with no sick, and with no casualty by drowning, or of any other description.' Truly a marvellous and unprecedented result in an arduous expedition, in which over 1,200 soldiers and 500 non-combatants were engaged.

On Wolseley's arrival at the north-west angle of Lake of the Woods, he found a note from General Lindsay, saying that he intended to embark for England on the 1st of October, and would be glad of his company. Wolseley immediately pushed on for Prince Arthur's Landing in his canoe, and on his arrival took ship to Collingwood. Hurrying through Toronto, he proceeded to Montreal, where the citizens entertained him at a banquet, and presented him with an address of welcome and congratulation.*

The citizens of Montreal, whose sentiments were echoed by the inhabitants of Canada, were capable of forming a just estimate of the arduous nature of the expedition brought

* In this address they said: 'In common with the entire people of Canada, we hailed your appointment to the command of the expedition with pleasure, and looked forward to your conduct of it with the most implicit confidence—a confidence which has been more than justified by the result. The difficulties of leading a considerable body of troops through an uninhabited territory without roads, and removed from any sources of supply, like that between Fort William and Fort Garry, were such as to tax the utmost skill; and that you have succeeded in overcoming them so successfully, without the loss of a single man, or any serious casualty, is the highest tribute that could be paid to your character and abilities as a soldier. The citizens of Montreal, who watched the progress of the expedition with the most anxious concern, will ever remember your admirable management of it with feelings of the warmest gratitude. We regret your departure from Canada, where your conduct as a soldier, and your character as a citizen, have won for you so many warm friends; and, in bidding you farewell, we can assure you that the citizens of Montreal will feel the deepest interest in your future career, and will learn with the greatest gratification of your future happiness and prosperity.'

to so successful a conclusion, as well as the advantages accruing to the Dominion; but it was otherwise with the people of this country. During the entire time occupied by the expedition, the attention of England, as of the whole civilized world, was riveted upon the tremendous drama then enacting on the banks of the Rhine, and so it happened that the labours and endurance of the soldiers, and the capacity and triumphant success of the leader of the Expedition to the Red River, were passed over with scarce one word of comment and eulogium on the part of the Press.

A point that always tells with the British taxpayer should not be omitted in summing up the successful features of this expedition, and it was one that tended in no small measure to consign it to oblivion. It has been generally stated—and Captain Huyshe himself, in his published work, repeats the error—that the cost of the expedition was about £400,000. We have it from the authority of the commander, however, that the entire sum expended was only £80,000, and as, according to the original agreement, the mother country was to defray one quarter of the amount, it follows that John Bull was only mulcted to the extent of £20,000. We know what a commotion was made over the Abyssinian bill of £9,000,000, and for years after a committee of the House of Commons was engaged inquiring into the items of expenditure. Doubtless, therefore, John Bull, in the case under consideration, somewhat illogically considered that his rewards and approval should be meted out in proportion to the expenditure and to the disturbance of his peace of mind on the score of his contribution.

Colonel and Mrs. Wolseley proceeded to England in the *Scandinavian*, and on their arrival in London, in October, 1870, his appointment of Deputy Quartermaster-General in Canada having been abolished with the withdrawal of all

British troops from the Dominion, he was placed upon the half-pay list of his rank.

Wolseley was not backward in expressing his sense of the conduct of the troops committed to his charge, and, in his final despatch of the 26th of September, after enumerating the difficulties overcome, adds: 'We were launched out into a desert of trees and water, carrying everything we required with us, unable even to avail ourselves of the assistance of horses or other draught cattle. Once cut adrift from our base at Prince Arthur's Landing, until we had forced our way through the 600 miles of forests that separated us from the inhabited country at the Red River, we were beyond the reach of all assistance from the outside world, and had to rely upon our own exertions solely to carry us through. Except that we were armed with superior weapons, the expedition might have been one of classic times, so primitive was our mode of progression, and so little assisted were we by modern appliances.'*

The success of the expedition was chiefly due to the master-mind, who infused into his subordinates some of his indomitable resolution and will, and who only encountered unforeseen difficulties to overcome them. A striking instance of this fertility of resource was afforded by him when, on finding the impossibility of utilizing the road to Lake Shebandowan for the transport of boats, he sent them up the Kaministiquia River—a route that had been pronounced impracticable. 'Had not this step been taken,'

---

* His Royal Highness the Duke of Cambridge, in a general order to the officers and men of the Red River force, expressed 'his entire satisfaction at the manner in which they have performed the arduous duties which were entailed upon them, by a journey of above 600 miles through a country destitute of supplies, and which necessitated the heavy labour of carrying boats, guns, ammunition, stores, and provisions over no less than forty-seven portages. Seldom have troops been called upon to endure more continuous labour and fatigue, and never have officers and men behaved better or worked more cheerfully, during inclement weather and its consequent hardships, and the successful result of the expedition shows the perfect discipline and spirit of all engaged in it.'

writes General Lindsay, 'the Regulars certainly would not have returned this season.' No one outside the expeditionary force knew better than the Lieutenant-General commanding the troops in Canada, the nature and extent of the obstacles so triumphantly overcome, and he says, in his final despatch of the 11th of October: 'The mainspring of the whole movement was the Commander, Colonel Wolseley, who has shown throughout great professional ability. He has the faculty of organization and resource in difficulty. He has served in many campaigns with distinction, and in this expedition he has shown great aptitude for command. His advance upon Fort Garry itself was conducted with skill and prudence, and his proceedings there in abstaining from all interference with civil affairs himself, seem to me to have been eminently judicious. I hardly think it possible to overrate the advantage Her Majesty's Government and Canada have derived from the employment upon this delicate as well as arduous service, of an officer of Colonel Wolseley's attainments, character, and discretion. I have esteemed myself fortunate in having such an instrument in my hand to carry out your orders with respect to the Red River Expedition. I therefore confidently recommend Colonel Wolseley to the gracious favour of Her Majesty.' Wolseley, while at Fort Garry, had learned in a letter from his old chief and friend, the late Sir Hope Grant, that his name would be included among the Companions of the Bath in the next *Gazette*, a tardy acknowledgment for his many and eminent services in four great wars; and now, at the bidding of his Sovereign, he 'rose up' Sir Garnet Joseph Wolseley, K.C.M.G.

On the 1st of May, 1871, after having been six months on the half-pay list, Sir Garnet Wolseley was appointed Assistant Adjutant-General, Discipline Branch, at the Horse Guards. His staff-service hitherto had been all passed in the Quartermaster-General's Department, which, dealing with the movement and supply of troops, as well as with other multifarious staff duties, was, according to the old *régime*, the most important of the administrative branches of the service.

In the following August the Duke of Wellington invited officers to compete for a prize of £100, for the best Essay on 'The System of Field Manœuvres best adapted for enabling our troops to meet a continental army.' The competitors were required to send in their Essays before the 1st of March in the following year, and Colonel E. B. Hamley, C.B., Commandant of the Staff College, and the distinguished author of the 'Operations of War,' consented to act as judge. Under the signature of 'Ubique,' Sir Garnet Wolseley competed for this prize; but he was not sanguine of success, as, owing to his onerous office-work at the Horse Guards, he was only able to give to the composition of the Essay such intervals of time as were snatched from his official duties. But though this hastily-written production of his pen did not carry off the prize, it was regarded with so much favour by the judge, that it was published by the desire of the Duke of Wellington.

It speaks not a little for Sir Garnet Wolseley's energy and love of his profession that he, who had made his name as a practical and successful soldier, should care to compete with Staff College students and other officers who had abundance of leisure.* This competition also affords an instance of his generosity; for when selecting his staff for the

---

* At the request of the late Sir Hope Grant, commanding the Division at Aldershot, he delivered a lecture at the Camp on the Red River Expedition, which was never published, and the MS. was burnt at the Pantechnicon. Again overcoming his rooted dislike to lecturing, at the request of his old commander and friend, in January, 1873, he read a paper before a large military audience at Aldershot on 'Railways in time of War.' As this important subject could not be treated exhaustively in one lecture, it was his intention to have delivered a second, but this resolve he was unable to carry out, and the *brochure* has been printed in its incomplete form.

WOLSELEY AT THE AUTUMN MAN

Ashantee War, he offered the appointr
Secretary to his successful rival, Lieutena
R.A. (Instructor of Tactics and Organiz...
Military College, Sandhurst); and on learning that, acc..
to 'the rules of the service,' the officer filling this position
on a General's staff must not be under the rank of a
captain, he appointed him his private secretary, and in that
capacity the successful essayist conducted his chief's official
correspondence with the Colonial Office in Ashantee.

During the autumn manœuvres of 1871, in the neighbourhood of Aldershot and Woolmer Forest, Sir Garnet
Wolseley held the post of Chief of the Staff to Sir Charles
Staveley; and, in the following year, he served as Assistant
Adjutant-General on the staff of the Southern army,
commanded by Sir John Michel, who, remembering the
capacity Wolseley displayed in the China War and in
Canada, requested him to conduct the duties of that
department. Sir Garnet was a member of the Committee
for the Reorganization of the Army, presided over by
General McDougall, and also frequently wrote minutes on
various military questions at the request of the Duke of
Cambridge and Mr. Cardwell, then Secretary of State for
War.

But the name and services of Sir Garnet Wolseley would
have remained in comparative obscurity had not one of
those crises arisen which this country, with her vast colonies
and dependencies, has so frequently been called upon to
meet, and once again 'the hour brought forth the man.'
When we survey the situation of affairs on the Gold Coast
in the autumn of 1873, and the difficulties that appeared to
militate against a successful invasion of Ashantee, difficulties
as to climate, transport, and the limited time disposable for

* This able and gallant officer is closely identified with the fortunes of
Lord Wolseley, under whom he served in Ashantee, Cyprus, South Africa,
and Egypt.

military operations, we may recall the anxiety with which every patriotic heart regarded the success of the expedition at the time it was despatched from these shores. We may bring to mind the telegrams and despatches in which was recounted the story of how these obstacles were manfully met and overcome, how the invading host of savages was rolled back across the stream over which the foot of a white conqueror had never yet been set, and then how the final advance on Coomassie was made with a handful of men, battling ten to one against a fierce and cruel enemy, who knew every tree and track of the forests surrounding their capital. When we recall these achievements of that small and daily diminishing band, achievements which equal in disciplined valour the deeds of Pizarro and Cortez, who fought in open country against an effeminate foe, and in a comparatively healthy climate, we may congratulate ourselves on possessing such soldiers, and 'lay the flattering unction to our souls' that while British officers volunteer in hundreds to encounter the perils of battle and disease, and the army can provide such a General to lead them to victory, the country has no cause to lament the decay of the spirit that led our fathers to conquer India and colonize so large a portion of the globe.

CHAPTER VII.

THE ASHANTEE WAR.

Preparations for the War.—Arrival at Cape Coast.—Operations South of the Prah.—The Action at Essaman.—Defence of Abrakrampa, and Retreat of the Ashantees.—Illness of Sir Garnet Wolseley.—Preparations for crossing the Prah.—The Advance into Ashantee.—Battle of Amoaful.—Action at Ordahsu.—Capture of Coomassie.—Return to Cape Coast.—The Treaty of Fommanah.—Sir Garnet Wolseley returns to England.—The Welcome Home.

THE Government of Mr. Gladstone, like others that had preceded it, was averse from entering upon an Ashantee War,* owing to the unpopularity attaching to such expeditions in England, and the knowledge that, in the event of failure, it was morally certain an adverse vote in Parliament would place them on the Opposition benches. But, though long-suffering, it was impossible that any Government not utterly destitute of public spirit could tolerate the continued occupation of the Fantee Protectorate and the practical blockade of the British forts by the savage hordes of Koffee Kalkalli; and, at length, the receipt of the news of the action at Elmina on the 13th of June, when Colonel Festing repelled the enemy, induced the Ministry to resolve upon undertaking military operations. Sir Garnet Wolseley was named for the command, and the Government wisely resolved to centre in his hands the supreme direction of civil as well as military affairs. In

* A detailed account of the events preceding the war may be found in 'Fantee and Ashantee,' by Captains Huyshe and Henry Brackenbury, R.A., and in the 'History of the Ashantee War,' by the latter officer, to which we are greatly indebted in the preparation of the following pages.

accepting the honourable and arduous task of pacifying the Gold Coast, Sir Garnet stipulated that he should not be required to remain as Civil Governor after the close of military operations; but his only other request, that he should be given an adequate force of Europeans, was not then complied with.

The Colonial Office, having also decided upon organizing a subsidiary expedition to Coomassie from the Volta, under the general control of Sir Garnet Wolseley, Commander Glover, R.N.,* formerly Administrator at Lagos, was appointed to the command. The chief object sought to be attained was to cause a diversion in the rear of the Ashantee army, and thereby to draw them from the Protectorate; and sanguine people, who were ignorant of the resources of the Ashantee King, even hoped that it might obviate the necessity of the despatch of any European troops.

When it was known that the Government had resolved upon an expedition to Coomassie, the Press was filled, as at the time of the Abyssinian War, with dismal prognostications, and one 'experienced' gentleman, in answer to a letter from Sir Garnet Wolseley as to necessary articles of outfit, replied that he would 'strongly recommend that every officer should take out his coffin.' 'One who was there,' as usual at such times, also made his appearance in print, and advocated a certain course, which others, who had likewise passed 'half their lives on the Coast,' laughed to scorn; indeed, had the proposals suggested by this multiplicity of counsellors been followed, anything but wisdom would have been exhibited by the authorities, and

---

* It is a singular circumstance that this able and gallant officer, who was thus thrown into such close relations with Sir Garnet Wolseley, received a severe wound near Donabew, on the Irrawaddy, in the disastrous attack on Myat-toon's position by Captain Loch, R.N., which led to Sir John Cheape's successful expedition, when Ensign Wolseley was severely wounded leading the storming-party, as already detailed.

SIR GARNET WOLSELEY'S INFORMANTS. 243

one of the few follies in the military preparations, undertaken on the advice of old *habitués* of the Coast, was the supply of rails to be laid from Cape Coast to the Prah. Among other doleful prophecies, Sir Garnet was assured by an officer who professed himself intimate with the country, that 'every soldier would require a hammock, and every hammock would require six men to carry it;' and he was even given to understand that after crossing the Prah, he would find a fine open country, though, as a matter of fact, the whole route to Coomassie north of that river lies through a dense forest.

The intelligence of the appointment of Sir Garnet Wolseley to the command of the projected expedition was received by the country with approval, and he speedily gave tokens of the wisdom of the selection in the infinite care and patience he took in organizing the details of the undertaking, as far as was possible at this early stage, and in gaining information on all points from anyone who had it to impart. He listened to all the gloomy vaticinations of his numberless correspondents and visitors, and answered the former with courteous rejoinders of thanks, or dismissed the latter with the assured smile of one who had visited many climes and encountered too many difficulties to be overcome with the terrors of travellers' stories. Though fully alive to the extreme difficulties of the undertaking upon which he was embarked, his confidence in his own resources and in his ability to triumph over them never deserted him. Before leaving this country, he informed his friends that he would be back in England, if he returned at all, by the 1st of April, and he was even more than usually punctual, for he landed at Portsmouth on the 21st of March.

Sir Garnet Wolseley was inundated with hundreds of applications from officers desirous of serving on the pestilential West Coast, and many distinguished by their scientific attainments resigned important and lucrative staff appointments to accompany him. In these days of competitive examinations, when an officer cannot be promoted from the junior regimental grades without 'passing,' the language of Ensign Northerton, or the Captain, in Swift's 'Hamilton Bawn,' does not represent the views of the profession :

> 'A scholard, when just from his college broke loose,
> Can hardly tell how to cry *bo* to a *goose;*
> Your Noveds, and Blutarchs, and Omers, and stuff,
> 'Fore George, they don't signify this pinch of snuff.
>
> 'To give a young gentleman right education,
> The army's the only good school in the nation ;
> My schoolmaster called me a dunce and a fool,
> But at cuffs I was always the cock of the school.'

The difficulty with Sir Garnet Wolseley was to select from so many suitable candidates; but he quickly succeeded in gathering round him an efficient staff of young, active, and able officers.*

Having digested all the information he could gather—the most reliable being that culled from the pages of Bowdich and Dupuis, who had visited Coomassie half a century before, and from whose itineraries a map was prepared at the Topographical Department of the War Office, which was afterwards found to be curiously inaccurate—Sir Garnet Wolseley laid before Her Majesty's Ministers a memorandum embodying his views of the objects to be attained, and the means necessary for their accomplishment. In this memorandum he proposed that two battalions of European troops,

---

* These were : Colonel J. C. McNeill, V.C., C.M.G., Chief of the Staff; Major T. D. Baker, 18th Royal Irish, Assistant Adjutant-General ; Captain G. L. Huyshe, Rifle Brigade, Deputy Assistant Quartermaster-General ; Captain R. H. Buller, 60th Rifles, Deputy Assistant Adjutant-General ; Deputy Controller M. B. Irvine, C.M.G., in charge of the Control Department ; Captain H. Brackenbury, R.A., Assistant Military Secretary ; Captain Hugh McCalmont, 7th Hussars, and Lieutenant Hon. A. Charteris, Coldstream Guards, Aides-de-Camp ; Lieutenant J. F. Maurice, R.A., Private Secretary. Of the preceding, Colonel McNeill, Captains Huyshe, Buller, and McCalmont, and Mr. Irvine, had served in the Red River Expedition.

PREPARATIONS FOR THE EXPEDITION. 245

numbering each 29 officers and 654 men, with detachments of other branches of the service, all specially selected for the duty, should be despatched to Cape Coast in time to commence operations on the 1st of December. The Government, however, influenced by the condition of the Marines, who had already been despatched to the Coast, and by the statements of the sickness that would decimate European troops taking the field, decided that the troops should be held in readiness for service, but that the question of their despatch should be reserved until Sir Garnet had reported to the Government, after investigating the condition of affairs on the spot.

From this date until his departure, Sir Garnet was fully occupied in the personal supervision of the details connected with the organization, transport, and fitting out of the force, the first portion of which was to consist only of Native allies and West India troops. He drew up memoranda and indents for the supply of stores and *matériel* of war, and decided upon the uniform and equipments of the Special Service officers, and of the men of the European regiments warned for duty, the important considerations of utility and comfort being only considered.*

The time having arrived for his departure, Sir Garnet Wolseley was invested with the local rank of Major-General, and appointed Administrator of the Government of the Gold Coast, with instructions as to his mission in the double capacity from the Earl of Kimberley, Secretary of State for the Colonies, and Mr. Cardwell, Secretary of State for War. The latter read much like the injunction addressed of old by the Egyptian task-masters to the Israelites, to 'make

---

* Officers' kit was limited to fifty pounds, and their uniform, which was made of grey homespun, consisted of the Norfolk jacket, with pantaloons, gaiters, shooting-boots, and cork helmet with the Indian puggree; their arms were the Elcho sword-bayonet and revolver. The rank and file were dressed in smock-frocks, trousers, long boots and helmets, and were armed with short rifles and the Elcho sword-bayonet.

bricks without straw,' as beyond a handful of Marines, Wolseley was given no European troops to enforce the 'lasting treaty' insisted upon by Lord Kimberley. The remainder of his troops consisted of a detachment of Houssas, and a West India regiment; and as for the 'allies,' so pompously paraded by his lordship, they were a mere rabble, whose cowardice had already been proved. Moreover, the whole responsibility of ultimately employing European troops, which 'nothing but a conviction of necessity would induce Her Majesty's Government to sanction,' was cast upon the Commander, who, nevertheless, cheerfully took up the burden, confident in his own resources, and animated by a single-minded determination to do his duty to the best of his ability.

On the 12th of September Sir Garnet Wolseley sailed from Liverpool for the Gold Coast, on board the West African steamship *Ambriz*, which also carried 27 Special Service officers. He had always been singularly unfortunate in the ships that had carried him to the scenes of his labours, and the *Ambriz* was to be no exception. She had been hastily prepared for sea, was badly found, had insufficient accommodation, and moreover, reeked with foul smells arising from bilge-water. The ship touched at Madeira and Sierra Leone, where Sir Garnet Wolseley landed on the 27th of September, and assumed the command of the land forces in the West African Settlements. As Sir Garnet had decided to raise two regiments of natives, who were to be placed under the command, respectively, of Colonel Evelyn Wood, V.C., 90th Regiment, and Major Baker Russell,* 13th Hussars, he despatched Captain Furze and Lieutenant Saunders to enlist men at Bathurst, on the Gambia, and Lieutenant Gordon was also left behind

* These two Special Service officers, who are so identified with Sir Garnet Wolseley, were now associated with him for the first time.

at Sierra Leone. The *Ambriz* touched at Monrovia, in the Republic of Liberia, and landing Commissary O'Connor at Cape Palmas with instructions to enlist Kroomen as carriers, cast anchor, on the 2nd of October, off Cape Coast, with its never-ending sound of :
> 'The league-long roller thundering on the reef.'

On the following day Sir Garnet landed under the usual salutes, the paucity of troops being manifested by the fact that the guard of honour of West India soldiers, after presenting arms at the landing-place, proceeded at the double, like stage 'supers,' to perform the same duty at Government House. On his arrival took place the ceremony of investiture, which simply consisted of the reading of his letter of appointment, followed by the usual swearing-in in the presence of the Chief Justice. On making inquiries, Sir Garnet found that the settlement was even more denuded of troops than he had expected, as Captain Glover, on his way to Accra, had taken with him the trained Houssa police. Thus the entire force of disciplined troops at his disposal, scattered between Cape Coast, Elmina, Secondee, Dixcove, Axim, Napoleon, Abbaye and Accroful, consisted of 700 men of the 2nd West India Regiment, of whom only 400 were available for service in the field, and scarcely 100 for the defence of Cape Coast itself. Besides these, Captain Thompson, of the Queen's Bays, who had been organizing the Fantee police, reported 10 men as the number really available for general duty ! There, were, also, only 13 officers on duty with the 2nd West India Regiment, and Sir Garnet Wolseley, who, while at Sierra Leone, had written requesting the Government to send him 12 additional Special Service officers, now urgently repeated his demand. Notwithstanding this paucity of officers and men, he took an encouraging view of affairs, and wrote to the Home Government on the 10th of October, that, with the fleet at his back, from which to draw in the event of an emergency, he was confident he could repulse any attack of the enemy. That such might be made at any moment, appeared no unlikely contingency, for the Ashantee army, nearly 40,000 strong, under their most redoubtable General, Amanquatia, was known to be encamped at Mampon and Jooquah, distant only a few hours' march, while well authenticated reports stated that large reinforcements had marched from Coomassie on their way to the Fantee territory. It is not surprising, therefore, that, though Sir Garnet Wolseley preserved his equanimity and spoke confidently to all around him, Cape Coast was in a state of panic, and the advent of a 'fighting' Governor was hailed with joy by the population.

In order to inspire confidence, and induce the Fantees to exert themselves, the General, on the day succeeding his landing, held a 'palaver' or durbar of the 'kings' of the Protectorate (as the petty chiefs of the West Coast are called), which took place in a large marquee pitched in front of Government House. The 'kings' began to arrive soon after three o'clock, and with the gravity becoming their exalted station, and the solemnity of the occasion, seated themselves on stools, carried by their attendants, some of whom also bore huge umbrellas, which denote the regal state among these African communities, while others carried swords and canes, and beat tomtoms to herald the approach of their potent masters.

On his arrival in the tent, he took his station upon a small raised daïs at one end, the British officers standing behind and around him. The kings and chiefs were now ushered in, and came crowding and jostling along like a crowd of schoolboys, or the members of the House of Commons when called to the bar of the Lords to hear the speech from the throne. Sir Garnet stood, while the kings

WOLSELEY HOLDS A PALAVER. 249

in succession were introduced to him, and received the conventional shake of the hand from the Queen's Representative. The presentations over, Sir Garnet, still standing, proceeded to address the crowded throng in an inspiriting address; each sentence, as it fell from his lips, being translated into Fantee by a German interpreter.

At the termination of his speech, which was received with respectful and eager attention, the present of gin, customary on these occasions, was made to each of the princes and chiefs, and, after a second hand-shaking, they retired to consult together, with instructions to return on the 6th. At this second meeting, which was conducted under the same formalities, they expressed their willingness to comply with the terms offered, and their readiness to collect their men, but with the indolence and cowardice that characterized their conduct throughout the ensuing operations, they delayed, from day to day, their departure from Cape Coast. These indolent Fantees viewed life like Tennyson's 'mild-eyed melancholy Lotos-eaters,' who said :

> 'Let us alone ; Time driveth onward fast,
> And in a little while our lips are dumb.
> Let us alone. What is that will last?'

At the request of the kings, the General appointed officers as Special Commissioners, with detailed instructions, to assist them in collecting their men. Several kings not having presented themselves, Sir Garnet wrote, requesting them to assemble their men at Dunquah.

Almost daily interviews took place between Sir Garnet and some of these chiefs, whom he strove to influence by considerations of profit, as 'honour' and 'patriotism' were unknown words in their vocabulary, to collect their men and fight the Ashantees. Bethinking him of the prevailing custom in this strange land, where the weaker sex belabour any men who remain behind when the tribes turn out for war, the General held a palaver of the ladies of Cape Coast at Government House. They attended the unusual summons in great numbers, all with elaborate *coiffures*, and decked out in gold rings and fastenings for the ample shawl which formed the sole covering of most of them; and the interview ended in their agreeing to take solemn vengeance against any faint-hearted males who failed to respond with alacrity to Sir Garnet's summons.

Nothing whatever had been done to prepare for the expedition, but the General and his staff soon supplied all deficiencies by their energy. The landing and storage of supplies first engaged the attention of Sir Garnet; and Cape Coast and Elmina, respectively under the command of Colonels F. Festing, of the Royal Marines, and Evelyn Wood, V.C., were placed in a position to resist any attacks of the enemy. Suitable sanitary arrangements were set on foot in Cape Coast, and a survey department was organized, under Captain Huyshe, who left headquarters for the advanced post, and made sketches of the road and of the positions of Accroful and Dunquah. His assistant, Lieutenant Hart, was engaged on the survey of the country about Cape Coast, and other officers surveyed the country between Elmina, Abbaye, and the Sweet River in the direction of Cape Coast. Within a few days of Wolseley's arrival, the entrenched outposts established at Napoleon, Abbaye, and Accroful (about fifteen miles northeast of Cape Coast), which were garrisoned by detachments of the West India troops, and those at Yancoomassie and Dunquah, held by Lieutenant Gordon and his armed police and volunteers, were all placed in postal communication with each other, and furnished with a week's supplies.

As, in order to inspire confidence, it was above all things necessary to act on the offensive, the preparations hitherto made only having for their object the defence of the British posts, the General instructed Captain R. H. Buller, 60th Rifles, in charge of the Intelligence Department, to gather all the information attainable regarding the positions and strength of the enemy. It had been Sir Garnet's earnest desire, since he landed on the Gold Coast, to prove to the people that the Ashantees were not invincible in the bush, a proposition which had come to be regarded as an article of faith in West Africa, and was even held by some people in England, who, while they allowed the superiority of European soldiers in the open, and were not prepared to deny that our officers could, under the same conditions, successfully lead native auxiliaries, yet would shake their heads when anyone argued that even British soldiers could fight and overcome, in the recesses of their own forests, the most dreaded of all the tribes of African warriors. Sir Garnet Wolseley resolved to take advantage of the first opportunity of showing what even Native troops could do in the bush, when properly handled and led, nor was this opportunity long in offering itself.

Learning that the Ashantees were drawing most of their supplies of food from Elmina, and the neighbouring sea-coast villages of Amquana, Akimfoo, and Ampenee, whence the supplies were conveyed inland through the village of Essaman, about four miles to the north-west of Elmina, the General directed Colonel Wood to write to the chiefs of these places, summoning them before him to appear at Elmina. The chiefs immediately sent off a messenger to the Ashantee camp at Mampon, asking for instructions, and were told to refuse compliance, as the Ashantees would protect them, and the white men, though brave in the open, dared not venture into the bush. Accordingly the Akimfoo chief alone came into Elmina. No answer was vouchsafed from Ampenee, and the Amquana chief sent word, 'I have small-pox to-day, but will come to-morrow,' though, instead of appearing, he betook himself to Mampon. Finally the chief of Essaman replied insolently, 'Come and fetch me; white man no dare go bush.' Sir Garnet resolved to undeceive these people, and as, to insure success, secrecy was essential, he only took into his confidence Colonels McNeill and Wood, Dr. Home, principal medical officer, and Mr. Irvine.

Much, indeed everything, depended on a first success, which would instil confidence into Europeans and Natives alike, and he now made use of a *ruse*, mention of which may be found in his 'Soldier's Pocket Book.' In that little work, speaking of newspaper correspondents, whom he stigmatizes as 'those newly invented curses to armies, who eat the rations of fighting men, and do no work at all,' he propounds a method by which they may be made of great utility in forwarding the plans of a General in the field. 'These gentlemen,' he says (p. 225), 'pandering to the public craze for news, render concealment most difficult; but this very ardour for information a General can turn to account, by spreading false news among the gentlemen of the Press, and thus use them as a medium by which to deceive the enemy.' Sir Garnet now proceeded to put into practice this *ruse*, and announced at breakfast on the 12th of October that he had received bad news from Addah on the Volta, where Captain Glover was in danger of being surrounded, and that he intended to proceed to his aid; and immediately proceeded to Elmina in the *Bittern*, with 140 Houssas, who had just been recruited at Lagos, a report having been allowed to spread that Colonel Wood expected to be attacked. The Houssas were drilled in the use of the Enfield during the two hours' voyage, and were landed at Elmina, where Sir Garnet had a conference with Colonel Wood, and, having imparted his plans to him

THE ACTION AT ESSAMAN.   253

under the seal of secrecy, returned to Cape Coast the same evening.

But as he could not take the field with the limited force at his disposal, he determined to solicit the assistance of Captain Fremantle, the senior naval officer, and, on the 12th of October, proceeded on board the *Barracouta*, ostensibly to return that officer's official visit. Captain Fremantle, having received instructions from the Admiralty which partially freed him from the restrictions as to the employment of his sailors and Marines, imposed by Commodore Commerell before his departure for the Cape, promised the General his hearty co-operation. The same day 250 labourers and the necessary stores and cots proceeded to Elmina, and Captain Peile, of the *Simoom*, landed with 40 seamen as a guard for Cape Coast. All the arrangements being made ostensibly to proceed to the aid of Captain Glover, on the evening of Monday, the 13th of October, the detachment of the 2nd West India Regiment at Cape Coast was embarked on board the *Decoy* (an appropriate name), expecting to sail for Accra; and at ten p.m. Sir Garnet and his staff embarked on board the *Barracouta*, in which were also 150 men of the Royal Marines. The two ships started about one a.m. on the following morning, and, two hours later, the General and Captain Fremantle landed at Elmina in the *Barracouta's* gig, and by half-past four the advanced guard moved off, the main body following soon after five. On their arrival at Elmina, Colonel Wood, who had posted a cordon of police round the town so as to prevent all egress, was placed in command of the column, the General accompanying it in order to show the Natives that, unlike preceding Governors, he held also the military command.

The force, accompanied by two chiefs and 20 guides, consisted of 20 Marine Artillerymen, with 1 7-pounder gun and a rocket tube, 129 Marines, 29 seamen, 205 of the 2nd West India Regiment, and 126 Houssas, besides 300 labourers.

The track from Elmina led through a swamp, knee-deep for almost eighty yards, and, later, through a very narrow bush-path, with high thick jungle on each side. After a halt, about 2,000 yards from a hill behind which Essaman was said to be, the Houssas were met by the enemy's scouts, and when Sir Garnet arrived at the front, he found them firing wildly into the bush, which was very dense.

Meanwhile, Captain Buller passed down the path leading to Essaman, and advanced into the village, where a number of armed men were collected. Captain Fremantle brought the gun and rockets up to the path and opened fire, and Colonel McNeill took some men into the bush to the left, and began working round the flank of the village. A heavy fire was opened by the enemy, and Captain Fremantle was shot through the arm, a slug penetrated the leather case of Captain Buller's prismatic compass, breaking the vane, and Colonel McNeill[*] was badly wounded in the arm. In order to clear the dense bush on the right, the General sent Captain Crease with some Marines into the bush, and while that officer cleared the hill on the right and protected the flank with some of his men, Captain Brackenbury and Lieutenant Charteris took the remainder into the village, and pushing on to the far end, posted a guard. Meanwhile the Ashantees employed their usual flanking tactics, and tried to turn the left of the West India Regiment, still on the brow of the hill; but the attack was repulsed, and the troops advanced on the village by a road cut by the axemen on the left.

At half-past eight the assembly was sounded, and the

[*] Colonel (now Major-General Sir J. C.) McNeill's wound was very severe, and necessitated his return to England. His loss was keenly felt by Wolseley, who applied for the services, as Chief of the Staff, of Colonel (now Major-General Sir G. R.) Greaves.

troops having breakfasted, marched off for Amquana, the heat being terrific. Amquana, like Essaman, was fired, and the column halted on the beach, the wounded being sent back to Elmina under an escort. At two o'clock a detachment of 150 West Indians, the Houssas, 12 blue jackets, with rockets, and 20 Marines, marched for Akimfoo along the beach, and met, half-way, the men of H.M. ships *Argus* and *Decoy*. Akimfoo was reached at 3.30, and burnt, and also Ampenee, half a mile further on.

The enemy opened fire from the bush behind the village, to which the Marines and blue jackets replied; but as it was too late to attack, Sir Garnet ordered the assembly to be sounded, and embarked on board H.M.S. *Decoy*, which steamed for Cape Coast Castle. The troops remained to cover the embarkation of the men of the *Argus* and *Decoy*, and then marched off, and picking up the Marines at Amquana, reached Elmina at eight p.m.

A more arduous day's work officers and men have seldom performed. The General, with his staff and the white troops, had been up all night, and had marched over twenty-one miles under a tropical sun, through a dense bush which prevented the circulation of a breath of air, while there were no forest trees to give shade. Yet, strange to say, there were only two cases of sunstroke; and Dr. Home reported : 'The occasion has shown that Europeans are quite equal to one very hard day's work in the bush, and that marches of half the distance could be easily borne by them.'

The moral effect created by this success was immense, and, in Sir Garnet's opinion, it was the turning-point of the war. It broke the spell regarding the invincibility of the Ashantees in the bush, which had not only enchained the cowardly inhabitants of the Protectorate, but was even tacitly acknowledged by those pessimists who are to be found among all communities: and, while it instilled confidence into every class, and taught officers and men that, when properly commanded and led, European troops could successfully compete with superior numbers in the densest bush, it also struck a terror into the hearts of our enemies, and shook the confidence of the Elmina people in their boastful allies from Coomassie.

The practical effect of this victory was apparent. On the following day, Amanquatia, the Commander-in-Chief, then at Mampon, called a meeting of chiefs, who resolved on retreat, though shortly before they had declared they would never return to Ashantee until they had driven away the Europeans.*

On the day Sir Garnet Wolseley started on his expedition to Essaman, he had penned two most important missives. One was a summons to Koffee Kalkalli, in which he required that potentate to withdraw all his troops into his own territory north of the Prah, by the 12th of November, to surrender all British subjects in his hands, and give guarantees for the payment of compensation for losses, failing which he was 'to expect the full punishment his deeds have merited.'

To this Amanquatia replied, by claiming the people of Assin, Denkera, Akim, and Wassaw, as vassals of his master (though forty years before the then King of Ashantee had, by treaty, renounced all claim to their allegiance), ending

* The experience gained by this hard day's fighting taught a valuable lesson to Sir Garnet Wolseley, and he says in his Report to the War Office: 'I have been shown how little reliance can be placed on even the best Native troops in this bush-fighting, where it is impossible to keep them under the immediate control of European officers. One point stands prominently from the experience of this day, viz., that for fighting in the African bush a very exceptionally large proportion of officers is required. Owing to the dense cover, an officer can only exercise control over the men close to him, and for this kind of work there should be, at least, one officer to every twenty men. A small body of very highly disciplined troops, well supplied with selected officers, would be of far greater service for warfare in this country than a much larger number detailed for service in the ordinary tour of duty.'

with the amiable asseveration, 'There is no quarrel with you. I send my love to you.'

The second letter Sir Garnet wrote, was to the Secretary of State for War, calling for the immediate despatch to the Gold Coast of the European troops,* whom, before his departure, he had requested might be held in readiness to join him. In this lengthy and able letter he gave an exhaustive exposition of the reasons that influenced him in taking a step deprecated by the War Office and Ministry; and, after adducing the experiences of his predecessors, and the reasons that militated against success on their part, he insisted on the 'possibility of undertaking a march of limited duration into the interior,' under such conditions as he proposed, and expressed his belief that 'the existing conditions of health of the troops on the station, show that such an expedition does not involve great risk.' He then, after adducing statistical proof that 'while sickness is diminishing throughout the whole Coast, it is far less in the camps inland than in the barracks on the Coast,' concluded with the opinions expressed in the report of Dr. Home, his responsible adviser on sanitary questions.

Though this letter was written the day before the action at Essaman, owing to no homeward-bound steamer calling at Cape Coast between the 9th and 27th of October, it was not forwarded to England until the latter date; by the same mail Sir Garnet despatched a second letter, dated 24th of October, applying for an additional battalion of European troops. Meanwhile, small detachments of recruits for Russell's and Wood's Native regiments continued to arrive, and ultimately the former was composed of six companies, consisting respectively of Houssas, Sierra Leones, Mumfords, Winnebahs, Opobos, and Annamaboes; and Wood's Regi-

* Two battalions of Infantry, 650 men each; detachment Royal Artillery, 60; detachment Royal Engineers, 40; Administrative Services, 50; total, 1,450 men.

ment, of four companies, viz., Cape Coast Volunteers, Elminas, Kossoos, and Bonnys. The raw material thus assembled seemed as unpromising as any ever raised for active service; but by dint of hard and unceasing toil, Russell and his officers at Cape Coast, and Wood and his coadjutors at Elmina, succeeded in instilling into the puzzled heads of their recruits a knowledge of the elements of drill, and eventually they proved serviceable and reliable auxiliaries. Captain Rait, R.A., assisted by Lieutenant Eardley Wilmot, had almost a harder task in making good gunners of the Houssas; but this difficulty also was surmounted by a combination of energy, tact, and hard work.

Very unsatisfactory were the results as regards the assembly at Dunquah, by the 20th of October, of the contingents from the Fantee and allied kings. If zeal and energy on the part of the officers accredited to these chiefs, or the employment of every argument addressed to their patriotism, an unknown sentiment in the Fantee breast, or their cupidity, which found a ready echo in every heart, could have moved these cowardly chiefs and people—whom it would seem as if the economy of nature had intended to be slaves, so dead are they to every manly sentiment—then some 50,000 fighting men, drawn from the entire confederacy, would have rallied round the standard of the British General to expel the invader from their soil. Far different was the result. The kings sent their men in driblets to Dunquah, where the entire number only consisted of 500 men and about 350 at Mansu, Napoleon, and Abrakrampa; the King of Annamaboe, the only one who displayed courage in the field, after much pressure from Captain Godwin, sent 287 men to Dunquah by the last week in October. Such were 'our allies,' and such the burlesque soldiers with whom Sir Garnet Wolseley, in conjunction with a few hundred Native levies, was expected to engage the disciplined and homogeneous

Ashantee hosts, and advance upon the capital of Koffee Kalkalli.

While the Control Department were busy landing stores, and sending them to the front, the Engineers were engaged making the road to Mansu. The outposts at Napoleon and Abbaye, and at Mansu, Dunquah and Accroful, on the main road, were fortified and garrisoned, and Abrakrampa, a town of 300 houses, was placed in a condition of defence.

On the 25th of October, in consequence of reliable information that Amanquatia had broken up his camp at Mampon, and intended retreating across the Prah in the direction of Dunquah, Sir Garnet Wolseley took immediate steps to harass the retreating army, and strengthen the force on the road, while the officers commanding the outposts on the main road and at Abrakrampa, were warned of the new turn affairs had taken. On the following day, Colonel Wood made a reconnoissance from Elmina, and the General marched to Assayboo, ten miles from Cape Coast, at the junction of the roads to Abrakrampa and Dunquah, with a force of 250 Marines and blue-jackets, under Captain Fremantle, preceded by 100 of Russell's Regiment, under their Commander, who was directed to select a site for their encampment. After a fearfully hot march, Assayboo was reached about nine p.m., and the men bivouacked for the night; the two small tents with the force being occupied, one by Captain Fremantle and some of his officers, and the other by the General and his staff—Charteris, Brackenbury, Baker, and Irvine.

In this connection, as the Americans would say, an amusing anecdote was told us, illustrative of Wolseley's *bonhomie* and kind thought for his officers. During his temporary absence one night on board the ship at Cape Coast, two gentlemen, holding high positions on his staff, slept in his room, and one of the General's servants, desirous of currying favour with his master, went off to the ship and reported the circumstance, adding that the matutinal tubs had been left unemptied and the beds unmade. 'Of course you cleared up my room?' asked the General. 'No, sir,' was the reply. 'Then,' added the former to the crestfallen domestic, in a tone which caused him to beat a hasty retreat, 'go ashore, and do so at once.' But *revenons à nos moutons.*

On receipt of reports that the Ashantees were moving past Abrakrampa, Sir Garnet sent orders to Colonel Festing at Dunquah to march in the direction of Iscabio, while he himself decided on moving on Abrakrampa, where he hoped to be able to attack the flank of some one of the bodies of Ashantees moving from Mampon towards Dunquah.

Colonel Festing, accordingly, marched early on the 27th of October, with 12 officers and 700 men, and surprised the enemy, who, to the number of about 5,000, were encamped about a mile from the village of Iscabio, and, having destroyed their camp, returned to Dunquah, his casualties being 5 men killed, and 5 officers, including himself and Captain Godwin, and 42 men wounded. The General proceeded on the same day to Abrakrampa, but the fatigued condition of the men prevented his attempting the march to Assanchi, 6 miles distant; on the following day he advanced with his whole force on that point, hoping that Colonel Festing, of whose success he was ignorant, would co-operate from Dunquah. But on his arrival at Assanchi, after a fatiguing march through a dense forest, or along a road nearly knee-deep in water, the enemy were found to have evacuated their camp; and, as there was no sign of Colonel Festing's column, the General returned to Abrakrampa, officers and men being thoroughly exhausted with the intense heat. As the path, owing to the overhanging creepers and branches, prevented the use of a hammock, Sir Garnet was obliged to walk almost the entire distance

OPERATIONS AGAINST THE ENEMY. 261

of twelve miles, and suffered much from his wounded leg, which still continued to trouble him if over-exerted. The Marines, after this march, had 29 men on the sick-list, suffering chiefly from foot-sores and weakness, due to exposure to the sun.

Sir Garnet returned to Cape Coast on the 29th of October, with the Marines, and blue-jackets, and issued a Proclamation to the native chiefs and people, apprising them of recent events, and urging them to exert themselves and strike the retreating enemy. But the call to arms fell upon dulled ears and slavish hearts, and there was no response to its stirring appeals. There can be no doubt that, owing to the want of one or two European regiments during this critical period of the campaign, a splendid opportunity was lost for striking a decisive blow and putting an end to the war.

As the only course the General could adopt, in view of his weakness, was to harass the retreating columns of the enemy, the garrisons at Abrakrampa and Dunquah were strengthened. At this date Colonel Festing had under his orders at Dunquah 100 of the 2nd West India Regiment, 2 guns, and 1,400 Native allies; and Major Russell, at Abrakrampa, 8 officers and 890 men, of whom 60 were sailors and Marines, and 100 Houssas. The headquarters of the 2nd West, under Colonel Webber, left Cape Coast for Mansu, thus denuding the seat of Government of troops, the military duties being performed by the armed police. On the same day (3rd of November) under orders from the General, reconnoissances in force were made from Beulah, Dunquah, and Abrakrampa, when the Native levies exhibited their wonted cowardice, and the army sustained a sad loss in the death of a gallant young officer, Lieutenant Eardley Wilmot, R.A.

On the 4th of November the Ashantees made their long-threatened attack upon Abrakrampa, and it was of a very determined character. On receipt of a despatch from Major Russell, Sir Garnet made the necessary dispositions for marching to his assistance, and sent orders by special runners to the officers commanding at Beulah, Assayboo, Accroful, and Dunquah, requesting them to act in co-operation. By nine a.m. on the 6th he was on his way with 22 officers and 303 seamen and Marines, and some rockets, under Captain Rait, R.A.

The march was a most distressing one to the men, the entire road between Cape Coast and Assayboo, a distance of ten miles, being almost destitute of shade, and more than 100 men fell out during the march, though only 32 were unable to rejoin during the four hours' halt at Assayboo. The General was eager to proceed, as he received here a despatch from Russell of that morning's date, reporting that the enemy were said to be advancing, and, about four o'clock, the march was continued by way of Butteyan instead of the main road, the garrison of Assayboo, consisting of 50 Marines, heading the column, which now numbered only 141 of the detachment landed in the morning. On the way they were joined by a party of the 2nd West Indians, and some Abrahs, under their king, by whom they were guided into Abrakrampa. On their arrival at the clearing in front of the position, Major Russell and other officers came out to receive the General, and the place was entered without any opposition from the enemy. Desultory firing continued during the night, but no further attack was made by the Ashantees, who were employed cutting the bush close to the Assayboo road. Had the enemy exhibited any enterprise they might easily have stormed the position, as the cover under which the garrison had lain for forty-eight hours was of the slightest description, but they feared to cross the cleared ground, some 40 to 100 yards in width.

On the 7th, Colonel Wood marched from Beulah with the Fantee levies, and Sir Garnet sent about 1,000 of them into the bush, when they exhibited a ludicrous spectacle of poltroonery. A crowd of officers assembled to watch these warriors creeping out like whipped hounds under the leadership of their chief, Attah, himself a despicable coward. Sir Garnet had addressed the Fantees when starting, to the effect that their conduct on the previous day had filled him with displeasure, and that he would give them this last chance of showing themselves fit to bear arms. To this they replied in their usual vein of bravado; but when it came to the point, hundreds of them lay down at the edge of the bush, which no persuasion or threat could induce them to enter. The General would not allow his officers to enter the forest with such curs, and this burlesque on the operations of war was brought to a conclusion by their charging them with sticks and umbrellas.

Sir Garnet sent in pursuit of the retreating Ashantees those of the Native levies that could be collected together; but, on approaching the Ashantee rear, they showed the usual cowardice, and fled in panic flight when there was no pursuit.* On the same day (8th of November), the General returned to Cape Coast, which he entered in a sort of impromptu triumphal procession, the state chair of Aman-

* In his despatch to Mr. Cardwell, Sir Garnet says of these levies, who were reported to him as being 'infinitely worse than useless': 'You will thus see that even the enemy's retreat cannot instil courage into these fainthearted Natives, and that they can neither be counted on to insure a victory nor to complete a defeat. They were ordered to pursue the enemy, remain in the field, and harass him in his retreat. The road was strewn with the *débris* of the retreating army; bodies of murdered slaves lay along the route; many prisoners were captured, the enemy's fire was silenced, and yet, such is the cowardice of these people, that they had to be driven into action, and after a success they became a panic-stricken and disorderly rabble. Still, hopeless as the task appears of stirring these tribes to any exertions, I shall not give up my efforts. Orders have been issued for the renewal of the offensive movement, and for the use of every possible method to keep the men at the front.'

quatia, together with a sacred cock, war-drums,* and other *spolia opima*, being carried in front of him, in order to impress the Natives and inflame their minds with a proper sense of patriotic ardour. Before leaving Abrakrampa, the General issued orders to Major Russell as well as to Colonels Festing and Webber, at Dunquah and Mansu, to harass the retreating columns of the enemy.

A lull now occurred in the operations, and it was fortunate indeed it happened just at this time, for the Director of the complicated engine of war and politics on the Gold Coast was stricken to the earth powerless as an infant. The ally that had suddenly arisen to fight on the side of the Ashantees was more potent for evil than even the cowardly Natives with whom the General was expected to effect their expulsion, and his plans, so far as he himself could have carried them out, came perilously near being frustrated. On the morning Sir Garnet quitted Abrakrampa, he felt the heavy hand of the African fever—induced chiefly by the trying exposure to the sun during the march up country —weighing him down with a feeling of lassitude and feebleness he in vain struggled to combat, and, on his arrival at Cape Coast, the fever took a turn that alarmed his medical advisers. He was first removed to the hospital hut at Connor's Hill, but the heat there was so intense that Dr. Home removed him to the hospital ship *Simoom*. The fever ran very high and caused great anxiety to Dr. Home,† who, though ill himself, came off to the *Simoom* three times

---

* These Ashantee war-drums were presented by the Headquarter Staff to the Royal United Service Institution, and have been deposited in the Museum, where they may be seen by visitors.

† Dr. Home wrote to us of this attack: 'Sir Garnet's illness was an attack of "ardent fever," caused by exposure to the sun on the march to the relief of the beleaguered village of Abrakrampa, on the 6th of November, and in the subsequent operations in connection with the affair. He had suffered from a degree of sunstroke, or insolation, in Burmah, and, as you probably know, a person who has once so suffered is ever after very susceptible of the sun. Sir Garnet's illness was very severe—dangerous—and Cape Coast was very anxious and troubled indeed until his symptoms mitigated.'

in the twenty-four hours to visit his patient, for whom he entertained the feelings of an old brother officer and friend. Not less devoted was Lieutenant Maurice, who nursed his chief day and night, and never quitted his side or took off his clothes for nearly a fortnight.

For two or three days a successful termination to the expedition appeared to be imperilled, as the British General lay sick of this fever, which has proved fatal to so many of our best and bravest before and since this war; and an Ashantee Cassius might have said of him, as did his Roman namesake of Cæsar:

> 'When the fever fit was on him I did mark
> How he did shake; 'tis true, this god did shake;
> And that same eye, whose bend doth awe the world,
> Did lose its lustre; I did hear him groan;
> "Aye," and that tongue of his, that bade the Romans
> Mark him, and write his speeches in their books,
> "Alas!" it cried: "Give me some drink, Titinius."'

On the 21st of November, Sir Garnet was sufficiently recovered to return to Government House, and his advent was hailed with joy by all classes, over whom a gloom had been cast by his enforced withdrawal.

At this time sickness had wrought considerable havoc among the Special Service officers who had come out in the *Ambriz*. On the 15th of November, within six weeks of their arrival in this country, of the staff of 10, 7 had been rendered ineffective by sickness; and, six days later, out of 64 officers 29 had suffered, of whom 7 were invalided and 1 died. The proportion among the seamen and Marines serving on shore was considerably less, only 18 per cent. being on the sick-list. The hospital-ship *Simoom* had become so saturated with malarious fever, owing to overcrowding and her unsuitability for the purpose, that she was little better than a plague-ship. She was, therefore, sent to St. Helena with 8 invalid officers.

Colonel Wood proceeded on the 22nd of November to

Mansu, to assume command of the advanced guard in the operations south of the Prah; and, on the 27th, pushed on to Faysowah with a small Native force, and came into collision with the Ashantees, but was forced to retreat, as the levies showed their usual unsteadiness. On the 5th of December the Ashantees crossed the Prah; and, on his scouts pushing on, the main Prahsu road was found strewed with their dead and dying, disease and starvation having decimated their ranks more than the sword. It is estimated that, of the 40,000 warriors who originally invaded the Protectorate, at least one-half perished. The remainder of Amanquatia's army was disbanded at Coomassie on the 22nd of December, and thus disastrously ended what we hope may be regarded in history as 'the last Ashantee invasion.'*

Renewed vigour was now displayed by all branches of the force, and while the transport of supplies and ammunition to the front engaged the attention of the Control, the medical department were busy establishing hospitals at Prahsu, Mansu, and Cape Coast, and the Engineers were engaged making the road to the Prah, and bridging the intervening streams. Owing to the exertions of Major Home, Lieutenant Bell, and their Sappers, the whole road from Cape Coast to Prahsu was in good order by Christmas

* In reporting to the Secretary for War the retreat across the Prah of the Ashantee Army, Sir Garnet Wolseley wrote on the 15th of December: 'The first phase of this war has thus been brought to a most satisfactory conclusion, without the assistance of any English troops, except the few Marines and the few available blue-jackets whom I found here on my arrival on the 2nd of October last. I submit that the happy change which has been since that time effected has been accomplished by the untiring exertions of the few carefully selected staff and Special Service officers who landed with me here at the beginning of October. In the second phase of this war, when the campaign is opened in Ashantee territory beyond the Prah, by a brigade of English troops, the operations may be more brilliant than those which have resulted in forcing the enemy to retreat into their own country; but I feel assured that they cannot entail upon those engaged in them the hard work, exposure, and privations that have been so cheerfully endured for the last two and a half months by the small band of officers of whom I speak.'

TRANSPORT DIFFICULTIES.

Day, when no less than 237 bridges of various sorts had been constructed. The difficulty of constructing bridges for crossing these small rivers and canals, and, indeed, of felling the timber across the tracks, was greatly increased by the size and hardness of the wood. Some of the trunks were four or five feet in diameter, and being of mahogany and iron-wood, the work of removing them was very heavy. The Engineers also cleared the camping-grounds,* in each of which huts† were constructed to contain 400 European soldiers, besides the huts of the garrison and of the Control and Hospital Departments.

No means were overlooked to insure the health and comfort of the European troops; and the General himself inquired into every detail of the Report‡ made to him on these vital questions by the principal sanitary officer, Surgeon-Major Gore, who, as well as Dr. Home, was invalided before the march commenced.

As the question of transport was likely to prove the chief difficulty in this expedition, the General, as soon as he landed from the *Simoom*, after his severe illness, turned his attention to it, and sought to grapple with the obstacles that lay in the way of organizing an efficient body of carriers. It may safely be said that these were greater than perhaps any Commander had before encountered, for here there was no

* These were : Inquabim, 7 miles from Cape Coast ; Accroful, 13¾ miles ; Yancoomassie Fanti, 24¼ miles ; Mansu, 35¾ miles ; Sutah, 46 miles ; Yancoomassie Assin, 58¼ miles ; Barraco, 67¼ miles ; and Prahsu, 73¾ miles.

† The huts each held 50 men, and were built with wattled sides and thatched with palm-leaves ; they were sixty by seventeen feet, with a height of five feet to the eaves. On each side was a raised guard-bed, made either of split bamboos or palm-stalks, for the men to sleep upon.

‡ The supply of rations was most liberal, and at daybreak, before starting on the march (the pace of which was even regulated), the troops partook of cocoa, biscuit, and quinine, and frequent halts were ordered, so as not to cause undue fatigue. Detailed arrangements were also made for the transport of the sick, who were carried by six bearers in the ordinary travelling hammock of the country, slung on a bamboo. At each of the six stations were thirty-five hammocks or cots, an average of thirteen miles being fixed as a day's journey, and with the column, in addition, were eighty-five cots, with a suitable retinue of bearers.

beast of burden of the size even of a goat, and everything had to be transported on the backs of the most indolent race in the world. However, the man who had conducted to a successful conclusion the Red River Expedition, with its manifold difficulties of transport by land and water, was not likely to be foiled by the still more arduous problem now presented for solution ; and though, at one time, the success of the expedition was seriously imperilled, the task was achieved.

Though a very large number of carriers was engaged by the exertions of the staff and Special Service officers— including a strong and willing brigade of women, and the 'picaninni' brigade of 400 boys and girls, who each carried a half-load of twenty-five pounds—they melted away ; and 'handing carriers over to the Control Department,' wrote the General, 'is like pouring water into a sieve ; they run away after making a single journey.' Sir Garnet Wolseley, recognising the extreme urgency of the question, ordered that 3,000 of the native auxiliaries should be disarmed and handed over to the Control for service as carriers, and, on the 10th of December, he informed the kings and chiefs at Dunquah, that unless 5,000 carriers were raised by the end of the month, he would not land the European troops who were daily expected. He also despatched Dr. O'Reilly to Elmina, where 700 men were raised in ten days, and Dr. Gouldsbury recruited with success in the windward ports ; thus, by supplementing the transport with the disarmed levies at Beulah, the unarmed men of the Abrah contingent, and the women carriers, there were, on the 22nd of December, when the department was placed in the hands of the late Colonel G. P. Colley, 6,000 carriers working between Cape Coast and the Prah.

Colonel Colley arrived at Cape Coast on the 17th of December, and immediately placed his services at the disposal of the General in any department they might be most conducive to the public advantage. From his special knowledge of army organization and administration Colonel Colley was peculiarly fitted to grapple with the transport difficulty, and the General appointed him Director of Transport, with 3 officers as assistants. Colonel Colley proceeded to Mansu on the 19th of December, and drew up a memorandum which showed that he had thoroughly mastered the question.

Between the 9th and 17th December the *Himalaya*, *Tamar*, and *Sarmatian* arrived with the troops requisitioned by Sir Garnet Wolseley; also Brigadier-General Sir Archibald Alison, Colonel G. R. Greaves, Chief of the Staff, 41 medical officers, and 10 Special Service officers.* The arrival of the *Himalaya*, on the 9th December, was the first intimation received by Sir Garnet Wolseley that his demand for the immediate despatch of European troops would be complied with by the Government. In Lord Kimberley's despatch of the 6th of October, he was informed of the desire of Her Majesty's Government 'to impress upon you that they would be most reluctant to sanction any expedition which would require that European troops should be sent from this country to the Gold Coast. A satisfactory state of things will be attained if you can procure an honourable peace, or can inflict, in default of such peace, an effectual chastisement on the Ashantee force.' Most officers, on receipt of this half-hearted despatch, would have considered that they had done enough in clearing the Protectorate, and inflicting an 'effectual chastisement' on the Ashantees. But if any doubts were entertained by Ministers as to the

* The following was the strength of the force: 2 batt. Rifle Brigade; 2 batt. 23rd Royal Welch Fusiliers and 42nd Highlanders, each 30 officers and 450 men; No. 1 Battery, 17th Brigade, Royal Artillery, 3 officers and 61 men; 28th Company, Royal Engineers, 4 officers and 68 men; Army Service Corps, 1 officer and 12 men; and Army Hospital Corps, 2 officers and 54 men. On the 29th December the 1st West India Regiment arrived at Cape Coast from Jamaica with a strength of 24 officers and 554 men.

desirability of loyally carrying out their agreement with Wolseley regarding the despatch of the European troops, on his responsibility, it was removed by the General's exhaustive letter of the 13th of October, demanding their instant embarkation. A Cabinet Council was held on the 17th of November, within a few hours of the receipt of the despatch in Downing Street, and, on the 19th, two regiments sailed from Portsmouth for the scene of hostilities, and the 42nd Highlanders followed on the 4th December in compliance with Sir Garnet's letter written after the fight at Essaman.

The *Sarmatian* brought a despatch from Lord Kimberley, dated 24th of November, limiting the time of employment of the European troops, at the very latest, to the end of March, before which it would be 'absolutely necessary' to withdraw them. This limit as to time would impose 'a corresponding limit upon the operations which it would be prudent or possible for him to attempt.' The decision on this point was left to Sir Garnet's own judgment to determine, but he was informed of the wishes of Her Majesty's Government. These were: 'That you should conclude a satisfactory peace as soon as it can be obtained; that you should advance no further into the interior than may be indispensable for the attainment of such a peace; and that after concluding, if possible, a treaty with the King of Ashantee, you should return with the least practicable delay to the sea-coast, and send home the European troops.' With respect to the relations of England with the Protectorate after the war, the Government, considering the cowardly conduct of the Fantee chiefs and people, held themselves entirely free 'to place them on such a footing as the interests of this country may seem to them to require.'

The European troops arrived rather inopportunely, for they were too late to strike a decisive blow—which lay in the General's power while the enemy were at Mampon, and he held Mansu on their main line of retreat—and they were too early for the march on Coomassie, the arrangements for which were not yet completed. In a letter to the Secretary for War, of the 15th of December, Sir Garnet said that it would be impossible to have the several halting-stages, including the depôt at Prahsu, completed, and a sufficient quantity of food and ammunition in the magazines at Prahsu, before the 15th of January, when he expressed his intention of crossing the Prah with the three European regiments, and a force of Native troops; and he concluded his letter by the assurance of his 'strong hope, bordering upon conviction, that in about six weeks from the date of our crossing the Prah, I shall be able to embark the European troops, having suffered but little loss from the effects of the climate.'

As the arrangements for the advance were incomplete, Sir Garnet, after landing the Army Service Corps, and a portion of the Royal Engineers, together with all the Staff and Special Service officers, sent the steamers, with the European troops, on a cruise. At this time he drew up a memorandum for the information and guidance of the soldiers and sailors about to take part in the operations north of the Prah, of which 100 copies were printed for distribution among the regiments. Nothing can be more concise and complete than these orders, which were found to meet every requirement and obviate every difficulty as they arose during the advance upon Coomassie. One innovation in the ordinary method of fighting was found of especial service, that by which the 'tactical unit' was changed, and it was enacted that 'every company will be at once divided into four sections, and each section will be placed under the command of an officer or non-commissioned officer. These sections once told off are not on any account to be broken up during the war.' As to the mode of fighting to be adopted by these sections, Sir Garnet directed that 'in action, as a general rule, three sections only of each company will be extended, the fourth will form a support in rear of the centre of the company's skirmishing line, and at forty to eighty yards from it.' At the most critical point in the action of Amoaful, on the 31st of January, these arrangements were found of the utmost vital utility; and Sir Archibald Alison, who commanded the advance, under 'one of the heaviest fires he ever saw,' declared that, notwithstanding the discipline and stubborn valour of the Black Watch, 'without the admirable sectional organization introduced by His Excellency, and thoroughly carried out by the company officers, it would have been impossible to prevent the men getting out of hand.' These 'Notes,' as forming the best code of instructions for bush-fighting, will be of value to any commander who may have hereafter to encounter a barbarous enemy under similar conditions.

Sir Garnet Wolseley's plan for the invasion of Ashantee, on the 15th of January, by several columns converging on Coomassie, was, briefly stated, as follows : On the extreme right, Captain Glover's force was to cross the Prah near Assim, and to move upon Juabin. The main body, consisting of the European troops and Native levies, was to advance from Prahsu by the main Coomassie road. As a connecting link between these columns, a column composed of Western Akims, under the command of Captain Butler, was to cross at Prahsu Akim ; while, on the extreme left, a force of Wassaws, Denkeras, and Commendahs, under the command of Captains Dalrymple and Moore, 88th Regiment, would advance on Coomassie by the Wassaw road. Theorists on the art of war might object that Wolseley, by this plan of dividing his force, violated the first strategical principles ; but the sequel showed that he was right, and

SIR GARNET AND CAPTAIN GLOVER. 273

that he possessed one of the chief attributes of a general, the power of estimating the strength of his adversary.

Had the General's movements on Coomassie been dependent on those of the three other converging columns, it is certain that the invasion of Ashantee would never have taken place, or that the attempt, if made, must have ended in failure. Captains Dalrymple and Butler failed to move the chiefs and people to whom they were accredited, and the latter gallant and able officer, who would have succeeded in his task if success was possible, after numberless delays, eventually persuaded 500 of the Western Akims —whom Captain Glover described as 'the best fighting men in the Protectorate'—to follow him a day's march through a deserted and devastated country, but at night their courage failed them, and they fled back across the Prah. Glover, by his conduct, showed himself to be a man of resource and capacity; but the people he had to deal with would have baffled the capacity of Cæsar himself, either to make them march or fight. The native kings and chiefs assembled at Accra on the 13th of October, promised to rally to Glover's standard with thousands of retainers within a stipulated time; but having ratified their oaths by accepting the usual presents of gin and large subsidies in money, they appeared to think they had fulfilled their share of the engagement.

The arrangements for the invasion of Ashantee were all planned, when, on Christmas Eve, to the dismay of Sir Garnet Wolseley, a despatch, dated the 22nd of December, was received from Captain Glover—who had written on the 14th, saying that he would cross the Prah on the 15th of January, with, 'at the lowest estimate, 16,000 effectives, possibly 30,000 men, all told '—in which he said : 'I should be misleading your Excellency if I stated that I saw any possibility of reaching the Prah before forty days, but I beg to assure you that no effort shall be left untried to carry a force to the point indicated.' Upon receipt of this despatch Sir Garnet Wolseley determined to take upon himself the responsibility of ordering Glover to cross the Prah on the 15th of January, and march on Coomassie with the Houssas and Yorubas, some 700 men; and, accordingly, the Chief of the Staff wrote, on Christmas Eve, to Captain Glover to this effect. That officer, in his reply of 28th December, promised compliance, but declined responsibility for the result.

In meting out the praise so justly due to Captain Glover for the energy and military skill he displayed throughout those eventful months in West Africa, it should be borne in mind that he thus formally declined to accept the responsibility for the course he adopted, and that Wolseley as formally accepted it. Had it not been for Sir Garnet's positive orders to Captain Glover to cross the Prah on the 15th of January, it is certain he would not have been on the northern bank of that river before the date of the capture of Coomassie; and then, as the General plainly informed him, he might, as far as being of any service in the prosecution of this Ashantee War was concerned, have been 'operating on the Zanzibar coast of Africa.'

Wolseley started for Prahsu on the 27th of December, and inspected the various camping stations on the road, and saw that all was prepared for the small army that was soon to follow. As far as Mansu, the fourth station, and thirty-two miles distant from Cape Coast, the road passed through low bush with little or no shelter from the blazing sun, but from thence to the Prah the pathway lay through the forest, the gigantic trees of which, festooned and encircled with creepers, rose more than 200 feet above the head of the passer-by, with a girth at the roots of between fifty and ninety feet. No colour lit up the infinite gradations of endless green which palled upon the jaded sight, the shades of the primeval forest were never penetrated by the sun's rays, and the silence was unbroken save by

> 'The moving whisper of huge trees, that branch'd
> And blossom'd in the zenith.'

Sir Garnet's old wound in the leg, received in the Crimea, had troubled him much since the march on the 28th of October, from Abrakrampa to Assanchi, and he was compelled to perform the journey to the Prah in a light American buggy, which was found at Cape Coast. This vehicle was left at Prahsu, and for the remainder of the march between the river and Coomassie, except at those frequent intervals when the nature of the road, or the proximity of the enemy, required that he should walk, Sir Garnet was borne by natives, seated in a wicker Madeira chair, fixed between two bamboos, and carried by relays of four bearers. On New Year's Day he arrived at Barraco—the last station from Cape Coast, from which it is sixty-three miles distant—where was stationed a detachment of the Naval Brigade. That night, over the huge camp fire, replenished by two or three entire trunks of trees, the sailors sang their forecastle songs and made the forest ring with choruses bawled out with stentorian lungs. There gathered on one side of the fire the General with his staff and the officers of the detachment, and, on the other, the sailors, who stepped out in succession and gave a selection of songs, sentimental and comic.

On his arrival at Prahsu on the 2nd of January, 1874, he found in garrison, 50 of Rait's Houssa Artillery (with 7 three-pounders, 2 howitzers, a Gatling gun, and 6 rocket-troughs), 70 men of the 2nd West, and Wood's and Russell's Native regiments, numbering 450 and 500 men respectively, who had been engaged making a clearing and cutting down acres of palm-leaves for thatching, and thousands of poles for uprights for the huts. By the 15th of January the camp at Prahsu was ready for the reception of the European troops, with the necessary accommodation for the stores and for thirty days' provisions for 3,520 fighting men and 3,000 carriers.

During Sir Garnet's stay at Prahsu, a correspondence took place between himself and the King of Ashantee. Scarcely had he arrived at the camp than two messengers from Coomassie made their appearance at Prahsu with two letters* from their master, dated the 25th of November and 26th of December, which, like those that followed, were signed by 'the mark' of Koffee Kalkalli and some of his ministers. As it was evident by the second epistle that the insignificant affair at Faysowah had been magnified into a great victory, the General wrote him a long letter, opening his eyes as to the true state of affairs, and stating the terms upon which a lasting peace could alone be concluded. The Naval Brigade, 22 officers and 250 seamen and Marines, which marched in on the 3rd of January, having left Cape Coast on the 27th of December, was paraded before the envoys, who were sent back to their master on the morning of the 6th of January with Sir Garnet's letter. On the 12th, an Ashantee envoy, with a suite of 15 persons and accompanied by Mr. Kuhne, a German missionary, arrived near the Prah with a letter from the King,† dated 9th of January, but Sir Garnet refused to see him, and reiterated his ultimatum to the King.

* These letters were written in English, at the dictation of King Koffee, by Dawson, a Fantee, who had been detained at Coomassie.

† From Mr. Kuhne it was gleaned that Amanquatia's army had reached Coomassie on the 22nd of December, and had been disbanded after defiling past the King in the great square with wild shouts and gesticulations, each chief dancing before the King as described by Bowdich in 1817. The King had sent for the missionaries, in whose presence Sir Garnet Wolseley's letter had been correctly interpreted to him by Dawson; and, when despatching Mr. Kuhne with his reply, he desired him to tell the British General of his earnest wish for peace.

DIFFICULTIES OF TRANSPORT.

The 2nd West India Regiment marched into camp a Prahsu, on the 4th of January, when the difficulties of transport, owing to the desertion of the carriers, which had been daily increasing, assumed such alarming proportions that the success of the expedition was imperilled. The number of troops fixed by Sir Garnet Wolseley, for whom transport was imperatively required, was 2,504 Europeans of all ranks, and 1,050 Native levies, including 200 of the 2nd West India Regiment.*

The ships, with the European troops, having returned to Cape Coast, as directed, the Rifle Brigade was disembarked on New Year's Day, and marched direct from the beach to Inquabim, which was reached in three hours. They were followed by the 42nd Highlanders and a half-battalion of the Fusiliers.

Colonel Colley expected a sufficient number of carriers to provide transport for the three battalions of Europeans, but, between the 31st of December and the 3rd of January, the Natives deserted by hundreds, and Sir Archibald Alison suspended the disembarkation of the second half-battalion of the Fusiliers and the Royal Artillery, which was in progress. On learning the position of affairs, Sir Garnet directed the re-embarkation of the Fusiliers, which had proceeded as far as Accroful, though, to soften the disappointment to many gallant men, the General arranged that the headquarters and 100 men should accompany him into

* For these troops the number of carriers required, on the lowest scale, was 3,500, being one carrier to every 3 European soldiers, and one to each officer, besides 240 for the cots, and others for the ammunition and camp equipment, which brought up the total for one battalion to 654. It was roughly calculated that to supply one European battalion daily with provisions 60 additional carriers were required for every day's march, and between 400 and 500 to keep up the daily supply at Prahsu from Cape Coast. 206 carriers were only required for each of the Native regiments, as the rank and file were their own carriers. In addition to this total, Colonel Colley estimated that he would require for the transport of the supplies and ammunition, and to carry back the sick and wounded, 5,000 local carriers, divided equally between the north and south banks of the Prah.

Ashantee, an equal number of the 42nd being re-embarked. Arrangements were made to employ Wood's Regiment as carriers, as a temporary measure; the Kroomen of the Naval Brigade were also sent back to Mansu for loads, and Russell's Regiment alone marched to the Prah to lead the advance. The Highlanders and Rifle Brigade were halted in their march up country, and Sir Garnet requested the chief magistrate of Cape Coast to put in force the law compelling the Natives to work. Only forty men were obtained by these means; but 270 men, in the pay of the merchants, were pressed by permission of their masters. Sir Archibald Alison at Cape Coast continued his efforts by doubling the allowance for rations, offering £50 to the chiefs for every 500 able-bodied men they raised, and 'driving' for carriers in the Elmina and the surrounding villages; while Sir Garnet issued a proclamation, that unless the native kings assisted the army in this matter of transport, he would re-embark his whole force, and leave them to the mercy of their enemies. Large additions were thus made by these means to the number of carriers, and, at length, Colonel Colley was enabled, on the 15th of January, to report that the transport difficulty had been surmounted. At that date he had collected 4,200 men and 1,250 women, 'local' carriers, exclusive of the regimental carriers, being 2,000 in excess of the numbers estimated as necessary to maintain communication with Prahsu. Under these circumstances, Sir Garnet Wolseley decided that the passage of the Prah, by European troops, should commence on the 20th of January, which was five days later than he originally projected.

The monotony and inaction of camp life at the Prah were beginning to tell on both European officers and men: twenty-two of the Naval Brigade were on the sick-list, and of the Staff, Major Baker, Mr. Irvine, Lieutenant Maurice, and the

WOLSELEY CROSSES THE PRAH. 279

two aides-de-camp, Captain Lanyon and Lieutenant Hon. H. L. Wood, were seized with fever, which carried off Captain Huyshe. This accomplished and energetie officer had been engaged up to the end of the year in surveying, and had just rejoined headquarters.

The first entry into the enemy's country was made on the 5th of January, by Russell's Regiment, 500 strong, and the scouts, which the General had placed under the command of Lieutenant Lord Gifford, 24th Regiment, Adjutant of Russell's Regiment. This young officer pushed on with 170 scouts to Ansah, and thence to the Foomoosu River, meeting with no opposition. On the 12th of January he occupied Accrofoomu, where he was joined by Russell's Regiment and the rocket-party, together with Major Home and the 28th Company of the Royal Engineers. The 2nd West India and Wood's Regiments, and Rait's Artillery followed on successive days; and on the 16th Lord Gifford reached the foot of the Moinsey Hill, the crest of which Major Russell occupied and fortified. On the 18th, Lord Gifford advanced to Quisah, the frontier town in Ashantee proper, which was occupied by Russell's Regiment.

In consequence of the enemy having thus evacuated the entire country to the south of the Adansi Hills, Sir Garnet Wolseley was gratified to find that the date he had originally fixed for reaching that point would not be departed from. Early the same morning, the General with his Staff, and the Naval Brigade under Captain Luxmoore,* crossed the Prah, and Colonel McLeod, 42nd Highlanders, pushed on to Quisah to take command of the advanced guard, now consisting of Wood's and Russell's Regiments, Rait's Artillery, and the headquarters of the 2nd West India Regiment,

* Captain Blake, of the *Druid*, who hitherto commanded the Naval Brigade with such credit to himself, died of dysentery.

the whole forming what was generally known as the 'Black Brigade.'

The General took up his quarters on the night of the 20th of January, at Essiaman in the old Assin village, situated on a hill surrounded by a small clearing. On the morning of the 21st he proceeded, by an admirable road, to Accrofoomu, where Major Home had constructed a work of the type of the New Zealand pah. Here he rested for the night in the store-shed, thatched with palm-leaves, a portion of the Naval Brigade encamping outside in their tents, where they made wattle-beds, well off the ground, of sticks gathered in the adjoining forest.

Commodore W. N. W. Hewett, V.C., C.B., commanding the squadron on the West Coast of Africa, arrived at Accrofoomu late in the day, accompanied by his flag-lieutenant, Lieutenant Rolfe, R.N., who, as his chief was present with the force *en amateur*, was placed on Sir Garnet's Staff, as Naval aide-de-camp. Captain Hunt Grubbe, commanding H.M.S. *Tamar*, now assumed command of the Naval Brigade. During the night, the Kroomen of the Naval Brigade, who, though of Herculean build, are abject cowards, fancying that the Ashantees were upon them, fled panic-stricken into the sleeping camp; the sailors stood to their arms with great promptness and presence of mind, but some time elapsed before the General and the officers, who all turned out, were able to restore order.

On the 22nd, headquarters marched to Moinsey, and the General proceeded to the summit of the steep Adansi Hill, whence a fine view was had of the surrounding country. It was with eager interest that every eye was turned northwards to the promised land of conquest, which stretched in the direction of Coomassie—a vista of hills, ridge upon ridge, all covered with the dense African forest, and partially shrouded by the mist which is never wholly dispelled by the sun. During the 23rd, the Rifle Brigade marched in, and envoys arrived from King Koffee, with the remainder of the white prisoners,* and a letter, dated 21st of January, in which, after promising acceptance of the British terms, he said : ' I beg also you would stop the progress of the forces, and let us go on with peaceful negotiation. I will make Amankwatia, who has acted contrary to my instructions, pay the amount your Excellency ask, if you can only keep patience and stop the advancement of the forces.' But the wily savage made a mistake when he calculated that Wolseley was to be taken in by specious promises, even though he had given, as an unwary general might have considered, a proof of his good faith in releasing the European captives. The Fantee prisoners were still retained, and Wolseley knew that these earnest and repeated supplications for delay were only made by the King to enable him to gather together his disbanded army for one final effort to save his crown and carry in triumph to his capital the soldier who, by defeating his armies and crossing the Prah, hitherto held inviolate from the foot of a white conqueror, had confuted the tradition which, for two centuries, had enchained the popular imagination. Still a considerable instalment of his original demand had been obtained by the release of the white prisoners; and the General, while not abating one jot of his determination to push on until his terms were satisfied in their entirety, despatched to Her Majesty's Government the following telegram :† ' King will pay indemnity I have demanded,

* These were M. Bonnet, a French merchant, and Mr. and Mrs. Ramseyer and their two children.
† This telegram was sent from Moinsey, at about six p.m. on the 23rd, by the hands of a police-runner, who reached Prahsu, thirty-two and a half miles distant, at daybreak next morning. Thence an officer was sent by Colonel Festing to Barraco, the nearest telegraph station, with orders to repeat the despatch, which was in two ciphers, to the Colonial and War Offices. By 10.30 the despatch had been repeated from Cape Coast ; and the same evening the *Sarmatian* sailed for Gibraltar, making the passage in nine days. Thence it was telegraphed to London, so that news from the

amounting to £200,000. He accepts the terms offered. The white prisoners are all now with us. Shall halt a few days at Fommanah, which is about thirty miles from Coomassie. Everything goes on well.'

Owing to the rapid advance of the troops, who had outstripped the transport, the halt at Fommanah was absolutely essential for the formation of a depôt of supplies by Colonel Colley, now in charge of the line of communication between the front and Cape Coast, and of all the posts on the road.

The delay also effected a double purpose, 'as it gave the appearance to the King of Ashantee of his halting in compliance with his request, so that every chance would be given him for carrying out his promises.' That Sir Garnet was not deceived by these promises, appears from the letter he despatched on the 24th, in which he said: 'I intend to go to Coomassie. It is for your Majesty to decide whether I go there as your friend or as your enemy.' If in the former capacity, he demanded certain hostages, the Fantee prisoners, and a portion of the indemnity. He then added: 'I shall then proceed to Coomassie with an escort of only about 500 English soldiers, in order to make a treaty of peace with your Majesty. The sooner I receive these guarantees, the sooner will my armies halt; and in order to allow your Majesty to fulfil my demands without trouble, I shall only advance very slowly with this army during the next few days. An officer of rank has conferred with your messengers, and I shall have much pleasure in conferring with your Majesty personally when I arrive at Coomassie.'

On the 24th, headquarters, with the Rifle Brigade,

Adansi Hills was published in the metropolis in less than ten days. When the telegram appeared in the daily papers on the morning of the 5th of February it was pretty generally pronounced to be an electioneering hoax to influence the fate of the Gladstone Ministry, then wavering in the balance.

followed Russell's Regiment to Fommanah, where Sir Garnet and Staff occupied the palace of Cobbina Obbin, the King of Adansi, 'a large building, consisting of several open courts communicating with each other, and each surrounded by rooms closed on three sides, but open on the fourth into the court.'

Sir Garnet inspected the Rifles on the 25th of January, when there appeared on parade 591 officers and men, out of a total strength of 784, 77 having been left behind sick, and 9 being in hospital at Fommanah. On the same day, the returns showed that in the Naval Brigade, 48 were sick out of a total of 250; 38 were sick in the 23rd Fusiliers, and 51 in the 42nd Highlanders. In consequence of this serious diminution in his fighting force, which included only 1,800 Europeans on shore, the General ordered that 10 officers and 200 rank and file of the Fusiliers should be landed and proceed forthwith to Prahsu, and this reinforcement was of the utmost service in keeping open the communications when the force pushed on to Coomassie.

Meanwhile Lord Gifford had scouted as far as Insarfu, and on receipt of information that the King of Adansi was at Borborassie with 1,000 men, Colonel McLeod, having received the General's permission to make a reconnoissance, started on the 29th of January, with a small force, which included the Naval Brigade. After a march of three hours from Kiang Boassu, the column reached the village, out of which the Ashantees were driven, though not without the loss on our side of Captain Nicoll,* who was shot dead while gallantly leading the advance of Russell's Regiment.

On this day headquarters arrived at Detchiasu, where

* On receipt of the news of the death of Captain Nicoll, who left a wife and family, a sum of £80 was subscribed at Sir Garnet Wolseley's table, the General himself heading the subscription list with £20; and when, some months later, the Company of Grocers in London placed at his disposal a sum of £250 for the benefit of the sufferers by this war, he presented Captain Nicoll's widow with half the amount.

Sir Garnet received two letters from King Koffee, reiterating his request that the British forces should stay their advance on his capital, to which he replied by repeating his demands and concluded as follows : ' I halted four days at Fommanah to please your Majesty. I cannot halt again until you have complied with my terms.'

On the 30th of January the advanced guard, consisting of Wood's and Russell's Regiments, moved from Insarfu to Quarman, holding the passage of the Dansaboo stream, and strongly intrenching themselves; also headquarters, with the Rifle Brigade, 42nd Highlanders, and Rait's Artillery, moved to Insarfu ; and the Naval Brigade, 23rd Fusiliers, with field hospitals and ammunition reserve, to Ahkankuassie, three miles in the rear. The 2nd West India Regiment also advanced a stage, and the 1st West India were ordered to the front from Essiaman.

The last day of January is memorable in the annals of the Ashantee War, as that on which the treacherous African monarch threw off the mask, and boldly staked his crown and *prestige* for invincibility on the arbitrament of battle. On that day the following was the position of the three other columns, which, as Sir Garnet Wolseley so candidly informed the King, would simultaneously invade his territories and converge upon his capital of Coomassie. Captain Butler proceeded in November, 1873, on a special mission to the Kings of Western Akim, to induce them to march with all their fighting men upon the flank and rear of the Ashantee army ; but though they crossed the Prah with him and Captain Brabazon, on the 20th of January, the entire force, 1,400 strong, bolted panic-struck, on the 30th, when, as he said, his junction with the main body at Amoaful 'was only a question of some hours.' Captain Butler joined headquarters at Agemmanu on the 7th of February, during the return march from Coomassie ; but though he failed in the main object of his mission, he created a valuable diversion by drawing away from the enemy's main army at Amoaful, the whole fighting force of Kokofoo, which assembled to bar his progress.

Even less was the measure of success that rewarded the efforts of Captains Dalrymple and Moore, of the 88th Regiment, who had been despatched on a mission to induce the Kings of Wassaw and Denkera to invade Ashantee by the Wassaw path, thus acting on the left flank of the main line of advance. On the 24th of January, when the British advance guard was at Fommanah, Captain Dalrymple had succeeded, in three weeks, in assembling at Kotakee only 50 men, and was compelled to give up the attempt in despair on the 30th of January. Though his mission collapsed even more signally than Captain Butler's, it was not wholly barren of results, for the King of Becquah, one of the tributaries of Koffee Kalkalli, assembled his men on the left flank of the invading army to oppose an advance.

But most important and successful, in every sense, was the diversion created by Captain Glover, who, in accordance with Sir Garnet Wolseley's orders, crossed the Prah on the 15th of January, with 740 Houssas and Yorubas. To do so— as he said in his lecture at the United Service Institution on the 17th of May, 1874—'he sacrificed clothes, provisions, and everything, to get up the ammunition.' On the 16th of January, the town of Abogoo was captured, and, on the 23rd, Lieutenant Barnard took Prahsu, and, on the 26th, Odumassie—which commands the road in the rear from Connomo to Juabin, and also that to Coomassie, from which it is some 25 or 30 miles distant. Captain Glover joined Barnard here, and, on the 1st of February, despatched Captain Sartorius across the Anoom river, to open communication with Captain Butler's force, which he supposed was operating between his own and the main army; and this gallant officer, with only 130 men, advanced through two large Ashantee camps, but, finding his rear cut off, despatched 40 Houssas back to Captain Glover, who sent Lieutenant Barnard to reinforce him with 150 men, when the combined force routed the enemy, and rejoined Captain Glover at Odumassie. To return to the movements of the main army under Sir Garnet Wolseley.

Lord Gifford reconnoitred the Ashantee position beyond Egginassie during the night of the 29th of January, and Major Home continued cutting the road up to within 100 yards of that village. As Colonel McLeod reported that the enemy in front were in great force, and it became evident that a general action was imminent, Sir Garnet Wolseley, on the 30th of January, issued his instructions* to the troops, who were formed into four columns facing outwards, similar to the four sides of a square. His design in adopting this formation is thus expressed by himself when reporting the successful result of his strategy : ' As the leading column advanced northward the left column, according to orders previously issued, cut a path diagonally to the left front, with a view of protecting the left flank of the front column ; and

* 'The troops will advance to-morrow, at an hour which will be hereafter decided, in the following order: 42nd Highlanders ; Rait's guns ; Naval Brigade ; Rait's rockets ; 23rd Royal Welsh Fusiliers ; Rifle Brigade. Wood's and Russell's Regiments, which are now in advance, will be drawn up on the side of the road, and will, on the above column reaching them, strike in between the 23rd Royal Welsh Fusiliers and Rifle Brigade. On approaching the enemy, the troops will be formed, the front line being commanded by Brigadier-General Sir A. Alison, the left flank by Colonel McLeod, the right flank by Lieut.-Colonel Wood, V.C., and the rear by Lieut.-Colonel Warren, Rifle Brigade. The regimental reserve ammunition will be inside the square on the road, that of the Rifle Brigade being in front of the battalion. Regiments must furnish a guard on their ammunition, and arrange for keeping their men supplied. The hammocks and bearers will also be inside the square. Every man of the force will carry one day's full ration of sausage and cheese. A reserve of supplies will be formed at Insarfu. The main road will be cleared as far as possible with the troops, by the Royal Engineers, who will cut roads on each side of, and 300 yards from, the main road. The 42nd Highlanders must be careful in their advance to lean in upon the guns, so as not to leave them without support.'

as it moved along this path, the right column, closing up, cut a path diagonally to the right to protect the right flank, while the rear column extended, so as to gain touch of the right and left columns, which were designed to follow the flanks of the front column, and, should it be outflanked, to face east and west outwards. My intention was to fight in the form of a square,* and so oppose the invariable flanking tactics of the enemy, which their superior numbers would probably allow them to carry out against any line which I could form.' The total force of all ranks and arms, numbered 134 officers, 1,375 European soldiers, and 780 Natives.

At daybreak, on the 31st of January, the advance column, commanded by Sir Archibald Alison, marched from the camp at Insarfu, and at 7.30, Sir Garnet Wolseley moved off with the detachment of the 23rd Fusiliers. Soon after eight, Lord Gifford's scouts received the first shot from the enemy, when they took the village of Egginassie with a rush. The two advance companies of the Highlanders, under Major Macpherson, now proceeded up the main road, and the heavy fire they quickly drew upon themselves showed that the Ashantees were in force; whereupon they were reinforced by a third company. As the enemy began thus early to resort to their favourite movement of turning his flank, Sir Archibald ordered two companies of the Highlanders, under Major Baird, to proceed along a path to the left, keeping three companies in reserve. On reaching a rise in the ground, he saw that the enemy had taken up a strong position in considerable force on a ridge beyond a low swampy hollow, through which a sluggish stream flowed. Major Baird at once attacked the ridge, which projected

* This formation of a square, with the sides facing outwards, is enjoined by Vegetius, in his 'Maxims,' 1,500 years ago, as the best, where your troops are superior in quality and *morale* to those of the enemy. It was the formation adopted by Lord Chelmsford at Ulundi.

forward in the shape of a semicircle, on the left completely enveloping the flank, and sweeping with its fire not only the path descending into the swamp, along which Major Macpherson was endeavouring to force his way, but the swamp itself, and the path on the other side. The fire at this time was tremendous, and it was fortunate indeed that the Ashantee arms and ammunition were of a wretched description. Major Scott was now directed to advance with two companies of the reserve, but still the enemy's fire could not be reduced. The Brigadier-General reported at nine o'clock to Sir Garnet Wolseley that he was 'heavily engaged with a large force in his front and left flank;' that six companies were in action, leaving only two in reserve, and that he would 'like some support.' A little later he asked for more surgeons at the front. Writing of this period of the action, Sir Archibald says in his despatch: 'The peculiarities of Ashantee warfare were now strongly developed. We were in the midst of a semicircle of hostile fire, and we hardly ever caught sight of a man. As company after company of the 42nd descended, with their pipes, into the ravine, they were almost immediately lost sight of in the bush, and their position could only be judged of from the sharp crack of their rifles, in contradistinction to the loud, dull roar of the Ashantee musketry.'

After describing some of the difficulties incidental to fighting with an unseen and numerous enemy in a dense bush, he continues: 'All these difficulties were, however, overcome by the wonderful coolness and discipline of the men, and the admirable way in which they were handled by the company officers. The orders to all were to regard the road as if the colours of the regiment were on it, and never to lose their connection with it; but without the admirable sectional organization introduced by his Excellency, and thoroughly carried out by the company officers, it would

THE ACTION OF AMOAFUL.

have been impossible to prevent the men getting out of hand. The Ashantees stood admirably, and kept up one of the heaviest fires I ever was under. While opposing our front attack with immensely superior numbers, they kept enveloping our left with a constant series of well-directed flank attacks.'

At this time Major Baird, Major Home, and a great number of men were wounded, and the Brigadier-General, who had applied to Sir Garnet for support, owns that he 'was getting very anxious as to the result,' when the two left detached flank companies, which had themselves been heavily engaged, most opportunely came in and joined the reserve, having been unable to force their way through the bush sufficiently quick to accompany the advance of the main column. Sir Archibald at once pushed the remaining reserve company into action, and, very shortly after, sent one of the flank companies, which had just returned, also to the front, and thus the 42nd had, at this time, seven companies engaged, and one in reserve. But as the enemy still 'held his ground stoutly in the front and left flank,' the Brigadier-General applied to Sir Garnet for some of the Rifle Brigade, as his men 'were getting tired from continuous fighting,' and his 'loss in wounded was pretty severe.' Half an hour later Sir Garnet received from him a second despatch, dated 'ten a.m., in front of Amoaful,' to the effect that the enemy held their ground steadily, and he had not yet been able to carry the village; and asking for a reinforcement of half a battalion of Rifles.

Sir Garnet immediately sent one company, but the enemy could not have been driven out of their strong position without very considerable loss, had it not been for Major Rait, who brought his guns into action with equal gallantry and judiciousness. Crossing the swamp and proceeding up the path under a hot fire, he quickly got one gun into action and fired fifteen rounds of case into the dense masses of the Ashantees. The Highlanders now carried the position with a rush; and, after Rait had well dosed the enemy, who had taken up a second position on a ridge behind it, the gallant 42nd again advanced, and this position also was carried. 'This,' said the Brigadier-General, 'was the last serious stand of the enemy. The breaking of their centre immediately diminished the severity of their flank attacks, which soon died away.'

Meanwhile, the flanking columns were not idle. Colonel McLeod, on the left, with the right wing of the Naval Brigade, under Captain Grubbe, R.N., and Russell's Regiment, had been busy cutting a path into the bush in a north-westerly direction and then north, according to the plan laid down by the General. Captain Buckle, R.E., encouraged his labourers both by word and example; but the fire they encountered while endeavouring to keep pace with the rapid advance of the 42nd to the hollow on the right, was very heavy, and that gallant officer fell mortally wounded. At length a path was cut to the crest of the hill, whence the rockets opened a destructive fire, and two companies of Russell's Regiment advanced and drove the Ashantees out of their camp. Colonel McLeod had cleared his front, but, having lost touch of the left of the front column, now cut his way in a north-easterly direction and came into the main road in rear of the Highlanders, about the same hour that the advance occupied Amoaful. 'I protected his left rear,' says Sir Garnet, 'by a detachment of the Rifle Brigade; our left flank was now apparently clear of the enemy.'

Colonel Wood, on the right, also advanced from Egginassie with the left wing of the Naval Brigade, under Commander Luxmoore, R.N., and his own regiment, and commenced cutting a path in a north-easterly direction;

A CRITICAL MOMENT. 291

but he encountered so heavy a fire that he directed his men to lie down, when they engaged in a musketry duel with the enemy. The two companies of Wood's Regiment, which had been left behind to hold Egginassie, having pushed on into the surrounding bush, were also engaged with the enemy, who kept up a heavy fire at this point, among those wounded being Colonel Wood himself.

When Sir Garnet arrived at Egginassie a little before 9.30, matters looked very serious, for the enemy had not given way at any point, while they were making persistent attacks with overwhelming numbers on both flanks of the village itself. But the General was calm and confident, and would not even allow the men he had with him to loophole the houses, 'lest the mere fact of this being done should make the troops consider that he thought it possible we might have to fall back upon the village, and act upon the defensive.' Urgent requests for reinforcements were received from all sides, and the General, who stood in the village personally superintending the movements, sent company after company to support the hardly-pressed advance column, and keep up the communication with the village. At length the tide turned when the Highlanders had passed the swamp, and though Colonel McLeod's column was but little advanced beyond the hill to the west of Egginassie, and Colonel Wood's column was still scarcely 200 yards east from the village, the fire of the enemy began to slacken. But so vastly superior in numbers were the enemy that they were enabled to break in upon the main road in rear of the 42nd, while they engaged the British front and flanks.

Sir Archibald Alison, having driven the enemy from their great camp, advanced upon the village of Amoaful, which was 'rushed' by the 42nd, after Rait's guns had searched it with a few rounds; and, soon after twelve, he reported to the

General that all was quiet on his right and left. Colonel McLeod's column now pushed across the swamp, but still no advance was made on the right, Colonel Wood being hotly engaged with the enemy; and it was not until 1.45 that the Ashantees were driven off and all firing ceased in the front, though they made heavy attacks in the rear.*

The action that was thus brought to a successful conclusion was hard fought, and the resistance encountered from the enemy much greater than was anticipated. Until the village of Amoaful was carried, says the Brigadier-General, 'the fighting was incessant; indeed it is impossible to conceive a more severe action than went on. The heavy loss suffered by the 42nd is the best proof of this, nearly every fourth man having been hit.' The loss of the enemy, he computed at not less than between 2,000 and 3,000 in killed and wounded. He adds, 'They stood admirably, came close up to our men, and evidently fought to win; but their final rout was complete.' The great Chief Amanquatia was among the killed, and the King of Mampon was wounded, while many other chiefs bit the dust. Admirable skill was shown in the position selected by Amanquatia, and the determination and generalship he displayed in the defence, fully bore out his reputation as an able tactician and gallant soldier.

The brunt of the fighting was borne by the 42nd Highlanders, of whom the Brigadier-General says, 'Their steadi-

* The Ashantees showed remarkable enterprise on this eventful day, for at 2.30 they attacked Colonel Colley while on his return to Insarfu, to bring up the regimental baggage, and escort the wounded to that post, and, at three o'clock, he reported that Quarman was 'warmly attacked.' On his arrival with reinforcements the enemy were repulsed, when he passed on to Insarfu, and, having collected the baggage and ammunition, which extended nearly five miles in length, started on his return to Quarman, which the Ashantees had again attacked, and fighting was continued on the road until late in the evening. Colonel Colley, having brought the baggage into Insarfu during the night, marched back to Quarman, and arrived at midnight at Amoaful, whither Sir Garnet had proceeded. At ten o'clock all the companies on the road between it and Egginassie were called into Amoaful, and Colonel Warren was left in command at Egginassie with four companies of the Rifle Brigade.

ness and discipline, the admirable way in which they were kept in hand by their officers, and the enthusiastic gallantry with which every charge was executed, exceed all praise.' Especial praise was due to Major Macpherson,* who, though wounded three times, refused to quit the field until Amoaful was carried; and to Major Scott, who succeeded in command, and Major Baird, who died of his wounds at Sierra Leone on his passage home. Others who distinguished themselves were Major Home, R.E., and Captain Buckle, R.E., who was killed; Lord Gifford, Colonel McLeod, Captain Rait, R.A., Captain Grubbe, R.N., and Colonel Wood, both of whom were wounded. Of the total force engaged, 1 officer, 2 privates of the 42nd Highlanders, and one native were killed, and 21 officers and 173 men were wounded; of these, 9 officers and 104 men belonged to the Highlanders, and 6 officers and 26 men to the Naval Brigade.

At daybreak on the 1st of February, the road between Insarfu and Amoaful was lined by the 42nd and Rifle Brigade, and the convoy of ammunition and baggage was brought to headquarters without opposition. At one o'clock the town of Becquah was carried by Lord Gifford, who received the Victoria Cross for his gallantry on this occasion and throughout the operations north of the Prah, when 'he daily carried his life in his hand.'

Sir Garnet having received the necessary supplies, determined to push on and give the enemy no time to rally. Accordingly, at daybreak on the 2nd of February, the whole force advanced from Amoaful, the advance guard, under Colonel McLeod, consisting of Lord Gifford's scouts, Russell's Regiment, detachments of Engineers and Artillery, and one company of the Rifle Brigade. Two days' rations were carried by the troops in their haversacks, the regimental transports accompanying with a similar

* This gallant officer again commanded the 42th Regiment at Tel-el-Kebir.

supply. The advance guard reached Aggemmamu at 12.40, without any serious opposition, and, soon after, the main body arrived, and halted. The General now pushed his pickets down the road towards Coomassie, and sent Colonel McLeod to scout Adwabin, which that officer occupied. In the meantime, Colonel Colley, who had proceeded back to Fommanah, found the small garrison hotly engaged with the enemy, who succeeded in penetrating the southern side of the village, but were repulsed with loss. During the attack, Captain North, 47th Regiment, in command of the post, was severely wounded.

The British force was now concentrated at Aggemmamu, with four days' supplies, and as Colonel Colley undertook that in five days' time a fresh convoy of provisions should arrive at that place, Sir Garnet Wolseley determined to advance forthwith upon Coomassie, some fifteen miles distant. It was a bold decision, as the enemy were known to be in force in the front; there was a river to be crossed, and his little army had been greatly reduced by casualties and sickness. 'Most generals,' says Colonel Wood, 'would have hesitated in such a conjuncture; but, with a happy audacity, Sir Garnet pressed on, and the result proved the wisdom of his decision.' As he determined, should he succeed in fighting his way into Coomassie, to quit the town within four or five days, whether he succeeded in making a treaty with King Koffee or not, he appealed to the men of the European Brigade to make their four days' rations* last, if necessary, for six days, and, as might be expected, they all responded most willingly in the affirmative. Accordingly, he issued orders to the force to march at daybreak on the following morning, each man carrying his greatcoat and a day's biscuit in his haversack.

* Colonel Colley, who joined headquarters during the forenoon on the line of march, brought 150 loads of provisions, thus completing the amount to between five and six days' supplies for the whole force.

THE ADVANCE ON COOMASSIE. 295

Leaving his tents and baggage at Aggemmamu, which had been strongly intrenched, Sir Garnet marched early on the 3rd of February. On the arrival of the head of the column at Adwabin, Colonel McLeod, with Lord Gifford's scouts in front, moved with the advanced guard on the path to the right of the main road to Coomassie. He soon encountered the enemy, when a detachment of the Rifle Brigade and Russell's Regiment drove them from the hill on which they were posted. In this affair the Rifle Brigade had six men placed *hors de combat*, Russell's Regiment ten, and the scouts eight.

Shortly before noon, two messengers, one bearing a white flag, and the other a golden plate on his breast, the symbol of his office, arrived with a letter from the King. The column was on the line of march, and the messengers were detained while Sir Garnet perused and replied to a letter from King Koffee, in the handwriting of Dawson, expressing his willingness 'to meet your Excellency's demands, but only your Excellency's very rapid movements puts me into confusion.' There was also a private letter from Dawson, petitioning him to halt, 'as no doubt we will all be killed, if your Excellency do not stay.' But nothing could change Sir Garnet's fixed determination to proceed to Coomassie. As, however, the Ordah, a deep and wide river, was still a considerable distance off, and it was evident that his troops could not reach Coomassie that night, he wrote the following brief reply to the King :

'12.10 a.m., February 3rd, 1874. On the march.

'You have deceived me so before, that I cannot halt until the hostages are in my possession. If you send them to me this evening, I will halt my army this side of the river Ordah. As time presses, I will consent to accept for to-day your mother and Prince Mensah. Both shall be well treated by me. You can trust my word. Unless you send them at once, my army shall march upon Coomassie.'

Sir Garnet continued his advance, and at three p.m. reached the banks of the Ordah, where he halted. Russell's Regiment crossed the stream, which was fifty feet wide and waist-deep, to act as a covering-party to the Engineers, who commenced to throw over a bridge. On a clearing being made on the north bank, the remainder of the advance-guard crossed the stream, the main body bivouacking on the south bank, or cowering beneath the meagre shelter afforded by hastily constructed huts of palm-stems and plantain-leaves, from a deluge of rain which never ceased throughout the night. Major Home and his Engineers continued to work during the pitiless storm, and by daybreak this indefatigable officer had completed an excellent bridge. The night before the capture of Coomassie must have reminded Sir Garnet Wolseley of that preceding the occupation of Fort Garry, and his mind was equally at ease as to the result of the operations of the morrow. As the prisoners had not arrived, Sir Garnet crossed the river with the main body of his little army.

Hardly had the advance commenced their march than the enemy opened fire, and Colonel McLeod pushed some of the Rifle Brigade and a 7-pounder, under Lieutenant Saunders, R.A., to the front, Lieutenant Bell, R.E.,* being engaged in clearing the bush on the left with his workmen. The attack gradually developed itself into a general action, and Sir Archibald Alison, who was engaged heavily on the right with the remainder of the Rifle Brigade and Rait's

* This gallant officer was awarded the Victoria Cross 'for his distinguished bravery and zealous, resolute, and self-devoted conduct at the battle of Ordahsu. By his example he made these men, his unarmed working-party of Fantee labourers, do what no European party was ever required to do in warfare—namely, to work under fire in the face of the enemy without a covering-party.'

THE ACTION OF ORDAHSU.

Houssa Artillery, reported that his 'whole right flank and rear were enveloped.' It was evident that the enemy were in great force, and were attempting their favourite tactics of surrounding their foe. Colonel McLeod, under cover of a gun, steadily continued his advance along the main road leading to Ordahsu, and at nine the village was carried by the Rifles. But it was not without serious loss, 7 of the 11 Houssas of Saunders' detachment being wounded, also Lieutenant Wauchope (severely), and Lieutenant Eyre (mortally), while urging on the Opobo Company of Wood's Regiment, of which he had been Adjutant throughout the campaign.

The Ashantees, quickly recovering themselves, now attacked the village of Ordahsu on both sides, and also made flank attacks down the road, where Wood's and Russell's Regiments, being unsteady, had been placed to guard communications. Sir Archibald, having pushed on the remainder of the Rifles to support Colonel McLeod, soon after joined him at Ordahsu, where the Rifles, Rait's guns, and the detachment 23rd, were concentrated. According to the Brigadier-General's request, Sir Garnet directed him to move on, and proposed to take his place at Ordahsu with the 42nd; but, before the Highlanders had time to occupy the village and relieve the advance-guard, the enemy attacked in force in front, on both flanks, and in the right rear. The General entered the village with the rear of the Highlanders, and immediately made his dispositions to bring all the baggage into the village, when he proposed, after leaving a strong guard for its protection, to push on for Coomassie, with all his available force, disregarding all flank and rear attacks.

At this time Ordahsu was encircled with a sheet of fire, and the enemy advanced to the attack with astonishing pertinacity and disregard of danger. They pushed boldly into the heart of the village, and the revolvers of the Staff-officers were called into requisition. Had the weapons and ammunition of the Ashantees been of a better description, many officers, who are the ornaments of the British army, would have fallen beneath the heavy fire, including the Commander of the Expedition, who narrowly escaped with his life. Sir Garnet Wolseley was sitting on a small native stool, and all the Headquarter Staff were seated round him on the ground; the noise of the firing was at its height, and Major Russell was in the act of leaning forward to say something in his ear, when a slug struck him, and passing obliquely through the puggree of his felt helmet, lodged between it and the hatband. The General was knocked off his chair, and both he and it rolled in the dust to the consternation of the Staff. But quick as thought he was on his feet again, and laughingly suggested that they should move into a somewhat less exposed place. On examination, this slug—which has been kept as an interesting memorial of a warm day's work—was found to be a square piece of tin, about the size of a dice, cut off from a bar. Had this projectile struck him on a vital part, or even on any portion of his helmet unprotected by the thick folds of an Indian puggree, it is probable that England might have had cause to mourn the death of a brilliant and successful soldier, who, like Wolfe and Abercrombie, fell at the moment when victory was about to reward his protracted efforts. Fortunately he escaped with no more serious injury than a severe headache for the remainder of the day.

Having completed his dispositions, about noon, Sir Garnet issued the order for the advance. The 42nd, as being fresher than the Rifle Brigade, who had been engaged in the van since daybreak, were to lead the advance, under cover of Rait's guns, and Colonel McLeod, who now took command of his own regiment, was directed to disregard all flank attacks and push on straight for Coomassie; while the Rifle Brigade were to follow in support as soon as the enemy were driven off from the village. Sir Archibald Alison describes in telling language the advance of the Highlanders, as Colonel McLeod rapidly passed the skirmishing companies through each other at intervals of fifty paces : 'On first debouching from the village, a tremendous fire was opened on the head of the column from a well-planned and strong ambuscade, six men being knocked over in an instant. But the flank companies worked steadily through the bush ; the leading company in the path sprang forward with a cheer ; the pipes struck up, and the ambuscade was at once carried. Then followed one of the finest spectacles ever seen in war. Without stop or stay the 42nd rushed on cheering, their pipes playing, their officers to the front ; ambuscade after ambuscade was successfully carried, village after village won in succession, till the whole Ashantees broke, and fled in the wildest disorder down the pathway on their front to Coomassie. The ground was covered with traces of their flight, umbrellas, and war-chairs of their chiefs, drums, muskets, killed and wounded, covered the whole way, and the bush on each side was trampled as if a torrent had flowed through it. No pause took place until a village about four miles from Coomassie was reached, when the absolute exhaustion of the men rendered a short halt necessary. So swift and unbroken was the advance of the 42nd, that neither Rait's guns nor the Rifle Brigade in support were ever brought into action.'

Up to this time, the enemy, encouraged by the presence of King Koffee, who was carried in his litter in rear, where no bullets could reach his royal person, had been making repeated attacks upon Ordahsu ; but, shortly before two, on the General communicating to his soldiers a despatch from Sir Archibald, reporting his capture of Karsi, a village four miles from Coomassie, the loud cheers, raised by Europeans and Natives alike, struck a terror into the hearts of the enemy, and they suddenly ceased firing.

The whole of the baggage having been now brought into the village, after some severe skirmishing with the enemy, who tried to cut the convoy off, our troops were drawn in and all communications severed with the rear,* a step rendered absolutely necessary owing to the available force being diminished by losses to 1,000 Europeans and 400 Natives, who, being supplied with five days' rations, were in a position to exist without connection with their base of supplies.

Sir Garnet attended the funeral of the gallant young Eyre, whose body was placed in a hastily dug grave, and, about 3.30, commenced his march on Coomassie with the whole of his force. Crossing two streams, and a pestilential swamp which surrounds the city, the General, mounted on a mule, and escorted by Captain Somerset's† company of the Rifles, at 6.15 arrived in the market-place, where he found the 42nd, and leading companies of the Rifle Brigade, which had entered the city three-quarters of an hour before, drawn up as on parade. Taking off his hat, he called for 'three cheers for the Queen,' which were given with such true British heartiness that the Natives fled in all directions; and thus was brought to a close one of the most singular and exciting episodes in the history of war.

Not less strange was the scene presented in the streets of

* Between this point and the Prah Sir Garnet Wolseley had established eleven posts, each of which was garrisoned with between 60 and 100 men; Fommanah, which was the largest post north of the Prah, having a garrison of 200 men. Thus at every advance his small force was weakened by establishing these posts, while his sick and wounded had increased daily, the carriers taking them back in one constant stream. Each post was fortified, the houses being loopholed, the ground cleared, and a parapet thrown up, and the garrisons daily patrolled half-way on either side until the patrols met.

† Captain Aylmer Somerset, an amiable and excellent man, died in the summer of 1882, much lamented by his brother officers and numerous friends.

Coomassie, where the old motto, 'Væ victis,' received the most singular of commentaries. With the coolest effrontery, the very men, with whom our soldiers had been engaged during the past four days in a fierce life-and-death struggle, on meeting the advance-guard, sauntered up to them with arms in their hands, and offered them water, with the remark, 'Thank you, thank you,' as if the whole thing had been a theatrical performance, in which all had equally well played their parts. The great main street of Coomassie,* which was full of King Koffee's warriors, who passed in front of the troops, carrying their arms and ammunition into the bush, commands both the town and the palace, and the Brigadier-General, on arrival, had thrown out pickets and placed the artillery so that it could sweep the streets ascending to the market-place. A party was at once sent down to the palace, but the King and all other personages of distinction had disappeared.

In the action of Ordahsu there were engaged 118 officers, 1,044 European soldiers and seamen, and 449 Natives; of this number Lieutenant Eyre and one man were killed, and 6 officers and 60 men wounded. The troops displayed, during the twelve hours' arduous marching and fighting, courage and endurance of a high order; though fainting with thirst, water being scarce on the route, and having no time to eat food, few if any of the force fell out, but all pressed on in emulous eagerness for the goal of their exertions. The enemy did not suffer so heavily as at Amoaful, which was owing to their resistance not being of so obstinate a character; and, after the capture of Ordahsu, they chiefly directed their energies to making fruitless flank attacks on the troops defending the village.

* Coomassie means 'the town under the tree;' so called because its founder sat under a broad tree, surrounded by his warriors, while he laid out the plan for the future town. This great fetish tree, singularly enough, fell down on the day Sir Garnet Wolseley sent his ultimatum of the 2nd of January to the King—an event which created a prodigious sensation among the townspeople.

It was almost dark before steps could be taken to quarter the troops, and Sir Garnet immediately issued stringent orders for the protection of the inhabitants and the safety of the town. The scene presented in the streets of the Ashantee capital was picturesque in the highest degree. The twilight quickly faded into night, which was lit up by camp-fires and torches, which threw a weird light on the crowds of Natives, while the sky was reddened by conflagration, the acts of incendiaries, principally Fantee prisoners, who took advantage of the confusion to pillage the houses. Captain Baker, Inspector-General of Police, and other officers, were engaged all night in extinguishing the fires, and restraining the plunderers, one of whom, caught red-handed, was summarily hanged, and several were flogged, which had the required deterrent effect. After seeing that strong outlying pickets were placed at all the main thoroughfares, Sir Garnet, with some of his Staff, took up his quarters for the night in a raised open recess, destitute alike of roof and front, which opened into the market-place.

A signal military success had been achieved; but, as political Chief of the Expedition, the laurels of the bloodless campaign of diplomacy remained still unplucked. Sir Garnet's chief anxiety now was to conclude a treaty of peace with the King: so before retiring to rest that night, he addressed to him a letter, offering the original terms, and expressing his readiness to accept hostages of rank in place of the queen-mother and heir. After an almost sleepless night, Sir Garnet rose early, and issued to the troops a 'Special General Order' of thanks,* and wrote his despatch

---

* 'Coomassie, February 5th, 1874.

'Soldiers, Seamen, and Marines of this Expeditionary Force,

'After five days' very hard fighting, under trying conditions, your courage and devotion have been rewarded with complete success. I thank you in Her Majesty's name for your gallantry and good conduct throughout these operations.

'In the first phase of this war the Ashantee army was driven back from

to the Secretary for War, on the operations since the action of February 2nd.

Accompanied by his Staff, the General proceeded to the King's palace, a huge building of irregular shape, in which 1,000 men might have been quartered. In one court was found a quantity of enormous umbrellas of various materials, including the state umbrella sent home to Her Majesty, and numerous litters, covered with silks and velvets or the skins of animals, in which the King was wont to be carried. In rooms upstairs were numberless boxes filled with articles of value and silks. As Sir Garnet Wolseley walked through these courts and apartments, containing a museum of articles from all countries, he must have been reminded of the scene at the Summer Palace, near Pekin, though the abode of the barbarous African monarch was a poor imitation of that edifice with its priceless contents. There were other articles in this palace that aroused feelings only of disgust and horror, such as the great death-drum, surrounded with human skulls and thigh-bones, and several stools 'covered with clotted blood, standing out from them in huge thick lumps, the blood of hundreds of victims.' As the flies rose in dense crowds from their foul repast, Sir Garnet beat a hasty retreat, and, after a brief survey of the King's bedchamber, with its heavy door, having many stamped plaques

---

the Fantee country into its own territory. Since then you have penetrated far through a dense forest, defended at many points with the greatest obstinacy. You have repeatedly defeated a very numerous and most courageous enemy, fighting on his own ground, in well-selected positions. British pluck and the discipline common to Her Majesty's land and sea forces have enabled you thus to overcome all difficulties and to seize upon the enemy's capital, which now lies at our mercy. All the people, both European and Native, unjustly held captive by the King of Ashantee, are now at liberty, and you have proved to this cruel and barbarous people that England is able to punish her enemies, no matter what their strength in numbers or position.

'Maintain on your return march to the coast the same admirable conduct you have hitherto evinced, and England may be as justly proud of having such soldiers, sailors, and marines as I am of having had the honour of commanding you throughout this campaign.'

of gold, and the gorgeous four-post bedstead, quitted the palace, over which he directed that a strong European guard should be placed.

Another of the 'lions' of Coomassie will not soon be forgotten by those who paid it a visit. Not far from the market-place, and hidden from the road by a fringe of rushes, was an open space, over an acre in extent, forming a receptacle for decaying corpses. The whole town was impregnated with the odour arising from the contents of this charnel-house, in which were lying, in all the hideous stages of decomposition, thousands of human bodies and skeletons. It was said that daily fresh victims were added to this Golgotha, and it must be a source of gratification to the victorious General to reflect that by the blows he inflicted in this short and sharp campaign, humanity has been the gainer in the abrogation in Ashantee-land of many of the so-called 'customs,' founded on the denial of the first principles that regulate society even among the most unenlightened communities.

During the day Sir Garnet received messengers professing to be sent by the King, with promises that he would come in immediately, and the General despatched emissaries urging him to meet him, when his palace would be placed at his disposal; but still there were no signs of his appearance, and, as it was evident that he was only carrying on his policy of dissimulation, the messengers, who were found collecting arms and ammunition, were arrested.

During the afternoon a terrible storm of wind and rain swept over the city, and in the night, a second tornado raged with fearful violence, converting the market-place into a pond. Major Russell reported that the bridge on the Ordah river was about eighteen inches under water, and, as it appeared that the rainy season was about to set in, the General determined to evacuate Coomassie and retrace his steps before the roads were rendered impassable. This determination was adversely criticized at the time, but there can be no doubt of its wisdom, for had he marched out and burnt the royal mausoleum at Bantama, and fought an action with his handful of men, his wounded might have been so greatly increased as to have placed it beyond his power to remove them back to Aggemmamu, there being no carriers or hammocks sufficient for the purpose. He knew also that the British soldier could battle against the insidious attacks of fevers while under the excitement of battle or anticipated conflict, but that when these influences had ceased he would become in that African forest an easy prey to disease. Acting under a sense of responsibility, from which his critics were relieved, and remembering the earnest injunctions of the Secretary for War, to avoid all unnecessary exposure of the white troops, he decided in the afternoon of the 5th of February on the course he should adopt. A report was circulated that, as the King had broken his promise, and failed to come in to treat for peace, the army would advance in pursuit of him, and it was given out that all Ashantees found in the town after six a.m. on the 6th of February, would be shot, an announcement which effectually cleared the town. Prize agents at once set to work to collect all they could before the morning, when the return march was to commence; but unfortunately, as the number of carriers placed at their disposal was but thirty, only a small proportion of the valuables was removed.* Meanwhile, through

---

* 'By the light of two candles,' says an officer, 'the search began. In one room were found those gold masks, whose object it is so difficult to divine, made of pure gold hammered into shape. One of these, weighing more than forty-one ounces, represents a ram's head, and the others the faces of savage men, about half the size of life. Box after box was opened, and its contents hastily examined, the more valuable ones being kept, and the others left. Necklaces and bracelets of gold, Aggery beads, and coral ornaments of various descriptions, were heaped together in boxes and calabashes. Silver plate, swords, gorgeous ammunition-belts, caps mounted in solid

the drenching downpour, the Engineers were hard at work making preparations for destroying the palace and firing the town, acts of retribution which the General determined to adopt in order that he might leave behind, as he says, 'such a mark of our power to punish as should deter from future aggression a nation whom treaties do not bind.'

Soon after six a.m. the troops, headed by the Naval Brigade, with the 42nd as the rearguard, marched off on their return, and the great rise in the Soubang swamp, at the entrance of the town, showed what might be expected at the rivers. The preparation of the eight mines at the palace took longer than had been expected, and the rear of the main body had moved off from Coomassie a full hour before they were ready; but at length the mines were exploded, and the palace was left in ruins. At the same time the town was fired, and soon the thick thatched roofs of the houses were burning furiously. As the dense masses of smoke formed a funereal canopy over his capital, and the flames leapt high into mid-air, King Koffee learned the full extent of the defeat and humiliation that had befallen his dynasty, and suffered at the hands of the British General an adequate punishment for the manifold wrongs inflicted for so many years on the subject-races of his Sovereign.

So quickly had the waters risen, that in one place that was knee-deep, there was now a reach of 200 yards of water, and the troops had to cross the deepest part by means of a felled tree. The Brigadier-General, who was riding a mule, was nearly drowned, the animal rolling over him. The river Ordah was two feet above the bridge, and was still

---

gold, knives set in gold and silver, bags of gold-dust and nuggets, carved stools mounted in silver, calabashes worked in silver and gold, silks embroidered and woven, were all passed in review. The sword presented by Her Majesty to the King was found and carried off, and thousands of things were left behind that would be worth fabulous sums in cabinets at home.'

THE RETURN MARCH.

rising. The carriers crossed with their bundles on their heads, and the greater portion of the European troops proceeded by the bridge, which, however, gave way in the evening, when the 42nd had to strip and ford, or swim across, their clothes being carried by Natives. By dint of great exertions the whole force, during the night, reached Aggemmamu, where the General halted on the following day with the 42nd, Rifle Brigade, and Rait's Artillery. The remainder of the column continued the march for Cape Coast, which they reached, on the 20th, without any noteworthy incident, when the 23rd Regiment embarked for England, and the Naval Brigade proceeded on board their respective ships.

While at Aggemmamu Sir Garnet Wolseley wrote despatches to the Secretaries for War and the Colonies, which were forwarded by special steamer to England, together with the previously written despatch announcing the fall of Coomassie. The bearer, his aide-de-camp, Lieut. Hon. H. J. L. Wood, who received promotion and the customary grant of £500, also conveyed the state umbrella of the King of Ashantee, as a present from the troops to Her Majesty, and a carved stool, from the King's palace, to the Prince of Wales.

On the 8th of February Sir Garnet proceeded to Amoaful, and on the 10th arrived at Fommanah. The 42nd and Rifle Brigade continued their march for the coast, the latter embarking on the 21st of February, and the Highlanders a few days later. Sir Garnet halted at Fommanah with the Native troops, with the double object of seeing the last convoy of sick and wounded across the Adansi Hills, and of negotiating wtth King Koffee, who had sent a messenger to express his desire for peace, and his willingness to accede to all the terms of the British Commander, coupled with a request that he would order Captain Glover* to halt his forces.

Sir Garnet agreed to waive the question of hostages, 'as the Ashantee kingdom had been already so severely punished,' but required before arranging the terms of a treaty of peace, that 5,000 ounces of gold-dust should be sent 'as an earnest of his sincerity and as a first instalment of the indemnity.' Cobbina Obbin, King of Adansi, sent messengers expressing his desire to migrate, with his whole tribe, into British territory south of the Prah, and, at Sir Garnet's invitation, arrived, on the 11th of February, at Fommanah, where he was quartered in his own palace, the only building left standing in the town.

On the morning of the 13th, messengers arrived from King Koffee, bringing 1,040 ounces of gold, consisting of gold-dust, large plaques with bosses in the centre, nuggets, nails, bracelets, knobs, masks, bells, and ornaments of every description, some entire and others broken up. They declared that the King could not at the moment produce

* Captain Glover had been detained at Odumassie, only two marches from Coomassie, for want of spare ammunition and reinforcements, his total efficient force on the 4th of February numbering only 262 Houssas and an equal number of Yorubas, while he was encumbered with 60 sick and wounded. On the 6th of February he was joined by Lieutenant Moore, R.N., with 2,000 Aquapims and Croboes, 3 guns, and some rockets; and on the 8th, having heard, meanwhile, rumours of the fall of Coomassie, he started to join Sir Garnet Wolseley at the capital. On the same day the King of Juabin sent in his submission to Captain Glover, who ordered him to present himself to the British General at Coomassie. His halt at Odumassie had been of essential service to the main army, for, while they were fighting on the Ordah, he had held in check on the river Anoom the contingent of the King of Juabin. On the 10th he halted, agreeably to his instructions that he was 'not to cross the Dah, nor to approach nearer Coomassie than ten miles without orders from the General;' and Captain Sartorius, who volunteered to take a letter to Sir Garnet Wolseley, proceeded, with 20 picked Houssas, from Akina to Coomassie, a distance of eighteen miles. Passing through Coomassie, which he found deserted and smouldering, he bivouacked at Amoaful, and rode into the British camp at Fommanah on the 12th of February. Glover, finding that Captain Sartorius neither came back to him nor wrote, crossed the Ordah on the 11th, and entered Coomassie on the following day, when he learned that the King had accepted Sir Garnet's terms. Proceeding on his return march, he arrived at Quarman on the 14th.

THE TREATY OF FOMMANAH.

more, and as the General considered that the main point was to obtain the treaty of peace, and that the money was important chiefly as a proof of complete submission, he accepted the gold, which was weighed out in the presence of European officers and Natives, who recognised in the scene an unqualified admission of defeat on the part of the African potentate. This concluded, Sir Garnet placed in the hands of the envoys the draft of the instrument known as the 'Treaty of Fommanah,'* to the provisions of which they agreed after some demur.

The envoys returned to Coomassie with the draft treaty, which was brought back to Cape Coast on the 13th of March, duly ratified by the King. Sir Garnet, having written to Captain Glover† desiring him to cross the Prah, quitted Fommanah on the 14th of February, and arrived at Cape Coast on the 19th.

The loot brought from Coomassie was sold by auction at

* By this treaty King Koffee agreed to the following summarized conditions:

'To pay the sum of 50,000 ounces of approved gold as indemnity. To renounce all right or title to any tribute or homage from the Kings of Denkera, Assin, Akim, Adansi, and all pretensions of supremacy over Elmina. To guarantee freedom of trade between Ashantee and Her Majesty's forts on the coast, and to keep the road from Coomassie to the river Prah open and free from bush to a width of fifteen feet. To use his best endeavours to check the practice of human sacrifice, with a view to hereafter putting an end to it altogether.'

Sir Garnet wrote to Lord Kimberley that it was very doubtful whether the balance of the indemnity would ever be obtained from the King; 'but,' he adds, 'as the payment of a few thousand pounds cannot be a matter of relatively so great importance as the maintenance of peace, I have caused the wording of this clause to be carefully so framed as to make it clear that the money is only to be paid in such instalments and at such times as Her Majesty may direct. The whole question of the money will thus be open for solution in any way Her Majesty's Government may think fit.' He had before, when forwarding to Lord Kimberley, from Prahsu, a copy of his letter to the King, said, referring to the amount of his demand of 50,000 ounces: 'Owing to the limited information at my command as to the amount of gold at his disposal, it is possible that during negotiations I may feel it necessary to reduce it.'

† Captain Glover received this letter at Quarman, on the 14th of February, and marched to the sea-coast with his force of 4,450 men, of whom 715 were disciplined troops, reaching Prahsu on the 17th, when the column was broken up.

Cape Coast, and realized nearly £6,000, exclusive of the gold ornaments received at Fommanah as part of the indemnity, which were brought over to London, where they were exhibited and re-sold by the purchasers, Messrs. Garrard. The loot sold at Cape Coast consisted chiefly of the gold ornaments of the King's wives, and included two of His Majesty's solid gold pipes, a curious silver coffee-pot of George I.'s time, which Sir Garnet purchased, and an ivory-hilted sword, bearing on one side of the blade the following inscription: 'From Her Majesty Queen Victoria to the King of Ashantee.' This weapon, which was left by King Koffee in his bed-chamber when he made his hurried exit from Coomassie, was purchased by the officers of the Staff, and presented by them to their gallant Commander, with the following inscription on the reverse of the blade: 'Major-General Sir Garnet Joseph Wolseley, G.C.M.G., K.C.B., from the officers of his Staff. Coomassie, 4th February, 1874.' Doubtless the victor of Amoaful and Ordahsu possesses no more valued souvenir of his distinguished military career than this sword, to which a peculiar interest must attach from the names of the original donor and recipient, and the circumstances under which it changed hands.

On his arrival at Cape Coast, Sir Garnet occupied the interval before his departure for England in a great variety of matters that pressed for solution. Among important papers he drew up a valuable Minute* in regard to the future defence of the Gold Coast, upon which Her Majesty's Government have since acted.

* In this paper he proposed that military posts, garrisoned by Houssa police, should be maintained at Prahsu and Mansu, in order to protect Ashantee traders from the insults and exactions of the Fantees; also that a garrison of 300 armed police, 12 to be trained as gunners, under 4 European officers, should be maintained at Cape Coast. Addah, Quettah, and Elmina should each be held by a garrison of 100 armed police, and Secondee, Dixcove, and Akim, by 50 men at each post. These posts to be provisioned for three months, and the total strength of the garrisons, including 25 men at Annamaboe, to amount to 975 armed police, who might ultimately be reduced to 800.

LOSSES DURING THE CAMPAIGN.

The troops rapidly left the country during the latter part of February, and Wood's and Russell's Regiments and Rait's Houssa Artillery were disbanded.

Sir Garnet Wolseley proceeded to Accra in H.M.S. *Active*, and making over the temporary charge of affairs to Colonel Maxwell,* C.B., commanding the 1st West India Regiment, sailed on the 4th of March in the *Manitobah*, a name of happy augury, and arrived at Portsmouth on the 20th. Though the campaign, now so successfully closed, had been short, some valuable lives had been sacrificed. Of the original party of 30 Special Service officers, who had accompanied Sir Garnet to Cape Coast, up to the date of the entry into Coomassie, four—Captains Buckle, R.E., and Nicol, Hants Militia, and Lieutenants Eyre, 90th Regiment, and Wilmot, R.A. — had been killed: three — Captain Huyshe, Rifle Brigade, and Lieutenants Hon. A. Charteris, Coldstream Guards, and Townshend, 16th Regiment—had died from the effects of climate; and seven had been wounded, while nearly all, including the General himself, had been hit by slugs and had suffered more or less severely from fever. The total of deaths among officers in this brief war was 43;† while, in less than two months, no less than 71 per cent. of the European force suffered from sickness.

* Colonel Maxwell soon died from the effects of climate, and under the new arrangements, by which the colony was made independent of the Governor-in-Chief of Sierra Leone, Captain (now Sir George) Strahan, R.A., was nominated Governor, on the recommendation of Sir Garnet Wolseley, whom he had accompanied out to the West Coast in the *Ambriz*.

† The following died of wounds or disease in Ashantee, or soon after their return to England: Colonel Maxwell, Majors Baird and Farquharson, 42nd Regiment, and Saunders, R.A. Captains Thompson, Queen's Bays; Butler, 1st West India Regiment, and Hopkins, 2nd West India Regiment. Lieutenants Dalgleish, Warner, and Cox, 2nd West India Regiment; Roper, Clough, Burke, Elderton, Huntingford, and Williams, 1st West India Regiment; Gray, Royal Marines; Johnstone, 23rd Regiment. Captain Blake, R.N., Staff-Commander Prickett, Lieutenants Wells and Hirtzel, and Sub-Lieutenants Mundy, Bradshaw, and Ficklin, Naval Brigade. Commissaries Marsh and Marsden; Assistant-Commissaries Reid, Harrymount, and Burke. Surgeons-Major Burrows and Kelly; Surgeons Clarke, Bale, and M'Carthy. Lieutenant Dillon, Army Hospital Corps.

Several histories of the Ashantee War have been given to the world, some being little more than the republication of the letters of special correspondents, and of one it may be said that the writer displays great presumption in laying down what 'ought' to have been done. It is amusing to read the dogmatic assertions of men, who

> 'Never set a squadron in the field,
> Nor the division of a battle know,
> More than a spinster,'

but who criticize the movements of one of the most accomplished and experienced soldiers of the age, and, filled with the sense of their own heaven-born aptitude for the science of war—a knowledge which the General acquired by laborious study and hard service in many climes—lay down the law on the art military with all the assurance of ignorant presumption. Such men think they have displayed great critical acumen by inveighing against the General for showing a want of prescience in not providing against the possibility of such an unforeseen incident as the desertion of the carriers, or for the hurried retreat from Coomassie, when the heavy rains warned the Commander that the return might be a matter of difficulty were it delayed for the purpose of accomplishing such an utterly useless measure, either from a political or military point of view, as the destruction of Bantama. Those sage critics who, before the campaign, went about town with long faces and shaking heads, giving vent to the gloomiest prognostications—just as occurred when Lord Napier was organizing his Abyssinian Expedition—were the same gentlemen who, after the first burst of public exultation at the brilliant success achieved by Sir Garnet Wolseley, began, in the press, in society, and at the clubs, to pooh-pooh the difficulties that had been overcome, and to decry any great merit in the General who had returned after carrying out to the letter the programme he had originally announced.

A passage in Wolseley's 'Narrative of the War in China in 1860' (Chapter VII.), bears with singular force on this habit of non-military critics, of seeking to lessen the public estimation of the services of a General if his successes have been achieved without incurring 'a heavy butcher's bill.' 'Non-combatants,' he says, 'are at all times anxious to push on and make light of military precautions. After any successful operation, it is easy to speak of the facility with which it is accomplished, and, adducing the smallness of your losses in proof thereof, to remark, 'Oh, you might have done it with half the number,' forgetting or ignoring the fact that the rapid success was very much to be attributed to the display of force, which ever carries with it great moral power in war, and that the precautions taken were the means of saving your soldiers' lives.'

Great permanent results may be expected to flow from Sir Garnet Wolseley's military achievement on the Gold Coast, and peace, which our Fantee Protectorate has not known for fifty years, will no doubt be enjoyed by that distracted land. As time goes on it will be found that the revolution, social and political, that has been wrought by the destruction of the ascendency of the Ashantee monarchy, will be far-reaching in its consequences; and Fantee and Ashantee alike will require no monument to remind them of the debt of gratitude they owe to their liberator from the deadliest and most debasing tyranny the world has seen.

The Ashantee Campaign has been frequently likened to the Abyssinian War, and the comparison obviously presents itself to the mind, though the conditions under which such striking successes have been achieved by two British Commanders, are as dissimilar as can well be. Though Lord Napier had to march 400 miles before he could strike at his savage enemy, and Sir Garnet Wolseley considerably less than 200 miles, and though the engineering difficulties that beset every mile of the advance were in both cases well-nigh insuperable, yet the climatic conditions were greatly in favour of the Indian General. Lord Napier's soldiers, numbering 12,000 men, after passing the narrow belt of low land near Massowah, marched over a succession of stupendous passes and gorges, with grand scenery to enliven the march, and the most bracing climate in the world to strengthen the frame, so that every breath of mountain air drunk in by the soldiers as they mounted higher and still higher up the chain of hills, until they attained the plateau in which was placed the stronghold of Theodore, was exhilarating, and every step of the long and toilsome march only invigorated their constitutions.

Far different was it with the small band—less than one-quarter the strength of Lord Napier's army, of whom only 2,000, owing to the want of transport, crossed the Prah into the enemy's territory—which, under the leadership of Sir Garnet Wolseley, assayed the task of restoring peace to the British Protectorate, and curbing the pretensions of the Ashantee monarch. The duty had to be performed in three months, or not at all; the transport with which the expedition would have to be conducted was limited to human agency, for the first time, perhaps, in the history of war; and, lastly, all this had to be effected in the most deadly climate in the world. European life on the Gold Coast, under the most favourable conditions as to diet, housing, and freedom from exposure, is held on so precarious a lease that insurance offices refuse risks, or charge exorbitant rates; but in this case, a military expedition had to march through a dense forest, the miasma arising from whose fever-laden glades and paths was even more fatal to health than the tropical heat that struck the men to the earth in scores when they made forced marches in the more open country south of the Prah, and the troops groped their way through the dense forest and brushwood, in which, at times, they had to march in Indian file, while the superiority of breech-loading arms was reduced to a minimum. As we have seen, the loss in officers was exceptionally heavy, for they exposed themselves freely, and suffered accordingly; indeed, that more officers did not succumb to the climate, was due to the precautions taken by the medical staff, and to the strategic skill of the General, by which, though the early part of the war was conducted by small columns acting from outposts, there were always supports ready to prevent the enemy from cutting off detached parties.

The fighting at Ordahsu and, particularly, at Amoaful, was very severe, and it is the opinion of those best qualified to judge, that had the Ashantees been armed with tolerable muskets and serviceable ammunition, the British force must have been forced to retreat, when their numerical inferiority might have precipitated a terrible disaster.

Critics describe the Ashantees depreciatingly as 'naked savages;' but that they were destitute of clothes was certainly no disadvantage in a climate where the frame of the European loses its elasticity so that any clothing is an aggravation of suffering and a listless apathy steals over the mind even of the most resolute and energetic. Again, writers have spoken slightingly of the discipline of the Ashantees, but the facts point to a different conclusion. Sir Garnet Wolseley is of opinion that the discipline of the Ashantee army that opposed him at Amoaful was 'perfect, death being the punishment of any infraction.' A Staff officer, who watched the march of a party of 150 Ashantees at Ordahsu, mistook them for men of Wood's Regiment. He says : 'Their arms were all sloped; every man was closed up to what we call fronting distance; the pace was quite regular, though much slower than our quick march, and except for that, and the fact that they were all talking, they moved as do our best drilled soldiers.'

As regards cost, a comparison of the Expeditions of 1868 and 1873-4 is in favour of the latter. The British tax-payer is not likely soon to forget the Abyssinian bill of nine millions he was called upon to pay; but, as gratitude is one of the least common of virtues, he has probably not sufficiently considered how greatly he is indebted to Sir Garnet Wolseley who, when successive Governors and Ministries had 'muddled' the country into an Ashantee War, brought us out of our difficulties at the very moderate charge of £900,000 —a large portion of which was swallowed up by Captain Glover's subsidiary expedition—being one-tenth the cost of the Abyssinian War. Yet, though drawing this comparison, we hope fairly, to Lord Napier's disadvantage, we would be the last to deny, in the latter case, the great risk incurred, where failure would have been fatal to our interests and *prestige* in the East, and the striking merit of the march to Magdala, achieved by as high-minded, brave, and accomplished a soldier as any wearing Her Majesty's uniform.

The Nemesis that overtook King Koffee Kalkalli, and wrought the destruction of the seat of his power, though its visitation was of a less dramatic character than that which induced the tyrant Theodore, in an access of frenzied despair, to take his own life, forms a striking episode of our Colonial history. The result, in both cases alike, was complete and crushing, and the flames that lit up the blackened rock of Magdala and the sombre forests of Ashantee, read a lesson to the savage tribes of East and West Africa, which they are not soon likely to forget; at the same time, also, the prowess of our soldiers and the skill of their leaders testified to the world that England was not so effete as her detractors, domestic and foreign, chose to imagine, but that British Generals and British soldiers, like their sires, could illustrate the art of war under conditions as novel as they were difficult.

Sir Garnet Wolseley, in his final despatch to Lord Kimberley, says of the Ashantee Power, 'that no more utterly atrocious Government has ever existed on the face of the earth. Their capital was a charnel-house; their religion a combination of cruelty and treachery; their policy the natural outcome of their religion.' And of the results of the war he says: 'I believe that the main object of my expedition has been perfectly secured. The territories of the Gold Coast will not again be troubled with the warlike ambition of this restless Power. I may add that the flag of England from this moment will be received throughout Western Africa with respectful awe, a treatment which has been of late years by no means its invariable fate among the savage tribes of this region.' That this end has been accomplished there can be no doubt, and that it has been effected at so small a cost in life and treasure, is due to the energy and skill of Sir Garnet Wolseley, who has added a page to our annals that may be read with pride by his countrymen, and studied with advantage by the student of military history.

The 23rd Royal Welsh Fusiliers, which sailed from England with a strength of 650 officers and men, landed at Portsmouth on the 20th of March, 503 strong, the difference representing the loss by death and sickness while on service on the Gold Coast for three months. The 42nd Highlanders, which sailed 687 strong, had, during their brief absence, besides losses in action, upwards of six-tenths of their strength in hospital, and landed from the *Sarmatian* on the 23rd of March, to the number of 570 of all ranks. The last to arrive at Portsmouth was the Rifle Brigade, who received similar honours to those accorded to their brethren in arms. The Rifles had landed at Cape Coast with a strength of 33 officers and 652 men, of whom no less than 22 officers and 298 men had been admitted into hospital. On their reembarkation at Cape Coast, only 16 officers and 277 men were returned fit for duty, owing to the marching being continuous since leaving Fommanah for Coomassie, on the 29th of January, and they landed on the 26th of March with a strength of 27 officers and 483 men. All three regiments were inspected within a few days of their arrival, by H.R.H. the Duke of Cambridge, who paid them a well-deserved compliment on the state of efficiency in which they had returned from active service.*

The *Manitobah* arrived at Portsmouth on the 20th of March, and, on the following morning, Sir Garnet Wolseley landed, accompanied by his Staff and most of the Special Service officers who had sailed with him in the *Ambriz*. At his request, his arrival and time of landing had been kept secret, so that, being in mufti, he was able to proceed by the first train to London without having to pass through the ordeal of a public reception or popular ovation.

On the following day, the General, having received the commands of Her Majesty, who had already telegraphed her congratulations to him at Madeira, proceeded to Windsor. On the 30th of March, the General and his little army received a double honour—the public approval of Her Majesty, as expressed by her reviewing the troops at Windsor, in the presence of the Legislature, and a vote of thanks from both Houses of Parliament, in which the two leading statesmen of the age vied with each other in praising the successful soldier.

---

* Lady Wolseley, as soon as intelligence arrived in London of the losses incurred during the three days' fighting before Coomassie, wrote a letter to the *Times*, on the 7th of March, initiating a subscription in aid ' of the widows, children, and families, generally dependent on the brave soldiers and sailors who have fallen in battle, or been victims to the climate in West Africa ;' and headed the list by a subscription of fifty guineas from herself, and a like sum from Sir Garnet Wolseley.

The review was held in the large open space between Queen Anne's Ride and the Long Walk, and after the inspection was over, the troops were formed into a hollow square, when Sir Garnet, having dismounted, was invested by the Queen with the insignia of the Grand Cross of the Order of St. Michael and St. George, and of a Knight Commander of the Bath. Sir Archibald Alison was then presented to Her Majesty, and also Lord Gifford, who was decorated with the Victoria Cross. The Duke of Cambridge, by command of the Queen, then expressed Her Majesty's thanks to the assembled troops, for their gallant services during the campaign; after which the Queen took her station beneath the royal standard, while her gallant soldiers marched past, headed by their Commander.

The march-past over, the troops were formed in line, with Sir Garnet Wolesley at their head. Slowly the long line advanced to within about fifty yards of the royal carriage, when the troops were halted, and Sir Garnet repeated the ceremony he so recently performed within the market-place of Coomassie. Under far different surroundings, in the presence of an assemblage as dissimilar as it is possible to imagine, the successful General raised his hat in the air, and calling for 'three cheers for the Queen,' received a response given with true soldier-like heartiness and precision, the multitude of spectators echoing this spontaneous ebullition of loyalty. As the Queen drove away, once more the strains of the 'National Anthem' burst forth, and the troops saluted. And so ended one of the most interesting of the many reviews that have been held in the Royal Park of Windsor.[*]

[*] Shortly after Her Majesty held a review at Gosport of the sailors and marines who had returned to this country; and, as a special mark of her approval of their conduct, the Queen, at Windsor Castle, conferred with her own hand upon nine men of the Naval Brigade the medal for conspicuous gallantry in the Ashantee War.

In the evening of the 30th of March, the benches and galleries of the Houses of Parliament were crowded, while the leaders of the Government proposed, in fitting terms, the vote of thanks to the gallant Ashantee army and its skilful leader, for the 'exemplary skill with which he planned, and the distinguished courage, energy, and perseverance with which he conducted, the recent expedition into Ashantee, resulting in the expulsion of the enemy's army from the British Protectorate, the defeat, by Her Majesty's forces, of the army of the King of Ashantee, and the capture and destruction of Coomassie.' The Duke of Richmond and Lord Granville having moved the vote of thanks in the Lords, the Duke of Cambridge addressed the House, in his capacity of Commander-in-Chief, and spoke of Wolseley as having always displayed 'the true instincts of a soldier.' Very happily conceived were the speeches in which Mr. Disraeli and Mr. Gladstone moved the thanks in the House of Commons.

The important question of rewards and honours to the officers and men of the expedition now came up for consideration, and it cannot be said that the Government erred on the side of illiberality. Five officers received the Ribbon of the Bath, twenty-five the C.B., and five the C.M.G. All field-officers and captains who had distinguished themselves received brevet promotion. As the amount realized by the sale of loot was inconsiderable, the troops and seamen received a gratuity of thirty days' pay, in lieu of prize-money. A medal was instituted for the Ashantee War, and Her Majesty testified the great personal interest she takes in all that concerns the interests of her soldiers, by making certain suggestions in the design.*

* On one side is the head of the Queen, with the legend 'Victoria Regina.' On the reverse side is a representation of a struggle in the Ashantee forest between some Native warriors in the foreground and a few British soldiers, clad in the uniform adopted for the Ashantee Expedition, in the background. There is a bar for 'Coomassie,' and another for 'Amoaful.' The ribbon is black and yellow, colours selected in honour of the Duchess of Edinburgh, as being those of the Russian national flag.

Sir Garnet Wolseley was offered the Grand Cross of the Order of the Bath, which, however, he declined, but accepted the second grade. Though he held the local rank of Major-General while employed on the Gold Coast, he was still only a Brevet-Colonel in the army, his substantive rank being 'Major half-pay, late 90th Regiment'; he was now promoted by Special General Order to the rank of Major-General,* 'for distinguished service in the field.' The Government, interpreting the wishes of the country, and the precedent usually followed in such cases, rewarded the successful soldier, who had extricated them from a serious and most perplexing difficulty, by the bestowal of something more substantial than ribbons and crosses, and, on the 20th of April, a motion was made in the House of Commons for the bestowal of a grant of £25,000. Mr. Disraeli also offered him a baronetcy, which was respectfully declined.

Perhaps the value of the offer was lessened by the consideration that at the time the Premier proposed an hereditary distinction to the victorious General, whose achievements he had described in picturesque terms, and of whose skill in the conception and execution of his plan of campaign Mr. Gladstone declared that history afforded no more striking example—at this very time the cynical author of 'Coningsby' conferred baronetcies broadcast among his followers and others, who had 'spent laborious days' in amassing large fortunes, which they expended in 'living at home at ease,' reserving a portion, mayhap, for profuse ex-

* The following are the dates of Sir Garnet Wolseley's various commissions in the army: Ensign 12th Foot, 12th of March, 1852; Ensign 80th Foot, 13th of April, 1852; Lieutenant 80th Foot, 16th of May, 1853; Lieutenant 84th Foot, 27th of January, 1854; Lieutenant 90th Foot, 24th of February, 1854; Captain 90th Foot, 26th of January, 1855; Brevet-Major, 24th of March, 1858; Major (half-pay), 15th of February, 1861; Major 90th Foot, 6th of August, 1861; Major (half-pay), 14th of January, 1862; Brevet Lieutenant-Colonel, 26th of April, 1859; Brevet-Colonel, 5th of June, 1865; Major-General (local), 6th of September, 1873; Major-General, March, 1874, ante-dated to 6th of March, 1868; Lieutenant-General, 25th of March, 1878; and General, 18th of November, 1882.

penditure in contesting a seat when the Conservative party sat on the left hand of the Speaker. Such public spirit, or that other form, which induces a Lord Mayor to lavish vast sums in entertaining a foreign sovereign, may only receive an adequate recognition in a baronetcy; but if so, there is nothing astonishing in the fact of a soldier, who had served his country in all quarters of the globe, respectfully declining the honour.

Not that there was any choice between the Conservative and Liberal Governments, the 'ins' and the 'outs,' in this question of hereditary rewards; for the latter, shortly before, rendered desperate by their sudden exodus from office, had signalized their exit by a perfect shower of baronetcies, conferred on political supporters with a haste that had its ludicrous, no less than its reprehensible, side. In the *sauve qui peut* which followed their retreat from the Treasury benches, a chosen few happily managed to find shelter from the wreck of the Liberal cause within the portals of the House of Lords, in the 'serene atmosphere' of which they will, doubtless, 'rest and be thankful.' But others were made peers and baronets, such as drawing-room soldiers, country gentlemen having the qualification of broad acres, or political supporters who had contested successfully—or unsuccessfully, as the case might be—vacant seats, and whose large expenditure of private means, and admirable consistency in voting according to the behests of the party 'whip,' called for some reward from their masters. But what services had these honourable and right honourable gentlemen rendered their country that they should be pitchforked into peerages and baronetcies? Has England so greatly benefited by the contentions of party and the haste of private persons to amass fortunes that hereditary distinctions should be lavished on political mediocrities and city mayors, while soldiers like Sir Charles Napier, the conqueror of Scinde;

Sir Henry Godwin, who gained the province of Pegu for the British crown; or Sir Hope Grant, who extorted an advantageous treaty for his country, should be suffered to pass away without such acknowledgments?

Sir Garnet Wolseley had no ambition other than to attain eminence in his profession; he was, before all things, a soldier, and to the military art he was devoted, not for the sake of the emoluments and honours usually attaching to success, but from a sense of duty. Hence he was able to refuse without a pang a baronetcy and the highest honours of the Bath, and, by adopting this course, he showed his wisdom in avoiding the acceptance of too many honours, which would only tend to excite feelings of jealousy among the less successful of his brothers-in-arms.

Sir Garnet Wolseley was not suffered to be any length of time in England before he was subjected to a very severe course of those public dinners, with the concomitant evil of speech-making, to which all eminent naval and military commanders are doomed on their return fresh from the field of their glory. The first public banquet was given at the Mansion House on the 31st of March, when he was accompanied by his Staff, and by a large number of the officers of the Ashantee army. It was the first occasion since his return from the scene of his successes that Sir Garnet had been afforded an opportunity of laying before the nation his own views on some of the matters that had engrossed the public attention during the past few months. He spoke with a fluency of diction and an ease of manner not frequently met with among officers of the service, who are usually more at home wielding the sword than when exhibiting their oratorical powers in the presence of a critical audience.

Two City Companies, the Clothworkers and Grocers, conferred their honorary freedom on Sir Garnet Wolseley, and entertained him at dinner, and the members of the United Service Club gave him a banquet, at which were present the Prince of Wales, the Duke of Cambridge, and about 140 noblemen and gentlemen, including the Secretaries for War and First Lords of the Admiralty of Mr. Gladstone's and Lord Beaconsfield's Administrations. The Duke of Cambridge having proposed the health of the guest of the evening, Sir Garnet made a speech, in which (not having the fear of the reporters before his eyes) he detailed the considerations that had guided him in quitting Coomassie so hurriedly, and which have been already placed before the reader when treating of that event. Sir Garnet Wolseley was a guest at the annual banquet of the Royal Academy, when he was honoured by having his health proposed in the most flattering terms by the heir to the throne. He was also fêted by his countrymen at Dublin, and received honorary degrees from the Universities on two successive days, the 16th and 17th of June, the occasions being those known as 'Commemoration' at Oxford, and 'Commencement' at Cambridge. The undergraduates of Cambridge cheered vociferously when Sir Garnet Wolseley was introduced to the Chancellor (the Duke of Devonshire); and his reception was not less enthusiastic at Oxford.

The Corporation of the City of London, having shortly after his return from Ashantee voted Sir Garnet Wolseley the freedom, accompanied by a sword of honour,* the pre-

* This sword is a beautiful specimen of the goldsmith's art, irrespective of its intrinsic value. The handle, of massive and handsome design, is formed of figures representing Wisdom and Truth, while recumbent figures of Fame and Victory form the guard. The scabbard is enriched with the arms and monogram of Sir Garnet Wolseley and of the city, with several groups of figures, representing the triumph of Valour over Tyranny, Britannia encouraging the Natives to energy and resistance, and trophies of Ashantee instruments of warfare. The blade bears the following inscription, surrounded by an ornamental border: 'Presented by the Corporation of London to Major-General Sir Garnet Joseph Wolseley, K.C.B., G.C.M.G., in recognition of his gallant services in the British army, and especially in reference to the distinguished ability and gallantry displayed by him in his

sentation took place, on the 22nd of October, at the Guildhall, and was conducted with all the ceremony usual on the rare occasions when potent sovereigns and successful generals have been similarly honoured. The list of the latter includes some of the greatest soldiers this country has produced—for the city authorities have ever jealously guarded the admission into their Valhalla of heroes—and reads almost like an epitome of our military history. The roll commences before the time of Monk and Marlborough, and, beginning with the first year of this century, includes the following names: Sir Ralph Abercrombie, fresh from his achievements in the West Indies, and just before he embarked for that expedition to Egypt, destined to be fatal to himself, but glorious to his country. Sir David Baird, who, with General Harris and Colonel Wellesley, beat down the power of Tippoo Sultan at Seringapatam, and wrested Cape Colony from the Dutch. The Iron Duke and his Lieutenants, Graham and Beresford, and others; the bluff old Blücher, called by his soldiers 'Marshal Forward;' Barclay de Tolly, and Platoff, the bold and remorseless leader of the Don Cossacks; and the Austrian General Swartzenburg, the victor of Leipsic—a remarkable group, the military representatives of the allied nations, whose sovereigns visited the Prince Regent in 1814.

Our Indian triumphs supplied some of the most noted recipients of civic swords of honour. Among these were Nott, Sale, and Pollock, the three veterans who upheld our honour in Afghanistan after it had been dragged in the mire through the incompetence of other commanders. Sir Charles Napier, a year later, earned his sword for his marvellous campaign in Scinde; and then came Lord Gough, who retrieved his

---

command of the Expedition to the Gold Coast, by which he obtained results conducive to peace, commerce, and civilization on the Continent of Africa.' The whole of the work, executed in silver-gilt, enriched with fine gold and enamel, is richly chased.

laurels at Goojerat, and Lord Hardinge, the hero of Albuera and Ferozeshur, where the sceptre of empire was nearly wrested from our hands by the soldiers of the Khalsa; and Sir Harry Smith, the victor of Aliwal. Sir William Williams was the next recipient for his defence of Kars, aided by Lake and Teesdale; and then there appeared upon the scene, to receive a reward he had earned by fifty years' hard service in Spain, America, China, India, and the Crimea, that fine veteran, Lord Clyde, who was quickly succeeded by his brother-in-arms and equal in fame, that Bayard of the Indian army, *sans peur et sans reproche*, Sir James Outram, both so soon to lie in the Abbey. Last on this roll of glorious names was Lord Napier of Magdala, the conqueror of Theodore, and the friend of Outram, whose high opinion of his military talents has been fully justified. And now there came into the city, to receive the civic honours, a General, young in years when compared with any of those who preceded him, but not unworthy to enroll his name among theirs as that of a soldier who had done the state some service on many fields and in varied climes.*

Soon after Sir Garnet Wolseley's return from Ashantee, he was appointed Inspector-General of the Auxiliary Forces, in succession to his friend Lieutenant-General the Hon. Sir James Lindsay. In February, 1875, he was called upon by the Government to proceed to Natal, and assume temporarily the direction of military and civil affairs. The colonists of Natal were much excited by the outbreak of Langalibalele's† tribe—a vexed question, the merits of which we would not

* During the present century 68 individuals have received the Freedom of the City of London, of whom 26 were distinguished soldiers and sailors, 12 representatives of royalty, the remaining 30 being eminent statesmen, travellers, judges, scholars, and merchants.

† Langalibalele was brought from Natal to Robben Island in August, 1874, and was soon after removed to the place on the mainland in the Cape Colony, where he has been since detained.

presume to discuss—and were irate at the efforts made by Bishop Colenso* to obtain from the Colonial Office a reversal of the sentence of banishment passed on that chief, who was accused of rebellion. Hence there was much soreness towards the governing powers in this country, and considerable tact and discretion were required to manage the colonists and remodel their institutions. Another object of his mission, not inferior in importance to the political problem, was to inquire into and report upon the question of military defence. The Zulu King, Cetewayo, was said to be restless and ambitious, while his army of 40,000 men, well disciplined and fairly well armed, were spoken of as the bravest and most athletic warriors in South Africa, and as desirous of 'washing their spears' in the blood of the English colonists across the Tugela.

* Bishop Colenso received as much abuse for his action in defending Langalibalele as for his famous work on the Pentateuch. Mr. Walter Macfarlane, Speaker of the Legislative Council, addressing his constituents, said of the Bishop: 'He runs amuck, like a drunken Malay, against everything Colonial; publishes a book in England, criticizing the Government and its acts; through his access to the public press, he gets his incorrect, one-sided views impressed on the people; converts, it is said, Lord Carnarvon to his views; upsets the Governor on charges which are not first submitted to that officer by the authorities in Downing Street for explanation or refutation; gets our whole Kafir policy altered, and takes or gets credit to himself among the ignorant and unreflecting for being the only English friend in South Africa of the much-injured Kafir.'

CHAPTER VIII.

THE NATAL MISSION.

Sir Garnet Wolseley proceeds on a Special Mission to Natal.—Reception at Durban and Maritzburg.—Natal Politics and Parties.—The Constitution Amendment Bill.—Triumph of Sir Garnet Wolseley's Policy.—His Progress through Natal.—Returns to England.—Is appointed High Commissioner and Commander-in-Chief of Cyprus.

SIR GARNET WOLSELEY was personally disinclined to accept the honourable, but not very grateful, task of reforming the administration of Natal; but in this instance, as throughout his career, he never suffered his private wishes to stand in the way of a manifest duty, and he left England at four days' notice. He could ill be spared from his important office at the head of the Auxiliary Forces, with the position and requirements of which he had become familiar, and it was rather singular that the Government could not find a Colonial ex-Governor, or a civilian of experience, to set Natal affairs in order; it was, however, considered desirable that the Colony should be placed in a state of defence, so that there might be no excuse for a repetition of the panic into which the white colonists—who only numbered 17,000 as against 350,000 Natives—had been thrown by the recent rebellion of Langalibalele, and Lord Carnarvon, instead of applying for the services of a military officer for this special duty, decided upon placing the supreme direction of civil and military affairs in the hands of a man who had recently been so successful in the dual capacity.

Sir Garnet Wolseley sailed in the *Windsor Castle*, in the latter part of February, accompanied by Mr. Napier Broome as Colonial Secretary, and the following Staff: Colonel G. P. Colley, C.B., who had special experience of Natal affairs between 1859-61; Major Butler, C.B.; Major H. Brackenbury, R.A., Military Secretary; and Lord Gifford, V.C., aide-de-camp—all of whom had been tried in the hard Ashantee school, and had certainly not been found wanting. The *Windsor Castle* made the passage to Cape Town in twenty-four and a half days, during which Sir Garnet and his Staff were very comfortable, the ship being well found by her owners, the Messrs. Donald Currie, differing greatly from his experiences in his voyages to China, Canada, and the Gold Coast. At Madeira Sir Garnet met the Channel Squadron, under Rear-Admiral Beauchamp Seymour, when the *Agincourt* saluted him with 17 guns. At the Cape, Wolseley and his Staff were hospitably entertained by Sir Henry and Lady Barkly, and drove to Constantia, which all visitors to the Cape know so well, with its beautiful prospect and delicious grapes, and rode 'round the Kloof,' not less celebrated for its fine mountain and sea views. A few days before Sir Garnet reached the Cape, the flying squadron had arrived from Monte Video, under the command of Admiral Randolph, who had received instructions from the Admiralty to conform to Wolseley's requirements, in the event of the outbreak of a Kafir war, which was anticipated, owing to the excited feelings of the Natives. In order to give due effect to the importance of the Natal Mission, the Admiral placed at the disposal of Sir Garnet H.M.S. *Raleigh*, of 22 guns, Captain G. Tyron, C.B., who had superintended the naval transport department in the Ashantee Expedition.

The *Raleigh* arrived at Durban on the 29th of March (Easter Monday), and, on the following morning, Wolseley landed, under the usual honours, while the inhabitants, official and non-official, gave him a most enthusiastic reception. It was only a few days before his arrival, that the colonists learned that the hero of Coomassie was coming to them as Administrator, and the prospect threw all classes into a fever of excitement. Sir Garnet Wolseley, in reply to a highly encomiastic address of the mayor, declared that his mission was to establish 'a firm Government that shall guarantee perfect security to the white settler, both in life and property, whilst the great Native population within your province shall feel that their interests are not forgotten.'

During his stay of two days at Durban, he entertained the chief Colonial officials, and took advantage of his visit to make the acquaintance of the principal inhabitants, and discuss with them the political difficulties of the Colony. Sir Garnet's position was all the more difficult as he was superseding Sir Benjamin Pine, a Governor of considerable experience and great popularity among the colonists, to judge by the many addresses expressing regret at his departure and approval of his policy.* But the Langalibalele difficulty, about which public opinion was so greatly excited, was soon placed in the fair way of settlement by the course adopted by Mr. Molteno, Premier of the Cape Ministry, who, in accordance with Lord Carnarvon's desire, agreed to introduce into Parliament a Bill for the release from gaol of the chief, and his location at Robben Island, so that he would cease to trouble Natal by his presence or the intrigues of his followers.

---

* Public opinion in England, however, was almost unanimous against the course of the Governor in the Langalibalele affair, and this notwithstanding that Mr. (now Sir Theophilus) Shepstone, an able and distinguished statesman—who had unequalled Colonial experience as guardian of Native interests for a quarter of a century—came to England to lay before Lord Carnarvon his view of the official case, in opposition to that of Bishop Colenso. 'There was,' said the *Times*, 'practically only one conclusion. Every one who considered the question, no matter what his prepossessions, ended by confessing that the colonists and their Government had been painfully misled.'

On the 1st of April, Sir Garnet Wolseley, with his Staff and Messrs. Napier Broome and Theophilus Shepstone, Secretary for Native Affairs, proceeded from Durban to the capital, Pieter-Maritzburg, in a four-in-hand break, doing the distance of fifty-four miles in a little over six hours, considered quite a feat, as the road was bad in places.

Sir Garnet was sworn in on the day of his arrival at Maritzburg, and, on the following day, held an Executive Council, when Mr. Napier Broome was appointed Colonial Secretary, and Major Brackenbury, Clerk of the Council. Colonel Colley was also nominated Acting-Treasurer and Postmaster-General, and Major Butler, Acting Protector of Immigrants, both without salary, the holders of these offices being given leave on full pay. To Lord Gifford were relegated the duties of Master of the Household, a post of no small importance in a mission where the exercise of tact and the influence of social amenities were almost as necessary in successfully carrying through the delicate work on hand, as talent and firmness. Soon after, another aristocratic addition was made to Sir Garnet's Staff in Lord Mandeville, eldest son of the Duke of Manchester.

The points upon which new legislation was required, were briefly: A sounder and fairer Native policy than that in operation; the security of life and property; the promotion of public works and immigration; and, lastly, the amendment of a Constitution which the elected members of the Legislative Council themselves declared to be unworkable. This was the *crux* of Sir Garnet Wolseley's Mission, and it was one that perhaps few men would have cared to undertake; failure, with which no man likes to have his name associated, was *almost assured*, and such an incident in a distinguished career would be peculiarly galling to an ambitious man like Wolseley, who could say of his diplomatic missions to Manitoba and Ashantee, no less than of his campaigns,

Veni, Vidi, Vici. He was still young, with a great future before him, and yet, without a thought of self-interest, he undertook a mission in which non-success was anticipated even by the Secretary of State, Lord Carnarvon, who was prepared, if need be, to adopt the extreme course of presenting a Bill to the House of Commons for forcing a new Constitution upon the recalcitrant Council.

The Legislative Council—as inaugurated on the 24th of March, 1857, since which seven Councils had been elected—consisted of 20 members, 15 elected and 5 nominated, the latter being the Colonial Secretary, the Secretary for Native Affairs, the Attorney-General, the Treasurer, and the Protector of Immigrants. These 5, with the Chief Justice and the Commandant of the troops, form the Executive Council, which sits under the Presidency of the Governor. The 15 elected members of the Legislative Council represented, at this time, an electoral body of only 4,000 electors, of whom less than half voted at a General Election—indeed, at the last, for a contested election for the return of 2 members for the county of Klif-river, there were only 124 votes recorded. The elected members easily preponderated in all divisions of the Council, and, in the previous Session, they had gone so far as to reject the votes of the nominated members, upon the passing of a Bill to amend and declare the Constitution of the Colony, upon the ground that their interest was remote and contingent.

But the chief obstacle to the system of responsible Government, sought for by the colonists, lay in the existence of the vast Native population, who would be governed and taxed by a Council, chosen by 4,000 electors, whose interests were diametrically opposed to those of the Kafirs. What the Council was capable of was shown in previous years, by the passing of a Protection Bill and a Census Bill, measures which would doubtless have brought on a Kafir War, had

DIFFICULTIES OF LEGISLATION. 333

not the Colonial Office disallowed them. On the other hand, it was only just that the Imperial Government should have a voice in the ill-considered legislation of these Councillors, as, in the event of an outbreak, the colonists would call for British troops to repress a disturbance caused by such measures as, for instance, that for 'utilizing Native locations.'

It is always a matter of difficulty to obtain a surrender of power from those who possess it, and this was the task Sir Garnet Wolseley undertook to accomplish. The European colonists were divided into several separate interests.* There was the sugar and coffee-growing interest on the coast, who required a cheap and constant supply of Coolie labour, and appealed to the Legislative Council for funds to introduce Natives from India. Then there was the up-country sheep-farming interest, which objected to the application of funds for the importation of Coolies, but clamoured for the introduction of white immigrants, and the breaking-up of the Native locations. There was also the trading interests of the towns, who approved the promotion of railways; and, finally, what may be called the 'vested interests' of the Legislative Councillors themselves, who received 17s. 6d. per day during the Session. Added to this, the Colony was torn by discordant opinions—literally, '*quot homines, tot sententiæ*'—on the Native Question, Responsible Government Question, the Coolie Question, the White Immigration Question, the Railway Question, the Land Question, and last, but not least, the Church Question, with its rival Bishops of Maritzburg and Natal.

To concede responsible government to a Colony thus circumstanced, would have been unwise; and Lord Carnarvon,

---

* There were four papers in the Colony, one of which—the *Natal Witness*, edited by a clever but violent councillor—went so far as to call upon the colonists to take up arms and fight for their liberties. The other papers were the *Natal Mercury*, a moderate and well-written organ, the *Natal Colonist*, and *Times of Natal*.

so far from doing so, had resolved to increase the number of nominated members in the Council, so as to secure the balance of power in the hands of the Crown, as the *ex-officio* members being united and permanent in their position, would be able to control the acts of their colleagues. The history of the past few years amply justified this course. The Government, thwarted by the Council, were compelled to enter into an alliance with the Coast members, the consideration being the supply of Coolies, and so matters went on in a discreditable, halting fashion. There were continual dead-locks, supplies were withheld, and the Councillors refused to argue questions, but 'decided in a caucus and voted in silence.' The Council, in the previous Session, themselves denounced the system as one which had failed to meet the requirements of the Colony, or to secure its good government, but whereas a minority clamoured for responsible Government, the mission of Sir Garnet Wolseley was in a contrary sense, namely, to strengthen the Executive, and institute a new Native Policy, by which gradually the influence of European magistrates would be substituted for the power of the chiefs.

During the month of April, Sir Garnet went on a tour of inspection to the coast, when Colonel Colley and Mr. Broome managed affairs during his absence. He visited some of the chief plantations, and while at Durban, besides transacting business, held levées, and attended regattas, inspections, and banquets, or gave balls and dinners in return. On the 23rd of April, he returned to Maritzburg to prepare for the Session, when a round of gaiety was instituted at Government House, and one of the opposition papers stated that the popular Governor was 'drowning the independence of the country in sherry and champagne.'

On the 5th of May, Sir Garnet Wolseley opened the Session of the Legislative Council, in a speech wherein he stated that a modification of the Council was necessary, in the sense of 'increasing and assuring the power of the Executive,' which was 'essential to the present safety and future progress of the Colony.' When the Governor had left the Chamber, one of the Councillors rose and called the speech an insult to the Colony, and declared that it merited no reply at all. A writer in the chief Maritzburg paper spoke of Lord Carnarvon, Sir Garnet Wolseley, and Mr. Broome, as three 'howling humanitarian fanatics,' and at a large public meeting it was resolved unanimously, that it was the duty of the Government to turn every Kafir out of Natal. Such were the amenities of the conflict upon which the new Governor had entered, and such the views of the Opposition in this Council and Colony.

In the following week the Constitution Amendment Bill, for increasing the nominated members of the Council from 5 to 15, was brought in, and the debate on the second reading, which lasted for three nights, was heated and acrimonious, though conducted with considerable ability on both sides. When passing through committee, the Government had to submit to a compromise—which was only carried by a majority of one, and that member was in such precarious health that he had to be carried into the House—by which the 10 aditional nominees were reduced to 8, who were to be chosen from colonists of two years' standing, with a £1,000 property qualification. A few days later the third reading was carried, and then the measure was sent home for the Queen's signature before becoming law. At one time, however, failure appeared so assured that Sir Garnet prepared his despatch to the Secretary of State, announcing his want of success. Much was due to the ability[*] of the

[*] The views of the Governor on the questions under consideration were represented in one of the Natal papers, which was purchased for six months, the leading articles being written by his staff, among whom were writers of commanding literary attainments, such as Brackenbury, Butler, and Colley.

Government advocates, Messrs. Broome and Gallwey (Attorney-General), Colonel Colley, and Major Butler, who was specially ready and amusing in debate; also to the high prestige attaching to the name of Sir Garnet, whose unbounded hospitality in entertaining the leading men and legislators of both political parties was the theme of praise, while his geniality and fascination of manner won all hearts. During the Queen's birthday-week were held the Maritzburg Races and Agricultural Show, to which Sir Garnet Wolseley gave prizes, as he had done at Durban for the Regatta, and also for essays on Colonial products. Altogether, what with the round of balls, banquets, and garden-parties at Government House, the ladies of the Colony will long remember the brief administration of Sir Garnet Wolseley, with his gay *entourage*, as the most brilliant in Colonial annals.

The Bill settled, the Governor, accompanied by Mr. Shepstone, Major Brackenbury, and Lord Gifford, went on an extended tour round the up-country districts and Native locations, while Colonel Colley and Major Butler proceeded on semi-official missions to the neighbouring states, the former visiting the Transvaal Republic and the Portuguese Settlement at Delagoa Bay, and Major Butler, the Orange Free State, returning *viâ* the Diamond Fields and Basuto Land.

According to the Natal mode of travelling, Sir Garnet journeyed in a 'buck-waggon,' drawn by eighteen oxen; this vehicle, which carries the supplies and *impedimenta*, goes creaking along between ten or twelve miles a day; but it is the only mode of conveyance practicable in this country, as those who have tried horses have found out to their cost. The 'buck-waggon' is large and roomy, and, if the traveller possesses sufficient patience to bear the slowness of the rate of progression, he can make himself comfortable at each 'out-span.' Sir Garnet took ponies with him, so that he was

A TOUR THROUGH THE COLONY. 337

able to ride about the country while the waggon was wending its way, and, the weather being perfect, the trip was most enjoyable. Only one accident happened on the road, at the Tugela River, where the huge vehicle slid down the bank and turned completely over, smashing the wine-cases and crockery, but luckily breaking no bones.

The first part of the journey lay along the base of the Drakensberg Mountains, and Sir Garnet proceeded to the location of Langalibalele, the famous chief and rain-doctor, the *teterrima causa belli*, whose tribe had been broken up in accordance with Lord Carnarvon's instructions, and personally inquired into their condition and that of the neighbouring Putili tribe, who had also been 'eaten-up'—that is, deprived of their cattle—for alleged complicity in the rebellion. Sir Garnet resolved to restore to them the value of their property in ploughs and seed, as well as cattle and sheep, and also decided to place in each location an European magistrate to whom the Kafirs could look for guidance, advice, and protection, thus superseding the influence of their chiefs, under whom progress was impossible. By bringing the Natives into contact with civilizing agencies, and by the construction of roads, the allotment of lands to settlers, and the formation of townships, the Kafirs, it was hoped, would be gradually reclaimed, while they would experience new wants, which could only be satisfied by the earnings of labour. But these changes had to be introduced with tact, or a Native war would result; and this was the problem which required solution at the hand of Sir Garnet Wolseley, who applied to the Home Government to station in the Colony an entire regiment, instead of a wing, with a battery of light mountain guns, and an increased force of mounted police. The Ministry were fully alive to the danger of the innovations about to be introduced, and directed the *Adventure* troop-ship, returning from

Japan, with a battalion of Marines, to call for orders at Durban.

One of the most interesting sights witnessed during his tour by the Governor was a Kafir war-dance performed, on the 3rd of July, at Ollivier Hoek, by 550 warriors of the Amangurana tribe, whose location lies between that of the Putili and the Tugela River. The Kafirs, who were dressed in wild and picturesque garb, were formed into seven companies, and on the completion of the dance, with its accompaniment of singing, Mr. Shepstone addressed them in an eloquent speech, which was greatly applauded, pointing out the special honour paid them by the Queen in selecting as her representative, one of her most redoubtable warriors. On the conclusion of the address, writes an eye-witness, 'a salute was given to the Supreme Chief, grand in its intensity and effect.'

After six weeks of 'trekking' and camping out, Sir Garnet returned to Maritzburg, and immediately commenced preparing for the Session of Council. About twenty-five Bills were draughted, dealing with almost every question affecting the welfare of the Colony. The principal measure was that relating to the construction of a railway, for which fresh taxes were raised, the Natives contributing £56,000 per annum, instead of £41,000, by the raising of the hut-tax from 7s. to 14s., the marriage-tax being remitted. There were also other measures dealing with the Natives; the Colonial estimates were prepared in a different and clearer form; a Committee on Public Departments, consisting of Mr. Broome, Colonel Colley, and Major Brackenbury, drew up a report full of practical recommendations for the facilitation of business; and Major Butler prepared an able report on European Immigration, by which the farms of absentee and do-nothing proprietors were dealt with. Thus, what with Committees and Commissions, added to the conduct of the ordinary business of the Colony, Sir Garnet and his 'brilliant Staff,' as the papers always called his officers, were hard at work from seven in the morning till late in the evening, and even the opponents of the recent reforms recognised the devotion and energy of this talented band of soldiers. At length, just five months from the date of his arrival, the task was completed, and Sir Garnet Wolseley handed over the conduct of affairs to Sir Henry Bulwer. The Mayor of Durban gave a banquet in his honour on the 1st September, at which he made his farewell speech, concluding with an eloquent peroration on the future of Natal.

Two days later, amid the regrets of the colonists,* Sir Garnet sailed for England, accompanied by his Staff, except Mr. Broome, the Colonial Secretary, and Colonel Colley, who proceeded to India to join his regiment. At Cape Town a public ball was given in his honour, Admiral Lambert and the officers of the Flying Squadron, which had arrived the day before, being present. On the 4th of October, the *Windsor Castle*, decked from stem to stern with flags, arrived at Plymouth, where Sir Garnet was received with hearty cheers on landing.

He now resumed his duties at the War Office, but, in November, 1876, was offered by Lord Salisbury, and accepted, a seat at the Council of India, where (as we were informed by a colleague) his varied military experience was of eminent service. During the past few years Sir Garnet frequently presided at lectures on professional subjects, delivered in the theatre of the Royal United Service Institution, when his remarks commanded the assent of the

* The *Standard and Mail* wrote: 'After all the bitter party-fights, Sir Garnet leaves the Colony with the high personal reputation with which he came, enhanced, and anything higher than this, in the way of praise, cannot be advanced.' The *Mercury* said he had 'gained the admiration, as well as the affection, of the whole body of colonists.' On the day of his departure he was overwhelmed with addresses and deputations, and the scene at the banquet in his honour, at Durban, will long be remembered by those present.

majority of his auditors, owing to the strong common-sense with which they were tinged. This was displayed, to take two instances, in the discussion on Lieutenant Graves's paper on 'Military Equipment,' when he spoke strongly against the present dress and appointments of the British soldier; and at a lecture delivered by Colonel Clive, when he argued against the proposed adoption of the Prussian system of 200 men to a company. Wolseley also wrote two articles in the *Nineteenth Century*, which received much attention. The first, a comparison of the French army in 1870 and 1877, was an exhaustive and detailed survey of the military condition of our neighbours; and the second, on the British army in 1854 and 1878, was an able and authoritative exposition of our resources and readiness to embark on a war in that year, as compared with our position at the time of the Crimean War. While taking a sanguine view of our military strength, he warned the nation of the 'terrible risks it runs under the present system of boy recruits,' which, he adds, 'is a question for the consideration of Ministers and Members of Parliament; our soldiers are helpless in the matter.'

It is a mistake to suppose that Sir Garnet is an advocate for battalions of 'boy' soldiers, though he prefers young soldiers, when properly trained, to older men. After the Secocoeni campaign in 1879, he wrote admiringly of the dash and gallantry of his 'young soldiers,' and again in the same terms in his Tel-el-Kebir despatch; but in both cases, though the bulk of his men were young soldiers, there was a leaven of veterans, and in his Egyptian victory the average service of the infantry was five years. The essence of the short-service system advocated by Sir Garnet Wolseley and others of his school, is the production of a reserve, and the full battalions first on the roster for foreign service are composed of what may be considered in these days seasoned soldiers. When the new system is fully inaugurated these latter will be ample

SIR GARNET SAILS FOR CYPRUS.

to provide for our little wars, while in a great war the reserves will bring up seventy battalions to a strength of 1,000 men each, a result unattainable by the old method, by which we had no reserve.

When war between this country and Russia appeared imminent, Sir Garnet Wolseley was nominated Chief of the Staff to Lord Napier of Magdala, Commander of the Expeditionary Army, and, on the 28th of February, 1878, the Press, in announcing the appointment, was unanimous in expressions of approval. But the war-cloud, which, at one time, looked so threatening, was finally dispelled by the labours of the Congress at Berlin; and when, on the 8th of July, the British public and the world were amazed by Lord Beaconsfield's great *coup*—the Protectorate of the Turkish Asiatic Empire, and the *quasi* annexation of Cyprus—the announcement in both Houses of Parliament was coupled with the intimation of Sir Garnet Wolseley's appointment as 'Her Majesty's High Commissioner and Commander-in-Chief' of this, the newest appanage to the British Crown.

On the following Saturday, the 15th of July, Sir Garnet* left England for Cyprus, *viâ* Brindisi and Malta, accompanied by Colonels Brackenbury, Baker Russell, and Greaves, who had all served under him in Ashantee; also Colonels Dormer and Maquay, R.E., and Captain McCalmont, 7th Hussars (who had served as a volunteer in the Red River Expedition); his second aide-de-camp being Lord Gifford, who joined him from Ceylon.

* Sir Garnet's Staff consisted of the following officers: Colonel G. R. Greaves, C.B., Chief of the Staff; Brevet Lieut.-Colonel Baker Russell, C.B., 13th Hussars, Military Secretary; Captains H. McCalmont, 7th Hussars, and Lord Gifford, V.C., 57th Regiment, Aides-de-Camp; Colonel Hon. J. C. Dormer, and Lieut.-Colonel H. Brackenbury, R.A., Assistant-Adjutant and Quartermaster-Generals, with Brevet-Major Hon. H. J. L. Wood, 12th Lancers, and Captain R. C. Hare, 22nd Regiment, their deputies; Colonel R. Biddulph, C.B., R.A., to command Royal Artillery; Captain J. F. Maurice, R.A., Brigade-Major R.A.; Deputy Commissary-General A. W. Downes, C.B., Principal Commissariat Officer; Deputy Surgeon-General Sir A. D. Home, V.C., K.C.B., Principal Medical Officer; and Mr. Herbert, Colonial Office, Private Secretary.

The task before him was great indeed, as government of any sort, in our acceptation of the term, it may be said there was none. Cyprus, like other dependencies of the Porte, was only valued for what could be squeezed out of it, and the most elementary requirements of a state had been denied to it, so that the new Governor would have to begin *ab initio*. But these conditions were just such as to call forth the powers of a man of Wolseley's temperament and boundless energy, and he was invested, by his instructions, with plenary powers on all matters, civil and military. Looking to his antecedents, great expectations were raised that if allowed time and afforded full powers and sufficient means, he would transform this fair island of the Levant—which in turn has been possessed by Phœnicians, Greeks, Romans, Saracens, Venetians, and Turks—into what the mightiest warrior of antiquity anticipated it would become in his hands. In a remarkable passage of Arrian (vol. i. p. 99) Alexander the Great says : 'And Cyprus, being in our hands, we shall reign absolute sovereigns at sea, and an easy way will be laid open for making a descent on Egypt.'

Sir Garnet Wolseley may, without flattery, be said to be indispensable to his country, for whenever the War or Colonial Offices have on hand some task of more than ordinary difficulty or delicacy, he is called from the post he may be filling, and despatched at a few days' notice to set matters right. Whether it is to conduct a military expedition through the untrodden prairies and lonely lakes of North America, or the gloomy forests of Ashantee, or whether it is to undertake a difficult task of practical statesmanship in Natal or Cyprus, the Government of the day, be it Liberal or Conservative, call upon this veteran soldier, who, mindful only of his country's weal, responds to the appeal without a moment's hesitation or thought of self-seeking. Though his career of unbroken, and almost unparalleled success has drawn upon him the usual amount of detraction from those who lack the qualities by which greatness is achieved, yet his countrymen appreciate his patriotism and talents, like the Romans, who, says Cicero, after a time ceased to applaud Cæsar, for 'obstupefactis hominibus ipsâ admiratione compressus erat, et eo prætermissus, quia nihil vulgare dignum Cæsare videri poterat.'

Critics who cannot gainsay Sir Garnet Wolseley's capacity, and rivals who view his success with an unworthy feeling of jealousy, speak of him as 'a very lucky man.' But truth should compel them to own that he has forced his way to the forefront of his profession by sheer hard work and good service, without adventitious aid, or the exercise on his behalf of interest or favouritism, and that he has chained Fortune to his chariot-wheels by seizing every opportunity to win her favours. It was no 'luck' that induced him, when all appeared lost, to volunteer to lead two storming-parties in one day, in Burmah, or that led him, after storming the Mess-house, according to Lord Clyde's orders, to break through the Motee Mahul, and be the first to make an entrance into the Lucknow Residency. These deeds were the result of courage and enterprise. Again, it was no 'luck' that induced him, when suffering from wounds and ill-health, to remain throughout that dreary winter in the trenches at Sebastopol, where, as an officer writes to us, 'he showed the highest capacity as a military engineer in the siege operations.'

Again, 'in China,' writes one who served with him there, 'he was one of the eyes of the expedition in the Quartermaster-General's Department. This was his *métier*, but it is one thing to fill an appointment, and another to fill it so evidently well, that, young as he was, people ranked him with the chiefs of the army.'

It was the reputation that is achieved by good service, and

not luck, that led to his selection for the command of the Red River and Ashantee Expeditions, and all the success was due to sheer capacity. When the former expedition, in its earlier stage, was on the verge of failure, which, indeed, was predicted even by the most sanguine, what was the quality that urged Wolseley to persevere? And was it luck, or soldierly intuition, that induced him, in spite of the adverse opinions of those best qualified to judge, 'to take his boats up the Kaministiquia River, and thereby,' as General Lindsay officially wrote, 'insured the success of the expedition.' Again, when in the Ashantee Campaign, with the aid of 'our allies' and a handful of sailors and Marines, he forced the enemy to cross the Prah, were his movements guided by the genius of luck or of daring strategy? When, later on, owing to the wholesale desertion of the carriers, he found his forward movements paralyzed, and the success of the expedition jeopardized, when he was forced to reduce his already small force, and leave behind a battalion of white troops and the detachment of European artillery, was it good fortune, or was it by the exercise of energy and resolution, that he overcame all difficulties and entered into Coomassie in triumph, within twenty-four hours of the stipulated time? We submit that no amount of luck—which indeed is another word for capacity—unless it were accompanied by judgment, readiness of resource, and able generalship, would have insured anything but a complete and ignominious failure.

The petty habit of depreciating a great success, which is repellent to every generous mind, is due to that frame of mind stigmatized by Thomas Carlyle, who says, 'Show your critics a great, and they begin to, what they call, account for him, and bring him out to be a little, man.'

In this record of Sir Garnet Wolseley's military career, enough has appeared to enable the reader to form an opinion of his character and professional qualifications; but we cannot forbear quoting the eloquent words of a distinguished officer, who has had the best opportunities of forming a judgment. Colonel Evelyn Wood* said of him, at a lecture delivered before a brilliant audience at the Royal United Service Institution : ' That the Ashantee Campaign did not end in failure, must be in part attributed to the spirit which animated the forces, and rendered them, like red-hot iron, fervent but pliable in the hands of the master-workman, and in part to the directing power of the master-workman, of whom may be said, as was said by Scott of Napoleon, " He was a sovereign among soldiers." His means were limited by time and circumstances ; with a handful of men he was required to accomplish a hitherto unattainable feat. In six months he had to re-establish our reputation, lowered by successive humiliations and failures, and to read a lesson in letters of fire to the arrogant and bloodthirsty race who had defied us so long by their weapons of distance, disease, and treachery. It is true of Sir Garnet Wolseley, as was written of Pitt, " Few men made fewer mistakes, nor left so few advantages unimproved." To all his other great qualities he joined that fire, that spirit, that courage, which, giving vigour and direction to his soldiers, bore down all resistance. In fine, our success was due to the leader and his choice of able subordinates, who all acknowledged their chief's superior military genius, as they loyally supported him in everything ; and he impressed on all his iron will and steadfast determination to take Coomassie.'

All who have once been on his Staff again offer their services when an opportunity presents itself, as witness the names of Butler, Brackenbury, Gifford, Greaves, Colley, Wood, Butler, Swaine, Stewart, Maurice, and Dormer. It must be no ordinary man who can thus bind to him some of the most distinguished officers of the service. One who knows him well, and has served with him in the field, an officer of

* Now Major-General Sir Evelyn Wood, V.C., G.C.B.

high rank, and a Knight of the Bath, writes to us thus: 'I have had the best opportunities of judging of the man, and I say he is the most perfect character I have ever met; no one can see much of him without having for him a regard which becomes perfect affection; no one could be more unspoilt by his rise; I know no difference in him now from the time when he was a very young captain—no franker, more magnanimous, fearless man, morally and physically, I think, ever lived.'

Other letters we have received from his old comrades in arms, breathe the same feeling of affection and admiration. Of one trait of character, his generous recognition of merit in others, a brother officer of the 90th Regiment gives an instance of which he was a witness. 'On entering Lucknow,' he writes, 'I well remember everyone saying, "Wolseley has got the Victoria Cross!" They heard he had gained it by storming the Mess-house. He said, "No, I was not the first man in; Bugler —— was!" The poor wounded bugler was forgotten by others, but not by his own Captain.'

In the prime of life, yet ripe with a military experience almost unrivalled in the British army; blessed with an equable temperament, and an iron constitution that seems proof alike against the assaults of a Crimean winter, or the torrid heats of the Gold Coast; gifted with sound judgment and a thorough mastery of the art of war, theoretically as culled from books, and practically as studied and illustrated in all climes and under varied conditions; possessing a chivalric courage that has extorted the admiration of witnesses, and a calm self-reliance, combined with that attribute which is an unerring indication of the presence of genius, a faculty for inspiring confidence in others—Sir Garnet Wolseley seems to be specially fitted to lead the armies of his country in a great national crisis, should any such unhappily arise.*

* This work, completed to this point in 1878, was published in that year.

CHAPTER IX.

THE ADMINISTRATION OF CYPRUS.

Occupation of Cyprus by the British Troops.—Condition of the Island and its Inhabitants.—The Reforms introduced by Sir Garnet Wolseley.—His Opinion of the Healthiness of Cyprus.—Sir Garnet Wolseley recasts the Administration of the Island.—Visit of some Members of the British Government to Cyprus.—Sir Garnet Wolseley and the War in Afghanistan.—Condition and prospects of Cyprus.—Sir Garnet Wolseley returns to England in May, 1879.

SIR GARNET WOLSELEY arrived in Cyprus in H. M. S. *Himalaya*, on the 22nd July, 1879, and took over charge of the island from Rear-Admiral Lord John Hay, who had received possession from the acting Turkish Mutasserif, or Governor, Bessim Pasha, and Samih Pasha, the bearer of the Sultan's firman, the Governor, Achmed Pasha, being under suspension for embezzlement. A force of some 10,000 men, including the Indian contingent brought to Malta by Lord Beaconsfield, as a warning to Russia, under Major-General Ross and Brigadier-Generals Macpherson, V.C., and Watson, V.C., was landed at the island under the superintendence of H.R.H. the Duke of Edinburgh, who officiated as Beachmaster.

Sir Garnet Wolseley, who took up his residence at Nicosia on the 30th July, held the supreme military as well as civil control. The military duties were never very arduous, and by the end of August the Indian troops had quitted the island for Bombay; but the civil and political work was responsible and pressing, for the condition of the island disclosed a state of corruption and misrule only to be found in other provinces under the rule of the Sultan of Turkey.

In undertaking the practical annexation of Cyprus,* and wresting it from Turkish misgovernment, Lord Beaconsfield was inspired by no Quixotic motives of benevolence. The prime object was a military one. It was designed as a 'place of arms,' and to complete the chain in our Mediterranean fortresses, though to attain this object a vast sum would have to be expended in fortifications and harbours.

The occupation of the island by the British was received with very different feelings by the nationalities comprising its population. While the official Turks, as the ruling class, were discontented at the cessation of their privileges and power to oppress, the lower order of Turks were gratified that they would in future be exempted from the conscription, and that there would be no more doubling of taxes on the outbreak of war on the Continent. The Greeks, forming two-thirds of the population, about 100,000 out of 144,000, hailed Sir Garnet Wolseley as a deliverer from the oppression of the Turks; and the British flag, after consecration at the convent of Nicosia, was hoisted in the presence of Sir Garnet Wolseley and of the Christian classes of the community with imposing ceremonial and amid hearty acclamations. But, with the greed of their race, the Greeks sought to make all the pecuniary gain possible out of their deliverers; and so exorbitant were the rents demanded for suitable residences

---

* Richard I. conquered Cyprus at the time of his expedition to Palestine, and when the Turks dispossessed the Venetians of the island in the war of 1570-73, Queen Elizabeth contested the usurpation, though her government took no military measures. It is also a curious circumstance that in the central shield on the frieze at the west end of Queen Elizabeth's tomb, in the north aisle of Henry VII.'s chapel in Westminster Abbey, is the quartering of the arms of Cyprus, heraldically described as 'barry of ten, argent and azure, over all a lion rampant gules, crowned or.' In the drawings of the funeral procession of Elizabeth in the British Museum, made by William Camden, Clarencieux King-at-Arms, may be seen an heraldic banner containing the blazon of the arms of Cyprus, of which Elizabeth was titular Queen.

THE CONDITION OF CYPRUS.

for the headquarters staff, that the Chief Commissioner established his camp at the convent, about two miles distant from Nicosia.

The Turkish law-makers profess to be guided by that fine axiom enunciated in Aristotle's 'Politics,' that 'he who bids the law to rule, bids God and the mind to rule; but he who bids a man to rule, sets up a beast, for desires and passion turn the best men wrong, while law is mind purified of appetite.' But these fine professions, while loudly proclaimed, have no existence in the Sultan's dominions; and though, theoretically, the law is no respecter of persons, the evidence of a Christian has no weight as against the statement of a Mussulman. To remedy this cardinal defect, and make equally admissible the evidence of any credible witness and the establishment of proof on the evidence of one witness, and to make other necessary enactments, Sir Garnet Wolseley issued a proclamation, in thirty articles, defining the vast changes to be introduced in the laws of Cyprus.

To each of the six districts into which Cyprus is divided, Sir Garnet appointed a Commissioner and Assistant-Commissioner. The central district, which contains the capital Nicosia, was placed under Colonel R. Biddulph, R.A., now Chief Commissioner of the island; and Captain L. V. Swaine, Rifle Brigade, now Military *Attaché* at Berlin, was appointed Commissioner of the Famagousta district.

The natural resources of the island are great, and, in ancient times, the great desert-like plain of Messaria, forming two-thirds of Cyprus, in which Nicosia and Famagousta are situated, was the chief cereal-producing portion of the island. Water is to be had in abundance within a few feet of the surface, and the one thing required to make this arid plain renew its pristine fertility, is that the cattle-wheel and other means of raising water should be applied, as in the delta of Egypt. But three centuries of Turkish misrule and oppression have crushed all enterprise out of the people.

At the time of our occupation the ruling Pasha extracted all the money he could out of the poor islanders, and sent it to Constantinople to minister to the luxuries of a dissolute court, while nothing was expended on public works.

Most exaggerated ideas were prevalent in England of the wealth and condition of Cyprus. But the country sacred to the worship of the Paphian goddess was found to be poverty-stricken; the groves in which Adonis hunted, and the bright waters by which he disported himself, had no existence. Its mythical and historic fame, the legends of its Assyrian settlers, Phœnician traders, and Crusading visitors, combined to dazzle the judgment of the English people, and the disenchantment was complete when the army of occupation found, on landing, that the island was denuded of trees except in places on the hills, and was bare of verdure save where a few fertile spots were watered with perennial springs.

In September Sir Garnet Wolseley made a tour of the island in H.M.S. *Raleigh*, with the object of visiting the principal towns on the coast. Having elaborated his plans, he announced, on the 27th September, at the public reception held on the first day of the Feast of Bairam, the appointment of a Legislative Council under his presidency. He also nominated an Executive Council, which held its first meeting on the 10th October. These important steps were taken in accordance with the Royal Order of Council of the 14th September, which constituted Cyprus a Crown colony, and defined the form of government and powers of the Chief Commissioner, who was empowered, at his discretion, to act in opposition to the advice of the Executive Council.

Sir Garnet Wolseley appointed as members of the Legislative Council three official members and three members chosen by himself from the inhabitants of the island: the first thus selected being a Turk, Mustapha Faid Effendi; a Greek merchant, Mr. Glykys; and an Italian, Mr. Mattei. The work before the Legislative Council was sufficiently arduous, and embraced a conversion of tithes, a customs tariff, the reorganization of the judicial system, including the appointment of a Chief Justice and Puisne Judge; also questions connected with the stamp duties, game licenses, and other matters of administration and social order.

At the time of the British occupation of Cyprus there was only one road, and that a bad one, between Larnaca and Nicosia. Such bridges as had been carried away by storm were suffered to remain in ruins; and what with the extortion of their rulers, the ravages of the locusts, and the uncertainty of the seasons, the Cypriotes were steeped in poverty. Unhappily the means for improving the condition of the people were limited, as the British Parliament was averse from affording pecuniary assistance to an island still under the sovereignty of the Sultan, to whom, by the terms of the Anglo-Turkish Convention, an annual subsidy was due, based upon the average surplus revenue of the past five years, which was only arrived at by the utter neglect of expenditure on public works.

At the time of the occupation it was anticipated that the exchange of the rule of the Englishman for that of the Turk would bear fruit in the greater prosperity of the people, and that the spectacle of a Turkish province thriving under wise government would be an example to the rulers of Turkey. On the whole this expectation has been achieved; but the great obstacle to its complete realization is the fiscal stipulations, under which, out of a net revenue of about £172,000, over £100,000 annually has to be paid to the creditors of the Porte. Notwithstanding strict economy, a bare sufficiency remains for the ordinary expenses of government.

The omission of any reference to the necessary expenditure on public works was a great flaw in the Anglo-Turkish Convention; but another point was not taken into consideration when regulating the amount of the tribute to the Sultan. The published cost of government of a Turkish province does not give an accurate account of the sum actually expended, or of what is necessary, because bribery and peculation in all departments of Turkish administration form, by unwritten custom, a supplementary fund for the maintenance of the cost of government. Thus the Justices of the Court at Larnaca received salaries of £24 a year, and as such a sum was inadequate to maintain them in respectability and independence, fees from suitors were openly accepted. Not only judicial officers, but all Government officials—officers of the Customs, Excise, and Police, as well as their subordinates—received through bribes the necessary complement to their fixed salary. It was, of course, the first duty of a British Governor to end such an evil. The salaries of all officials were raised, and in the courts of justice British assessors were appointed, who took care that no fees were received by the Cadi and his coadjutors. Hence the cost of the administration of Cyprus largely exceeded the sum set apart by the Convention with Turkey.

The revenue of the first year of the occupation of the island compared unfavourably with that of the previous year. Thanks to a bountiful harvest, the tithes of 1878 had been sold for over £70,000; whereas in 1879, owing to the scarcity of rain, they did not reach £50,000, and Sir Garnet Wolseley was constrained to sanction the expenditure of over £6,000 in the distribution of seed-corn to the people.

Soon after taking possession of the island the Indian

troops were withdrawn, and by the end of November the island was garrisoned by the 71st Regiment and two companies of Sappers, who were all accommodated in huts. One of Sir Garnet's first steps was to organize a police force, at first numbering 500 men, under Major Grant, who, on his returning to England in August, was succeeded by Colonel Brackenbury, R.A., who completed the organization of the corps. Though the Porte, in the Convention with England, signed on the 4th June, 1878, divested itself of legislative functions in Cyprus, Sir Garnet Wolseley—having, as law adviser, first Sir Adrian Dingli, from Malta, then Mr. Cookson, Consular Judge at Alexandria, and afterwards Sir L. Phillips —and his officers, acting as assessors to the native courts, were called on to administer Turkish laws, and the industry and patience they displayed in acquiring and dispensing justice under such novel conditions were beyond all praise.

The establishment of a judiciary and of municipal government throughout the island occupied the Chief Commissioner's thoughts, and engrossed his time equally with the question of the destruction of the locusts* and the planting of the island with trees to increase the rainfall, the absence of which was, in a large measure, due to the improvident conduct of the Turkish rulers in cutting down the forests. One of his first acts was to establish district dispensaries throughout the island, where the poor could obtain medical advice free of charge, and drugs at a cheap rate. The work of the revenue survey of the island was put in hand by November, and a reform was instituted in the collection of tithes, formerly a source of great abuse, but which, under the guidance of British District Commissioners, was now effected without complaint or disturbance of order.

---

* These locusts are an annual plague, and since our occupation of the island as much as £28,000 has been expended in one year in exterminating them.

Under Turkish rule tithes were either sold to rich farmers, whose influence allowed them unlimited means of exaction, or were collected in kind by Government officials equally extortionate. The assessment upon the crops was now made at a convenient time for the peasants, who were permitted to pay the tithes later in the year, which was found to work well, as the crops were not exposed to damage while awaiting the call of the collector or the farmer for the tithe, and the peasant was free to harvest his fields at his own time. Under the hand of the new Governor the police, or zaptiehs, who formerly ground down the poor peasants, became only an object of fear to evildoers, and the villagers actually requested their presence. By properly paying the native judges, and rigorously punishing peculation or bribery, these evils were banished from the judgment-seat, and justice was impartially and promptly administered. Also by his measures on the currency question Sir Garnet Wolseley succeeded, during his year of office, in introducing the English pounds and shillings, with the Turkish piastre, thus placing, as he wrote, 'the currency of Cyprus on a footing nearly equal to that of Great Britain.' Finally, there was the land question.

One of his first steps was to appoint a Land Commission, under the Presidency of Mr. W. Baring, brother of the present Finance Minister in India, whose functions were, briefly, to ascertain the law, as practically applied in the island, relating to the different tenures of land, and to determine the extent of the various classes of land held under those tenures—a most complicated task, as, according to Turkish laws, land is divided mainly into five kinds, some of which—as wacouf, applied for religious uses, and mulk, land held in fee-simple—comprise many subordinate divisions.

The duties of the Chief Commissioner were thus multifarious and novel, and would have tested the capacity of a civilian administrator of the highest stamp. He had to work with native officials brought up in the worst school of corruption and tyranny. A new administration had to be established; radical changes of a more or less experimental character to be initiated. And he had to consider many contending interests the treatment of which required tact and consideration. Of course, where abuses and intrigue had flourished from time immemorial, there were complaints, but these were due either to disappointed adventurers who, at the time of the British occupation, descended upon the island like a cloud of its indigenous locusts;* or to those inhabitants having Hellenic aspirations, who thought that by villifying British administration they would promote the annexation of the island to Greece, as was done in the case of the Ionian Islands. But the people could not be brought to abet these intriguers, and the obvious reply to those who wished to substitute the rule of the King of the Hellenes for that of the Queen of England was to point to the reforms carried into effect with such striking results for their well-being. Such were the reductions in the taxation, and the abolition of all export duties; the removal of the onerous restrictions on the wine trade, and the equalization and reduction of the tax for military exemption. True, the expenditure was greater than under the Turkish *régime*, the total, exclusive of that on public works and prisons, being £72,731 against £29,093;

* One example of the speculation mania will suffice. The morning after the signature of the Anglo-Turkish Convention for the cession of Cyprus to England, Mr. Zarify, the Sultan's private banker at Constantinople, despatched to Larnaca by the Austrian Lloyd's packet one of his employés with sealed instructions, which he was not to open until he arrived in Cyprus. The instructions proved to be an unlimited credit and authority to purchase everywhere all the agent could get hold of, whether houses, lands, or cattle. The agent, with assistants, succeeded in buying property to the extent of £40,000, consisting of houses, shops, lands in town and country, cultivated fields, cattle, etc., all of which were obtained at very low rates, owing to the prevailing misery. Within four months this property was worth more than £300,000, though there was soon a great and disastrous depreciation, due to the greed of the sharp-witted financiers.

but, as we have shown, the Turkish officials were underpaid and corrupt, and did little and defective work in return for their salaries. The revenues and expenditure balanced, however, during the one year of Sir Garnet's administration.

The Home Government appreciated the ability and devotion displayed by the Chief Commissioner and his subordinates. Speaking in the House of Commons in May, 1879, Sir Stafford Northcote, the Chancellor of the Exchequer, expressed his opinion that 'those who had been administering the island during the last twelve months had done a work which would bear comparison with the achievements of many founders of states and legislators in bringing about great reforms.'

Many visitors of note, including Sir Samuel Baker, Mr. and Mrs. Brassey, Sir George Elliott, M.P., Sir Henry Holland, M.P., and Lord Colville, came to Cyprus and received a hospitable welcome at Government House. Much interest was displayed by the people and Press of England in the condition and prospects of our new dependency, the acquisition of which was the subject of numberless questions in Parliament and speeches out of it on the part of the Opposition in the House of Commons, from Mr. Gladstone downwards, and specially afforded a fertile theme for the wit and invective—that 'ornament of debate,' as Lord Beaconsfield once called it—of Sir William Harcourt. During the recess, Mr. Smith, the First Lord of the Admiralty, and his coadjutors, and Colonel Stanley, the Secretary of State for War, paid Cyprus a visit, to see for themselves the condition of the island, and the advance it had made during the few months it had been under the new administration.

They visited the monastery camp near Nicosia, where Sir Garnet Wolseley had established his seat of government, owing to the exorbitant rents asked by the speculators, who had bought up all the valuable house property in the island;

THE CLIMATE OF CYPRUS. 357

and thence proceeded to the military camp at Mathiati, seventeen miles distant, situated among the slopes of the southern hills, and, returning to Larnaca, proceeded round the island, visiting Famagousta, Kyrenia, Papho, and Limassol. The inspection much gratified them, and Sir Garnet Wolseley, writing to us on the 6th November, 1878, from Larnaca, says: 'I have just returned from a trip round the island, in H.M.S. *Himalaya*, with the Secretary of State for War and the First Lord of the Admiralty, both of whom are very much pleased with all they saw.'

Much was said in the Press and Parliament, at the time of our occupation of Cyprus, of its unhealthiness and the sickness among our troops. The island had, from the earliest times, an unenviable notoriety for its heat; and Martial writes: '*Infamem nimio calore Cyprum.*' But the fever prevailing in 1878, an unusually unhealthy year, was due to two causes—one temporary, and the other preventible by more care. The soldiers were kept in the plains and exposed to the heat of the sun, and, owing to the hasty manner in which they were despatched from England, were quartered in 'bell-tents,' which were of limited capacity and afforded no protection from the sun. The Indian troops were provided with pâl-tents, which are of much thicker texture, and every way more suited for a torrid climate than the bell-tents, which were found adequate for autumn manœuvres on Salisbury Plain. By the 24th August all the Indian troops, except some Bombay and Madras Sappers, had left the island on their return to India, and Sir Garnet Wolseley retained a sufficient number of pâl-tents to accommodate their European brethren-in-arms until huts were erected in healthy sites. That the island does not deserve all the opprobrium that has been heaped upon it, is shown by the medical returns of the troops stationed there the first year of our occupation, and from the fact of the authorities having selected it as a sanitarium for the sick troops during the recent operations in Egypt. For the last two years, of all the numerous stations where we have garrisons, Cyprus has been the healthiest for our men. The army annual returns prove this conclusively. The following was the opinion expressed to us by Sir Garnet Wolseley, writing from Cyprus during the winter of 1878 : 'We are now enjoying delightful weather, so much so that anyone arriving here now for the first time would be astonished to learn that the island had ever at any season proved unhealthy. All round the Mediterranean sea, fever at certain seasons is prevalent, especially in the eastern portions. We had a bad type of fever at Malta, and why anyone should wonder that our men, living in belltents under the piercingly scorching sun of summer in Cyprus, should have suffered, seems strange to me.' Early in the following year he wrote : 'The fever of Cyprus, of a malarious type, is not to be met with at any elevation above 5,000 feet over sea-level; and before the hot weather sets in this summer, I shall have the huts erected in the mountains, about 5,500 feet above the sea. If I had known of this place in July last, we should, I feel convinced, have avoided all the sickness we had in the summer and autumn. There are now in the island 944 of all ranks, of whom only 32 are on the sick-list, which is under $3\frac{1}{2}$ per cent., a rate lower than we have even in England.'

Of the good results of his administration he wrote : 'In some districts there was a considerable amount of crime before our occupation; now I do not believe we have a possession where there is less crime than in Cyprus. I feel and know that our administration of justice suits the people, and gives general satisfaction. Technically, from a lawyer's point of view, it may not be everything it might be, but I assert that the people have had substantial justice administered to them ; and this has been effected without any call upon the

Imperial treasury. Everything promises a good, fair average harvest this year. We shall have no more tithe-farming, and I hope to collect all the taxes in future in money, instead of in kind, and to do so in a manner that will be agreeable to the people. I am now planting 20,000 eucalyptus trees of one and two years old each. Even supposing half of them die, I shall have made a good start towards replenishing the island with timber. It is a mistake, however, to imagine that no forests still exist; we have a good deal of timber in the mountains, and I have stopped the cutting of trees everywhere. I am giving employment on the roads to all those who formerly earned a livelihood by forest-work; and as I have taken off all import-duty on wood and timber, I hope to give our forests some years of rest. The people are easily governed, and are a quiet and orderly lot. Turks and Christians live together on amicable terms.'

Sir Garnet Wolseley had been highly gratified by his appointment to the government of Cyprus, and the task of carving order and good government out of chaos and mal-administration was one suited to an energetic temperament, to whom difficulties only acted as an incentive to fresh exertion. Had his country remained at peace he would have been content to have continued the task until perfect success had crowned his efforts, and Cyprus was as well governed as Mauritius, or Ceylon, or any other Crown Colony. But in the latter part of 1878, a few months after his arrival, the Indian Government was embroiled in a war with Shere Ali, Ameer of Afghanistan, and, by the 1st November, our armies were in motion for the invasion of that country from three different points. The soldier-diplomatist ruling in Cyprus at this time was 'a statesman if you will, but a soldier above all,' and was anxious to be in the thick of the fray; his eager, heroic nature, to whom war, with all its turmoil and excitement and soul-stirring incidents, was as a second nature, panted to exchange the labours of the administrator for the risks and responsibilities of the General. He wrote to us on the 6th November with characteristic enthusiasm: 'All our thoughts here are now turned to the Afghan frontier, and I long to be in the saddle leading our men through these passes which former wars have made so familiar to us in history. I like being the Governor of a new place like Cyprus during peace, but when "the blast of war blows in our ears," I long to run to the sound, and take my fair share of its dangers and excitements.' But he was denied the opportunity, and for nearly two years the war continued in Afghanistan without his participating in its chequered history of victory and defeat, though another sphere of activity opened to him before Sir Frederick Roberts's crowning achievement—the march from Cabul to Candahar and the victory of the 1st September, 1880—ended the war. Then once again Sir Garnet Wolseley was in the saddle, cheering on British troops to victory.

The Eastern proverb has it, 'Everything will come to him who waits;' and though Sir Garnet Wolseley fretted at his enforced inaction while the Afghan War was in progress, the disaster of Isandlwhana gave him the required opportunity, and the demand made in the Press for the appointment of Sir Garnet Wolseley to the supreme military command in South Africa was at length favourably responded to by the Government. As usual, there were some unworthy comments on the appointment of 'our only General,' as his detractors sneeringly styled one whose uniform success in war they attributed to 'luck;' but Sir Garnet Wolseley had the wisdom to treat such remarks with contempt, agreeing with Hudibras, who says:

'——— that man is sure to lose
That fouls his hand with dirty foes;
For where no honour's to be gain'd,
It's thrown away in being maintain'd.'

CHAPTER X.

SERVICES IN ZULULAND AND THE TRANSVAAL.

Sir Garnet Wolseley is appointed to the Chief Political and Military Command in Natal and the Transvaal.—Arrival in Zululand.—Pursuit and Capture of Cetewayo.—The Settlement of Zululand.—Departure of Sir Garnet Wolseley for the Transvaal.—His Reception at Pretoria and the other Towns of the Transvaal.—Declaration of British Policy with respect to the Country and its Effect on the Boers.—The Campaign against Secocoeni.—Capture of the Chief's Stronghold on the 28th November, 1879.—Sir Garnet Wolseley and the Boers.—His opinion on the Basuto question.—Return to England of Sir Garnet Wolseley.

On the 21st May, 1879, Sir Garnet Wolseley landed in England, having been summoned from Cyprus by the Government to proceed to South Africa, to undertake the conduct of military operations from the hands of Lord Chelmsford. The war with the Zulu King was still dragging its slow length along, and the unsepultured bones of our brave officers and men yet whitened the plain under the fatal hill of Isandlwhana. That disastrous encounter was fought on the 22nd January. By the end of May there were at the seat of war in South Africa, as appears by a Ministerial statement in Parliament, 19,959 British troops, and 4,453 colonial troops, in addition to 850 seamen and marines—over 25,000 men in all, being a larger army than Lord Clyde undertook to capture Lucknow and reconquer Oude.

Sir Bartle Frere, in vindicating his conduct in sending an ultimatum to Cetewayo involving this country in war with the Zulu monarch, invoked the opinion of Sir Garnet Wolseley on the military danger to Natal by the Zulu despotism on its borders, while on the political question he quoted the sanction given to his measures by Sir Henry Bulwer, Sir Theophilus Shepstone, and Mr. Brownlee, Commissioner for Native Affairs to the Cape Colony. It was quite true that Sir Garnet Wolseley declared that the Zulus were 'a great danger to our colony, and to all South Africa;' but he was of this opinion three years before, and while warning the Government to be prepared, did not advise that we should go to war and precipitate the very danger we were anxious to guard against, being satisfied that a policy of firmness and preparedness would ward off hostilities. The Government had been in fault in neglecting to take the military measures of defence recommended by Sir Garnet Wolseley when in Natal, and then in going to war with an insufficient force; Sir Garnet having, in a memorandum on the invasion of Zululand, expressed an opinion that 20,000 men would be necessary to subjugate Cetewayo's forces, an estimate that was borne out by the result.

Sir Garnet Wolseley was appointed 'Commander-in-Chief of the forces in South Africa, and High Commissioner for Natal, the Transvaal, and the neighbouring countries,' Sir Henry Bulwer and Sir Owen Lanyon being placed under his orders, and Sir Bartle Frere remaining Governor of the Cape Colony. On the 21st May, Sir Garnet arrived from Cyprus, having travelled *viâ* Paris and Brindisi; and on Monday, the 26th May, statements were made in both Houses of Parliament, in his presence, announcing his appointment; that in the Upper House being made by Lord Beaconsfield. A sense of relief was felt by all classes of his countrymen when the appointment was made known, and *Punch* gave expression to this feeling in some verses on the similarity between his name and that of the great Duke of Wellington:

> ' When Wolseley's mentioned, Wellesley's brought to mind ;
> Two men, two names, of answerable kind :
> Called to the front, like Wellesley, good at need,
> Go, Wolseley, and like Wellesley, greatly speed.'

ARRIVAL IN NATAL.

On the 29th May Sir Garnet, accompanied by his staff, left London to assume his important functions. At Paddington numerous friends assembled to bid him farewell; and he was accompanied as far as Didcot Junction by Sir Michael Hicks-Beach, the Colonial Secretary. Travelling all night, he arrived at Dartmouth at four a.m., and, on the following morning, embarked on board Donald Currie and Co.'s ship *Edinburgh Castle*, which arrived at Cape Town on the 23rd June, after a pleasant voyage. The first news that greeted Sir Garnet and his fellow-passengers as the ship cast anchor was the death of the Prince Imperial, which, with the attendant circumstances, created a painful impression on all on board. Sir Garnet landed at Cape Town, where he was the guest of Sir Bartle Frere; and on the following day, Tuesday, 24th June, sailed in the *Dunkeld* for Durban, putting in at Port Elizabeth for news.

To a man of the eager temperament of Sir Garnet the days and hours occupied on the voyage from England had appeared interminably long, and it was an inexpressible relief when he found himself nearing the goal of his anticipated triumphs; for the possibility of failure never entered into his philosophy. But he was destined to suffer the disappointments that had awaited all connected with this lamentable South African War, though in his case, at least, they were none of his making.

Amid the hearty cheers of his fellow-passengers and a display of bunting from all the ships in harbour, he landed at Durban at six a.m. on the 28th June, and after greeting many familiar faces among the crowd awaiting him, and receiving and replying to an address from the mayor and corporation, started at nine o'clock, by special train, for Maritzburg, where he was obliged to proceed in order to be sworn in according to the terms of his patent. There was a break in the line, and the remaining distance of 35 miles, over a break-neck road, was traversed in carriages at a hand-gallop, so that Sir Garnet arrived an hour before he was expected. At Maritzburg he was received by the Lieutenant-Governor, Sir Henry Bulwer, Major-General Clifford, commanding the line of communications, and other officers, and duly installed as Governor—the first the colony had received. Sir Garnet would have at once struck across country by Rorke's Drift and joined the army in the field near Ulundi, but his horses, purchased at the Cape, had not arrived, and he came to the resolution to return to Durban and proceed by ship to Port Durnford, on the coast of Zululand, near which were the headquarters of the First, or General Crealock's, Division.

After a visit to the hospital, where he spoke a kind word to the wounded—among whom was Major Hackett, of the 90th Regiment, who lost the sight of both eyes at Kambula—and making arrangements for raising a corps of 4000 carriers for General Crealock's column, and to assist in landing stores, forage, and ammunition at Port Durnford, he installed Sir Henry Bulwer as his *locum tenens*, and at six a.m., on the 1st July, left for Durban. The driver of the train, who bet he would do the distance of 37 miles in one hour and 20 minutes, won his wager by three minutes; a feat, owing to the curves and ascents, described by one who was present, and had seen war in many climes, as so perilous that 'he did not think anyone alive was ever in greater danger.'

Sir Garnet at once embarked on board H.M.S. *Shah* Captain Bradshaw, which arrived off Port Durnford on the following morning. Captain Bradshaw considered that the surf was too high to render a landing possible, and Sir Garnet was constrained to put off the attempt. On the following morning matters had scarcely improved; but the Commander-in-Chief would brook no further delay, and

END OF THE ZULU WAR.

made the attempt in a surf-boat. But it was impracticable, and after running considerable danger, the party had to return to the *Shah*, which proceeded back to Durban, where she arrived at 2.30 p.m., on the 4th July, the day Lord Chelmsford fought his decisive action at Ulundi. On the following morning Sir Garnet proceeded by train and on horseback to Fort Pearson, on the Lower Tugela, where he remained for the night. Here he received intelligence of Lord Chelmsford's victory. On the following day he rode to Fort Chelmsford, halting by the way at Fort Crealock, and on the afternoon of the 7th reached the camp of the First Division at Port Durnford.

On his arrival Sir Garnet Wolseley telegraphed to the Home Government that 'the war was over,' and directed the return to England of the reinforcements on their way, and a large portion of the troops in the field. For this action he was taken to task by critics, who called it 'precipitate;' but, as has happened throughout his career, his military intuition was not at fault, and he took a juster measure of the requirements of the situation than his censors. Sir Garnet issued a final order, dated 18th July, cordially acknowledging the success achieved by his predecessor; and thus the more active phase of the Zulu difficulty was terminated. Meanwhile Lord Chelmsford, immediately after the battle of Ulundi, instead of following up the beaten Zulu army, and effecting the capture of the King, fell back with the Second Division to Entonjanini, 10 miles from Ulundi, where wood and grass were abundant. On the 15th his lordship arrived with the Flying Column at St. Paul's Mission Station, where he was met by Sir Garnet Wolseley, who reviewed the Division under its gallant leader, Sir Evelyn Wood, and conferred the Victoria Cross on Major Chard, R.E., the hero of Rorke's Drift.

On the 19th July Sir Garnet Wolseley held a great meeting of Zulu chiefs, 20 of whom attended, including Dabulemanzi, who commanded at Rorke's Drift; Somapo, the King's father-in-law; Magwende, and other influential leaders, whom he addressed at length on the settlement of the country, inviting their opinions, which were given, and the important question of the reorganization of the country discussed. After inspecting, on the 21st July, the Naval Brigade, under Captain Campbell and Commander Brackenbury, which re-embarked on board ship, Sir Garnet Wolseley, accompanied by his staff, including Brigadier-General Pomeroy Colley, who had joined him from Simla, where he was military secretary to Lord Lytton, Viceroy of India, left the 1st Division, encamped at Fort Durnford, for Maritzburg. During the next few days all the senior officers of the army proceeded on leave to England, including Lord Chelmsford, Major-Generals Newdigate, Crealock, Marshall, and Sir Evelyn Wood, and Colonels Buller and Drury-Lowe. At Maritzburg Sir Garnet Wolseley remained till the 30th July, transacting important business as Governor, and then returned, *viâ* Rorke's Drift, into Zululand, having elaborated his measures for effecting the capture of Cetewayo, as no confidence could be felt among either Europeans or natives until he was a prisoner. With this object he organized two small columns, under Brigadier-General Clarke, 57th Regiment, and Colonel Baker Russell,* 13th Hussars, an officer of whom Sir Garnet entertained a high opinion, which was justified by subsequent events.

Escorted by a troop of the 1st Dragoon Guards, Sir Garnet Wolseley, after crossing the Tugela at Rorke's Drift, visited the battle-field of Isandlwhana, where so many of England's sons fell a victim to their gallantry and the incapacity of the General who left them in small force and unlaagered

---

* This officer had served with him in Ashantee and Cyprus, as had also other members of his staff—Colonel Brackenbury, R.A., Majors Wood and McCalmont, Lord Gifford, and Captain Maurice, R.A.

THE PURSUIT OF CETEWAYO. 367

to defend a vast camp, and bear the brunt of the attack of the whole Zulu army while he was decoyed away by a wily foe. All the bodies of our dead had been buried, but some native corpses still lay festering where they fell; other memorials of the fatal 22nd January were plentiful in the books, soldiers' pocket-ledgers, and Bibles lying about, with ammunition-boxes, boot and horse brushes, the latter numerous on the site occupied by the Artillery camp.

On the 10th August Sir Garnet reached Ulundi, where he was joined on the afternoon of the following day by the column under Brigadier-General Clarke.* In his plan for capturing the Zulu King, and completing the work only partially achieved at Ulundi, Sir Garnet provided for the safety of the western and southern borders of Natal and the Transvaal by stationing the 21st, 24th, and 58th Regiments at Landsmann's Drift, Utrecht, and Koppie Allen respectively, while Brigadier-General Clarke reoccupied Ulundi, a strong entrenched camp being thrown up at Entonjanini, ten miles distant, with a garrison of 400 men, and Colonel Baker Russell, with a flying column, entered the Intabankulu valley, in order to prevent Cetewayo from breaking away into the difficult country between Ulundi and Luneburg. In co-operation the Swazies were to descend from the north, under Captain McLeod, and Burghers from Utrecht, and Oham's friendly Zulus, under Colonel George Villiers, from the west, so that the escape of the Zulu King would be impossible. At Ulundi Sir Garnet received messengers from Cetewayo, who offered to submit and pay taxes, provided his

* Clarke's column consisted of 2 nine-pounders, a battery of Gatlings, 2 troops of Lonsdale's Horse, Barrow's Mounted Infantry, 57th Regiment, 3rd Battalion 60th Rifles, 5 companies 80th Regiment, and the 4th Native Contingent. The communication between Ulundi and the sea was maintained by small posts at St. Paul's and Kwamagwasa, the 90th Light Infantry and a body of Artillery holding Port Durnford. Baker Russell's flying column consisted of a squadron 1st Dragoon Guards, a battery of Artillery, 6 companies of 94th Regiment, 400 irregular cavalry, and 200 Native Horse.

position was recognised; but they were told that unconditional submission would be exacted.

On the 12th August, the cavalry captured, in a donga eight miles beyond Ulundi, the two seven-pounder guns lost at Isandlwhana. Stores of gunpowder and arms were also found by reconnoitring parties, and the effect of these vigorous movements was soon apparent in the submission of Umnyana, the Prime Minister; Tyingwayo, who commanded the Zulu army engaged with Sir Evelyn Wood at Kambula; Sirayo, whose raid into Natal was the ostensible cause of the war, and other important chiefs.

The pursuit of Cetewayo was now taken up under Sir Garnet Wolseley's orders, and there was no rest for the King or the flying columns. For sixteen days these detachments of cavalry and natives followed closely in his footsteps, until, on the 28th August, he was captured on the confines of the Ngome Forest. In this pursuit Major Barrow, and his second in command, Lord Gifford, aide-de-camp of Sir Garnet Wolseley, were specially prominent. Captains Herbert Stewart and Barton also commanded small columns; but the capture of the Zulu King was actually accomplished by Major Marter, of the King's Dragoon Guards.

On the morning of the 14th, Major Barrow reached the kraal which Cetewayo had left the previous afternoon, and continued the pursuit the same day with 120 picked men, arriving at the kraal where the King had slept on the previous night. On the following morning, as soon as the moon rose, he reached the kraal where the fugitive monarch had been during that night, and searched the neighbourhood, sending Lord Gifford, with the mounted natives and Natal Police, to seek for the tracks of the King. The people were friendly, furnishing guides and supplies, but no reward could induce his immediate attendants to deliver him up, his prestige being great, notwithstanding that he was defeated and a

THE CAPTURE OF CETEWAYO.

fugitive. From the 15th, Lord Gifford, with Jantze, the Natal chief, and his 25 Caffres, 6 Mounted Infantry, and 7 Colonial Volunteers, was never quite off the track, more than once passing close to Cetewayo's hiding-place; but on the 27th he obtained certain information which enabled him to proceed to the very kraal in which Cetewayo proposed sleeping on the following night. To obtain this information he had recourse to a ruse. Two of Umnyana's men who had been taken by Lord Gifford, being blindfolded, were led some distance apart, and a volley fired between them. Each man thought the other had been shot, and told all he knew about the King. On this information a rapid march was made by Lord Gifford, who, on the night of the 27th, travelled over, as he said, the most difficult country he had ever seen. At times it appeared an impossible task for the horses to keep their feet; but at daybreak he arrived within sight of the King's kraal. Lord Gifford now unsaddled, and sending the horses back a short distance, kept well out of sight behind a ridge, while he sent two Caffres to reconnoitre the kraal. Having ascertained that it was occupied, Lord Gifford determined to remain quietly on the watch till nightfall, when he intended surrounding the kraal and securing the King. Meanwhile a party of the King's Dragoon Guards, under Major Marter, and eight men of Lonsdale's Horse, under Lieutenant Werge, arrived on the hill overlooking the kraal on the opposite side. Without loss of time Major Marter descended to effect the capture of the King. The kraal, along its north side, by which Major Marter approached, is bordered by steep and rocky ground, rising in one place to a sheer precipice. All the ground is thickly wooded and rugged, and the descent from the summit of the hill to the level of the kraal occupied an hour and a quarter, during which two horses were killed and one of the troopers broke his arm. Cetewayo's scouts, on seeing the movement, rushed back to warn the King; but some of Barton's Native Contingent, accompanying the Dragoons, followed so quickly on their heels, that the kraal was surrounded before the occupants could escape. On the arrival of the Dragoons, Cetewayo came out of his hut and surrendered to Major Marter, conducting himself with great dignity and composure, as, indeed, he has done during the whole time he has been a captive.

Fortune was hard upon Lord Gifford, who had followed up the King with unwavering pertinacity; but the gallant officer received the encomiums of his chief, who sent him to England with his despatches announcing the conclusion of the war.* Cetewayo was removed to the camp at Ulundi, where he arrived under escort on the morning of the 31st August. On the same day Sir Garnet Wolseley, without seeing the ex-King, sent him off to Port Durnford, whence the steamship *Natal* conveyed him to Cape Town. The capture of the dreaded Zulu monarch created a great impression among the native races of South Africa. Usibebe, the most important chief still holding out, and all others of note, gave in their submission to the authority of the Queen, and English prestige was raised immensely until the humiliating events in the Transvaal lost all the ground that was gained.

On Monday, the 1st September, the anniversary of the day in 1873 when Cetewayo was crowned King by Sir Theophilus Shepstone, and on the same spot, Sir Garnet Wolseley held a great meeting of chiefs, when he announced the dismemberment of the kingdom and his arrangements for its future government.† Of the thirteen chiefs selected by him to rule

---

* In accordance with custom, Lord Gifford received the reduced sum of £300 for bringing home the despatches, and Major Marter was promoted to the brevet rank of Lieutenant-Colonel.

† These, briefly, included the appointment of a Resident in Zululand, the abolition of the practice of witchcraft, the taking of life except after fair trial, the maintenance of a standing army, and the purchase of rifles.

THE SETTLEMENT OF ZULULAND.

the territories into which Zululand was to be divided, there were present seven, including John Dunn, Cetewayo's English friend and adviser, who had rendered good service to the British cause throughout the war, the other six having mistaken the way, or, owing to bodily infirmity, were represented by their councillors. Before procuring the signature to the terms, which were signed by Sir Garnet Wolesley and by each chief concerned, in duplicate, all but John Dunn signing with a cross, his Excellency described briefly the nature and grounds of the settlement he had determined upon. He warned them not to stir up trouble, and said that as sales or pretended sales of land had been in the past a fertile source of dispute, in future no land must be parted with to white people. The only chief who refused to sign the agreement, on the ground that the extent of the territory assigned to him was too limited, was Umnyana, the late Prime Minister, and accordingly Sir Garnet informed him that the district should be given to another, which was done. On the following day the two chiefs who had mistaken the day of meeting signed the terms; and a few days later, on the march from Ulundi, Seketwayo signed; and at Conference Hill, on the 8th and 9th, Oham, the King's brother, and Taku, attested in due form, as did also Ulube, the Basuto chief, to whom was allotted Sirayo's territory.

As the Home Government would not permit annexation, and the restoration of Cetewayo was at this time out of the question, the settlement effected by Sir Garnet Wolseley was probably the best that could be made; and when we consider the state of anarchy to which the country was reduced by the war and the deportation of the King, the wonder is not that there has been occasional fighting and bloodshed, but that the settlement has worked fairly well.

Having arranged for the appointment of a Resident and three Commissioners, under the presidency of Colonel Hon.

George Villiers, to settle the boundaries of the thirteen independent chiefs, Sir Garnet Wolseley marched from Ulundi on the 4th September, Brigadier-General Clarke's column moving into Natal, and Colonel Baker Russell proceeding to compel the submission of the semi-independent tribes inhabiting the north-west corner of Zululand and the disputed territory there bordering on the Transvaal. This was completed without fighting, and by the end of the month all the British troops had quitted Zululand, Colonel Baker Russell proceeding to Leydenburg, in the Transvaal, the Natal native levies and irregular bodies of European horse enlisted during the protracted operations against the Zulu King being disbanded. With a general order to the troops on the capture of Cetewayo, and the surrender of Manyanyoba, who had caused some trouble on the Zulu border of the Transvaal, the Zulu War was at an end.

On his arrival at Utrecht, in the Transvaal, on the 10th September, Sir Garnet Wolseley received an address of welcome from the inhabitants, to whom he made a conciliatory reply, and inspected the 24th Regiment, conferring the V.C. on Major Bromhead, of Rorke's Drift fame. On the 13th he was at Wakkerstroom, and he also visited Standerton and Heidelberg, and on the 27th arrived at Pretoria. Here and elsewhere on the road, when addressing gatherings of Boers, he stated to them that the act of annexation was irrevocable; and at Standerton, on the Vaal river, he told the people that the sun would cease to shine, and the Vaal would flow backwards through the Drakenburg, before the British would withdraw from their country. He promised that everything should be done to satisfy their just requirements, short of independence; but the Boer Committee, numbering seventy members, who assembled near Heidelburg, under the chairmanship of Mr. Pretorius,* replied by

* Mr. Pretorius wrote in temperate terms to Sir Garnet Wolseley, calling attention to the fact that these representatives of the people had been

a resolution declaring that nothing could satisfy them but the retrocession of their country, and a mass meeting was called for the 9th November. Mr. Joubert, one of the Boer delegates to England, a man of great influence and wealth, who later on played so important a part, visited Sir Garnet Wolseley, by invitation, at Standerton, and reiterated that nothing short of independence would satisfy the people, and that compromise or conciliation was out of the question ; to which Sir Garnet replied that he was prepared to listen to the wishes and aspirations of the Boers, but he declined to enter upon the question of annexation.

At this time there were in the Transvaal 5 battalions of infantry, 2 batteries of artillery, and the 1st Dragoon Guards ; but 2 battalions of foot and a battery were under orders to leave the country later in the year, and the remaining battery of artillery was to be divided between the Transvaal and Natal. On the 29th September Sir Garnet Wolseley was sworn in as Governor of the Transvaal, the Government of which had been administered under his orders by Colonel Sir Owen Lanyon, who, in the latter part of 1878, had succeeded Sir Theophilus Shepstone. Sir Owen Lanyon had been very successful as administrator of Griqualand West ; but from various causes, chief of which was his having to carry out the odious task of enforcing the collection of taxes in arrears, he became very unpopular with the Boers.

On the 29th September* Sir Garnet Wolseley issued a

---

recognised by her Majesty's Government upon occasions when delegates were sent home by the Boers, and had official dealings with Sir Bartle Frere. He begged, therefore, that Sir Garnet Wolseley would favour him with a signification of the British Government's intentions in regard to the unanswered memorial praying for the restoration of the country to the Dutch. He added that the people's committee was stated by Sir Bartle Frere to comprise gentlemen of the highest repute in the country, and their memorial was forwarded by his Excellency as ' deserving the earnest consideration of her Majesty's Government.' This consideration the committee understood the memorial had been receiving, and the decision had now been long anxiously awaited.

* On the same day, in consequence of the massacre of the Cavagnari Mission and the renewal of the war in Afghanistan, his Chief of the Staff,

proclamation to the people, which was published in the *Transvaal Gazette*, announcing 'that it is the will and determination of her Majesty's Government that the Transvaal territory shall be, and shall continue to be, for ever an integral part of her Majesty's dominions in South Africa.'

On the 3rd October Sir Garnet Wolseley issued a proclamation constituting an Executive Council for the Transvaal, to consist of five official and three non-official members, to be appointed by the Governor or Administrator, whose duty it would be to advise the Government; and one of the first matters the Government intended to submit to them was a scheme for the constitution of a Legislative council. But other matters of more immediate moment engrossed the attention of Sir Garnet Wolseley.

A chief of Basuto origin, Secocoeni by name,—inhabiting a district about 120 miles north of Pretoria as the crow flies, and 200 by the road, through Middelburg, lying between the Olifant and Steel Poort rivers,—was in arms, and refused to acknowledge British authority, being satisfied of his ability to defy any force sent against him in his stronghold situated in the Lulu Mountains. And he had good cause for his opinion, as he had not only defeated a Zulu army, but in 1878 compelled 3,000 Boers, under President Burgers, assisted by Swazies, to retire from his country; and, finally, in November, 1878, Colonel Rowlands, V.C., with a British force, consisting of 6 guns, 450 men of the 13th Regiment, 430 cavalry, under such leaders as Carrington and Redvers Buller, failed to compel the submission of Secocoeni, owing to the drought and want of forage, and retired harassed by the victorious chief, who had 5,000 fighting men under his command, besides levies from the

---

Sir George Colley, left for India to resume his duties on the Viceroy's staff; whence he returned to South Africa as Sir Garnet's successor, and lost his life in seeking to coerce the Boers, whose powers of resistance, like so many others, he underrated.

neighbouring chiefs. Sir Owen Lanyon, a few months before, had assembled a force of 2,000 men, including 700 Mounted Volunteers, to compel the submission of the Basuto Chief; but Sir Garnet Wolseley, considering the force too weak, and desirous of settling one difficulty at a time, directed him to refrain from undertaking hostilities. To this redoubtable warrior Sir Garnet now turned his attention; and before commencing military operations which, owing to the difficult nature of the country and the strength of the mountain fastness to be attacked, promised to be hazardous, despatched Major Clarke, R.A., who had been Commissioner of the northern portion of the Transvaal since our acquisition in April, 1877, with an ultimatum demanding his submission, also the payment of a fine of 2,500 head of cattle, and consent on his part to receive a military force in his territory, warning him that Cetewayo's fate would be his unless he recognised the authority of the Queen, and paid taxes to her representatives.

Meantime the Boers, finding their demands unheeded, began to give trouble; and in October a large body made a threatening demonstration against British rule at Middelburg, and being refused permission to purchase ammunition seized it, leaving payment on the counter with the storekeeper.

According to the local law of the Transvaal, which Sir Theophilus Shepstone's proclamation of 12th April, 1877, expressly maintained unimpaired, no person was allowed to purchase ammunition without a permit signed by a justice of the peace. This provision was originally directed against the natives, whom the Boers were unwilling to supply with the means of waging war upon the small European minority. But since the British occupation of the country it was turned against the malcontent Boers themselves. Sir Garnet Wolseley, after his proclamation of the 29th September, found that one of the principal difficulties with which the British administrative authorities had to deal was the refusal of the Boers to pay taxes, which were difficult to enforce over a wide and sparsely peopled tract of country. He accordingly gave orders that no permit for the purchase of ammunition should be granted to any applicant who was unable to produce his receipt for taxes. As the Boers who assembled at Middelburg to make a threatening demonstration against the jurisdiction of the British courts, were banded together by a resolution not to pay anything to the 'usurping' Government, nor in any other way to recognise its rights, they held no permits and were accordingly refused ammunition by the storekeepers. Thereupon they proceeded to seize it, and committed other riotous acts, but dispersed on the arrival of Sir Garnet Wolseley, though similar acts of violence were repeated at Potchefstroom.

Negotiations having failed with Secocoeni, who relied on the strength of his mountain fastness, Sir Garnet, having completed his preparations for attacking that chief, and received the report of Colonel Harrison, R.E., who had made a close reconnoissance of the Basuto stronghold, resolved at once to take the field. The troops, numbering about 1,400 British infantry, 400 Colonial Horse, and 10,000 natives, were placed under the immediate command of Colonel Baker Russell. The attacking force, styled the Transvaal Field Force, was divided into two columns—the Eastern, under Major Bushman, 9th Lancers; and the Western, which the General accompanied, under Colonel Baker Russell.* Sir Garnet Wolseley, leaving Sir Owen

* The Western Column consisted of 2 seven-pounder guns, manned by men of the 80th Regiment, and 2 Krupp guns, manned by Colonial Volunteers, under Captain Knox, R.A., who had organized the artillery; Ferreira's Horse, 100 strong; Transvaal Mounted Rifles, 116 men; Border Horse, 100; and 34 Mounted Infantry: the whole under Major Carrington, 24th Regiment, an officer of approved gallantry, who had been carrying on successful border warfare with Secocoeni, harrying his country and carrying off his cattle. The infantry was 6 companies of the 2nd battalion 21st Regi-

Lanyon in charge at Pretoria, took his departure for the front, and encamped at Fort Weber on the 28th October. Before starting for the campaign from Pretoria, he had written to the Secretary of State for War, to the Duke of Cambridge, and to many others, giving in detail the whole of his plans for bringing it to a rapid conclusion. In each and all of his letters, he fixed the dates when his troops would be at certain places and in named positions, winding up, to each of his correspondents, with the assurance that he would take his afternoon tea in Secocoeni's house on the 28th November. *These arrangements were literally fulfilled*, and the afternoon of the 28th November saw him in Secocoeni's mansion.

At Fort Weber Sir Garnet Wolseley found that the supplies he had ordered had not been collected, thus disarranging his plans. He accordingly changed his base from Fort Weber to Fort Olifant, on the river of the same name, distant about twenty-four miles from Secocoeni's town. The line of supply, therefore, had to be taken by the bush veldt road from Pretoria. In this brief campaign—as before, in the Red River, and Ashantee, and later in Egypt—the supply departments, whether commissariat or transport, were the weak points of military organization, as it ever has been in our defective system. The plan

---

ment and 6 companies of the 94th Regiment; also 21 men of the Royal Engineers. The natives with the column were the Rustenburg levies, 500 men; Mapoch's Caffres, 600; and 700 men from Zoutspanberg. The Eastern or Leydenburg Column, which was ordered to concentrate at Fort Burgers, was commanded by Major Bushman, 9th Lancers (Major Creagh, 80th Regiment, having fallen ill), with Captain Yeatman Biggs, R.A., as staff officer. It consisted of 94 men of the 80th Regiment; 170 men of the 94th Regiment; the Leydenburg Mounted Rifles, 40 men; Captain Eckersley's natives, 250 strong, and about 10,000 Swazies. The Headquarter Staff consisted of Colonel Brackenbury, R.A., Chief of the Staff since the departure of Brigadier-General Colley; Mr. Herbert, Private Secretary; Major McCalmont, 7th Hussars, and Lieutenant Creagh, R.A., aides-de-camp; Surgeon-Major Jackson; and Captain Maurice, R.A., Camp Commandant. Captain Stewart, 3rd Dragoon Guards, was staff officer to Colonel Baker Russell, and Captain Fraser, 60th Rifles, orderly officer.

of operations was for the cavalry, under Major Carrington, to push forward on the night of the 23rd and seize a small hill commanding Secocoeni's water supply, about three miles from the town. This position, called the Water Koppie, was to be strongly entrenched. Two days later the main body of infantry from Fort Albert Edward, by Mapeshlela's Drift, on the Olifant river, were to advance to support the force holding the Water Koppie. The Eastern Column, marching from Leydenburg, and due at Fort Burgers on the 23rd November, was directed to advance simultaneously along the south-eastern base of the Lulu Mountains, halting about five miles from the mountain spur at the rear of Secocoeni's town, upon which, and his stronghold, called the Fighting Koppie, a combined attack was then to be made.

When all was ready Sir Garnet marched, on the 21st November, from Fort Weber, reaching Fort Olifant on the following day. On the 23rd he crossed the Olifant river, and recrossing it at Fort Albert Edward, established his headquarters there. The same day an advance column captured and burnt the kraal of Umgirane, one of Secocoeni's chiefs, and a post was established near there, called, from its distance south of Fort Albert Edward, the 'Seven-mile Post.' Thence a reconnoissance was made up the valley towards Secocoeni's town and the Fighting Koppie, or citadel, 600 yards distant from it. This natural fortress is of singular formation and strength. Formed of huge boulders and rocks, covered with trees and brushwood, and honeycombed with galleries and caves and passages, it rose out of the plain to a height of about 150 feet; and if garrisoned by a handful of well-armed and determined men could have defied an army unprovided with siege artillery as long as food and water held out.

The force garrisoning the 'Seven-mile Post'—now the advanced position—numbering 1,140 Europeans and natives,* was further strengthened on the 24th; and the same night 150 men of the 21st and 94th Regiments, conveyed in mule-waggons, one company from each of these regiments on foot, 20 men of the Royal Engineers, and 300 Colonial Cavalry and Mounted Infantry, the whole under Major Carrington, started from the 'Seven-mile Post,' and seized the Water Koppie, some seventeen miles up the valley, and within three miles of the town and citadel of the Basuto chieftain, who, seemingly confident of repelling an assault on his virgin fortress, made no effort to take the offensive. Here a fortified post was established, which was named Fort Alexandra.

On the 26th Sir Garnet Wolseley set out from Fort Albert Edward with the main body of his force and a convoy; and, after a short halt at the 'Seven-mile Post' to make inquiries, pushed on to the front. The road, or track, was very bad, being partly covered with dense bush, and very narrow, and commanded by rocky and wooded hills. During the night a heavy storm of rain broke upon the weary column, which continued doggedly to plod on across swollen rivers and heavy mealie fields, where they bivouacked as best they could.† If the night was wet and

* It was from this koppie, or hill, that Colonel Rowlands was compelled to retire in his unsuccessful expedition in the previous year.

† Dr. W. H. Russell, the correspondent of the *Daily Telegraph*, says: 'The wind howled, the lightning flashed, the thunder rolled incessantly, the rain poured down in torrents, and at each side of us there was a dense forest of bush, wherein a concealed enemy could hide and start out, or pour in a volley at any moment, and get away to the hills before any attempt could be made to punish them. It was impossible to throw out flankers or cover the advance; and such a march could and would only have been made in face of such an enemy as the Caffre. About midnight Sir Garnet came to the spot where Colonel Russell was enjoying his bivouac without a fire; and all that night and the following morning and the whole of the day up to 3.30 the march went on, full of delays and ups and downs—waggons sticking, oxen falling, mules dropping, and the cries of the drivers and the crack of the cruel whips rang for ever through the valley. The oxen were sixteen hours in yoke without food or water. The men of the 21st must have been under arms for twenty-four hours continuously, and those of the 94th nearly as long, and the rearguard were especially harassed by frequent

miserable, the day was equally trying, for the heat was excessive, as it was the height of summer. Sir Garnet Wolseley pushed on in advance of the main column, and, on the morning of the 27th, arrived at Fort Alexandra, twenty-four miles distant from Fort Albert Edward. Here a small force of natives was left in garrison, and the whole force advanced up the valley in order to take up their positions for the capture of Secocoeni's town, which extended a mile and a half in length, and the assault on the Fighting Koppie at its base.

As soon as the main column had arrived Sir Garnet Wolseley, accompanied by Baker Russell and his staff, rode over to the Eastern Column, commanded by Major Bushman, occupying a position some miles on the further side of the Lulu range of mountains. This column consisted of 260 men of the 80th and 94th Regiments, 40 Colonial Horsemen, 250 natives of Eckersley's contingent, and some 10,000 Swazies—fine, athletic warriors, who presented a very picturesque appearance with their head-dress of glossy plumes, their heavy kirtles of leopard and wild-cat skin, and the roll of leopard or other fur around their foreheads.

By the plan of attack elaborated by Sir Garnet Wolseley Major Bushman was directed to lead his force up the eastern slope of Secocoeni's mountain during the night of

---

halts; in fact, the storm nearly frustrated the whole movement for twenty-four hours, and tested the endurance of the troops to the uttermost. The test was bravely encountered, and I am bound to say, after all I have written in a sense which might be taken as adverse to the efficiency of the army out here, that the 21st and 94th behaved in the most creditable manner, and marched with the utmost spirit, cheerfulness, and steadiness, notwithstanding the evident exhaustion and fatigue of many of them before they came into camp. If their clothes were in rags and of many colours, their rifles were clean: but I confess that I felt some uneasiness as to their fitness for action the following day, as I saw them late on the 27th straggling on towards their camping ground. Sir Garnet Wolseley, however, had no fears on the subject; he is all for young soldiers, as the world knows, and he certainly can show reasons for the faith that is in him as far as the troops of Russell's little force went.'

THE PLAN OF ATTACK.

the 27th, in readiness to attack by four a.m. on the following morning. The main body was divided into three separate columns. Major Carrington, with the Border Horse and the Transvaal Mounted Rifles, 161 strong; the Mounted Infantry, 34 strong; and the Zoutspanberg natives, under Captain Dahl, was entrusted with the left, or northern attack; Colonel Murray, 94th Regiment, with the 21st and 94th Regiments, and the artillery, commanded the centre attack: and Commandant Ferreira, with his two troops of horse, Mapoch's natives, and a company of Rustenberg natives, was to make the right, or southern attack. The three attacking columns were to be in position at four a.m.

By the night of the 27th Sir Garnet Wolseley was in readiness to carry out, and did carry out, the programme he had marked out for himself when planning the campaign at Pretoria; displaying, as in his Ashantee and Egyptian combinations, a mathematical exactitude in carrying into effect the complicated operations of war.* Here, as on a larger scale in Egypt, he had changed his base of operations from Fort Weber to Fort Albert Edward on the Olifant, requiring a change of the line of supply from Pretoria.

Though the column had performed an arduous march from the night of the 26th to the afternoon of the 27th, and had suffered considerably from the inclement weather and fatigue duties of the previous days, nevertheless by 2.30 a.m. on the 28th November not a tent was standing, and half an

* On this point Dr. Russell says: 'On the evening of November 27th Colonel Russell's force was massed on the plain, within a mile and a half of the enemy's towns, which was to be attacked on the day indicated by Sir Garnet some time previously. Now that was by no means so easily accomplished as one might suppose who knows what money has been spent on the war. When Sir Garnet Wolseley arrived at Fort Weber on the 28th October he found, to his disgust, that, instead of two months' supplies for 1,900 Europeans, 1,200 natives, and 475 horses being stored there, as he had been led to believe by Assistant Commissary-General Philips, there were only 5 slaughter oxen, 5200 lb. preserved meat, 21 days' rations of bread, and 3 days' rations for horses. He had to buy slaughter cattle, send to Marabastad, seventy miles off, for Indian corn, and to order the forage ration to be reduced.'

hour later everyone was at his post ready for an attack that promised some desperate fighting. The moon was visible at intervals in a cloudy sky when the whole force was put in motion, and Sir Garnet Wolseley accompanied the troops out of the laager to a level piece of ground in front of the Fighting Koppie, where he and his staff dismounted. Before four the entire force had taken up its several positions, and were waiting in silence and darkness for the signal to begin.

This was given, at 4.15, by the discharge of a shell at the Fighting Koppie, when the scene was lit up, as if by magic, by musketry-fire from the enemy, who yelled and blew their war-horns, as though to evoke their courage and strike terror into their foes. The bullets whistled round the battery and over the head of Sir Garnet, who, with his staff, had taken up his station within 800 yards of the citadel. The 21st and 94th Regiments were directed to make no reply, as, before attacking the Fighting Koppie the plan of operations required that the town at the base of the hills should be captured. To effect this, Major Carrington and Commandant Ferreira led their men into action from two opposite points.

The latter fired his first shot at 4.25, when, having waited in vain for Mapoch's men, who never joined him throughout the day, he charged the schanzes, or stone breastworks, with his handful of 80 dismounted troopers, and fought his way gradually from rock to rock and bush to bush, upward and forward, to a point commanding Secocoeni's town, which occupied the base and upper steeps of the mountain-side. Having reached this point at 6.20, he commenced a brisk fire on the masses of the enemy, and, at 7.30, when dense bodies of Swazies showing above on the sky-line announced to him that aid was at hand, his men descended and burnt a part of the town. These martial allies, who had declined Major Bushman's invitation to march from the rendezvous at the time agreed on, and were one and a half

THE ATTACK ON THE KRAAL. 383

hours behind time, did good service when their leaders, Captains Macleod and Randolph Campbell induced them to move. Through some misunderstanding, Major Bushman did not bring the detachments of the 80th and 94th Regiments into action, but kept them on the top of the ridge, spectators of the fighting. The Swazies now swarmed down on the enemy, and a terrible hand-to-hand fight ensued, in which the assegai and musket-stock did its sanguinary but silent work. Hundreds died here struggling on the narrow ledges, and dragging one another over the precipices; among those who were killed being Captain Campbell, a soldier of fortune, and described by Sir Garnet, as 'one of the bravest and most recklessly daring men that ever lived.'

In the meantime Major Carrington did equally good work with his column, consisting of the Border Horse, Mounted Infantry, under Lieutenant O'Grady (94th Regiment), and Transvaal Mounted Rifles, under Captain Macaulay, formerly an officer of the 9th Lancers—in all 200 men, with 300 Rustenburg natives. As usual, the latter left the fighting mostly to their white allies, who, advancing from the north along the ridge near Secocoeni's town, were hard pressed by superior forces until the timely arrival, about 6.20, of the Swazi left wing enabled them, after some severe fighting, to descend towards the central part of the town, to which they set fire. The losses were considerable, and the few officers of the column freely exposed themselves, as is essential when leading irregular troops into action. Captain Macaulay was killed, and Captain Maurice, Camp Commandant, who had volunteered his services, and Lieutenant O'Grady were wounded. By eight o'clock the enemy had been driven by Ferreira out of their posts on the south of the town, and by Carrington on the north, and the Swazies were at work about the higher ridges of the mountain.

The time had now arrived for attacking the citadel, the

Fighting Koppie, hitherto impregnable to black and white foes alike. Sir Garnet Wolseley determined to trust to the bayonet to effect this object, and, accordingly, the British infantry was called into requisition. The centre column, commanded by Colonel Murray (94th Regiment), consisting of the 21st and 94th Regiments, was to be supported by Carrington and Ferreira, who had led their men into the valley after the arrival of the Swazies. The attack was made on the centre by the regular troops, on the south-east by Carrington's dismounted men, and on the west by Ferreira's irregulars, who were supported by a company of the 94th. The guns had been shelling the Koppie for nearly four hours, and whenever a puff of smoke appeared, a dozen bullets were fired in response from the infantry, the range being little more than 600 yards, at which Colonel Baker Russell's horse was killed under him. But it was uncongenial work for Sir Garnet Wolseley, and a feeling of relief pervaded every officer and man of the little army when the order was given that the Fighting Koppie must be carried by assault. The signal was to be two rockets, the first to prepare, the second to advance.

The scene at this time, with mountain, valley, and forest lit up by the sun's rays, was picturesque, and formed a panorama of extraordinary beauty and interest—the town, having a frontage of one and a half mile, in flames, the yells and blowing of horns on the hills as the murderous conflict still raged, the shells hurtling overhead, and the sharp crackle of musketry from the orderly lines encircling the grim-looking Koppie, red-coats, dismounted horsemen, and dense masses of Swazies, all waiting to rush upon the works, swarming with men, and spitting forth fire from every cave and cranny.

The first rocket was fired, and then the second, and as the thin column of smoke ascended into the serene sky, Sir

STORM OF THE FIGHTING KOPPIE. 385

Garnet Wolseley's eye flashed with the light of battle, while, in a voice calm as if making an ordinary observation, he exclaimed : 'Mark the time. I make it 9.45.' In an instant the quick rattle of musketry was stilled, and a ringing cheer rent the air as the British infantry started to its feet and made straight for the hitherto impregnable fortress of boulders and rocks and caves, within whose confines many hundreds of desperate men awaited their onset. It was a thrilling moment, and the inspiriting sight held as if spellbound the Swazies, who had begun to regard with contempt their red-coated allies, who had done nothing as yet but fire on the Koppie at long range, or line the crest of the ridge while they descended and engaged in close conflict.

Seeing them standing and making no sign, Sir Garnet Wolseley rode up to them, and, pointing towards the Koppie, exclaimed in ringing tones : 'Come on, you fellows ; come on. Is there no one to make them understand ?' But though they did not understand the homely English, no interpreter was required to explain ' the eloquent gesture of the outstretched hand and the language of the kindling eye ;' and in an instant the dense mass, brandishing their assegais, gave the required response. Like Hector,

> 'Through all his host, inspiring force, he flies,
> And bids anew the martial thunder rise !'

Little wonder the savages displayed such enthusiasm when the British Commander-in-Chief and Governor of Natal and the Transvaal himself led them in the deadly charge, right up to the base of the rocks. Then ensued the race between Briton and native for the goal which was to bring death or glory to the competitors. Led by Baker Russell, Anstruther and Hazelrigg, by Carrington and Ferreira, by Brackenbury, McCalmont, Stewart and other members of the staff, and by their own officers, the 21st and 94th Regiments, volunteers and Swazies, all ran with eyes fixed on the beetling crags of the Koppie, only eager to be first at the death. Opinions differed as to whether it was a white or a black man who first set foot on the goal that formed their honourable emulation. The Swazies, in their costume of feathers and skins, and armed only with the stabbing assegai, had the advantage of the British soldier, and ran like greyhounds slipped from the leash; but, nevertheless, Sir Garnet Wolseley, who intently watched the scene, was of opinion that the latter was first on the rocks.

Having regard to the picturesqueness of the surroundings, the diversity in the actors, and the attendant circumstances, the scene was one that never could be effaced from the memory of the spectators. The encircling hills, the burning town, the rush of the stormers, the wild cheer and the skirl of the pipes of the Scots Fusiliers, answered by the blare of the war-horn, and the defiant yell of the Basutos in the brief interval ere the whole array of regulars, volunteers and Caffres were in their midst, must have formed a picture such as a De Neuville or Gerome would have longed to paint.*

The Basutos were quickly driven into the caves and clefts, whence they kept up a biting fire which caused some loss. The light spare savages excelled with the rifle, but had no chance at close quarters with the powerful Swazies.

* In a speech made by Sir Garnet Wolseley, at a public banquet given in his honour by the inhabitants of Pretoria, he said: ' In the action we lost heavily; but the number of dead is far less than I had contemplated or anticipated. I am glad to say the Basutos were very bad shots—nearly as bad as the Zulus. There was one peculiar feature in the engagement. For some time past we have fought in South Africa only on the defensive, especially in Zululand. We waited behind our slight intrenchments or waggon-laagers, for the rush of the enemy—they the assailing, we the defending party. Attacking parties are naturally expected to lose much more than those who act on the defensive, and accordingly I made arrangements for a considerable number of wounded. My arrangements were, I am glad to say, not wanted so much as I expected they would be. Sixty white men killed and wounded, and about 500 natives, constituted our loss. In the operations the white men were greatly assisted by the natives. The large force of Swazies discharged the duties for which they were employed to my entire satisfaction.' Sir Garnet Wolseley has since informed us that the loss of the Swazies in killed and wounded was subsequently ascertained to be 1,000 men.

BRITISH LOSSES.

Our loss during the day was 3 officers and 7 European non-commissioned officers and men killed, and 6 officers and 43 non-commissioned officers and men wounded. The officers killed were Captain Lawrell, 4th Hussars, Staff Officer to Colonel Baker Russell; Captain Macaulay,* late 12th Lancers, commanding the Transvaal Mounted Rifles, and Captain Randolph Campbell. The officers wounded were Captains Willoughby and Gordon, 21st Regiment; Captain Beeton, Rustenburg Native Contingent (severely); Lieutenants O'Grady, 94th Regiment, commanding Mounted Infantry, and Dewar, King's Dragoons, attached to Mounted Infantry (both severely); and Captain Maurice, R.A., acting

* 'Captain Macaulay,' writes one who knew him well, 'had all the pluck and adventure which spread the fame of England across the world. He was singularly cool and daring in fight, and no body of irregular horse were better in hand than his motley corps of half-breeds. He was some time at the gold-fields before the annexation, and was returned by that constituency as a member of the Volksraad of the South African Republic. He will be mourned, not only in South Africa, but in many parts of Australia, especially in Queensland, where he lived some years and had many friends.' There were many narrow escapes when storming the Koppie. The enemy stood their ground among the rocks and schanzes until our men were very close upon them. One Basuto crouched behind a tree until Mr. Herbert, of the Colonial Office, Sir Garnet's private secretary, who was storming with Ferreira's men, was within 12 yards of him, when he then threw his assegai, which passed over Herbert's shoulder and bent itself in the ground. The following was the manner of Captain Lawrell's death. When Colonel Baker Russell, leading the infantry charge, went straight up the Koppie, he was accompanied by Captain Brackenbury, R.A., Captain Lawrell, and a number of his staff. As Captain Lawrell mounted the rocks, a shot from a cave struck him in the throat and killed him. He toppled over backwards, and fell down the rocks some twenty feet. Upon the other side, an almost similar shot struck a troop-sergeant-major of Ferreira's Horse. The ball passed in at the throat and out at the back of the head. Two men of the 94th Regiment, serving with the Mounted Infantry, Privates Fitzpatrick and Flawn, received the V.C. for their gallant conduct in assisting Lieutenant Dewar, who was wounded in the groin and lay helpless, during the fighting at Secocoeni's town. 'Some of our natives were helping him down the mountain, when, seeing about 40 of the enemy approaching, they deserted the officer and ran. Fitzpatrick and Flawn were near, and rushed to his assistance, barely saving him from the assegais of the enemy. They drove the enemy back by the fire from their rifles, and then took turns to support the wounded officer and to hold the hovering enemy in check with a rifle. When one was exhausted with the fatigue of bearing the helpless body, the other took his place, releasing his comrade to maintain the fire upon the enemy. Thus step by step Lieutenant Dewar was rescued by the gallantry of two men from an overwhelming force.'

Staff officer to Major Carrington, who was in the thick of the fighting with his commanding officer, and received a bullet-wound through the shoulder. The loss of the Swazies, as subsequently ascertained was 1,000, most of them being killed. But they considered themselves repaid by being permitted to retain the cattle they had captured, which forms the chief source of wealth among the natives of South Africa. As to the Basutos, the tribe was almost exterminated, and Secocoeni, as he looked around him, found that all his chief warriors had fallen in obeying his behests.

> 'Round the battlements and round the plain,
> For many a chief he look'd, but look'd in vain.'

The *spolia opima* that fell to the victorious Swazies was not limited to the cattle, of which thousands were captured, but they took possession of the Basuto women. Sir Garnet Wolseley, however, sternly ordered that these should be set free, and that, if necessary, force should be used to prevent this cruel appropriation of the spoils of victory.

Within fifteen minutes—a *mauvais quart d'heure* for the Basutos—of the time Sir Garnet Wolseley gave the signal for the charge, the Fighting Koppie had changed hands, thus foreshadowing in its fate, mode of capture, and time occupied in the assault, the storming of the lines of Tel-el-Kebir. But though the position was practically won, within its cavernous bowels a large body of Basutos had taken refuge with several hundred of their women and children. Hence they kept up a desultory fire on our men, stationed on the rocks above them and forming a cordon at the base, and only surrendered on the 1st December, impelled by the pangs of hunger and thirst, and the intolerable stench arising from the dead bodies in the caves.

Meanwhile, at four a.m. on the 30th November, Ferreira proceeded with his men up the mountain to effect the capture of Secocoeni, who had taken refuge in a cave some distance up the ravine beyond his town. Sir Garnet Wolseley essayed to accompany the force, but the old wound in the leg he had received in the Crimea prevented him from ascending precipitous paths, and he had to return to the plain. Ferreira was joined higher up the mountain by two companies of the 21st and 94th Regiments and some natives; and after a tiresome ascent under a scorching sun, at eleven o'clock the party reached the mountain-top and burnt a kraal. The cave, in which the chief lay hid with some 600 followers, was discovered and blockaded; and ultimately, on the morning of the 2nd December, Secocoeni, ill and with his followers suffering from want of food and water, surrendered to Major Clarke, R.A.

The conduct of officers and men throughout the day was most exemplary, and there was no failure anywhere, all ranks being animated by the example of their leader and his able lieutenant, Colonel Baker Russell. A word of special praise is due to the services rendered by Colonel Brackenbury, R.A., Chief of the Staff, and Captain Herbert Stewart,*

* An officer who was present throughout the campaign, says: 'After the Water Koppie had been occupied on the 25th, Captain Stewart, having accompanied the advanced guard, started in quest of the eastern column, taking with him an escort of Ferreira's Horse. The eastern column had orders to advance from Fort Burgers, and occupy a position some five or seven miles on the eastern side of the mountain, accordingly as water might be found. This column arrived in position the same morning, and made a fort, called Fort George, at a distance of five miles from the eastern base of Secocoeni's mountain, and at about the same distance from Fort Alexandra. Captain Stewart, having ridden round the northern spur of the mountains bounding Secocoeni's valley on the east, on his way to this column, passed its patrol, though the two bodies thus crossing were unseen one by the other, owing to the wooded and hilly nature of the ground. Thus the movements of the two columns advancing against Secocoeni, though they had been without the means of exchanging communications for eight days, had so precisely conformed to calculation that they occupied their respective bases of attack within a few hours of each other.' On the 27th, Captain J. C. MacGregor, R.E. (who was killed in the campaign with the Boers), with a signalling party of the Royal Engineers and 94th Regiment, supported by 100 of the Zoutspanberg levies, established a heliograph station upon a neck or ridge to the east of Fort Alexandra, near the Water Koppie, and secured communications by flashing signals with Major Bushman's column at Fort George.

3rd Dragoon Guards, Staff officer to Colonel Russell. This officer displayed untiring energy and a singular tact in dealing with men such as formed the component parts of this heterogeneous force, which marked him out as a capable soldier. These qualities received even more conspicuous illustration in the Egyptian campaign.

On the 4th December Sir Garnet Wolseley, accompanied by an escort of Border Horse, and taking Secocoeni with him, set out for Pretoria, where his presence was urgently required to deal with the Boers. The 94th Regiment remained in the valley, garrisoning a post on the Lulu Mountains, until the submission of the remaining chiefs and adherents of the Basuto chief. Sir Garnet Wolseley arrived at Pretoria* on the 9th December, with his captive, who was the second great African potentate that he had captured within six months. The rival of Cetewayo and his companion in misfortune, the fate of Secocoeni was more tragic than that of the Zulu King. Released, like the latter, he returned to his native country and sought to revive his influence. But though he could rebuild his desolated kraal, his prestige had vanished, and he was murdered by Mampoer, an influential rival chief, who has since found an asylum with Mapoch, the chief who co-operated with us in the attack on Secocoeni's stronghold.

On his arrival at Pretoria, Sir Garnet Wolseley found that the Boers, though much impressed by the striking success

* A more pleasant event in Sir Garnet Wolseley's administration of affairs in Natal and the Transvaal than wars and political troubles was the opening of telegraphic communication between England and South Africa by the completion of the line between Aden and Zanzibar. On the 25th December, 1879, the Queen telegraphed to him from Windsor Castle, congratulating him and the Colonies under his government 'on this happy event;' and two days later he replied from Pretoria, expressing his 'sincere thanks to her Majesty for her gracious telegram of the 25th, received that afternoon.' Another incident that occurred during Sir Garnet Wolseley's administration was the visit of the ex-Empress Eugenie to South Africa for the purpose of making a mournful inspection of the scene of the death of her son. Sir Garnet Wolseley received the unhappy consort of Napoleon III. on her landing at Durban on the 23rd April.

achieved against the powerful chief who had so long defied their armies, were as irreconcilable as ever. For many reasons, they had hoped and anticipated that success would reward their efforts to obtain independence without having recourse to arms. Besides the encouragement given to them to persevere in passive resistance, by their friends in the British Parliament and Press, they had hopes of a reversal of the policy of annexation from the words of a covering despatch to the British Colonial Secretary of State, addressed by Sir Bartle Frere in the preceding April, when he received the Boer committee.* Sir Bartle Frere showed this covering despatch to five members of the Committee, who drew encouragement from the passage in which he said that in his opinion, 'their representations are worthy of our earnest consideration.' Whatever Sir Bartle Frere meant by these words, they were interpreted by the recalcitrant Boers to recommend the restitution of their independence, and greatly increased the difficulties under which Sir Garnet Wolseley now laboured, as showing that the annexation was not irreversible. Thus the people were in a state of passive rebellion already, and in June Mr. Piet Joubert, afterwards Commander-in-Chief at Laing's Nek, refused to take the

---

* This was after the third mass meeting held by the Boer leaders to lay their grievances before their rulers, On a previous occasion—in March and April, 1879, at the time Colonel Lanyon became Administrator—some 5,000 or 6,000 Boers assembled to receive and consider the answer brought by Kruger and Joubert, the delegates composing the two deputations to England. Colonel Lanyon's reply to the deputation was not conciliatory in form or substance. It was then proposed that they should take up arms ; but as Sir Bartle Frere was coming to the Transvaal, it was decided to await his arrival. Sir Bartle was at first, and until his visit to the Transvaal, under the belief that the Boer agitation was partial, and thought to allay it by argument and the offer of a constitution similar to that at the Cape ; but the Boer Committee would listen to no compromise, and finally, finding that the malcontents represented ' the very great majority of the Boer population of the Transvaal,' he consented to forward a memorial, and support it with a letter to Lord Carnarvon, giving it as his opinion that it 'demanded the most serious attention of her Majesty's Government.' Then followed the lull which Sir Garnet Wolseley, acting under instructions from the Home Government, dispelled by his uncompromising language.

oath of allegiance and pay arrears of taxes due from him; and other Boers of wealth and position followed his lead.

Sir Garnet Wolseley clearly perceived the storm that was brewing, and, on the 29th October, addressed the following words to Sir Michael Hicks-Beach, the Colonial Secretary: 'I am compelled to recognise the continuance of grave discontent. I am informed on all sides that it is the intention of the Boers to fight for independence. . . . There is no doubt, I think, that the people are incited to discontent and rebellion by ambitious agitators; but I am compelled also to allow that the timid and wavering, who are awed into taking sides against us, are comparatively a small party, and that the main body of the Dutch population are disaffected to our rule.' The result amply vindicated Sir Garnet Wolseley's judgment, but his views were not shared by experienced politicians and Press writers,* who were of opinion that the protests and threats of the Boers would end in their doing nothing.

On the 10th December, the day after Sir Garnet Wolseley's return to Pretoria, the Boers, openly displaying the flag of the South African Republic, assembled in camp at Dornfontein, a place on the main road from Pretoria to Potchefstroom, and about equidistant between those places and Heidelberg. Here were gathered 3,000 men, and 510 waggons—the adult male population of the country being about 8,000—and resolutions were adopted, demanding that the Vice-President, Mr. Paul Kruger, should, in the absence of Mr. Burgers, the President at the time of the annexation in 1877, convoke the *Volksraad*, asserting their independence and their determination to 'sacrifice their lives and shed their blood for it;' and requiring the National Committee,

* The *Times* correspondent at Pretoria, writing on the 15th December, after the great Boer demonstration held in that month at Heidelberg, says: 'The party which professes to desire fighting is very small, and if any fighting was probable, would grow smaller still.'

as soon as possible, to take the necessary steps for the recovery of independence. Mr. Pretorius, an ex-president and chairman of the meeting, sent a copy of these resolutions under his own signature to Sir Garnet Wolseley, with a request that they might be communicated to the Home Government. To this demand Sir Garnet made reply by causing the arrest of Pretorius and Bok, the secretary, on a charge of high treason. The former was brought to trial, but the proceedings were discontinued after lasting three days.

Sir Garnet had taken ample military precaution to guard against a rising. As early as the middle of November he had constructed redoubts at Wakkerstroom and Standerton, each for defence by two companies; and at Heidelberg and Middelburg for one company; three months' supplies of everything for their garrisons being kept in each fort. In readiness for the Boers resorting to arms, after their meeting on the 10th December, he concentrated at Pretoria a force, consisting of the 80th Regiment, seven companies of the 4th Regiment, six companies of the 58th Regiment, and a squadron of the King's Dragoon Guards. Thus overawed, the *Volkstein*, the Boer organ in Pretoria, strongly urged on the farmers not to give Sir Garnet Wolseley any excuse to attack them, but quietly to disperse and await the departure of his Excellency and the troops, meanwhile persisting in the attitude of passive resistance and refusal to pay taxes. This advice the Boers followed, with what success is well known.

Early in 1880 Sir Garnet Wolseley promulgated the new constitution, which had been promised three years before. By it, besides the Executive Council he had already announced,—which was to consist of the Governor, or Administrator, and four leading members of the Government, with three non-official members nominated by the Governor,

—the Legislative Council was constituted, to consist of the Executive Council, the Chief Justice, and six nominated members. This constitution, which was framed by Sir Michael Hicks-Beach upon lines recommended by Sir Bartle Frere, was a sham; as not only were the members of both the Executive and Legislative Councils removable at the Governor's pleasure, but power was reserved to the Governor to act without consulting, or in opposition to, the Council, if he judged it expedient; and questions affecting the revenue could only be proposed in the Legislative Assembly with the Governor's permission. Moreover, any legislation the Council might pass could always be disallowed or repealed by the Queen's authority. The only apology for this constitution is that it was temporary; but much of the odium attaching to it fell upon Sir Garnet Wolseley, though it will be seen he was not responsible for its conditions.

At this time Mr. Pretorius was in frequent correspondence with Sir Garnet, and promised to join his Government a little later on, when the country had quieted down, as Mr. Pretorius then thought it would in a short time.

That the hostilities which broke out in December, 1880, did not occur at this time, was due to the fact of the presence of Sir Garnet Wolseley and the large force of troops still remaining in the country, and also to the apprehended change of Ministry in England, which actually took place in the following spring. The Boers had sympathizers in the Radical Press and Parliament, among the most able and consistent being Mr. Leonard Courtney, now Under-Secretary for the Colonies. Mr. Gladstone also, in his Midlothian addresses, expressed his disapproval of the policy of annexation, thereby encouraging the Boers to hope, if he came into power, that the question of their independence might be reconsidered. In this hope it was determined to wait and endeavour to influence the Cape Parliament against agreeing to any step in furtherance of South African Confederation. Kruger and Joubert proceeded to Cape Town on this errand in the spring of 1880. In the meantime the elections took place at home, and the Liberals came into office. Advantage of the change of Ministry was immediately taken by the delegates to memorialize Mr. Gladstone; but the answer of the Liberal Government, dated June 8th, gave the final blow to the hopes which alone had induced the Boers to refrain so long from open rebellion. It was in these terms—'Our judgment is that the Queen cannot be advised to relinquish the Transvaal.' Doubtless, in time, the whole question would have been examined, and the wishes of the people conceded; but the Afghan, Irish, and other questions of domestic interest, were considered more pressing, and the Boers, finding their aspirations unsatisfied, took up arms. The unwisdom of reducing the garrisons of the Transvaal, a country as large as France, to two weak regiments of infantry, the 58th and 94th, without any cavalry, while matters still remained unsettled, bore its legitimate fruits; and when the troops were handled in a manner that betrayed extraordinary military incompetence, a succession of disasters ensued, happily without parallel in our recent military history.

Before leaving South African questions, we may refer to one in which Sir Garnet Wolseley offered advice equally creditable to his sagacity and sense of justice. We refer to the Basuto question, which was so unwisely raised by the Cape Government during the time he was administering the affairs of the Transvaal, and which appears to be still unsettled after the expenditure of much money and many valuable lives. The Basutos, who became British subjects in 1869, had enlisted under our banners in the hostilities against the Baphuti chief, Moirosi—whose mountain was carried by assault on the 20th November, 1879—and during the Zulu War, when, specially at Isandlwhana, they served with great gallantry. But when hostilities were over, Mr. Sprigg, the Prime Minister of the Cape Government, who had borne testimony to the loyalty of the paramount chief, Letsea, brought in a measure, called the Peace Preservation Act, enforcing their disarmament; and in a speech in the House of Assembly, on the 1st June, gave as his reason for its introduction, his fear that these arms would be used to make war against the colony.* Sir Garnet Wolseley indignantly protested against this treatment of loyal allies after the danger that had called for their services had passed away. On the 10th March he wrote to the Secretary of State for the Colonies: 'That the Cape Colony is endeavouring to take the arms from its natives, regardless of whether they had or had not been previously loyal, is a species of news that soon spreads far and wide beyond our frontiers, and is calculated to raise the bitterest of feelings against our rule. . . . This disarmament policy will array against us the native sentiment in every part of South Africa; and should it result in a Basuto war, every native, from the Zambesi to Cape Agulhas, will feel that every shot fired in it against us has been fired in his interests.'

Two and a half years have passed since Sir Garnet Wolseley wrote this warning, during which the Cape Ministry have failed to enforce their policy, though large armed forces have been in the field, and much blood and treasure have been expended. By the last news, General Gordon—

---

* Of course there was some question of annexation concerned, and the Quothing district of Basutoland, occupied by Moirosi's tribe, was to be annexed, notwithstanding the strong protest of Mr. Griffith, the Government Agent, who said that 'to cut it off and dispose of it in any other way would, in my opinion, be acting most unjustly to the Basutos, and would entirely shake their confidence in the British Government. . . . I fail to see why the Basutos, who have staunchly supported us, should be punished for the acts of the rebel chief Moirosi and his followers, who have paid the penalty of their crimes with their lives.'

'Chinese Gordon,' the friend of subject races and a man of chivalric honour—who had been called in to settle the Basuto difficulty, has resigned, as he does not approve the course pursued towards Masupha, the chief who has successfully resisted the disarming policy of the Colonial Government.

Early in April Sir Garnet Wolseley quitted Pretoria on his return to England, Colonel Bellairs being left in command of the troops on the departure of General Clifford, and Sir Owen Lanyon, Administrator, under the orders of Sir George Colley, the new Governor of Natal, who had resigned his position on the Indian Viceroy's staff, and came out from England with instructions that the Transvaal was to be retained.

Sir Garnet Wolseley rode the distance of 350 miles from Pretoria to Maritzburg in three days, accompanied by Major Herbert Stewart, now his Chief of the Staff. He arrived at Maritzburg on the 8th April, and on the following day he and Sir Henry Bulwer, the retiring Lieutenant-Governor of Natal, were entertained at dinner, when he expressed a hope that the colony would soon be confederated with the Cape. Sir Garnet proceeded to Grahamstown, where he received a hearty reception, and, after a brief stay at Cape Town, sailed thence for England on the 4th May, accompanied by his staff, in the Royal Mail steamer *Conway Castle*. On the 25th May, 1880, the ship cast anchor in Plymouth Sound, and receiving the inevitable address from the mayor, he proceeded to London the same day, having successfully accomplished the mission with which he had been entrusted.

Sir Garnet Wolseley received no reward for his services, and surely the pacification of Zululand and the restoration of the prestige of our arms in South Africa by his victory over Secocoeni may be regarded as such. True, he was gazetted a G.C.B., in common with Lord Chelmsford;

but this honour he had declined on his return from Ashantee, and he might well have anticipated that the local rank of General, conferred on him on leaving for South Africa, should be made substantive; but this was denied, from motives that do not bear consideration.* Sir Garnet, however, did not look for reward as an incentive to serve his country, and bore this treatment in dignified silence; but he had friends who were more outspoken.

* Sir Garnet Wolseley was too plain-spoken to please the Horse Guards, who resent anything like independence; but his position was too assured, and the opinion held of his services by his countrymen too high, for those in authority to do more than retard the advancement which he ultimately wrung from them. At the Newspaper Press Fund Dinner in June, 1880, he spoke his mind in a way that gave great offence at the Horse Guards. He said: 'To the Press generally the British army now looks with the greatest anxiety and the greatest interest; for the rising men of the army feel that it is only the power of the Press which can bring useful light to bear upon the dark parts of our military system, which they believe not to be in unison with the spirit of the age or with modern military science. You alone have sufficient power to enable us to correct and reform what we believe to be wrong, and to remove from the path of progress those great boulders of prejudice and superstition which now impede the way. You alone can enable us to put new wheels to the military coach, which by its creaking tells us of its present dangerous condition, and which is only with difficulty maintained in an upright position at all.' Again, at a banquet at the Mansion House he said: 'He was surprised when the shortcomings of the army were attributed to the short-service system by those who remembered how an army raised under the long-service system totally disappeared in a few months under the walls of Sebastopol. He contended that the short-service system had made the army popular, and in consequence of it we were now in a position to obtain any number of recruits we might require. If the system were intelligently carried out it would create a reserve which would prevent such catastrophes as occurred in 1855. At the same time he believed, with many rising soldiers, that the army needed many reforms; and he trusted that the required changes might be effected within no distant time, so that the army might be brought to such a state of efficiency as would make it worthy of the Queen whom it served, and the nation for whose protection it existed.'

CHAPTER XI.

THE EGYPTIAN CAMPAIGN.

Sir Garnet Wolseley as Quartermaster-General.—Attends the German Autumn Military Manœuvres.—Is appointed Adjutant-General.—Nomination of Sir Garnet Wolseley to the Command of the Expedition to Egypt.—He proceeds to Alexandria.—Change of the Base of Operations to Ismailia.—Transport Difficulties.—Advance of Sir Garnet from Ismailia.—The Action at Tel-el-Mahuta.—Capture of Mahsameh.—The Action at Kassassin on the 28th August.—Preparations for the final Advance. The Action of the 9th September.—The Night March on the 12th September.—The Battle of Tel-el-Kebir.—The Surrender of Cairo.—Operations of the Cavalry.—Sir Garnet Wolseley in Cairo.—Return to England.—Conclusion.

ON his return from South Africa, Sir Garnet Wolseley was nominated Quartermaster-General, and assumed the duties of his office on the 1st July, 1880. He had not long been installed when, on the 28th July, news arrived in England of the disaster at Maiwand, involving a recommencement of hostilities in Afghanistan. Sir Garnet was at Freshwater, in the Isle of Wight, and posted up to London on the following day. Public opinion in England pointed to him as the best man to retrieve the disaster, and even in India the *Times* correspondent at Calcutta telegraphed that the news of his appointment 'would be hailed with delight by soldiers and civilians alike from one end of the country to the other.' But his time had not yet come, and indeed, as the event proved, there was no occasion for his services, as the Indian Government had at their disposal, in Sir Frederick Roberts, a General competent to deal with the crisis and rehabilitate the tarnished honour of his country.

Instead of the stern realities of war, Sir Garnet Wolseley found himself nominated for the duty of attending the German Autumn Military Manœuvres. It was a high honour to represent the British army at the great school of modern war; though at a time when his country was engaged in active hostilities, to be a spectator of mimic warfare, even though some of the most accomplished soldiers of the age were the exponents, was a duty scarcely congenial to one who was conscious of his own capacity for demonstrating the teachings of war. The manœuvres commenced, on the 10th September, with the parade of the 3rd, or Brandenburg Army Corps, before the Emperor William, and were continued with the manœuvring of this and the Guard Corps. Sir Garnet was treated with special honour by the German Emperor and Crown Prince, and attracted much interest among the Generals, including Count von Moltke and Prince Frederick Charles, who commanded the Brandenburg Corps in the terrible battle of Thionville, after Bazaine's retreat from Metz, when 62,000 Prussian soldiers repulsed the whole army of the Rhine, mustering 125,000 men, losing one-fourth of their number.

Early in the present year Sir Garnet Wolseley was appointed Adjutant-General in succession to Sir Charles Ellice. With the causes or with the results of the war in Egypt we will not deal in this work, as Sir Garnet Wolseley's mission to that country was purely military. His task was to defeat and disperse the forces under Arabi Pasha in rebellion against the authority of the Khedive Tewfik, and to restore that prince to the throne. It was a task, having regard to the climate, time of the year, and difficult nature of the country in which operations would be conducted, that was calculated to test his claims to be regarded as a great General. It was so recognised at the time of his appointment; and when a delay occurred before the final advance from Kassassin, hostile and ignorant critics who had predicted a lengthened campaign, or even failure, pointed to the approaching verification of their prophecies. It is, therefore, only just that when success crowned Wolseley's strategy, a full and unstinted measure of credit should be accorded to him.

These croakers, whose wish in some instances was father to the thought, had some grounds for their vaticinations in the previous history of the Egyptian army. They might have drawn attention to the prowess of the Egyptian contingent engaged in the Russo-Turkish War of 1828, when they were decimated in the gallant resistance they offered to the passage of the Danube by the army of General Paskievitch; and again when the Soudanee regiments displayed heroic devotion when fighting against enormous odds during the Abyssinian War, as related in a recent work written by an American officer in the Khedive's service. The readers of Palgrave's 'Travels in Central Arabia' know what deeds were performed by Ibrahim Pasha's Egyptian soldiers against the Wahabees of Derryah, who overran the countries of Asia from the Persian Gulf to the Red Sea, and conquered even the sacred places of Mecca and Medina; and but for the English at Acre, in 1840, Mehemet Ali, the father of the same great General, would have dictated terms to the Sultan himself at Stamboul. Let, then, our English General and his brave soldiers wear the laurels they have well earned, and if foreign critics, envious of their glory, chose to impute to British gold the victories achieved by British valour and the genius of a British General, it were a disgrace to any of our countrymen to write or say aught to give them encouragement in such an unworthy course. History tells a different tale.

Bonaparte himself, though assisted by such soldiers as Kleber, Lannes, Berthier, Dessaix, Davoust, Marmont, and

Murat, did not achieve a more rapid and striking success in his memorable expedition in 1798 than did Wolseley in 1882, and the difficulties encountered by the latter were far greater. Bonaparte was opposed by an army of Arabs and Mamelukes, armed with scimitars and 'large pistols from London,' as he wrote to the Directory; whereas the British General was required to combat a vastly superior force of disciplined troops, probably not less than 60,000, armed with Remington rifles and Krupp guns. The hardships endured by Wolseley's soldiers in the march across the desert from Ismailia to Cairo were much greater than those suffered by Napoleon's army of 25,000 men in their march between the 6th and 23rd July through the fertile Delta from Alexandria to Cairo. By any test that may be applied the campaign of 1882 exceeds in brilliancy that of 1798. Wolseley's losses, reduced to a minimum by his able strategy and rapid advance, were greater than those incurred by Bonaparte, and the actions of Tel-el-Mahuta, Kassassin, and Tel-el-Kebir were more sanguinary than those of El-Rahmânyeh, Chobra Keit, and the Pyramids, in the last of which Bonaparte lost 30 killed and 120 wounded to Wolseley's 60 and 400 respectively.

The political results of the campaign of 1882, which have given us the command of the road to India and predominance in Egypt, exceed those attained by the French in 1798, which were of a transitory character, unless the future has in store for us such defeats as Nelson and Abercromby inflicted on the invaders of Egypt at the Nile and Alexandria, and expulsion from that country. As for the financial results, Europe had no business relations with Egypt in 1798, while now she is Egypt's creditor for one hundred millions of debt, besides all the vast amount of capital invested in commercial undertakings, rescued by the British General's victories from total loss. The lapse of years and the halo surrounding a mighty name should not prevent us from instituting a just

WOLSELEY'S DEPARTURE FOR EGYPT.

comparison between the deeds of a countryman and those even of the greatest master of the art of war.

On the 11th June took place the massacres at Alexandria, followed by others scarcely less sanguinary at Tantah and elsewhere; and, in that month, Admiral Sir Beauchamp Seymour, having in vain warned Arabi Pasha and the Government of which, though only Minister at War, he was virtually the head, that further strengthening the defences of Alexandria would involve the bombardment of the forts, effectually carried his threat into execution. This was followed, two days later, by the landing of some seamen and marines from the fleet, who were reinforced on the 18th July by the 1st South Staffordshire (38th Regiment), and 3rd King's Royal Rifles (60th Rifles) from Malta, and on the 24th by a battery of Garrison Artillery and half battalion of the 1st Sussex (35th Regiment) from Malta, and the 2nd Cornwall (46th Regiment) from Gibraltar, their places being taken by other troops from England. Sir Archibald Alison assumed command of all the land forces at Alexandria, which he retained until the arrival of Sir Garnet Wolseley. It was not until the 25th July, when a vote of credit was taken by the Government, that this country was committed to a war with Egypt. On the following day the reserves were called out by proclamation, and on the 29th the French Chamber of Deputies refused the vote of credit proposed by M. Freycinet to enable his Government to take part in the expedition to which England was now irrevocably committed. No one experienced a greater sense of relief on hearing of this step than the British Commander-in-Chief, who witnessed in China the disastrous results of co-operating with a French army commanded by the incompetent Count Montauban de Palikao. His hands would now be free to act as he thought proper, without consulting with allied generals, or being hampered with considerations for the susceptibilities of a proud nation. The dangers of co-operation were not, however, finally dispelled until Italy declined the offer of our Government, and the Sultan, after an extraordinary display of vacillation and mendacity, first declined the proposal to send his troops to Egypt to coerce Arabi as the mandatory of Europe, and when the war was practically over accepted the offer of our Government to despatch a division to act in virtual subordination to the British General.

Before leaving England Sir Garnet Wolseley himself saw to the proper appointment, in all its branches, of the army entrusted to his command, and the arrangements for their embarkation and disposition. Not only this, but he prepared his plan of campaign, from which he deviated in no particular, but carried it out to the letter, and even to the day he fixed before his departure, thus reducing the conduct of military operations in a country 3,000 miles distant, to the precision of a mathematical problem. The troops despatched to Egypt from this country and the Mediterranean before his departure from England numbered 1,010 officers and 21,200 non-commissioned officers and men, with 54 guns and 5,600 horses; and reinforcements, including depôts and drafts to Cyprus, were subsequently sent out or prepared for despatch to the number of 280 officers and 10,800 men. To carry this large army, including all the stores, provisions and material (about 41,000 tons up to 30th September), a fleet of transports was employed having an aggregate burthen of 147,000 tons. Besides these troops, the Indian contingent, including the reserve at Aden, consisted of 7,270[*] officers and men, which included two British regiments, the 1st Seaforth Highlanders and 1st Manchester, and two batteries of artillery. The three native cavalry regiments had each a strength of 550 of all ranks,

[*] This was exclusive of camp followers, 3,500 men. Also 1,700 horses, 840 ponies, and nearly 5,000 mules for the guns and transport.

and the native infantry of 822. The grand total of the Egyptian expedition was 40,560 officers and men, being the largest, as it was certainly the best equipped, army ever despatched by this country.

The one department in which the expedition was defective, as so often happens in our wars, great or little, was the land transport; only 500 pack animals being sent from England. The defect, due to the system by which the land transport service is not maintained at a serviceable strength, was sought to be remedied during the campaign, and thousands of mules from Spain, America, and elsewhere, were purchased, but they arrived when the war was over. From Ismailia, whence Sir Garnet intended to advance on Cairo, there is a railway* to the capital; but the enemy succeeded in removing most of the railway plant and all the engines, except one that was broken-down, so that until this defect was remedied by the arrival of four engines from England and some inferior ones from Alexandria, he had to fall back on the few pack animals in his possession and the Sweet Water Canal; the Indian contingent alone being supplied with sufficient transport, due to the system in force in that service.

When all was ready and the Commander-in-Chief was about to sail from England, the success of the expedition

* The railway from Ismailia, which Sir Garnet Wolseley adopted as his base, proceeds in one direction to Suez, 55 miles distant, with the Fresh Water Canal running parallel and close to it the whole way; and in the other to Cairo, 85 miles. The first station from Ismailia is Nefiche, 2½ miles, where the Fresh Water Canal bifurcates, one branch to Ismailia, and the other, passing through two locks, follows the line of the Maritime Canal, to Suez. After leaving Nefiche, the first station on the line (which runs parallel to the Sweet Water Canal), after passing Magfar, is Mahsameh, 14 miles, where are irrigating sluices, and at Kassassin, the next station, is a lock. Then follow in succession the stations of Tel-el-Kebir, Abd-el-Hamed, and Zagazig, an important place with a population of 35,000 souls. Here the Fresh Water Canal, which divides 8 miles from Tel-el-Kebir, is met again, the other branch going off to Belbeis, and thence to Cairo. The railway station after Zagazig is Burden, 7 miles distant, and then comes Belbeis, 6 miles, Shebeen-el-Kanater, 17½ miles; Kalioob, 12 miles; and Cairo, 10 miles.

was jeopardized by his illness. In Ashantee Sir Garnet Wolseley suffered from the fever so prevalent on the West Coast of Africa; and now, at this critical time, he was again prostrated with this fever, which recurred at a later period when he was at Cairo. Sir Garnet, accompanied by Sir John Adye, chief of the staff, and his divisional and brigade generals, proceeded, on the 28th July, to Osborne, to take leave of the Queen, and on the following day he was seized with illness, which temporarily incapacitated him from work at the War Office. On the evening of the 31st July, feeling slightly better, he insisted on transacting business of importance at his own house in connection with his command. On the following day the Prince of Wales called on him to inquire after his health and take leave.

Sir Garnet had intended proceeding to Alexandria, *viâ* Brindisi and Cyprus, there to inspect the depôts, but his state of health debarred him from undertaking so fatiguing a journey. He resolved, therefore, to proceed to his destination by sea, and embarked in the *Calabria*, which conveyed two squadrons of the 2nd Life Guards and Horse Guards. Sir Garnet drove to the Albert Docks in a brougham, and his appearance as he walked on board, muffled up as though it was the depth of winter, indicated at once his weak state of health and the strength of the patriotic resolution that animated him. On the ship arriving at Gibraltar, Lord Napier of Magdala went on board to visit Sir Garnet, with whom he had campaigned at the relief and capture of Lucknow, under Sir James Outram at the defence of the Alumbagh position, and in China. By this time Sir Garnet had quite recovered from the fever, and was daily gaining strength, so that when the *Calabria* cast anchor at Alexandria, on the night of the 15th August, he was restored to his ordinary health.

On the following morning he held a conference with

Admiral Sir Beauchamp Seymour, Sir John Adye, who had preceded him on the 10th August, and the other generals. He then landed, and, in company with Sir E. Malet, visited the Khedive, and in the afternoon accompanied by the Duke of Connaught and Generals Sir Archibald Alison and Graham and a large staff,* inspected the British lines at Ramleh, and made a more lengthened examination of the positions of the enemy. He was dressed in the blue tunic he wore throughout the campaign, with brown boots, gauntlets, large black goggles, and the solar topee of India. On the following day, the 17th August, the Khedive returned the visit of the British Commander-in-Chief on board H.M. despatch-vessel *Salamis*, which he had made his headquarters.

Sir Garnet issued a proclamation in Arabic to the inhabitants, declaring it to be the mission of the British army to re-establish the authority of the Khedive, inviting the people to furnish supplies, which would be paid for, and promising that the persons and property of those peaceably disposed would be respected.

Before leaving England, Sir Garnet had arranged his plan of campaign, the chief feature of which was the removal of the base of operations from Alexandria to Ismailia; but beyond apprizing H.R.H. the Commander-in-Chief, the Secretary for War, and the First Lord of the Admiralty, he

---

* Sir Garnet Wolseley's personal staff consisted of : Military Secretary, Major L. V. Swaine, Rifle Brigade ; Private Secretary, Major A. C. F. Fitzgeorge, 11th Hussars ; Aides-de-Camp, Lieutenant Wyatt Rawson, R.N., Captain F. M. Wardrop, 3rd Dragoon Guards, and Lieutenants E. S. E. Childers, R.E., A. G. Creagh, R.H.A., and J. Adye, R.A. ; Medical Officer, Brigade-Surgeon R. W. Jackson, C.B. Of these officers, Major Swaine had served under him in Cyprus as Commissioner ; Lieutenant Rawson in Ashantee, and was wounded at Amoaful ; and Lieutenant Creagh, and Dr. Jackson in South Africa, on his personal staff. It has been asserted that Sir Garnet gave little opportunity for the exercise of new talent, but as a matter of fact, in the Egyptian campaign, out of 140 staff appointments, including those of the Indian Contingent, only 17 officers had been with him in Ashantee.

kept his plans to himself: and when, on the 17th August, he issued instructions for the embarkation of the 1st, or General Willis's, Division,* giving out that the forts at Aboukir were his destination, no one was in his confidence except Sir John Adye, even the divisional and brigade commanders being in the dark. Alexandria was full of Arabi's spies, and, in making the newspaper correspondents the medium for misleading the enemy, Sir Garnet only repeated the stratagem he had adopted in Ashantee with such success, and which is recommended in the following passage in his 'Soldiers' Pocketbook,' written in 1871 : 'Without saying so directly, you can lead your army to believe anything; and, as a rule, in all civilized nations, what is believed by the army will very soon be credited by the enemy, having reached him by means of spies, or through the medium of those newly-invented curses to armies—I mean newspaper correspondents.' Sir Garnet was very severe on 'travelling gentlemen, newspaper correspondents, and all that race of drones who,' he declared, 'are an encumbrance to an army; they eat up the rations of fighting men, and do no work at all.' Further on he writes, 'An English general of the present day is in the most unfortunate position in this respect, being surrounded by newspaper correspondents, who, pandering to the public craze for "news," render concealment most difficult.' But Sir Garnet throughout his career has made excellent use of these 'drones;' and in the present campaign he established a press-censorship, under Colonel Hon. Paul Methuen, which

* The 1st Brigade of the 1st Division was commanded by H.R.H. the Duke of Connaught, and consisted of 2nd Battalion Grenadier Guards, 2nd Battalion Coldstream Guards, and 1st Battalion Scots Guards. The 2nd Brigade, commanded by Major-General G. Graham, V.C., C.B., consisted of 2nd Battalion Royal Irish (late 18th Regiment), 1st Battalion West Kent (late 50th Regiment), 2nd Battalion York and Lancaster (late 84th Regiment), and 1st Battalion Royal Irish Fusiliers (late 87th Regiment). The divisional troops were two squadrons 19th Hussars, 2nd Battalion Duke of Cornwall's Light Infantry (late 46th Regiment), A and D Batteries 1st Brigade Royal Artillery, and 24th Company Royal Engineers.

worked remarkably well, and supplied the English public with news without enlightening the enemy on material points such as the numbers and disposition of his troops.

On the 18th July, the 1st Division embarked and sailed on the evening of the following day, the transport agents being supplied with sealed orders, which were only opened after the ships were under weigh. The whole armada, consisting of twenty-six ships of war and transports, with Sir Garnet Wolseley in the despatch-vessel *Salamis*, anchored off the Aboukir forts at 3.30 p.m.; the ships of war had their topmasts struck in readiness for action, but at about 10.30, in the darkness of night, the fleet silently got under weigh, and steamed full speed for Port Said. On the following morning, Rear-Admiral Hoskins at Port Said, acting under orders from Sir Beauchamp Seymour, effected the seizure of the Maritime Canal. Commander Edwards with boats of the squadron seized the portion between Port Said and Ismailia, Captains Fairfax and Fitzroy occupying these places with seamen and marines; and, at the same time, Rear-Admiral Sir William Hewett, commanding at Suez, sent H.M.S. *Seagull* and *Mosquito*, under Captain Hastings, with 200 of the Seaforth Highlanders under Major Kelsey, into the lower portion of the canal, and, after a skirmish, in which the enemy suffered great slaughter from the shell-fire of the ships, Shalouf was occupied, which gave the British the command of the Fresh Water Canal. The important operation of seizing the canal throughout its length of 99 miles was completed by the British navy between three and eight a.m. of Sunday, the 20th August, when Sir Garnet arrived at Port Said with the 1st Division.

No operation could have been more rapidly and effectively performed, and the greatest credit was due to Admirals Hoskins and Hewett, and their subordinates, Captain Hastings, at Shalouf; Captain Fairfax, who occupied Port

Said, and disarmed the garrison; Commander Edwards, who seized the upper portion of the canal and the telegraph station at Kantara; and Captain Fitzroy at Ismailia. This latter officer had a specially difficult and delicate task to perform. Landing with 565 seamen and marines from the *Orion*, *Coquette*, and *Carysfort*, he seized the town of Ismailia, the proposed base of operations, being ably seconded by Captain Stephenson, of the *Carysfort*, Commanders Moore and Kane (who was wounded when seizing the railway and locks), and Major Fraser, R.E., whose professional assistance in entrenching the advanced position was of great service. Arabi had strong guards in Ismailia and the Arab town, as well as 2,000 men, with 6 guns, in camp at Nefiche, and during the day he sent 3,000 more men towards Nefiche from Tel-el-Kebir to re-occupy the town, upon which the ships bombarded the railway station, destroying the camp and wrecking two of the trains, and compelled the enemy to withdraw. At 10.30 p.m. the same night, General Graham, commanding the 2nd Brigade, arrived with the advanced guard of the army, and, assuming command, reinforced the different positions in the town; and, at eight a.m. on the following morning, the 21st August, he occupied Nefiche with two battalions. Meanwhile the canal was closed against the admission of all vessels, except British ships of war and transports, which proceeded as rapidly as possible to Ismailia, where the troops were quickly landed.

On the 21st August Sir Garnet Wolseley arrived at Ismailia. He soon found that he would be compelled to advance beyond Nefiche before his preparations were complete, owing to the gradual, but continuous, fall of water in the Sweet Water Canal, which denoted that it had been dammed. It was, as he wrote, of 'paramount importance' that he should 'secure possession of that part of the water-supply of the desert lying between Ismailia and the first cultivated portion of the Delta;' and accordingly, although his cavalry and artillery horses had been less than two days ashore after a long voyage, and he was averse from 'placing the strain of a forward movement upon the recent and partially organized supply service,' he determined to push forward with such of his available cavalry and artillery as had been landed, to a point in the neighbourhood of Tel-el-Mahuta, about nine miles west from Ismailia.

At four a.m. on the 24th August, Sir Garnet Wolseley marched from Ismailia with the Household Cavalry, under General Drury-Lowe, and accompanied by Colonel Harrison, R.E., assistant to General Earle, commanding the lines of communication; Colonel W. F. Butler, C.B., and Major J. F. Maurice, R.A., respectively Assistant and Deputy-Assistant Adjutant and Quartermaster-General; Major L. V. Swaine, Military Secretary, and his four aides-de-camp. At daybreak the Commander-in-Chief arrived at Nefiche, whence General Graham marched in support with his infantry, consisting of the Royal Marines and York and Lancaster Regiment, and the Mounted Infantry. Following the general line of the railway, Sir Garnet arrived at 7.30 a.m., on the north side of the canal, at a point midway between El-Magfar and the village of Tel-el-Mahuta, where the enemy had constructed his first dam across the canal. A little skirmish took place, the Household Cavalry delivering their first charge in the campaign, and from this point the enemy could be observed in force, about one and a half mile farther ahead, his vedettes holding a line, about 2,000 yards in front, extending across the canal and lining the crest of a ridge which curved round to the British right flank. The canal and railway, which are carried through deep cuttings at Tel-el-Mahuta, were strongly entrenched and held in force, and communication was kept across the canal by a dam, and across the railway by an embankment, but in rear the latter was at work bringing up reinforcements from Tel-el-Kebir.

The enemy was in great force, consisting, as afterwards ascertained, of a regiment of cavalry, nine battalions of infantry (7,000 men) and 12 guns, with a large body of Bedouins; while the British General had with him only three squadrons of cavalry, less than 1,000 infantry, 34 Mounted Infantry, and 2 guns of N Battery A Brigade R.H.A., which only arrived at nine o'clock, the men and horses being much exhausted with bringing the guns through the heavy sand. Sir Garnet sent Lieutenant Adye to bring up the Duke of Cornwall's Light Infantry from Nefiche, and the brigade of Guards, and the remainder of the N Battery, and A Battery of 1st Brigade, as soon as they could be pushed on from Ismailia, and Colonel Harrison went back to organize the supply arrangements. The enemy opened a heavy artillery fire, and his infantry advanced in regular attack formation, halting and forming a line of shelter trenches, about 1,000 yards from the British position, and within 900 yards of the dam on the left, held by the York and Lancaster Regiment. But this gallant corps and the Marines maintained their ground with great spirit, while nothing could exceed the stubborn determination with which the detachment of Horse Artillery, under Lieutenant Hickman, posted on a line of sand-hillocks, replied to the overwhelming fire of the Egyptian gunners.

'The enemy's guns,' writes the General, 'were served with considerable skill, the shells bursting well among us.' The first shell went a few yards over the head of Sir Garnet, who had dismounted, breaking the leg of a horse, on which he ordered all the horses to be led behind the hill. The shells fell thickly around, but fortunately they were fitted with percussion-fuzes, and sank deep in the soft sand before exploding, so that few splinters flew about; and the shrapnel were equally harmless, owing to the time-fuzes being badly cut. While the guns and infantry were actively engaged, the Household Cavalry and Mounted Infantry moved forward at right angles on the extreme right to check the enemy's advance on that side, but the horses were in no condition to charge. The latter most useful corps particularly distinguished itself, under the command of Captain Hallam Parr (who, as also Lord Melgund, was wounded), and again demonstrated its great utility in war.*

The heat was excessive and told especially on the gunners, who had to run up the guns each time they recoiled through the heavy sands; but nerved by the encouraging messages sent to them by Sir Garnet Wolseley, and later in the day assisted by some of the Marine Artillery, they nobly stuck to their work. The position at this time was undoubtedly such as to cause anxiety, but the Commander had perfect confidence in his men, and they justified his good opinion. Most, if not all, of them had never before been under fire, but the calm cheerfulness of their General never more self-possessed than amid the turmoil of battle, reassured them that all was right.

At noon a serious danger arose, the enemy having placed 4 guns completely taking the front of the position in flank,

* Sir Garnet Wolseley has always been an advocate for the employment of Mounted Infantry. In the last edition of his 'Soldiers' Pocket-book,' completed just before his departure for Egypt, he expresses an opinion that they ought to form a component part of an army. Regarding his views as to artillery, Sir Garnet, whose experience of shell-fire is only equalled by those who like him had served in the trenches of Sebastopol throughout the siege, has always been of opinion that their effect is more moral than material. He says: 'An immoderate number of guns with any force is most embarrassing, for any guns that cannot be brought into action are most injurious in their effects upon the result, as they block up the roads and hamper every movement.' At Gravelotte, out of every hundred casualities, only six were caused by artillery. 'Campaigns,' he says, 'can be carried out without cavalry or artillery, but nothing serious can be effected without the aid of men fighting on foot.'

and exposing the force to a cross fire; but at this time a party of sailors from H.M.S. *Orion*, under Lieutenant King-Harman, opportunely arrived with 2 Gatlings, and aided by one of the 2 guns met this new attack.

At one p.m. the Duke of Cornwall's Light Infantry arrived from Nefiche, and at 3.30 the Household Cavalry and Mounted Infantry, under General Lowe, again moved forward on the extreme right, forcing the enemy to partially withdraw his attack on that flank. Soon after five, the enemy again advanced his left, pushing 4 guns over the ridge, but at this time Sir Baker Russell arrived with 350 men of the 4th and 7th Dragoon Guards, and the remaining guns of N Battery, and 2 guns of N Battery 2nd Brigade R.A.; at six, the Duke of Connaught appeared on the scene with the Brigade of Guards, which, leaving Ismailia at 1.30 p.m., suffered severely from the great heat of the desert march. It was too late to make an offensive movement, which Sir Garnet resolved to defer till the morrow, but he spent the last two hours of daylight by riding round all the positions and thanking the troops of all arms for their exertions.

The army bivouacked on the ground, and Sir Garnet rode back to Ismailia, which he quitted at 3 a.m. on the following morning, the 25th August, accompanied by Sir John Adye and the headquarter staff, and the remaining squadron of the Household Cavalry, which had just been landed. The Commander-in-Chief had given orders to General Willis for a general advance at daybreak, and on his arrival at 5.30, found that the whole of the 1st Division, with the cavalry, 8 guns, and the 3rd Battalion King's Royal Rifles, had quitted their bivouac and were advancing on the enemy's position.

Pushing on he joined them, when the advance was continued in the following order: The cavalry and Mounted Infantry on the extreme right on the sand-hillocks, then the artillery towards the high ground between Ramses and Mahsameh Stations, and the infantry on the left in *échelon* from the right upon Mahuta, the Guards leading. Sir Garnet's plan was to pivot on his left at the dam captured the day before, about half-way between Magfar and Mahuta, and swing round his right so as to take the enemy's position in flank and drive him into the canal, sending the cavalry completely round his position to occupy the railway. The enemy, however, did not await the onset, but abandoned his earthworks at Mahuta, and retired along the canal-bank and the railway line towards Mahsameh, using also the trains for assisting the movement.

At 6.25 the guns came into action, and as it was of the utmost importance to secure some engines, Sir Garnet directed the cavalry to push forward with that object. But the horses were in bad condition after their long voyage and rapid and fatiguing march of the previous day, and as Sir Garnet observed, 'there was not at this time in the whole cavalry brigade a troop that could gallop.' They, however succeeded, notwithstanding considerable resistance, in getting into the rear of the enemy, and capturing Mahsameh with its extensive camp, 7 Krupp guns, vast quantities of ammunition and supplies, and seventy-five railway carriages laden with provisions. The enemy, who were commanded by Rashid Pasha, fled along the railway and canal banks, throwing away their arms with every appearance of demoralization, and among those captured was Mahmoud Fehmy Pasha, Arabi's chief engineer.

The results of the two days' operations were such as to satisfy the Commander-in-Chief, being the capture of the strong entrenched position on which 7,000 peasants had been compelled to labour, the clearance of the canal for more than half the distance between Ismailia and the Delta, thus securing the water-supply, the capture of the railway line for a distance of 20 miles from the base, and the seizure of an important strategic position. All this was accomplished by troops most of whom had never before been in action, marching over a desert without roads and under a blazing sun. Owing to the advance being made before the railway or telegraph lines had been repaired, or the canal cleared of its obstruction, or any regular system of transport organized, the men were without tents and suffered severe privations as regards food, which they bore with cheerfulness. The British loss was slight, 5 killed and 25 wounded, among the latter, Major Bibby, 7th Dragoon Guards, and Captain Parr and Lord Melgund of the Mounted Infantry, and there were forty-eight sunstrokes in the ranks.

On the following day Sir Garnet occupied Kassassin Lock, two and a half miles west of Mahsameh; and having placed in command of this advanced post General Graham, an officer in whom he had every confidence, which later events fully justified, he returned to Ismailia, to push on, with all the energy and administrative ability of which he was possessed, the organization of the transport department, which offered no ordinary difficulties. But with his experience in the Red River and Ashantee Expeditions, his energy, and power of infusing his spirit into his own subordinates, these difficulties were vigorously combated until success rewarded his efforts. When the removal of the locomotive engines by the enemy threw difficulties not wholly unexpected in his path, the Navy—under the leadership of his two old friends and comrades in arms, Sir Beauchamp Seymour, who served with him in the second Burmese War, and Sir William Hewett, in the Crimea and Ashantee—zealously co-operated with the sister service. Captain Rawson, R.N., the naval officer in charge of the disembarkation, assisted by Captain Brackenbury, R.N., worked with untiring energy in co-operation with Sir Owen Lanyon, commandant of the base of operations, under Major-General Earle, in supreme charge of the lines of communication, his assistants being Majors Sartorius and McGregor, who distributed and forwarded from Ismailia the stores as they were landed from the ships. From Ismailia there was a service of mules towing pontoons filled with stores; and the Navy organized in the Fresh Water Canal a service of steam-launches towing ships' boats, which were of assistance also in bringing back from the front the sick and wounded. A tramway was constructed from the beach to the railway station, but there was a deficiency of labourers, and for a considerable time over 1,800 soldiers, chiefly Guardsmen, were engaged in the irksome and uncongenial work of common navvies, while their more fortunate comrades were fighting at the front. No blame for this deficiency of transport was attributable to Commissary-General Morris, but it was due to political causes, as the Government wished to avoid any expenditure requiring a Parliamentary vote, in order to obviate the necessity of entering into inconvenient explanations of policy.

When the press and public at home grumbled at the so-called delay at Ismailia, it was not known that it was expected by the sagacious Commander-in-Chief before he left England. The prime object was to seize the canal and railway with the rolling-stock. This was accomplished by the actions of the 24th and 25th August, and between that date and the 29th, the advantages gained by those successes were in course of development, so that events followed their normal and anticipated course.

Much delay and inconvenience was caused until the arrival of the railway plant from Alexandria and England, the former being old, and in bad repair; but by the first week in September there were in use seven engines, including four sent from England in the *Canadian*, and abundance of rolling-stock, including the seventy-five carriages captured at Mahsameh on the 25th August. The tonnage of the railway plant sent from England was 15,500, the administrative staff consisting of the 8th company of Sappers and Major Wallace, R.E., and Captain Scott, R.E. (both of whom had great experience in this department in India and served under Sir Frederick Roberts in Afghanistan), and Lieutenant Willcock, R.E., all of whom did special good service.

After the successful action of the 25th August had placed Kassassin Lock in the hands of Sir Garnet Wolseley, he returned to Ismailia, leaving General Graham in command with a force* of 1,728 infantry, 127 cavalry and Mounted Infantry, and 2 guns. In rear, at Mahsameh, four and three-quarter miles distant, General Drury-Lowe was stationed with the Household Cavalry, 7th Dragoon Guards, the four remaining guns of N Battery, and a battalion of the Royal Marines. The brigade of Guards, under the Duke of Connaught, was stationed at Tel-el-Mahuta, where General Willis had his headquarters.

About 9.30 on the morning of the 28th August, the enemy's cavalry appeared in force on the left of General Graham's position, when he turned his troops out and heliographed to General Drury-Lowe, who brought his cavalry within two or three miles of the camp, but as the enemy, about 3 p.m., appeared to be retiring, and the men were suffering much from the heat, the cavalry and other troops returned to their camps. An hour and a half later, however, the enemy advanced in great force, estimated at 1,000 cavalry and 8,000 infantry, supporting the attack with a heavy fire from 12 guns. General Graham's position astride the canal, with a ridge within range which he was too weak to occupy, was not easily defensible, but it was determined by the necessity for

* This force consisted of N Battery A Brigade R.H.A., 40 officers and men and 2 guns ; 4th Dragoon Guards, 15 of all ranks ; 7th Dragoon Guards, 42 ; Mounted Infantry, 70 ; 2nd Battalion Duke of Cornwall's Light Infantry, 611 ; 2nd Battalion York and Lancaster, 690 ; Marine Artillery, 427.

holding the lock. That veteran soldier made his dispositions with skill, placing his infantry in irregular *échelon*, right thrown back, the Marine Artillery on the south of the canal, the Duke of Cornwall's in the centre, and the York and Lancaster on the right. The troop of 7th Dragoon Guards were on the flank and the 2 guns under Lieutenant Parsons on the ridge. Owing, however, to the latter being only supplied with the ammunition in their limbers, they had soon to cease firing; but the fire was gallantly taken up by a captured Krupp gun, manned by Marine Artillery under Captain Tucker, who maintained an unequal duel with the enemy's artillery throughout the action. The Mounted Infantry and detachment of 4th Dragoon Guards acted as infantry, and did gallant service, Lieutenants Pigott and Edwards of the Mounted Infantry being wounded. General Graham again heliographed to General Lowe for assistance, and despatched Lieutenant Pirie, 4th Dragoon Guards, with a request to send forward the Royal Marines, and 'bring round his cavalry under cover of the hill and fall upon the left flank of the enemy's skirmishers and roll up his line.' How brilliantly this order was executed is well known. General Graham gave the order to his whole line to advance on the enemy at 6.45, about the time of the expected cavalry charge, which was executed about an hour later by the fitful light of the moon. After a few rounds from the guns, the Household Cavalry, under Colonel Ewart, and 7th Dragoon Guards—the whole gallantly led by the Brigadier, Sir Baker Russell, who gave the order, 'Now we have them—charge!'—guided by the flash of the rifles of the hostile infantry, which continued to advance, charged through and utterly scattered the enemy, capturing 7 or 9 guns, which they were unable to secure, owing to the darkness. General Graham had already, unaided, compelled the retirement of the enemy, but this brilliant charge completed their discomfiture. On hearing of it at 8.15, he ordered his infantry to fall back, and all the troops returned to camp, where the Marines had arrived an hour before. The loss sustained by Graham's Brigade was one officer, Surgeon-Major Shaw, and 7 men killed; 5 officers and 66 men wounded. The Cavalry Brigade had one officer—Lieutenant Gribble, 3rd Dragoon Guards, orderly officer to Sir Baker Russell—and 6 men killed, and one officer, Major Townshend, 2nd Life Guards, and 18 men wounded. Thirty horses were killed and wounded, and Sir Baker Russell had his charger shot under him. The enemy fought with great determination, probably inspired by the presence of Arabi, who was present on the field, and brought up reinforcements about 8 p.m., evidently in the expectation of overwhelming the British.

Generals Drury-Lowe and Graham are somewhat at variance in their accounts as to the enemy being in retreat before the cavalry-charge was made, but as one conversant with the incidents remarked to us, both were right, for the main portion of the enemy opposed to Graham were actually in retreat; but there was another portion detached to the flank, which were unbroken at the time of the cavalry-charge, by which they were effectually dispersed.

On the following day, the 29th August, Brigadier-General Wilkinson marched in with a portion of the cavalry of the Indian Contingent, which had made the distance of eighty-three miles from Suez in four days.* Reconnoissances were

* The cavalry consisted of two troops of the 2nd Bengal Cavalry, under Captain Martin, two of the 6th Bengal Cavalry, under Colonel Upperton, and three of the 13th Bengal Lancers, under Colonel Macnaghten. The Indian Brigade, completely equipped, with transport, supplies for five days, and ambulance corps, left Suez at 2 a.m. on the morning of Thursday, 28th August. On arriving at the edge of the desert an unavoidable delay occurred, as Admiral Hewett, at the last moment, thought it unadvisable that Suez should be protected only by the small force of cavalry told off for the purpose. But overnight the *Tenasserim* arrived with the 2nd Bengal Cavalry, and the column struck camp at 1 a.m. on the 25th and marched without incident to Shalouf, eleven miles distant. On Saturday the column was again on the march by 5 a.m., and Gennafeh, seventeen miles distant,

almost daily undertaken by these fine troops in the direction of Tel-el-Kebir, where Arabi had thrown up strong defensive works. The troops at Kassassin now consisted of the whole of the 1st Brigade of cavalry, seven troops of Indian cavalry, five battalions of infantry, and five batteries of artillery.

The Highland Brigade,[*] consisting of four battalions, under Sir Archibald Alison, with Sir Edward Hamley commanding the 2nd Division, arrived from Alexandria at Ismailia on the 1st September, but were kept on board ship until their services were required at the front. On the same day Colonel Redvers Buller arrived from England to take charge of the Intelligence Department,[†] of which Lieutenant-Colonel Tulloch had been so efficient a head, and conducted reconnoissances of the enemy's lines at Tel-el-Kebir.

On the morning of the 2nd September, Sir Garnet Wolseley, accompanied by Sir Beauchamp Seymour, Admiral Hoskins, the Duke of Teck, and other officers, started from Ismailia for the front, proceeding as far as Tel-el-Mahuta in a steam-launch, and the remainder of the journey in a train. The

---

was reached early in the day. Next day the distance covered was thirty miles, the march being unbroken at Serapeum, and the troops reached Ismailia at 1 p.m. in perfect condition, and on Tuesday arrived at Kassassin.

[*] 1st Battalion Royal Highlanders (late 42nd), 2nd Battalion Highland Light Infantry (late 74th), 1st Battalion Gordon Highlanders (late 75th), and 1st Battalion Cameron Highlanders (late 79th).

[†] The officers of the Intelligence Department were among the most capable in the army. Colonel (now Sir Redvers) Buller's name is a household word, not only in England, but in South Africa, where he and Sir Evelyn Wood were confessedly the heroes of the Zulu War. 'In this campaign,' says Sir Garnet, 'he displayed his usual and thorough-going soldier-like qualities.' Of Colonel Tulloch, 69th Regiment, he says: 'No man could evince more untiring zeal for the public service than he has done since his arrival in Egypt some months ago.' Of Major Ardagh, R.E., who also did good service at Alexandria, he says: 'In addition to his regular duties he rendered valuable assistance in the organization of our railway system from Ismailia to Kassassin. Always willing to undertake any service, no matter how difficult or trying, he had proved himself to be a most excellent officer in the field.' Major Hart, East Surrey Regiment, the other officer of the Intelligence Department, assisted in pioneering General Graham's brigade on the eventful night of the 12th September.

party reached Kassassin at 1.30, and Sir Garnet, after a hasty inspection, left again at three, taking in the train some wounded prisoners. The engine, one of those from Alexandria, was in a wretched condition, and, after many halts, finally broke down within two miles of the camp at Mahuta. All the generals, admirals, and their staffs had to trudge on foot through the desert until horses arrived from the Guards' camp, and would have afforded a fine haul to any roving body of Bedouins, parties of whom had been seen prowling about, and had killed a European soldier. The remainder of the distance to Ismailia was performed in a steam-launch.

Beyond an expedition on the 6th, by General Graham, along the south bank of the canal in the direction of Mahsameh, against these bands of marauding Bedouins, and reconnoissances towards Tel-el-Kebir, no military operations were undertaken at Kassassin until Saturday, the 9th September, when the enemy tried to force the Commander-in-Chief's hand by taking the offensive.

On the morning of the previous day a reconnoissance was made by the three arms towards Tel-el-Kebir, when the Mounted Infantry* bore the brunt of the skirmishing. Arabi replied by a reconnoissance in force on the 9th, and the affair almost assumed the proportions of a general action. Lieutenant-General Willis was now in command of the troops at Kassassin, and his dispositions for preventing a surprise were certainly not such as might have been expected from an officer of his experience and reputation as an Aldershot strategist.

At 4 a.m. that morning Lieutenant-Colonel Penning-

* The Mounted Infantry was now commanded by Captain R. C. Lawrence, 5th Dragoon Guards, son of General R. C. Lawrence, C B., of the Indian army, and nephew of the late Lord Lawrence and Sir Henry Lawrence. The gallant officer was a worthy successor of Captain Hallam Parr and Lieutenant Pigott, who had both been wounded, and, like them, he received the high approval of his commander.

ACTION OF THE 9TH SEPTEMBER.

ton left camp with two pickets, about 60 men, of the 13th Bengal Lancers, and found himself in presence of a force of three squadrons of cavalry and some infantry. Pennington first dismounted his men to keep the enemy in check while Colonel Macnaghten, commanding the regiment, galloped back to camp to bring up the rest of his men, and then, finding that they still advanced, made a gallant charge on the cavalry, killing 10 of them.

Meantime the enemy, commanded by Ali Fehmi Pasha, Arabi being present on the field, advanced in great force from Tel-el-Kebir, a detachment from Salahieh co-operating on the flank. The enemy's force was seventeen battalions of infantry, several squadrons of cavalry, and a few thousand of Bedouins, with about 30 guns, and an easy victory was anticipated, as Arabi thought General Willis had only a weak advanced guard. The British camp was soon astir, and all arms had a hot day's work. The Household Cavalry charged the detachment from Salahieh and captured a gun; and two companies of the Marines, under Captains Wardell and Coffin, captured 2 guns in gallant style. The battalion had 25 men wounded, of whom several died. Other regiments that distinguished themselves were the York and Lancaster, the King's Rifles, which had 2 killed and 28 wounded, and the Duke of Cornwall's Light Infantry. The Naval Brigade worked a forty-pounder in a railway truck, and Lieutenant Purvis, R.N., in command, was wounded in the foot, which had to be amputated. Major Hart, East Surrey Regiment, of the Staff—brother of Major Hart, V.C., R.E., aide-de-camp to General Graham—did excellent service on this day, and was wounded in the arm.

The enemy could effect nothing, though their shells at one time fell within the camp, and at length the steady fire of the infantry and two batteries of artillery compelled them to give ground, and they retreated in some confusion towards

Tel-el-Kebir. General Graham followed until Arabi, having arrived within one and three-quarter miles of his works, drew up, and our army also halted, when the two remained surveying each other, the artillery only exchanging an occasional shell. About 10.45 Sir Garnet Wolseley arrived from Ismailia, and, having carefully surveyed the position, decided to withdraw his troops into camp.

Much disappointment was felt among the eager young spirits in the camp, and even among those more experienced in war, at this step of the Commander-in-Chief. The *Times* correspondent wrote : ' It is understood that more than one distinguished officer in the field on Saturday was anxious to push right into the works with the rebel troops;' adding that ' if an advance had then been ordered, it seems to be generally believed that Arabi's troops would have made no stand.' But this was what Sir Garnet Wolseley wished that they should do. As he says, 'My desire was to fight him decisively where he was in the open desert, before he could retire to take up fresh positions more difficult of access in the cultivated country in his rear, which is practically impassable to a regular army, being irrigated and cut up in every direction by deep canals.' It was because this object could only be effected by a surprise that the Commander-in-Chief held his hand, and decided not to strike the blow until it could be made crushing and decisive. Many of the newspaper correspondents, and a section of the London and foreign press, inveighed against Sir Garnet Wolseley for want of enterprise and judgment in not following up the success of the 9th September; but looking at the results of abstention from pushing his advantage, probably in no action of his military career did he display in so remarkable a manner the self-restraint and judgment which are among the chief attributes of a really great commander. It was true military genius that showed him, after a rapid glance at the

THE EVE OF THE BATTLE.

situation, that the time had not yet come for the final advance. His carefully elaborated plans for following up the victory on which he surely counted, could not be put into execution so certainly and effectually as if he waited for all his reinforcements, including the Highland Brigade, and struck his blow at such an early hour of the day that time would be given for the pursuit, and for following up the advantages of the victory, chief among which were the seizure of Zagazig and the rescue of Cairo from the fate of Alexandria.*

The troops in the rear were now moved up to the front. The Guards arrived from Mahuta, and the Highland Brigade, under Sir Archibald Alison, from Ismailia; also the remainder of the Indian Contingent, commanded by Sir Herbert Macpherson, consisting of a battery of sevenpounders (screw guns), the 1st Battalion Seaforth Highlanders (72nd Regiment), and detachments of the 7th Native Infantry, 28th Punjaubees, and 29th Belooches.† The first day's march of the troops from Ismailia was eight miles; the second, after a bivouac in the desert under a blistering sun until 4 p.m., nine miles; and on the third day eight miles, which brought the column to the camp at Kassassin. The troops left in garrison at Ismailia were the Sussex and Manchester Regiments, and some Native Infantry.

All was now ready for the great blow which was to make or mar the success of the Egyptian Expedition, and on which the reputation of Sir Garnet Wolseley was staked. Were he

* On this point General Drury-Lowe said, in reply to an address in England: 'Before I left the ship in which I sailed from England, I knew that my duty with the cavalry was to get to Cairo; that was all planned by Sir Garnet Wolseley before we left England.'

† The infantry of the Indian Contingent was commanded by Brigadier-General O. V. Tanner, Bombay Staff Corps, who did such good service at Khelat-i-Ghilzye, during the recent Afghan War. The officer commanding the cavalry, Brigadier-General Wilkinson, also held a command in the Candahar division; and the services of Sir Herbert Macpherson at Cabul and in the march thence to Candahar are historical.

to fail, the wiseacres who always say, 'I told you!' the armchair critics who censured his strategy, and the numerous mediocrities who, after the manner of their kind, view with jealousy the success of one they could not hope to rival, would join in a chorus of condemnation; and the fickle public, who only judge by results, would hurl from his pedestal the commander generally acknowledged to be the most enterprising and able in the army. All this was staked on the hazard of the die; but nevertheless Sir Garnet, having, with characteristic self-reliance, matured his plans unaided, awaited with perfect confidence the result. While anxiety was depicted on the faces of those in high command, and it was generally agreed that the formidable works, behind which was entrenched a numerically superior army with a powerful artillery, could only be carried after desperate fighting and heavy loss, the leader, on whom would fall the responsibility for the loss of every life sacrificed by false strategy or defective arrangements, was never more calm. His face was the best augury of success, for no one who doubted the result of the impending movement could feign the cheerfulness which was apparent to every eye.

On Monday, the 11th September, Sir Garnet Wolseley reconnoitred the ground in front of the enemy's works, and at daylight of the following day, accompanied by all the Generals and Brigadiers, rode out of camp, and having inspected the enemy's position, explained to them his intended mode of attack, and gave to each one a sketch showing the formation in which it was to be effected. The enemy's position was a strong one, and extended from a point on the canal one and a half miles east of the railway-station of Tel-el-Kebir, a distance, almost due north, of three and a half miles. Between the camp at Kassassin and the enemy's lines extended the desert, affording no cover of any kind. The general character of the ground over which the army had to advance was that of gently undulating and rounded slopes, rising gradually to an open plateau about ninety feet above the valley through which runs the railway and canal. 'To have marched over the plateau,' says Sir Garnet, 'upon the enemy's position by daylight, our troops would have had to advance over a glacis-like slope in full view of the enemy, and under the fire of his well-served artillery, for about five miles. Such an operation would have entailed enormous losses from an enemy with men and guns well protected by entrenchments from any artillery fire we could have brought to bear upon them. To have turned the enemy's position either by the right or left was an operation that would have entailed a very wide turning movement, and therefore a long, difficult, and fatiguing march; and, what is of more importance, it would not have accomplished the object I had in view, namely, to grapple with the enemy at such close quarters that he should not be able to shake himself free from our clutches except by a general fight of all his army.'

The General's plan was, briefly, to make a night march and carry the position at dawn at the point of the bayonet. A plan apparently so full of difficulty and danger could never have been entertained save by an original mind; nevertheless, it was the least hazardous, if it could be done as a surprise. An assault after a bombardment afforded a doubtful chance of success, and would be accompanied by heavy loss, while a flank attack would be fatiguing in such a climate; moreover, both these methods afforded the great disadvantage of prolonging the war, which, as we have seen, Sir Garnet wished to finish at one blow.

Though a close and ardent student of the art of war, he was not a slavish adherent of precedent. Such men never can attain to the position of the real masters of the art, that bright and gifted band whose names illustrate the history of the world by achievements which less original minds can neither conceive nor carry out. Sir Garnet Wolseley, in maturing his plans for a great *coup* like the battle of the 13th September, brought to his aid the resources of a daring mind, vast experience, and a nice adaptation of means to end. Only a highly disciplined enemy could have withstood a bayonet-charge at early morning, when suddenly waked out of sleep, and having made the discovery that Arabi withdrew his pickets and outposts after midnight, he turned his knowledge to account. A surprise was, on the whole, the best way of capturing his formidable works, which extended line behind line, and would have required an enormous expenditure of life to attack by any other method. That there was a surprise has been denied by some, but Arabi himself acknowledged to his conqueror that the first he knew of an attack was the firing, and that the surprise was complete and absolute.

To conduct to a successful issue such a difficult operation as that on which he had embarked, required a rare combination of fortune and good management. Sir Garnet's star was in the ascendant when Arabi, having (it is said) received information from his spies that an attack was intended on the night of the 12th, actually sent out his vedettes to reconnoitre shortly before midnight, when they returned with the intelligence that the British army had not quitted its encampment, the fires in which were brightly burning. Lulled into a sense of false security by this report, which was true at that hour, Arabi suffered his troops, who were fatigued, having been on the *qui vive*, to turn in shortly after midnight, at the very time that his skilful opponent had begun the march that was to shatter his army and bring irremediable ruin on his cause.

The force at the disposal of Arabi consisted of 59 guns, distributed along the line of works, twenty-four battalions of infantry (about 20,000 men), and three regiments of cavalry, together with about 6,000 Bedouins, besides a force of about 5,000 men, with 24 guns, at Salahieh. To defeat this large army and storm a double line of intrenchments, with redoubts, the British General could only place in line about 11,000 infantry, 2,000 cavalry, and 60 guns.* This force was disposed in the following order: on the extreme right marched the Cavalry Brigade, under General Drury-Lowe, consisting of the Household Cavalry, 4th and 7th Dragoon Guards, Mounted Infantry, 2nd and 6th Regiments of Bengal Cavalry, and 13th Bengal Lancers, with two batteries of Horse Artillery. General Drury-Lowe's orders were to sweep round the northern extremity of the enemy's works after they had been captured, and charge the broken masses as they attempted to escape.

Next to the cavalry, and forming the right of the infantry, which was directed to move in line of columns of half battalions, was the 1st, or General Willis's, Division, of which the 2nd, or Graham's, Brigade, was in the front line. The regiments of this brigade were in the following order from the right: 1st Royal Irish (18th Regiment), 2nd York and Lancaster (84th Regiment), 1st Royal Irish Fusiliers (87th Regiment), and Royal Marine Light Infantry. In support was the Brigade of Guards, under the Duke of Connaught. Next in line to Graham's Brigade, and covering a front of 1,200 yards, were massed seven batteries of artillery, 42 guns, under Brigadier-General Goodenough. Then came the 2nd, or Sir Edward Hamley's, Division, with the magnificent Highland Brigade leading, under Sir Archibald Alison. The Brigade consisted, in the order named, from the right, of the 1st Royal Highlanders (42nd Regiment), 1st Gordon Highlanders (75th Regiment), 1st Cameron Highlanders (79th Regiment), and 2nd High-

* The official returns show that the entire force at Sir Garnet Wolseley's disposal on the 13th September was 12,277 infantry, 2,785 cavalry, 60 guns, and 214 men of the Naval Brigade with 6 Gatlings.

land Light Infantry (74th Regiment). In support of the Highlanders were the Duke of Cornwall's Light Infantry (46th Regiment) and the 3rd Royal Rifles, brigaded under Colonel Ashburnham.

Across the canal—along which moved the Naval Brigade, 214 men, with 6 Gatlings, under Captain Fitzroy—marched the Indian Contingent, consisting of a Mountain Battery, a squadron of the 13th Bengal Lancers, 1st Battalion Seaforth Highlanders (72nd Regiment) and 2 companies of the 2nd Battalion (78th Regiment), detachments of the 7th Bengal Native Infantry, 20th Punjaubees, and 29th Beloochees, under Major-General Sir Herbert Macpherson, who received orders to march one hour after the leading brigades, as an earlier advance would have given the alarm to the enemy, owing to the number of villages in the cultivated land south of the canal. Sir Garnet Wolseley, whose escort throughout the campaign was a company of Royal Marines, under Captain Heathcote, himself marched in rear of the 2nd Division, with the Royal Marine Artillery and a squadron of the 19th Hussars, forming the reserve, and maintained telegraphic communication with the Indian Contingent throughout the night by means of an insulated wire through Kassassin.

To pilot the two leading brigades, officers of great and acknowledged capacity were told off. Brigadier-General Goodenough performed this duty for the Artillery Division under his command. Colonel Buller—so well known as a leader of irregular horse, or chief of the Intelligence Department of an army in the field—Major Hart, and Captain W. H. Holbech, Brigade-Major, directed the march of Graham's Brigade; and Lieutenant Wyatt Rawson, R.N., Naval aide-de-camp to the Commander-in-Chief, whose knowledge of the stars had been called into requisition during the Arctic expedition under Sir George Nares,

THE START FROM KASSASSIN. 431

piloted the Highlanders. This noble young seaman, not satisfied with this duty, was among the first in the enemy's works, and sacrificed his life for his country, in whose cause he had already bled in Ashantee.

The operation on which Sir Garnet Wolseley had now embarked was difficult and hazardous as any in the range of warfare. To conduct, in the darkness of night, the simultaneous advance of an army whose front covered nearly four miles of ground, was no easy feat of administrative and tactical skill. The distance to be traversed from the camp at Kassassin was about seven and a half miles, and no tree or landmark of any description—beyond a line of telegraph poles placed by the Engineers along the first portion of the route—pointed out the way over the trackless desert and low sandy hillocks which intervened between the British camp and the Egyptian lines. To regulate the march of the extended lines of the three arms so that at a given moment—for a delay of even five minutes might be fatal to success—the combined assault of the Infantry Brigades could be made, was a task that offered a crucial test of the capacity of the Commander who elaborated the plan to its minutest detail.

At 6.15 on the evening of the 12th September, all tents were struck, and, with the regimental baggage, were collected along the line of railway for transmission after the anticipated victory. All bugle and trumpet calls were forbidden, and, an hour later, when darkness had fallen on the busy scene, the corps and batteries marched out of Kassassin in perfect order, and took up their regulated positions on a range of sand-hills, about two miles from the camp, in which the fires were left burning. Brigadier-General Nugent, R.E., with the 1st West Kent (50th Regiment) and 19th Hussars, was left in command of the camp, to cover the rear of the army and protect that position with all its stores and depôts from the enemy's force at Salahieh, which, as mentioned, numbered 5,000 men and 24 guns.

On arriving at the regulated positions, a halt was called, and the men lay down on the bare sand and snatched what sleep they could. It was a weird and solemn scene, without even the moon's silvery light to cheer the ranks of the soldiery. No fires were permitted; even smoking was prohibited; and silence was enjoined in the ranks stretching in endless line along the star-lit desert. Under such circumstances a man's reflections would be turned inward, and thoughts of home must have filled the hearts of the gallant array awaiting the signal which was to change this scene of ghostly silence and grim darkness for the stirring incidents of the battle and the garish light of day.

> 'All heaven and earth are still—though not in sleep,
> But breathless, as we grow when feeling most;
> And silent, as we stand in thoughts too deep.'

So passed the night, and at 1.30 the army rose from the ground and started for the march that was to place them in position to storm the enemy's works at daylight.

The formation of the Highland Brigade, which numbered 3,000 bayonets, was in half-battalions, formed with two companies in front and two in rear, at deploying intervals, the lines being about fifty yards behind each other. The supporting brigade, 1,500 yards in rear, was formed in line of quarter-columns; and in order to maintain touch with the Highlanders, a company of the Rifles was extended between in files about fifteen yards apart. The formation of General Willis's Division, which was about three-quarters of a mile to the right of the 2nd Division, was somewhat different, each half-battalion of the leading brigade being formed in a column of companies, thus presenting the appearance of a line of eight columns, each four companies deep. Before the march was begun connecting files were put between the battalions and brigades, and between the first and second lines.

The difficulty of so large a body of men, marching with such an extended front, keeping touch, now became apparent, but the arrangements of the Commander-in-Chief met all obstacles, and his staff officers, as able a body of men as ever served any leader, intelligently carried out the instructions of their chief. At one time one of the brigades was diverging from the line, but at the critical moment Sir Garnet appeared through the darkness, and the difficulty was overcome and touch was maintained. As the night advanced the men were occasionally halted, when some lay down and rested, though all were glad to be on the move again, as the cold night air chilled to the bone, and the condition of expectancy was not conducive to rest. The final halt before the rush at the enemy was made at four o'clock.

Meanwhile, at midnight of the 12th, the Cavalry Division, under General Drury-Lowe, commenced its march so as to get on the left flank and rear of the enemy's lines at the moment of the assault, the 2nd Brigade, consisting of the three Indian cavalry regiments, leading, followed by the 1st Brigade, formed of the Household Cavalry, the 4th and 7th Dragoon Guards, and Mounted Infantry. The march was first to the north, and then they bore to the west, and at two a.m. the Cavalry Division halted about three miles short of the enemy's extreme left flank. After a rest of two hours, during which the men lay on the sand holding their horses by the bridle, they advanced in squadron columns until the time for action arrived.

To return to the movements of the main column.

The great difficulties of a night march by an army covering so large a front was strikingly illustrated by an incident mentioned by Sir Edward Hamley, in an article in the *Nineteenth Century*. Soon after the Highland Brigade, after a brief halt, resumed the march, there was a rumour that horsemen were in front. The centre battalions halted, while the wings moved on until they faced each other at a distance of fifty yards, and the companies of the wings were thrown into disorder. Fortunately, it was discovered before a fatal collision took place, as there was no telling in the darkness whether they were friends or foes.

Sir Garnet, in his plan of attack, determined to assault about five a.m., just when the first streaks of dawn began to appear. But three-quarters of an hour before this, occurred a circumstance that, on after-consideration, must have exercised a powerful influence on the minds of the superstitious Orientals slumbering behind the earthworks of Tel-el-Kebir, who were about to experience so fearful an awakening, and which nearly had a disastrous effect on the fortunes of this war, so full of dramatic incidents and telling situations.

Frequently through the night the General consulted his watch, and at 4.15, to his surprise, saw what appeared faint streaks of dawn in the east behind the backs of the advancing army. By observation it had been ascertained that five was the hour the 'rosy-fingered' Goddess of Day first showed above the horizon; so if this was daybreak, his chances of success in assaulting the enemy's works, which were yet some distance ahead, would be materially lessened by the miscalculation. But as this phenomenal light continued at the same intensity it soon became apparent that there was no real cause for anxiety at its appearance, which was due to the presence of the great comet, which appeared for the first time this night, as though to denote (so might the superstitious read it) that the stars in their courses fought for the favourite of Fortune who led the white soldiers from over the sea. As Byron apostrophized the

THE FINAL HALT. 435

stars on the banks of Lake Leman, so might Arabi and his fellow-conspirators or patriots (as we, according to oui divergent views of the justice or wickedness of the cause he championed, choose to dub the leaders of this national movement) address these heavenly lights on this night, so big with the fate of their country:—

> 'If in your bright leaves we would read the fate
> Of men and empires—'tis to be forgiven
> That in our aspirations to be great,
> Our destinies o'erleap their mortal state
> And claim a kindred with you.'

The Commander-in-Chief was reassured, and the great array of men, and horses, and guns continued its march with mechanical precision; and as the hand of his watch pointed to the hour of five, and the dawn began to break, every man and gun was in its allotted place, and the leading brigades of each division came under the enemy's fire within a few minutes of one another.'[*]

[*] An officer, speaking with authority, thus explains the cause of this difference, which lay in the movements preceding the attack: 'Neither brigade had precisely carried out the original conception of Sir Garnet. His intention had been to attack in a series of short lines, with a series of supporting short lines behind them. But he had not the opportunity of training his army according to his own ideas. The only form of attack which had been known and practised beforehand was either what is called the Aldershot formation for attack, or the old English continuous line. Accordingly, one brigade took for granted that its business was to form line and so attack; and the other, after an impossible attempt to advance in a continuous line and an inevitable relapse into company columns of fours, had under fire adopted as the one formation the "Aldershot formation of attack." The successive changes had delayed the advance of the right brigade, and hence a disparity of time in the actual moment of attack, which gave opportunity to the intervening batteries to bring an effective and close fire upon the lines of the enemy at the moment of the attack of General Graham's Brigade. We have now the clear evidence of independent observers who have recently crossed the ground, that the shells of as many as thirty cartridges are to be seen in heaps where the Egyptians stood to fire against General Graham's Brigade, while not more than five or six mark the rounds that were fired against the Highland Brigade. Moreover, the tracks of the artillery-wheels show clearly where the several batteries came into action, and it is evident that Colonel Schreiber's two batteries were directing their fire in the first instance precisely upon the part of the line which the 2nd Brigade attacked. But though men now know that at the actual moment when the assault commenced the Highland Brigade was considerably nearer than the 2nd Brigade, it is pretty clear that the whole of the 2nd Brigade had crossed the enemy's lines and commenced to advance before the whole of the Highland Brigade had done so.'

One who was present, describing the wonderful precision with which this difficult movement was effected, says : 'The evidence of Sir Archibald Alison, and of the officers who were with him, is clear that the attack was delivered at the most happy moment that could have been chosen ; for, as they say, had the attack been any earlier, there would not have been light enough to follow it up within the works, and had it been later, the troops would have been exposed to severe fire before attacking.' But to effect this precision of movement required a very nice calculation of the time required for the march across the desert, and pre-supposed high intelligence on the part of the staff and regimental officers concerned.

The orders were that the leading brigades were not to fire a shot, but were to carry the entrenchments by the bayonet. Nothing finer than the *élan* with which these orders were executed is to be found in the history of war. Like the contending hosts before Troy :—

> 'Rank on rank the thick battalions throng,
> Chief urg'd on chief, and man drove man along.
> Far o'er the plains in dreadful order bright,
> The steely arms reflect a beamy light.'

Just when the stars began to pale, but before daylight had broken, a few shots were heard, followed by a bugle sounded in the enemy's lines. 'In a minute or two,' says the commander of the 2nd Division, 'the whole extent of entrenchments in our front, hitherto unseen and unknown of, poured forth a stream of rifle-fire.' The Highland Brigade, who had not even loaded their rifles, instantly advanced to the charge with levelled beyonets, and so murderous was the fire with which they were met, that, though they had only a narrow strip of 150 yards to cross, 200 men were shot down, the Highland Light Infantry alone losing 5 officers and 60 men before gaining the ditch, six feet wide and four feet deep, beyond which rose the parapet, four feet high. The first line was quickly into the ditch, and engaged in a hand-to-hand struggle with the enemy on the parapet, 'behind which, on either flank, was an elevated battery armed with guns, enclosed throughout by its own separate parapet, and a ditch ten feet deep.' The Highland Light Infantry found themselves opposed to a 4-gun battery, and the Royal Highlanders to one mounted with 6 guns, almost enclosed by an entrenchment, and forming the highest point of the position. The centre battalions, meanwhile, pushed on through the outer entrenchments, a distance of 200 or 300 yards, into the centre of the works.

The Highland Light Infantry were at one time compelled to recoil from the battery on the left flank opposed to them; but soon Colonel Ashburnham's Brigade came up, and the whole carried the work with a rush, and joined their comrades of the centre, who were assembled on a low hill 300 yards within the outer line. The division now advanced against the second or inner line, and, entering by a gap in the entrenchment, took the defenders in reverse at all points. The Egyptians were shot down in hundreds as they fled, and a battery of artillery coming up opportunely, assisted in cutting up the fleeing foe. Pushing on, Arabi's camp was captured by a party led by Sir Archibald Alison on foot, and also the railway station with 100 carriages; and by 6.30 the last shot was fired by the Highlanders—one hour and twenty-five minutes after the first.

In that time, says Sir E. Hamley, 'The Highland Brigade had captured two miles of works and batteries, piercing the enemy's centre, and loosening their whole system of defence, and finished by taking the camp and railway station.' The division lost 258 men killed and wounded,[*] of whom 23

[*] The following were the casualties in the Highland Brigade: Royal Highlanders, 2 officers—Lieutenant Graham-Stirling and J. C. McNeill—and 7 men killed, 6 officers (including Lieutenant Park who died) and 37

were officers, and their leader claims for them that they bore the brunt of the fighting, as evidenced by their losses.

Meanwhile, equally gallant and successful was the 2nd Brigade of the 1st Division, which advanced, says General Graham, 'under what appeared to be an utterly overwhelming fire of musketry and artillery.' The brigade came under fire when distant between 800 and 1,200 yards. Its formation was in *echelon* of half battalions from the right, which placed the Royal Irish (18th Regiment) in advance. Thus 'they were,' says an officer of the regiment, who was wounded, 'the first corps over the trenches,' and received the honour of a special mention from Sir Garnet Wolseley in his official telegram announcing the victory. 'About fifty yards in rear of these trenches,' says the same officer, 'between the front of the 18th and 84th (York and Lancaster Regiments) stood an elevated redoubt, which was taken conjointly by these two corps.' Not less dashing was the advance of the Irish Fusiliers (87th Regiment) and the Royal Marines.* This latter corps, which had taken a prominent part in every action of the war, advanced, says Colonel Howard S. Jones, in attack formation at the 'double,' taking up the 'quick' once or twice to let the men get their breath, and it was not until the fighting line was within some 150 yards of the enemy that he ordered the battalion to halt, fix bayonets, and open

---

men wounded, and 4 missing. Gordon Highlanders, 1 officer—Lieutenant H. G. Brooks—and 5 men killed, and 1 officer and 29 men wounded, and 4 missing. Highland Light Infantry, 3 officers—Major Colville and Lieutenants D. S. Kays and L. Somervell—and 14 men killed, and 5 officers and 52 men wounded, and 11 missing. Cameron Highlanders, 13 men killed, and 3 officers and 46 men wounded.

* The following were the losses of this brigade: Royal Irish Fusiliers, 2 men killed, 34 wounded, and 3 missing. York and Lancaster, 12 men wounded. The Royal Irish, 1 officer, Captain C. N. Jones, and 1 man killed and 2 officers and 17 men wounded. Royal Marines, 2 officers—Major H. H. Strong and Captain J. C. Wardell—and 3 men killed, 1 officer and 53 men wounded.

SERVICES OF THE ARTILLERY. 439

fire, the supports to reinforce it, and the whole to advance by rushes. By thus keeping the line in movement the fire of the enemy was to a great extent diverted.

The Guards, who supported the 2nd Brigade, were subjected to a heavy shell-fire, and had they been only five minutes later in passing over a slight elevation on which the enemy's guns were trained, at a range of 2,000 yards, their loss would have been very considerable. As it was, they escaped with the loss of only 1 man killed and 20 wounded, besides 3 officers, of whom one, Lieutenant-Colonel Balfour, died of his wounds after his arrival in England.

The nature of the attack left little for the artillery to effect. The division of seven batteries, under Brigadier-General Goodenough, stationed between Alison's and Graham's Brigades, deployed into one line, and after the entrenchments had been penetrated, some of the batteries inflicted heavy loss upon the enemy. N. Battery 2nd Brigade, commanded by Lieutenant-Colonel Brancker, did special good service. Assisted by the Royal Highlanders, the artillerymen levelled the parapet in one spot and the guns were brought within the enemy's lines, opening fire on the retreating Egyptians with shrapnel and canister; they limbered up and came into action every 300 or 400 yards, and enfilading the line of entrenchments, drove the enemy out of some redoubts. Pushing on to the top of a hillock, Colonel Brancker again brought his guns into action, and opened fire on the railway station in which three trains were standing, with engines attached. As the first was starting off, a shell from the battery, fired at a range of about 1,400 yards, blew up the fore portion of the train, which apparently contained ammunition. Soon after, the 13th Bengal Lancers, under Colonel Macnaghten, entered the station and seized the remaining trains, the enemy fleeing along the railway and canal.* The Infantry Brigades, supported by the Guards and Ashburnham's Brigade, advanced rapidly through the enemy's works, and took possession of the vast camp, the Highlanders, following the 13th Bengal Lancers, occupying the railway station, which contained much stores and ammunition.

On the extreme left, the Indian Contingent, numbering, with a squadron of cavalry and a company of Madras Sappers, about 1,500 men, with 6 seven-pounder screw-guns, conduced to the success of the day by its steadiness and admirable marching-powers. Their advance along the south side of the canal was held back so as to ensure the success of the intended surprise by the main column. Crossing the Fresh Water Canal by pontoon bridges, they took up their prescribed position on the south bank, and soon after three a.m. the troops and long train of mules, carrying ammunition and stores, commenced the march in perfect order. Heading the column were two companies of the Highlanders, while the Naval Brigade, under Macpherson's orders, acted in support on the northern bank of the canal. As dawn broke, the enemy opened fire from his

* The following is an account given by an officer of Arabi's army of the battle of Tel-el-Kebir: 'On the 12th we were informed that a general attack would be made that night. We were all under arms and at our posts shortly after sunset. During the night scouts were sent out with orders to fire in the air as a signal if any body of troops were approaching. They three times reported all quiet. We had given up all expectations of attack; we were tired, and the officers were beginning to lie down, when three scouts were sent out as a last reconnoissance. We had expected that the attack would begin at about 2,000 yards. Our guns were sighted for this range. Arabi exhorted his officers to wait ten minutes for the result of this last reconnoissance; but hardly had he left the camp when they heard the signal. Instead of 2,000 yards, they must have been 200 yards off. We fired, but most of our shots must have gone over their heads. Almost at the same moment, it seemed so quick, they were scrambling over us—first over our right, then rolling over all down the line like a wave. We never expected war like this. Our soldiers stood fire at a distance very well. On the 5th August many were killed, and they were not afraid of shells; but these men came close up to us, and the only way to save life was to run away. The native soldier has never exercised this close way of fighting. No soldiers but the English could fight like that.'

redoubts, and a shell exploded in the midst of the General's staff, hurling Captain Melliss to the ground. At this time the infantry, with the Highlanders extended in line leading, was advancing along an excavated roadway lying along the base of the causeway by the side of the canal. On the left the mountain battery shelled a native village, occupied by Arabs, who were driven out; and the Naval Brigade poured a hot fire into some of the enemy's works near the canal. Soon the column reached a battery consisting of 4 seven-pounders, outside the causeway, and the General directed the Seaforth Highlanders to storm the work. This was gallantly done, Lieutenant Burn-Murdoch, R.E., being the first man in. Pushing on, the Highlanders, supported by the Native Infantry, captured a second battery of 8 Krupp guns, which was abandoned. Two redoubts or batteries on the north side of the canal, apparently covered from the main attack by the intervening hill, were shelled, also the retreating Egyptians on the same side of the canal, the Naval Brigade affording valuable assistance with their Gatlings. The contingent then continued its advance, and cleared the fields on the left of the causeway; and Arabi's camp was shelled at a range of about 1,200 yards, as also by artillery from the main attack which came over the hill, until the infantry marched down and took possession of the camp. The squadron of 6th Bengal Cavalry did good service at this time in pursuing the enemy through the village of Tel-el-Kebir.

Sir Herbert Macpherson's dispositions were completely successful, and the Commander-in-Chief attributed the small loss sustained by the contingent—1 man killed and 3 wounded in the Highlanders — to his 'excellent arrangements.' These might have been anticipated from an officer having the vast and varied experience of General Macpherson, who served as Adjutant of the 78th Highlanders, under

General Havelock, at the Relief of Lucknow, and was the right hand of Sir Frederick Roberts from the time of his advance on Cabul to the battle of Candahar. As Sir Garnet said of him at the conclusion of the war : 'He is a pillar of strength in any army with which he serves. His varied experience of war, and the confidence he inspires in all under his command, mark him out as a divisional leader to whom the honour of our arms and the lives of her Majesty's soldiers can at all times be safely entrusted.'

Sir Garnet Wolseley arrived on the bridge over the canal at Tel-el-Kebir almost at the same time as Sir Herbert Macpherson, to whom he gave instructions to proceed with the Indian Contingent to Zagazig, twenty-five miles distant from the camp at Kassassin. Accompanied only by his staff and about 30 men of the 6th Bengal Cavalry, about four p.m. he rode into this large and important town, the principal cotton centre of the Delta. No resistance was offered, and the small party pushed on to the railway station, and their temerity was rewarded by the capture of five trains filled with soldiers, which were on the point of steaming out of the station—one was actually leaving, but Lieutenant Burn-Murdoch, R.E.,* threatened the driver with his revolver. The soldiers leaped from the trains, and throwing away their arms, made good their escape.

The telegraph was now put into action and communications opened with Cairo, announcing the capture of Tel-el-Kebir, the total defeat of the army, and the occupation of Zagazig by her Majesty's troops in force *en route* for Cairo. Within an hour a telegram was received from Ali Rouby Pasha and his colleagues, announcing, in the name of the nation, the

* This young officer affords a proof of the truth of the saying that 'adventures are to the adventurous.' He served with distinction in the Afghan War, under Sir Frederick Roberts, and was wounded in action at Cabul, in December, 1879, on which occasion his conduct was mentioned in despatches as 'most gallant.'

CAPTURE OF ZAGAZIG. 443

entire submission of the army to the will of the Khedive, and entreating that further hostilities might cease. The remainder of the squadron of cavalry, with the infantry and mule battery, arrived at Zagazig by six p.m., having no supplies* but what they carried in their haversacks, the Highlanders and artillerymen having made a march which, considering the distance traversed and the climate, and that they fought a battle on the way, has seldom been equalled by British troops. The feat was even greater than any performed by the Seaforth Highlanders during the memorable march they made, under Sir Frederick Roberts's command, from Cabul to Candahar, two years before. In his report, General Macpherson drew special attention to the fact that not a man of the infantry fell out or had to be carried during the day, probably an unprecedented circumstance in a forced march of over twenty-five miles under a tropical sun.

The advance on Zagazig was a bold stroke, and equalled in dash anything of the sort chronicled of the famous Prussian Uhlans in the Franco-German War. But the action of the Cavalry Division was another instance in this brief but memorable campaign equalling if not surpassing it in daring, and the inception of both alike was due to the master-mind who infused into his subordinates the eager spirit that animated him. But we must follow the course of events in their proper sequence.

As Sir Garnet Wolseley rode through the conquered position, a redoubt on the extreme left, near the canal, which had not yet been captured, continued its fire, enfilading the works. Colonel Schreiber, R.A., ordered up a battery and soon silenced the work and blew up the magazine. The Cavalry

* A great impression was created among the natives of Zagazig by the punctilious honesty of Sir H. Macpherson and his staff. At the railway station they came upon a great find in the shape of wine, beer and provisions, and the General directed every officer who partook of those luxuries to inscribe in a book his name and the amount appropriated, with the view of future payment.

Division on the extreme right swept round the northern extremity of the enemy's lines and charged them as they endeavoured to escape. With praiseworthy humanity General Drury-Lowe ordered that those of the fugitives who threw down their arms and begged for mercy should be unmolested, and suffered to go free, as to make them prisoners would have prevented him from pushing on to Cairo. But no less than 1,500 of Arabi's soldiers died for the faith, the free exercise of which, they were given to understand, was menaced, and having fought the good fight,

'In Elysian valleys dwell,
Resting weary limbs at last on beds of Asphodel.'

Within thirty-five minutes of the first shot being fired, the British flag flew over the entrenchments of Tel-el-Kebir, and the victorious Commander, riding through the enemy's camp and works, which lay line within line, met his Generals on the bridge over the canal and concerted measures for making the victory decisive. While Sir Herbert Macpherson was directed to push on to Zagazig, whither the Highland Brigade followed him on the following day, General Drury-Lowe received instructions to make a forced march to Belbeis and thence to Cairo, to save the city from experiencing the fate of Alexandria.

In the very hour of his triumph, and amid the hurry of giving the necessary orders for pushing his great success, Sir Garnet Wolseley did not forget one who was dying in faithfully carrying out his instructions. Lieutenant Wyatt Rawson, R.N., his Naval aide-de-camp, who had pioneered the Highland Brigade during the night march, with 'marvellous accuracy,' as Sir Edward Hamley said, was shot through the body while scaling the entrenchments among the foremost, and Sir Garnet rode back some miles to see his faithful friend and follower for the last time. Entering the tent where the wounded young officer lay, he knelt by his side, and taking his hand, strove to cheer him, though he himself was much affected, for he knew there was no hope. The dying man asked, with a proud satisfaction lighting up his features, racked with pain: 'General, did I not lead them straight?' It was the old spirit that flamed up in the dying Nelson when, amid the throes of dissolution, he summoned up sufficient strength to thank God he had done his duty. 'Yes,' was the reply—as the leader pressed the hand of the subordinate who had sacrificed his life, with all its hopes of distinction, just as they were on the point of realization, and even the happiness of those nearest and dearest to him, in fulfilling his orders—'I knew you were well to the front all the time, old fellow.' He spoke these words cheerfully, but he knew his friend was mortally wounded,* and before leaving promised to telegraph to his wife.

While the Indian Contingent and cavalry pushed on to Zagazig and Cairo respectively, Sir Garnet Wolseley occupied the camp with the rest of the army. There was ample accommodation, and Arabi's tent was specially luxurious; and it may be mentioned as an interesting circumstance, that one of the carpets found therein, and appropriated by the Duke of Connaught, was used by Her Majesty the Queen, who stood upon it when decorating the officers and men at Windsor Castle on their return from Egypt.

* Lieutenant Wyatt Rawson died on the morning of the 21st September, on board the *Carthage*, hospital ship, as she was entering Malta harbour. He did not live to know that the Admiralty, with commendable promptitude, had promoted him to Commander. The Queen wrote a letter to the widow, expressing her sympathy, and Sir Garnet spoke in the following terms of his late Naval aide-de-camp: 'During the many journeys I made by night, I found him of great use in directing our march correctly, through his knowledge of the stars. On the 13th instant I consequently selected him to conduct the Highland Brigade during the night to the portion of the enemy's works where I explained to him I wished them to storm. This duty he performed with the utmost coolness and success, but lost his life in its execution.' Sir Garnet keenly felt the death of Lieutenant Rawson, for whose services he had specially applied to the Admiralty, and wrote of him: 'No man more gallant fell on that occasion.'

Early on the following morning telegraphic communication was established with Zagazig, and Sir Garnet, on ascertaining that the line was open to Cairo, resolved to proceed thither without delay. Accompanied by the Duke of Connaught, and escorted by a company of Guards and one of Marines, he was on the platform ready to start at noon, but owing to a slight accident on the line, did not leave the station of Tel-el-Kebir until five p.m. In consequence of the line being blocked by artillery, infantry, and stores, Zagazig was only reached at 9.30, and as it was not deemed advisable to go any further in the dark, the Commander-in-Chief and the Duke of Connaught, with their staffs, passed the night in great discomfort at the deserted railway station. At 5.30 on the following morning (the 15th of September) the journey was resumed, and at seven, on reaching the important junction at Benha, a deputation was found awaiting the Commander-in-Chief from Cairo, announcing that Arabi had surrendered, and that the notables of the capital were expecting his advent with eagerness. After partaking of some refreshment, which was freely brought by the inhabitants, who took care to make their deliverers pay handsomely for the same, Sir Garnet proceeded to Cairo, where he arrived at ten a.m., and was received by a great crowd, who thronged to see the General who had defeated their hero and scattered his boasted battalions to the winds with an ease and rapidity that savoured of magic.

On the previous day the cavalry had secured the surrender of the capital and some 8,000 troops in garrison. General Drury-Lowe, without drawing bridle, marched rapidly with the whole of his cavalry and Mounted Infantry, and Lieutenant-Colonel Borradaile's battery of Horse Artillery, and pushing the pursuit along the canal, by the side of which arms and munitions of war were thickly strewed, arrived that evening at Belbeis, twenty-five miles distant from Kassassin.

THE MARCH OF THE CAVALRY.

After exchanging a few shots, the railway station here was occupied, and it was found that Arabi had only passed through a quarter of an hour before; and indeed, soon after their arrival, a telegraphic message was received from him from the next station, asking what troops had reached Belbeis. The town was requisitioned for food, but little was obtained, and on the morning of the 14th, after a cheerless bivouac, the division was again on the march by the south bank of the canal. A halt of two hours was made at Syriakus, and General Drury-Lowe then pushed on for Cairo, which he desired to approach by the desert near the barracks of Abbassyeh.

On nearing Cairo he formed his small division into two lines, as its strength was reduced to a portion of the Indian Cavalry, 4th Dragoon Guards, and Mounted Infantry, the Household Cavalry, 7th Dragoon Guards, and guns being in the rear, unable to keep up through the heavy sand. The advance was made in two lines, *échelloned* from the right, and each line itself in *échellon* of regiments from the right. The Mounted Infantry led, being thus the right corps of the first line. In order to make the force look stronger, the rear rank was put into the same line as the front rank— a formation called 'rank entire'—and at 4.45 the cavalry halted about a mile from the great barracks of Abbassyeh, when General Lowe sent in a flag of truce, under Colonel Herbert Stewart,* 3rd Dragoon Guards, demanding the surrender of the barracks and citadel with its garrison. The view of Cairo from the point presented to the troops, who, by their rapid march, had saved it from fire and rapine, was one of extraordinary beauty. The city, with its palaces and mosques interspersed among gardens, the graceful minarets

* Colonel Stewart was one of those officers whose selection displayed Sir Garnet Wolseley's remarkable discrimination. He had served under him in South Africa, and his services during the present war at Kassassin and Cairo, as Assistant Adjutant-General to the Cavalry Division, fully justified the good opinion formed of him by Sir Garnet.

soaring into the bright cloudless sky, and the heavy battlements of the citadel frowning on the fair landscape at its feet, is unsurpassed in the East. Titus's address to his soldiers before Jerusalem, in Milman's noble poem, rise to the mind as descriptive of the scene on this evening, so fateful for Cairo.

> 'There bright and sumptuous palaces,
> With cool and verdant gardens interspersed ;
> There towers of war, that frown massy strength—
> While over all hangs the rich purple eve.'

While Colonel Stewart was occupied settling the terms with some representatives of the enemy, the sun set, and the cavalry soldiers lay down, bridle in hand, quite exhausted with the great heat, and half famished, having had nothing to eat the whole day. Terms of surrender were at length arranged with the Egyptian generals, and, soon after, the Prefect of Cairo arrived and surrendered the citadel and town. About 10.30 Arabi Pasha and Toulba, who commanded the Egyptian troops garrisoning Alexandria at the time of its bombardment, were brought by the Prefect, and gave up their swords to General Drury-Lowe, who, throughout the difficult negotiations, had displayed equal tact and firmness. That night the extraordinary spectacle was witnessed of a strong garrison of horse, foot, and artillery laying down their arms to a handful of exhausted troopers, and surrendering a citadel of great strength, mounted with heavy guns.

At 9 p.m., a detachment of 150 troopers of the 4th Dragoon Guards and Mounted Infantry, under Captains Lawrence (commanding the latter) and Darley (4th Dragoon Guards), piloted by Captain Watson, R.E., of the Intelligence Department, the only British officer with the cavalry who spoke Arabic, quitted Abbassyeh, and, threading their way past the tombs of the Caliphs, drew up before the citadel, without passing through the city or attracting the notice of the people. On arriving at a point opposite the

THE SURRENDER OF THE CITADEL.

great gate of Sultan Hussein's mosque, the little band tranquilly awaited the surrender of the garrison of 6,000 men, and of the vast citadel whose battlements, bristling with guns, frowned defiance upon them. Presently the commandant, Yusuf Ali Bey, presented himself, and after a few words exchanged with the British officer, gave directions for the evacuation of the fortress. Then took place the astonishing spectacle—not the first of the kind in our island story—of an army surrendering to a handful of Englishmen, around whose brows shone the reflected might of the resistless array that won the entrenchments of Tel-el-Kebir. For two hours the long line of disciplined troops, sullen and silent, defiled out of the fortress before the conquerors; and at 12.30 the last scene in the surrender of the Egyptian capital was consummated by the British troops, weary and famished after forty-eight hours passed in the saddle, marching in through the gate, and taking possession of the citadel. Before midnight, the rebellion had collapsed by the surrender of Arabi Pasha, that famous subject of the Khedive, the *fons et origo* of the war. A more detailed account of the services of the several Brigades of the Cavalry Division will be not inappropriate at this point of the narrative.

At the battle of Tel-el-Kebir, the Cavalry Division, commanded by General Drury-Lowe, was divided into two Brigades. The Indian Cavalry Brigade, under Brigadier-General Wilkinson, forming the first line, consisted of the 2nd and 6th Bengal Cavalry and 13th Bengal Lancers; and the second line, composed of the Heavy Brigade, under Sir Baker Russell, consisted of the three squadrons Household Cavalry and the 4th and 7th Dragoon Guards. Immediately after the result of the action was made known to General Drury-Lowe, he pushed forward the Indian Brigade and the Mounted Infantry, which seized the lock a few miles above Tel-el-Kebir; and after a halt of half an hour, General Wilkinson started for Belbeis, sixteen miles distant, by the north bank of the Sweet Water Canal. Crowds of fugitives were passed, who offered no resistance, but threw away their arms; and it was not until within about six miles of Belbeis that shots were exchanged with a body consisting of some hundreds of infantry and cavalry, who were dispersed after a smart skirmish. About noon the Indian Cavalry and Mounted Infantry entered Belbeis, distant twenty-five miles from Kassassin by the route north of Tel-el-Kebir. On his arrival General Wilkinson opened the lock-gates, and let the water into the lower part of the canal. About five p.m. General Lowe arrived with the 4th Dragoon Guards, and at 4.30 on the following morning, he marched with that regiment and the Mounted Infantry; the 2nd Bengal Cavalry and five troops of the 13th Bengal Lancers taking the route by the south, or desert, bank of the canal. On reaching Syriakus Lock, about twelve miles from Cairo, General Lowe halted for two hours, when Brigadier-General Wilkinson not having arrived, he set out on his march with the 4th Dragoon Guards and Mounted Infantry, and diverging to his left, reached Abbassyeh Barracks, about three and a half miles from Cairo, at 4.30 p.m.

Meanwhile, shortly after General Lowe left Belbeis, General Wilkinson marched with the 6th Bengal Cavalry, one troop 13th Bengal Lancers, and some Mounted Infantry, and keeping straight along the Sweet Water Canal, arrived during the night of the 14th at the railway bridge, some few miles short of the station. At daybreak on the 15th, under instructions from General Drury-Lowe, who had arranged for their surrender, he occupied the railway station and telegraph office, and remained in possession until ordered by General Lowe to move out to the Abbassyeh Barracks, a detachment of the 4th Dragoon Guards afterwards re-occupying the railway station. The Heavy Cavalry Brigade, with the guns,

THE SERVICES OF THE CAVALRY. 451

did not arrive at Abbassyeh until the 15th, marching in the desert sand being very trying for the stalwart troopers and their heavy horses.

The gallant services rendered by the Household Cavalry at the ever-memorable charge of Kassassin on the 28th August have been the theme of many pens, and with their dramatic surroundings will form a brilliant page in contemporaneous military history. The 4th Dragoon Guards rendered not less distinguished service, and, as we have seen, was the only regiment of British Cavalry (excluding the Mounted Infantry) that possessed the staying power to hold its own with the Indian Cavalry, which was quite at home in the heated sand of the Egyptian desert. The 19th Hussars, as Divisional Cavalry, were split up throughout the campaign, providing escorts and holding the line of communications. On the 13th September a portion of the regiment was placed, under Brigadier-General Nugent, R.E., in charge of the camp, and a squadron, under Major Taylor, formed, with the battalion of Royal Marine Artillery, the Reserve, under Sir Garnet Wolseley's personal command. The services of the 7th Dragoon Guards were of a more active description, but nevertheless, this gallant regiment did not play so conspicuous a part as some of its officers could have wished.*

* Every regiment of the Cavalry Division, British and Native, has received a meed of praise except the 7th Dragoon Guards. The Household Cavalry has been belauded for the brilliant charge at Kassassin, in which the 7th participated; and the 4th Dragoon Guards, led by that popular officer, Major Denne, has received the equally well-merited praises of the Duke of Cambridge, as the first cavalry regiment to enter Cairo, an honour it shared with the Mounted Infantry. Nevertheless this gallant regiment (the old ' Black Horse') did well, as the following brief record of its services, supplied to us by the able and indefatigable Adjutant, Captain de Burgh, will show: ' On the 28th August, on the third occasion of our turning out from our camp at Mahsameh, judging, from the heavy artillery-fire over the camp at Kassassin, that the small force there was heavily attacked, about half an hour before sunset we left the camp in the following order : *First line,* four squadrons 7th Dragoon Guards, followed by N Battery A Brigade Royal Horse Artillery, and with three squadrons Household Cavalry in support. On attaining the crest of the ridge over Kassassin, the sun went down ; and

Captain (now Brevet-Major) R. C. Lawrence (5th Dragoon Guards), who commanded the Mounted Infantry from the 1st of September, gives us the following account of the movements of this force, which formed the advanced guard of the Cavalry Division, and, with a detachment of the 4th Dragoon Guards, received the surrender of the citadel. 'At the battle of Tel-el-Kebir, the Mounted Infantry, under my command, consisted of 6 officers, besides myself, and 130 non-commissioned officers and men, divided into four troops. At one a.m. on the 13th September, the Cavalry and Mounted Infantry, with a battery of Royal Horse Artillery, left Kassassin. Striking off into the desert at once, and making a considerable *détour*, we halted about two miles from, and opposite, the left flank of the enemy's position at Tel-el-Kebir. Dismounting, we lay down, and tried to rest beside our horses. We must have been here for at least an hour and a half. At daybreak we mounted and moved on rapidly, and the Horse Artillery, taking up a

---

shortly the enemy perceived the cavalry in the moonlight advancing, and turned their guns on us at once. An order was sent to the 7th to open out from both flanks to enable the Royal Horse Artillery to come into action ; this they did, supported on the left by the fire of a dismounted troop of the 7th. When General Lowe sent an order to charge the guns, the Household Cavalry came up in the interval made by the 7th for the Royal Horse Artillery to come into action. Thus the enemy was attacked with a line formed by the Household Cavalry in the centre, one squadron 7th on their right, two squadrons 7th on their left, while the fourth squadron remained as escort to the Royal Horse Artillery. From their central position, the Household Cavalry got among the enemy's guns. The casualties of the 7th were Lieutenant Gribble (3rd Dragoon Guards), attached to the 7th, killed (his body was found on the 9th September), 3 men wounded, and 3 horses killed.

'At Tel-el-Kebir, on the 13th, the 7th were engaged in the pursuit of the enemy, and pushed on to Cairo, *viâ* Belbeis, with the Household Cavalry and N Battery A Brigade Royal Horse Artillery. We bivouacked in the desert, nine miles east of Belbeis, on the night of the 13th, and about fourteen miles east of Cairo on that of the 14th, where two squadrons were left in escort to the battery on the morning of the 15th. The remaining two squadrons with the Household Cavalry (three squadrons), commanded by Sir Baker Russell, marched into Cairo at nine a.m. on the 15th, the two other squadrons marching in about two hours later, having been delayed by a portion of the road having to be repaired to enable the guns to traverse it.'

position on some rising ground to our left front, came into action. During this time we heard the incessant rattle of musketry, and owing to the partial darkness, could see the flashes of shells bursting in the air. We now passed in front of a work on the enemy's extreme left, out of which they ran on seeing us approaching, and soon came upon hundreds of Egyptians, many badly wounded, who were walking slowly across the desert away from us, or in the direction of El Menair. Those we overtook threw down their arms, but many of those in the distance turned round and fired shots at us. General Lowe sent me off to look after these latter, and I dismounted a couple of troops, who fired two or three volleys, and thus stopped this firing on the part of fugitives.

'General Lowe now moved with the British Cavalry, under Sir Baker Russell, close up to the rear of Tel-el-Kebir, taking away one troop of my Mounted Infantry. I went on with the rest, and together with the advanced parties of the 2nd and 13th Bengal Cavalry, the whole under General Wilkinson, seized the first work (Abu Hamed, I think). We then pushed on along the north-west side of the canal, as it branches towards Cairo, riding sometimes in sections along the bank, sometimes in column of troops along the open ground between the canal and cultivation. We could see numbers of fugitives retreating along through the high growth of millet and cotton covering this irrigated land. About one and a half mile short of Belbeis about 150 of the enemy made a short stand behind some heaps of sand on the desert, or opposite, side of the canal, and opened a sharp fire on the advanced parties. These dismounted under cover of our bank (both sides of the canal had a high bank here, with a path between it and the water-side), and I pushed the Mounted Infantry under this cover. We replied briskly to their fire, knocking over a lot of them, and in about ten minutes the rest bolted. About 1.30 p.m. we reached Belbeis, and the Mounted Infantry were established in and about the lock-keeper's house.

'About five or six p.m., General Lowe joined us with the 4th Dragoon Guards. I sent a picket to take charge of the railway station, and about one a.m. (14th) was awakened by Colonel Herbert Stewart, with orders to send back three trustworthy men with a message to Colonel Ewart to bring up some guns to join us. At five a.m. we all crossed at the lock to the desert side of the canal, and advanced on Cairo, delivering the Khedive's proclamation at the villages on the way. After going about fifteen miles, we halted for about fifteen minutes, and then continued our march. At Syriakus General Lowe bought large supplies of bread and coarse forage for the troops from the villagers, and we halted in the shade for an hour. We then turned sharp to our left across the irrigated land—here about a mile broad—and skirting outside Birket-el-Hadj (I think), we advanced on Abbassyeh. About five miles from Cairo, near the ruins of Heliopolis, a flag of truce was sent in, demanding the surrender of the city, under Colonel Stewart, whose escort was a detachment of the Mounted Infantry and 4th Dragoon Guards (I think), the two Egyptian officers who had accompanied us the whole way going with us. We then moved slowly on till within one mile of Abbassyeh.'

Captain Lawrence, the senior cavalry officer of the party that took possession of the citadel, fully recognised the dangers of the situation, and is of opinion that had a single shot been fired on either side, the whole of his small detachment must have been massacred. Indeed, it is manifest that nothing but good management and the bold face he and Captains Watson and Darley put on matters, averted a catastrophe. He writes to us as follows of the events of that night: 'At nine p.m. we left Abbassyeh, and making a

SERVICES OF THE MOUNTED INFANTRY. 455

circuit by the desert road, arrived before the citadel at 10.30, under the guidance of Captain Watson and an Egyptian officer, Hussein Bey, who was sent to communicate to the Governor the order to march out. My men were so utterly exhausted that they lay down at the heads of their horses, and when the time came to take possession of the citadel, some of them had to be kicked up before they could be aroused. We formed in an open space (between the main gate and archway, leading through an interior line of wall) facing inwards, the 4th Dragoon Guards, two squadrons (in single rank), under Captain Darley, and the Mounted Infantry (81 men).

'The Egyptian troops (about 6,000 or 7,000) formed by battalions in the inner barrack-yard, and were marched out by a smaller gate in the lower part of the citadel near the mosque of Sultan Hassan, and leading more directly into the native town. This was done to avoid any confusion or possible danger that might have arisen from their passing our men, it being improbable that they would have quietly submitted to be turned out had they known our numbers. On the completion of the evacuation, we proceeded to lock the gates and place guards over them, two from the Mounted Infantry and one from the 4th Dragoon Guards. I now found that the prisoners had been let loose by the departing Egyptians. Having broken into an armourer's workshop, they had seized a number of tools and began knocking off their shackles, they being mostly fastened in couples by long fetters. With the assistance of two dragoons I drove them back into their prison, and Captain Watson told them that anyone attempting to escape would be shot. I considered this necessary, as some of them had gained possession of arms which the troops had left lying about. Having got as many of them as I could see into the two prisons, I placed a guard of the 4th Dragoon Guards on each, and the prisoners gave no further trouble, though they appeared to continue knocking off their shackles all night.* Watson and the Egyptian officer now left for Abbassyeh, and I locked the last gate.

'It was quite dark when we arrived, so that there were many nooks and corners that had to be explored. I therefore got a lantern, and went round and about the whole place. In some places I found stragglers from the Egyptian regiments, whom I turned out by the nearest gate; in others, a few prisoners whom I confined with the rest. None of these made any show of opposition, but all were ready to go in any direction I pointed out to them (with a revolver). As soon as the Egyptian troops had moved out, the Mounted Infantry picketed their horses in the open way before referred to, just inside the main gate, and I sent the 4th Dragoon Guards into the inner yard. We found a large dirty room with divans round it, apparently some officer's quarters, inside the inner yard, and here the officers lay down. About three a.m. I woke up Lieutenant Hore, 1st Stafford Regiment (38th), one of my officers, who relieved me in patrolling for one hour. I then called Lieutenant Harrison, 11th Hussars (attached to 4th Dragoon Guards), to do the same for one hour, and got up again myself at five a.m. At six I saw Ali Bey about rations for the troops, and he sent for an Egyptian police official (zaptieh), who got me rations on requisition. This man told me he knew of Midshipman de Chair's whereabouts in the town, so I sent him off at once to bring him in, thinking it would be safer to do so. About eight or nine a.m. young De Chair arrived, looking well and glad to get back to friends and countrymen. About half-past nine

* 'During the night,' says Captain Lawrence, 'one of the prisoners tried to escape, but was shot, and, I believe, mortally wounded, by one of my sentries. I handed him over to a Guards' doctor next morning. Two other prisoners shackled together were, I believe, injured in trying to escape by jumping a wall, but neither was killed. Some of the prisoners appeared to be of the cut-throat class, and others were harmless political offenders.'

or ten a.m. on the following morning (the 15th September), the Duke of Connaught arrived with the Scots Guards and relieved me at the citadel, and I marched out to the Kasr-el-Nil Barracks.'

During the succeeding few days, the Guards arrived from Benha; also the Highlanders, who had been halted at Belbeis after quitting Zagazig, and the Artillery, General Graham's Brigade and the Indian Contingent.

If the capture of the lines of Tel-el-Kebir was a remarkable feat of war, even more extraordinary was the manner in which the fruits of that victory were reaped by the successful General, to whom, in his capacity for correctly estimating the real strength of an enemy, might be applied the words pronounced by the Roman historian on Hannibal : *'Bene ausus vana contemnere.'*

The cavalry had fought an action and made the distance of sixty-five miles in two days,* and if the credit of storming the entrenchments of Tel-el-Kebir, and capturing 59 guns and vast quantities of military stores and supplies of all sorts, belongs almost exclusively to the infantry, to the mounted branch of the service is due the honour of a forced march rarely equalled, whether we regard the place and circumstances under which it was made, or the vast interests subserved by its accomplishment. The events of the past forty-eight hours were indeed startling in the rapidity of the incidents and the dramatic character of the *dénouement.* Whether we regard the skill of the General, who placed his men in front of the lines of the enemy at the exact moment of time, neither sooner nor later, that was essential for success, or the gallantry of the troops, we, as a nation, may echo the words of their leader : ' I

* One troop of the 6th Bengal Cavalry, which only left Ismailia on the evening of the 12th, were present at the battle of Tel-el-Kebir on the 13th, and were at Cairo on the following day, eighty-five miles from Ismailia, not a horse or man having fallen out.

do not believe that at any previous period of our military history has the British infantry distinguished itself more than upon this occasion. I have heard it said of our present infantry regiments that the men are too young, and their training for manœuvring and for fighting and their powers of endurance are not sufficient for the requirements of modern war. After a trial of an exceptionally severe kind, both in movement and attack, I can say emphatically that I never wish to have under my orders better infantry battalions than those whom I am proud to have commanded at Tel-el-Kebir.'

The critics who disagree with Sir Garnet Wolseley in his estimate of the young soldiers who now compose the major portion of the British army, and contemptuously dub them 'immature boys,' forget that the average service of the victors of Tel-el-Kebir was five years, while that of the vanquished at Majuba Hill was seven years. With the Reserve, that essential and integral part of the short-service system, it will always be possible in war-time to place any battalion in an efficient condition by adding as many reserve men as are necessary to take the places of the recruits. It must be considered a good test of the efficiency of the new system, of which Sir Garnet has been so warm an advocate, that, including the troops on their way to Egypt, 41,000 men were equipped for service without embodying a single battalion of Militia, and with the aid of less than one-fifth of the Reserves, and Mr. Childers has stated that 'twice that number of efficient soldiers could be despatched from this country, leaving an ample force at home, within a month of the expedition being approved by Parliament; and this without its being necessary to embody more than half the Militia, or to obtain any aid from India.' This is certainly a gratifying state of things, and compares favourably with the condition of the army

RETROSPECT OF THE CAMPAIGN. 459

at the time of the Crimean War, or even ten years ago.

To achieve this great victory,* the losses, though con-

---

* The following are chief among the officers who conduced to this great success, with the terms in which they are spoken of by the Commander-in-Chief:—Sir John Adye, to whom, he says, 'I was indebted, from the beginning to the termination of this war, for the cordial, loyal, and efficient assistance I have at all times received from him. His ability as an administrator is well known to you, and the highest praise I can give him is to say that his soldier-like qualities are fully on a par with his administrative capacity.' Sir Archibald Alison, 'whose services rendered at Alexandria previous to my arrival are already well known to you. No one could have led his brigade more gallantly or with greater skill than he did on the 13th inst., when he showed it the way into the enemy's intrenchments. He is both zealous and capable.' General Graham, 'to whose lot fell the brunt of the fighting throughout the campaign, and it could not have been in better hands. To that coolness and gallantry in action for which he has always been well known, he adds the power of leading and commanding others.' General Drury-Lowe, 'who commanded the Cavalry Division with great skill and success throughout the campaign, and I have great pleasure in strongly recommending him to your favourable consideration. His pursuit of the enemy and occupation of Cairo the day after the battle of Tel-el-Kebir is worthy of every praise. I believe the preservation of the city is owing to the splendid forced march made by the cavalry on that occasion.' Brigadier-General Dormer, the officer second in rank belonging to the Head-Quarter Staff. ' He has had long and varied experience on the Staff. He thoroughly understands our army system in all its phases, and adds great tact and judgment to his other many high military qualities.' Sir Baker Russell, 'whose soldier-like qualities are so well known that it is unnecessary for me to enlarge upon them. He is a born cavalry leader.' Colonel Rollo Gillespie, 'who is a first-rate Staff-officer.' Colonel Herbert Stewart, 'one of the best Staff-officers I have ever known, and one whom I feel it will be in the interest of the army to promote.' Colonel H. S. Jones, commanding the Marines, who did his duty at all times with zeal and ability.' Brigadier-Generals Wilkinson and Tanner and Colonels Gerard and Pennington, of the Indian Contingent, also rendered good services, and were strongly recommended by Sir Herbert Macpherson. Other excellent officers, favourably mentioned in the despatches were Colonels Stockwell, Maurice, Swaine, Ewart, Richardson, Wilson, Stevenson, Macpherson (who led his regiment, the 42nd, at Amoaful as well as at Tel-el-Kebir), Gregorie, Tuson, and Graham, and Major Denne, who commanded the 4th Dragoon Guards at Tel-el-Kebir and on the march to Cairo.

The Railway and Intelligence Departments have already been referred to in the preceding pages ; and we have also spoken of the services rendered by Sir Herbert Macpherson, General Earle, Colonels Buller and Butler, Sir Owen Lanyon, and the naval officers engaged in the occupation of the Suez Canal, and the services they and the navy generally rendered to the army, of which Sir Garnet Wolseley spoke in no stinted terms. Finally, of the rank and file the Commander-in-Chief wrote : 'It only remains for me to add how much I feel indebted to the non-commissioned officers and rank and file, who have borne the trying hardships of this desert campaign without a murmur, and in the most uncomplaining spirit. Their valour in action and

siderable, were not near so numerous as Sir Garnet Wolseley anticipated. The casualties were 9 officers and 48 men killed, 27 officers (of whom 3 died) and 353 men wounded, and 22 men missing—giving a grand total of 459 of all ranks.

To his despatch of the 24th September, eulogizing those officers who had done good work during the campaign, objection has been taken that every officer holding a prominent position, or commanding a corps or battalion, has been praised; but in pursuing this course the Commander-in-Chief only followed precedent. All had done well, and therefore all received the meed of approval. But while none had fallen below what was expected of them, it is not difficult to read between the lines of the despatch, and detect the names of those officers who displayed singular capacity, or seized opportunities of distinction as they arose. These are the men to whom the country will look in future emergencies, and hence this despatch possesses a national interest. Such are, in an exceptional degree, Generals Sir John Adye, Sir Archibald Alison, Sir Gerald Graham, Sir D. Drury-Lowe, Sir Evelyn Wood, and Sir Herbert Macpherson; and Colonels Sir Baker Russell, Stewart, Buller, Gillespie, Butler, Maurice, and others. The war did not afford much opportunity for the display of exceptional talent, for the reason that so perfectly were its contingencies provided for by the Commander-in-Chief, that the ultimate issues were not left to chance, or to the interposition of a *deus ex machinâ* in the shape of a general or staff-officer.

Sir Garnet Wolseley has always recommended himself to the favour of the English public by the economy with which he has conducted the expeditions under his command, unlike some distinguished commanders, who have displayed a

---

discipline in quarters have shown them to be worthy successors of those gallant soldiers who, in former days, raised the reputation of England to a very high position among nations.'

lordly indifference to financial considerations. As we have seen, the entire charge for the Red River Expedition was £80,000, and of this John Bull only paid out of his pocket one-fourth. The Ashantee War was conducted at a cost of £900,000. Even more remarkable is the economy displayed in the conduct of the Egyptian Campaign. When we consider that 33,000 men proceeded to the seat of war up to the 14th September, and that 41,000 were despatched from this country and India, the English taxpayer must have regarded with feelings of dismay the fiscal prospects before him. But having regard to the vast European and Asiatic interests that have been safe-guarded—on the one hand our road to India and the far East, and on the other the re-establishment of the prestige of this country throughout the world as a power that will do more than bluster and talk when its vital interests are concerned—the actual cost to the nation of the expedition down to the 1st of October, when the state of war was succeeded by an armed occupation, has been only £3,360,000.* This is exclusive of the charge for the Indian Contingent, which was estimated at £1,880,000, but has only reached £1,140,000. Thus the total cost of the war has been £4,500,000, exactly half of that of the Abyssinian Expedition, though the number of troops landed in one case was only 12,000, and in the other 33,000. This economy in expenditure, which forms so striking a feature in the expeditions conducted by the subject of this memoir, is, of course, chiefly due to the rapidity with which he has con-

* The vote of credit taken on 25th July was for £2,300,000: War Office, £900,000; Admiralty, including Transport, £1,400,000. This vote on account is thus increased by only £1,060,000, made up by War Office charges £750,000, and Admiralty £310,000. The charge for the Indian Contingent, borne in the first instance by the Indian Government, will be adjusted at a later date between it and the Home Government.

From the 1st October the extra charge for the pay and maintenance of the Army of Occupation—in the above account are included only the special allowances, and the whole extra charge connected with the war—will be borne entirely, or chiefly, by the Egyptian Exchequer.

ducted the military operations—seven weeks from the date of the vote of credit, and four weeks to the day from his landing at Alexandria ; but it is also owing to the intimate knowledge he possesses of the requirements of war as waged in the four quarters of the globe, and his unequalled mastery of the administrative details of the several departments of the complicated military machine in Pall Mall.

The British Government instituted a medal in honour of the Egyptian War, to be granted to all troops who served in that country between July 16th and September 14th, with clasps for Alexandria and Tel-el-Kebir. The decorations and rewards to officers were conferred in accordance with Sir Garnet Wolseley's recommendations, and it cannot be said that they were given on an illiberal scale. The officers of the army received one G.C.B., ten K.C.B.'s, and fifty-six C.B.'s ; also one K.C.S.I., one K.C.M.G., and two C.M.G.'s. Sir Garnet Wolseley was created a peer, with the title of Lord Wolseley of Cairo, and a pension, and was promoted to the rank of General, 'for distinguished service in the field ;' Sir Archibald Alison was made a Lieutenant-General, and Brigadier-General Hon. J. Dormer, Deputy-Adjutant-General, a Major-General. In the combatant branch sixty-two Majors were promoted to Brevet Lieutenant-Colonels, and forty-three Captains to Brevet-Majorities. Eighteen officers in the non-combatant branches received promotion ; and Brigade-Surgeon R. W. Jackson, C.B., who served on Sir Garnet's Staff as medical attendant in South Africa as well as in Egypt, was knighted. Seven officers were made Aides-de-Camp to the Queen, with the rank of Colonel ; and three —Brigadier-General Goodenough, R.A., Colonel Stockwell, C.B., Seaforth Highlanders (who had served with his regiment in Afghanistan, under Sir Frederick Roberts, and commanded it, on the death of Colonel Brownlow, at the battle of Candahar), and Colonel D. Macpherson, C.B., Royal

Highlanders (who had commanded the regiment at Amoaful)—were awarded a distinguished-service pension. The prodigality with which rewards were given in this and recent campaigns affords a contrast to the niggardliness of a previous generation. Lord Wolseley's early career offers a case in point. After serving in the Burmese War, where he headed a storming party and was severely wounded; and throughout the siege of Sebastopol, where he was again severely wounded, and was as often under fire in the trenches as any officer in the British army, and was specially mentioned in despatches by Lord Raglan—for these services he received neither promotion, nor brevet, nor any other reward.

Sir Garnet Wolseley* received at the hands of the Khedive the Grand Cross of the Turkish Order of the Osmanieh; and a distribution was made of the five different grades of this Order and of the Medjidie to every officer of rank, and to one field-officer, one captain, and one subaltern of each corps and battery. His Highness also followed the example of the British Government, and instituted a medal for the Egyptian Campaign, in silver for the officers, and copper for the men.

Sir Garnet Wolseley, on his arrival at Cairo on the 15th September, in company with the Duke of Connaught, took up his quarters, with his Staff, in the Abdeen Palace, which was placed at his disposal by the Khedive. One of his first acts was to issue a general order to his troops in the following terms: 'The General Commanding-in-Chief congratulates the army upon the brilliant success which has crowned its efforts in the campaign terminated on the 14th

* The notables of Cairo have recently presented Lords Wolseley and Alcester with magnificent swords, subscribed by, and presented in the name of, the nation. The value of these weapons, which are of ancient manufacture, and were worn by famous Sultans of Turkey, is stated to be £3,500. The notables have also presented General Drury-Lowe with a costly pair of pistols.

inst. by the surrender of the citadel of Cairo and of Arabi Pasha, the chief rebel against the authority of his Highness the Khedive. In twenty-five days the army has effected a disembarkation at Ismailia; has traversed the desert to Zagazig; has occupied the capital of Egypt; and has fortunately defeated the enemy four times—on August 24th, at Magfar; on the 25th, at Tel-el-Mahouta; on September 9th, at Kassassin; and, finally, on September 13th, at Tel-el-Kebir—where, after an arduous night-march, it inflicted upon him an overwhelming defeat, storming a strongly entrenched position at the point of the bayonet, and capturing all his guns, about sixty in number. In recapitulating the events which have marked this short and decisive campaign, the General Commanding-in-Chief feels proud to place upon record the fact that these military achievements are to be attributed to the high military courage and noble devotion to duty which have animated all ranks under his command. Called upon to show discipline under exceptional privations, to give proof of fortitude in extreme toil, and to show contempt of danger in battle, general officers, officers, non-commissioned officers, and men of the army, have responded with alacrity, adding another chapter to the long roll of British victories.'

In spite of the complete overthrow of Arabi and the cause he represented, the lower orders of Cairo were insolent in their bearing, and, on the 23rd, Sir Garnet directed the whole Cavalry Division* to march through the city to impress on the people the reality of the change of masters. Meanwhile the effects of the great victory achieved at Tel-el-Kebir were becoming apparent in the surrender of the fortified places on the coast, and the submission of the

* The loss of troop-horses during the Egyptian Campaign was exceptionally heavy, considering its brief duration. The Household Cavalry lost 90 horses, being 30 per squadron; the 7th Dragoon Guards lost 72; the 19th Hussars, 50; the Horse Artillery, 96; and the 4th Dragoon Guards, which marched over 70 miles in 48 hours, without unsaddling, 267 horses.

COMPLETE SUBMISSION OF EGYPT. 465

rebel chiefs who, lately the servile tools of Arabi, now cringed at the feet of the Khedive. The conduct of the notables and priests was as subservient to the triumphant Khedive as it had lately been to the Colonel of Infantry who had usurped his functions, and of whom they now professed, in words applied by his quondam sycophants to Sejanus, commander of the Prætorian Guard of Tiberius, '*Nunquam, mihi credis, amavi hunc hominem.*'

The forts at Aboukir were evacuated and occupied, but Abdelal, the commander in Arabi's interest at Damietta, refused to surrender, and Sir Evelyn Wood proceeded with some troops to attack the forts, which the fleet was directed to bombard. However, Abdelal discovered the hopelessness of resistance when his men refused to obey him and deserted in great numbers, and, on the 23rd September, he surrendered himself to the British General at Kafr-el-Battikh, a station five miles from Damietta, and by noon the forts and city were occupied by British troops. The services of Sir Evelyn Wood and the 4th Brigade should not be overlooked in this brief retrospect of the Egyptian War, for not only did they receive the surrender of Damietta and the large force entrenched behind the lines at Kafr-Dowar, but they kept at bay, and prevented from swelling the ranks of Arabi, probably not less than 30,000 of his best troops.

On the 25th September the Khedive, accompanied by Sir E. Malet and his ministers, arrived at Cairo from Alexandria. Preparations were made on a grand scale for his reception. The streets, which were densely crowded, were lined with troops, and, on his alighting at the station, a salute was fired, and the band of the Grenadier Guards played 'God save the Queen.' Sir Garnet Wolseley and the Duke of Connaught received his Highness, who, having warmly expressed his thanks to the General who had restored him to the throne, entered his carriage in company with the Prince, Sir Garnet and Sir E. Malet, and drove to the Ismailia Palace, where he decorated Sir Garnet with the Grand Cross of the Osmanieh. How different were the circumstances under which, on the 12th of July, he quitted his capital, with Arabi sitting in the carriage by his side to protect him from the very people who now cheered and illuminated in his honour!

On the following day the Khedive held a reception of British officers, the Diplomatic body, and natives—the latter crowding in numbers greater than was ever known before, some 4,000 being present. Sir Garnet was unable to be present owing to his being laid up with illness, caused by catching cold when visiting the Pyramids; but, under the watchful care of his friend and medical attendant, Dr. Jackson, he was able to resume his duties in a few days, and, on 1st October, reviewed his magnificent army of 18,000 men and 60 guns, in presence of the Khedive. The Abdeen Square, in which the review was held, had been the arena of a far different scene when, on the 9th October in the preceding year, Arabi—who now witnessed the stirring military spectacle from a window in his prison-house in the square—with 4,000 men, enforced his own terms on Tewfik, besieged in the palace whence his wife and family were now watching the march of the soldiers who had replaced him on the throne.

The troops, now that they were no longer kept up by the excitement of active service, began to suffer from the effects of the hardships they had undergone, and the unhealthy climate.* The greater portion of the force was necessarily

* The entries into hospital from the time of the landing at Ismailia to the 25th October, a few days after Sir Garnet quitted Cairo, were, out of a total of 25,092 officers and men, 462 wounded and 7,038 sick. The following is a list of the military officers killed and died from wounds and the climate in the Egyptian Expedition: Colonel Beasley, 87th; Lieutenant-Colonel Balfour, Grenadier Guards; Major Strong, Captain Wardell, and Lieutenants Coke, Hickman, Colvin, Marshall, and Parkinson, Royal Marines; Major Colville and Lieutenants Kays and Somervell, 74th; Captain Baynes and Lieutenant Brooks, 75th; Lieutenant Bayly, 2nd Dragoon Guards (attached to 7th Dragoon Guards); Lieutenant Gribble, 3rd Dragoon Guards; Lieutenant Weyland, 1st Life Guards; Captain Jones,

encamped around Cairo, on sandy soil, with dust-storms all day, and fogs from the river at night. The Abbassyeh and Abdeen Barracks were found in such a condition of indescribable filth that, until they were cleansed, a process which took some weeks, they could not be occupied. With the exception of the Guards, which encamped in front of the Abdeen Barracks, and occupied the citadel, the infantry were stationed in the Island of Boolak, and the cavalry and artillery at Abbassyeh.

As Her Majesty's Government decided to reduce the army of occupation to 12,000 men, the expeditionary force was broken up; and on the 4th of October, Sir Garnet issued the following general order to the troops: 'The army in Egypt being broken up, and about to separate, the Commander-in-Chief wishes to thank all ranks for the manner in which they have done their duty during the war. After the crowning success of Tel-el-Kebir, he had the pleasure of thanking them for their endurance, courage, and gallantry in the field. To these high military virtues the troops have since added steadiness of conduct in garrison, have maintained the character of the distinguished regiments to which they belong, and shown the people of Cairo that Her Majesty's soldiers, British and Indian, are as conspicuous for their good behaviour in camp and quarters as they had already proved themselves gallant troops before the enemy. Her Majesty has every reason to be proud of the soldiers who have served in Egypt, and in her name and on her behalf he thanks them for their valour and discipline. For himself, Sir Garnet Wolseley begs to assure them that he will ever remember and prize to the utmost the

---

88th; Lieutenant Howard-Vyse, 60th Rifles; Lieutenants McNeill, Graham-Stirling, and Park, 42nd; Lieutenant Pirie, 92nd; Captain Doyle, 2nd Dragoon Guards (A.D.C. to Sir H. Macpherson); Lieutenant Peters, 11th; and Surgeon-Major Shaw, Army Medical Department.

fact that he had the honour and good fortune to command them in this short campaign.' With reference to the discipline, steadiness and good conduct of the army under his command, it should be noted that this was the first occasion in which a British general was called upon to maintain discipline in an army in the field without recourse to the lash. As regards their good conduct in quarters, Sir Garnet has since stated that, during his stay in Cairo, which extended over six weeks, he did not see a single drunken soldier—truly a remarkable testimony to the sobriety and discipline of the army under his control.

The Commander-in-Chief, during his stay, was busy reviewing brigades and regiments, inspecting hospitals, visiting the unequalled mosques and edifices of this famous Oriental city, and attending fêtes and banquets in his honour. Of these, the entertainment given on the 17th of October, by the Sheikh-i-Bikri, carried off the palm for interest, and the scene resembled the descriptions we read of the fêtes that rendered memorable the reign over Baghdad of 'the good Caliph Haroun-al-Raschid.' The narrow lanes leading to the Sheikh's palace, which those who have visited this most picturesque of Eastern cities will remember, were converted into long arcades, ablaze with lights, and spanned by triumphal arches, and the old palace, with its courtyard and gardens, was illuminated with Oriental taste and profusion.

The only *contretemps* that happened during Sir Garnet's stay in Cairo was the great fire at the railway station, supposed to be the work of incendiaries, when a vast amount of ammunition and stores was destroyed.

One other occurrence is worthy of chronicle, and that was the grand parade, on the 5th of October, of the British troops, in honour of the 'holy carpet,' annually sent to decorate the Kaaba at Mecca, held in the presence of the Khedive and the principal British officers. Much discussion arose in the

Press, and questions were asked in the House of Commons, regarding the salute given by British troops on that occasion; but, as explained in a memorandum by Sir Garnet Wolseley, the honour had not been paid to the carpet, but to the howdah, or litter, which is supposed to represent the Sultan, and received the same salute as is paid to the Queen's colours.

On the 10th of October, Sir Garnet Wolseley reviewed the Guards' Brigade, now reduced to 1,400 bayonets; after which he addressed a few words to the Duke of Connaught and the Colonels of the three battalions. On the following day, he received a farewell visit from the Khedive, who reiterated his unbounded thanks; and at eleven p.m. the same night, left for Alexandria, on his return to England. All the Egyptian ministers, the Duke of Connaught, and the British Generals and Staff were present at the station to see him off, and as the train moved out, the august assemblage gave 'Three cheers for Sir Garnet.'

On arriving near the lines of Kafr-Dowar, on the following morning, the Commander-in-Chief got out of the railway carriage and examined the formidable works constructed with such labour by Arabi. On the following day he inspected the four regiments composing the garrison of Alexandria, and, on the 21st of October, sailed in H.M.'s despatch vessel, *Iris*, for Trieste, nine weeks and two days after landing at that port with the arduous Egyptian military problem to solve.

It was truly a wonderful retrospect, to look back at the relative positions of Arabi and the Khedive then and now, and to consider the vast change that had come over the political world, not only of Cairo and Constantinople, but of London and Paris, and of every Court in Europe; for it is certain that the consequences of the victory of Tel-el-Kebir will exercise a momentous, and perhaps permanent, change in the relations of the Great Powers as regards the Eastern Question, no less than on the well-being of the Egyptian people.

Sir Garnet Wolseley was received with special honour by the Austrian military authorities at Trieste, and a large crowd assembled to see him depart, a special carriage being placed at his disposal by the railway company. Travelling direct to Paris, he landed in England on Saturday, the 28th of October. He received an enthusiastic reception at Dover, where he was met by Lady Wolseley and his daughter, and was presented with an address by the Mayor and Corporation. In his reply he expressed his pleasure on being thus greeted on his return home, and added, 'I hope the time may never come when I shall have the vanity and self-conceit to make me blind to the fact that for this honour I am indebted to the valour, the endurance, and the high state of discipline of that army of which I have recently had the command in Egypt.' On alighting at Charing Cross Railway Station, the successful soldier received the congratulations of numerous friends, including the Duke of Cambridge and Mr. Gladstone, and great crowds of his countrymen assembled to welcome him. In obedience to the Queen's command, Sir Garnet left London on the following day for Balmoral, and, after a most gratifying reception by Her Majesty, returned to town, receiving both going and coming a popular ovation at Perth, Aberdeen, and other places where he was recognised. Immediately on arriving in town, on the 1st November, he proceeded to the War Office and resumed his duties as Adjutant-General of the forces from that date.

The thanks of the Legislature have always been regarded as among the most coveted distinctions conferred on a successful Commander, and Sir Garnet Wolseley and his brave army had no cause to complain of the terms in which, on the

THE THANKS OF PARLIAMENT. 471

26th of October, the leaders of the great parties in the State conveyed their appreciation of their services to him and his army. Lord Granville gave a concise sketch of the campaign, and Lord Salisbury enlarged on Sir Garnet's 'peculiar and characteristic genius—namely, a vast and most accurate knowledge of detail'—while the Duke of Cambridge exposed the fallacy, if it required exposing, that attributed delay to him in advancing from Ismailia after seizing the Sweet Water Canal.

But Mr. Gladstone's speech in the Lower House was, as might be anticipated, the most complete exposition of the war, and the most eloquent panegyric of the Commander. In describing the change of base, he spoke of his possessing the virtue 'of keeping his own counsel, thus throwing off the scent the prying eyes which do so much to entertain the public, and sometimes to perplex or even disturb the action of a General.' In speaking of his wise determination to delay his final attack when, on the 9th September, he could have made it 'with a moral assurance of victory,' the Prime Minister said : 'There are some victories which are nothing more than the commencement and the inauguration of prolonged struggles. There are other victories which in themselves at once assure the consummation of the great work which the General has in hand; and it was the wise delay of Sir Garnet Wolseley, and his determination, whatever storm of criticism might come upon him, not to stir and not to touch the enemy till he could effectually crush him, and attain at once the objects of the war,—it was that quality which caused Sir Garnet Wolseley to wait until he had such a force at his command, until he was able to throw forward right and left such a strength of cavalry for the purpose of surrounding the defeated enemy that he might perform that great operation I will describe in the single phrase of converting a victory into a conquest.' That phrase, 'converting a victory into a conquest,' conveys with epigrammatic terseness the feature that places this campaign among the most remarkable in modern times. Finally, Mr. Gladstone dwelt on the great characteristic of the assault on Tel-el-Kebir,—that it was effected with a smaller loss of life than could have been anticipated, considering the strength of the works and the numerical superiority of the enemy. In the words of Shakespeare, from whom an apt quotation can be drawn for any and every contingency of thought and action, 'A victory is twiçe itself when the achiever brings home full numbers.' Dwelling on this happy circumstance, one for which many households in the United Kingdom will bless 'the achiever' with more heartiness than for any of the other military qualities he displayed, the orator added: 'Sir Garnet Wolseley will feel the consolation in his life and in his death that the fulness of those numbers was not owing to accident or to the weakness of the enemy, but to a deliberate and well-laid combination—a skilful comparison of means to ends, a judicious arrangement of every step of his measures, and the realization in actual experience of all that he had planned.'*

A sword of honour was voted to Sir Garnet Wolseley by the

* A noteworthy feature in this campaign—to which we drew attention in a professional journal on the formation of the Staff of the Expeditionary Army, and to which reference has been made by Lord Wolseley in a speech since his return to this country—was the selection of officers of the Royal Artillery and Royal Engineers for high commands and important posts on the Staff. It has never been the custom in the British army, though it is common enough in India and in all Continental armies, for officers of these branches of the service to command divisions and brigades; but in the expedition to Egypt Sir John Adye, the second in command, and Sir E. Hamley, commanding a division, were artillerymen, and General Graham, who commanded what Lord Wolseley termed 'the fighting brigade,' as it bore the brunt of the work, belonged to the corps of Engineers. Moreover, of 25 officers on the Headquarter Staff, 12 were in the Artillery or Engineers. In India some of the most successful commanders of armies belonged to the 'scientific' corps, including Sir George Pollock, Sir John Whish, Sir Archdale Wilson, Lord Napier of Magdala, and Sir Frederick Roberts; and had the rule that obtained until lately in the British service regulated that of France, the great Napoleon himself would never have risen beyond the grade of Divisional General of Artillery.

Corporation of London—the second he had received from the same body; and dinners and receptions were given in his honour by the Duke of Cambridge, the Prime Minister, and the Secretaries for War and India. He was also entertained at a banquet by the members of the United Service Club, at which were present the Prince of Wales and the Dukes of Edinburgh, Connaught, and Cambridge. When replying to the toast of his health, he took the opportunity to explain that he had been misunderstood in the views attributed to him regarding our regimental system, since the publication of his article in the *Nineteenth Century;* and added, 'that but for the regimental officers, and the way the men were led by them, the success of Tel-el-Kebir could never have been achieved, and that it was his knowledge of and faith in the regimental officers and their men that induced him to plan such an attack.' That an opinion should have been generally entertained that one who gained his first steps on the ladder of fame in Burmah and India by his services as a regimental officer, could have been capable of maligning the class, was due to the malevolence of his detractors; for his published 'Soldier's Pocket-Book' is witness that it had no claim to credence. In this work he writes: 'The issue of every fight depends upon the infantry, and their conduct depends upon the company officers, who, of all others, are the most important men in any army. At that final moment of actual conflict the result is in their hands. Drawn from the gentry of England, their courage has never been impugned, even by the most Radical of newspapers. Hence, in a great measure, our unvarying success in infantry and cavalry charges.' That under the old system of purchase there were officers who bought a commission in the army without any intention of remaining in it as a profession, but merely as a passport to society, or a gentlemanly way of passing a few years until coming into the family estate, and that some such even yet exist, especially in the Household troops, we fancy few will have the temerity to deny.

A fitting sequel to the Egyptian campaign was the review, on the 18th November, of the troops who had returned from the seat of war. Londoners will not soon forget the brilliant spectacle, and, indeed, no military pageant at once so interesting and splendid as the triumphal procession through the streets of 8,000 men of all arms and branches of the service, and 36 guns, has been seen in the metropolis in this generation, if ever.* The scene—as Her Majesty, accompanied by the Princes of her house and the Commander who had illustrated her reign by his martial deeds, and now for the last time commanded the soldiers who had so faithfully obeyed his behests, arrived on the parade-ground at the Horse Guards, when the fog lifted as though by magic, like the curtain at a theatrical performance—was one never to be forgotten; but in interest it was eclipsed by the procession through the crowded streets of the soldiers who had swarmed over the ramparts of Tel-el-Kebir, and compelled the surrender of Cairo.† So much has been said of the immaturity

* The only scene of a similar character witnessed in this century was in 1814, when the Prince Regent, accompanied by the allied Sovereigns, reviewed, in Hyde Park, a portion of the troops who had served at Waterloo, including the Household Cavalry, who formed so conspicuous a feature of the display of 1882.

† The following general order to the troops was issued by command of the Queen after the review: 'His Royal Highness the Field-Marshal Commanding-in-Chief has received the Queen's command to convey to General Sir Garnet Wolseley, G.C.B., G.C.M.G., and the officers, non-commissioned officers, and men of all branches of the expeditionary force, Her Majesty's admiration of their conduct during the recent campaign, in which she has great satisfaction in feeling that her son, Major-General his Royal Highness the Duke of Connaught and Strathearn, took an active part. The gallantry displayed by the well-organized contingent of her Indian army and by the Royal Malta Fencible Artillery, as well as by her sailors and Marines, has not failed to attract Her Majesty's attention. The troops of all ranks, in the face of obstacles of no ordinary character, have shown a marked devotion to duty. For a time without shelter in the desert, under a burning sun, in a climate proverbially adverse to Europeans, their courage and discipline were nobly maintained throughout, and to this, under brave and experienced leaders, may be attributed the success which has distinguished this campaign. The defeat of the enemy in every engagement, including the brilliant cavalry charge at Kassassin, culminated

SIR GARNET RAISED TO THE PEERAGE.

of our soldiers, that no little surprise was evinced by the spectators of the stately show at the stalwart appearance of the men whose years apparently averaged from twenty-one to twenty-seven—an age than which Count von Moltke wrote, 'I could not desire anything better,' for such a battalion 'has sufficient age for stamina.' The crowd who came to see what manner of men were they who had overrun the land of the Pharaohs in a few weeks, went away satisfied that the soldiers for whose maintenance they paid taxes had not deteriorated in physique from the standard of those who, twenty-six years before, received an equally enthusiastic welcome from their countrymen on their return from the Crimea. The campaign served the useful purpose of testing the efficiency of the army under the new system of short-service soldiers, and it must be allowed by all candid critics that, on the whole, it came well out of the ordeal.

On the 20th of November, Sir Garnet Wolseley was created a Peer of the United Kingdom, by the title of 'Lord Wolseley of Cairo, and of Wolseley in the county of Stafford,' the ancestral seat of the family; thus, though the surname, so well known to his countrymen, has not been merged in the title—the familiar prefix, 'Sir Garnet,' has ceased to be borne by him. On the 22nd, his lordship proceeded to Windsor, 'kissed hands' on being raised to the peerage, and, in company with about 350 officers and men of all ranks of the army and navy, who had served in Egypt, including the detachment of the Indian Contingent,

---

in the action of Tel-el-Kebir, in which, after an arduous night-march, his position was carried at the point of the bayonet, his guns were captured, and his whole army, notwithstanding its great numerical superiority, was completely dispersed. It is, therefore, with the greatest gratification that His Royal Highness conveys Her Majesty's welcome to the troops whom it was her pleasure to review on the 18th instant, and His Royal Highness, at the same time, has to express Her Majesty's thanks to the entire force for the brave and exemplary conduct displayed by all, individually and collectively, during the campaign.'

received, at the hands of Her Majesty, the Egyptian War Medal, the massed bands of the 2nd Life Guards and Coldstreams playing 'See the conquering Hero comes,' as the Sovereign pinned the medal on his breast. On this occasion the Queen addressed the recipients of the medals in the following terms : ' I have summoned you here to-day, to confer upon you the well-earned medals commemorative of the short and brilliant, although arduous, campaign, in which all have done their duty with courageous and undaunted devotion. Tell your comrades that I thank them heartily for the gallant services they have rendered to their Queen and country, and that I am proud of my soldiers and sailors, who have added fresh glories to the victories won by their predecessors.'

A distinguished officer who has served on his Staff, writes to us of the characteristics of Lord Wolseley : " What I observed chiefly was his extraordinary power of imparting confidence to all around him, and also the influence that he can exercise to win over the most cantankerous of mortals. I have known old colonels more than once, who had never before seen him, who were jealous of his success, and whose bristles were all up, come out after an interview with their prejudices shaken, and added to his devoted admirers. His power and rapidity of doing business is also, as you no doubt know well, one of his greatest traits. When another man would be fussy and solemn, he will be chatty and amusing, and even renders the most dry of official details interesting by his remarks. Official document after official document may come under his notice with a 'Yes,' or a 'No,' or an 'All right' for an answer; but no sooner is a knotty point raised than he seems to grasp at once the bearings of the case without an effort. His freedom from any sort of prejudice is also remarkable in a profession which is full of it.

' In South Africa, taken generally, what I noticed chiefly

REMINISCENCES OF LORD WOLSELEY.

was the change that came over the soldiers after his arrival. It is not too much to say, that in the Zulu War great portions of the army were really almost demoralized, and the very name of a Zulu was enough to make them rush behind the nearest waggon. The same men, but a month or two afterwards, thought themselves individually equal to 50 natives, and in the operations against Secocoeni exhibited this in a marked degree. Lord Wolseley's determination was also very great. Upon one occasion he determined to ride to Newcastle from Prætoria ; he used troopers only. He left Prætoria at seven a.m., and reached Heidelburg, fifty-six miles, a little before one p.m. Pushing on from here, he was caught in a violent thunderstorm, arriving at the next stage, McHatty's, eighteen miles, drenched through and through. Although the storm had not ceased, he endeavoured to push on from here, with a result that he lost his way in the veldt, and was wandering in rain and darkness until two a.m. the following day. At six a.m. he was away again with a very similar day to follow, determined to arrive at Newcastle as he had arranged. I attribute the rising of the Boers, in the winter of 1880, very much to the influence of his absence. During the whole time he was at Prætoria he held them comfortably in check. Their chances of success were great, and the position would have been awkward had they risen when Sir Garnet was *en route* to Secocoeni, but his influence was quite sufficient to restrain them.

'In Egypt, the day that struck me most, or rather where his individuality had the greatest play, apart from Tel-el-Kebir, was the 24th August. Starting in the morning to make a small reconnoissance, he came upon the Egyptians in considerable strength. As their numbers developed and their guns came into play, as their irregulars threatened our flank, and their main body formed up, apparently to come on, I believe that nine men out of ten would have thought how to retire judiciously. I remember so well his expression at the time when things looked worst : " I shall turn their left flank and roll them into the canal." The late arrival of reinforcements, owing to the heat of the march, prevented his doing this on that day eventually ; but I shall never forget the sublime confidence of the man under the circumstances, a confidence that had a great influence—in my opinion, the very greatest—on the course of the campaign.'

As has been said of him, the three chief characteristics of Lord Wolseley are—'dash, discretion, and foresight.' A singular similarity may be traced in the successes he has achieved—the same careful elaboration of plan, with a rapid execution that gives no time for rallying or a prolonged resistance. Thus it was in the brief campaign against Secocoeni, when the night-march preceded the attack at daybreak. The advance on Coomassie affords an even more striking instance, and a passage in his despatch of the 13th of February, 1874, summing up the results of the war, might almost have been written of the recent campaign. 'Our success,' he writes, 'does not lie merely in our having defeated the enemy's army and occupied his capital, but in our having thoroughly established in this kingdom a wholesome fear of the British power, and a knowledge of the advantages of an alliance with Her Majesty.'

Remarkable as have been the achievements of Lord Wolseley's career, his last was the most striking of all. Military opinion is unanimous that the conception and execution of the plan for the capture of the lines of Tel-el-Kebir stamp the originator as a soldier of genius. Such competent critics as Baker Pasha and Colonel von Hagenau, the German officer attached to the Headquarters of the British Army in Egypt, who have studied the ground marched and fought over, have expressed an opinion that the method of attack adopted was at once the most bloodless for the assailants, and the most certain to be decisive that could have been delivered.* The plan was not less unique than daring, and the ability with which it was carried into execution proclaimed the hand of the master-workman skilled in the use of the tools placed at his disposal. The very completeness of the success has tended to lessen the credit due to the Commander, and the writers who spoke despondingly of the difficulties of the campaign are the same men who later wrote disparagingly of its merits.

Had Lord Wolseley carried the lines of Tel-el-Kebir after a sanguinary struggle, the measure of his success and the greatness of the victory would, in the eyes of such critics, have been guaged by the extent of his losses. But in this instance, as throughout his career, his object was to effect his purpose with as little effusion of blood as possible, and he was successful where a general of inferior skill would have suffered heavy loss. Had the surprise not been complete, and the arrangements perfect, the intrenchments could not have been carried without great slaughter; and indeed the issue was doubtful in the opinion of many experienced officers, and no one anticipated success without a heavy casualty-roll. The selection of the plan of attack was only determined after much careful consideration, and on observing several days in succession that the enemy's outposts were withdrawn during the night, and only posted after

* An officer who traversed the field writes: 'I think the more we inquire into the conditions under which Sir Garnet Wolseley was obliged to act, the more his admirable tactical foresight will strike us, and the greater will be our admiration for his exceeding skill, both as a cautious, careful leader, and a bold and rapid strategist. What he wanted, above all things, to effect was the complete destruction of Arabi's army, involving the safety of Cairo, and the utter collapse of all defensive schemes at Kafr Dowar, Aboukir, and Damietta. I declare to you, as I rode over the desert, and tried to conjure up the night-march, the silent, fireless bivouac, the advance in the early hours ere dawn, and then the terrible rush on the startled enemy, I was filled with a sort of awe at the audacity and wonder at the success of the enterprise. Did any General before this, in all your reading, think of directing the march of his army on the enemy by the stars of heaven?'

daybreak. From his great experience of warfare with many and varied nationalities, he knew that a sudden attack at night on an unprepared army, even if made by a small body of men, offered a favourable opportunity for delivering a blow. But this blow, to be decisive, must be struck at dawn; and his familiarity with the difficulties attending a night-march, taught him that even the best troops are liable to fall into confusion or suffer from a sudden panic. Leaving nothing to chance, he therefore decided to assault with two columns, so that in the event of failure on the part of one, the other should not be thrown into confusion. Hence Graham's and Alison's Brigades made *distinct* attacks, and the Artillery force of 42 guns planted between them afforded yet another chance of success, a third string to his bow, as in the event of both columns being driven back, with their supports and reserves, the fire of the massed guns, concentrated on a single spot, might give time for the infantry to rally and clear a way for a fresh advance. His plans were, in fact, based on the assumption that if even a small force made its way within the intrenchments, the blow could be followed up and success achieved. The flanks of the main attack were well watched by the Indian Contingent on the left, to complete the security of the movement, and, being fresher than their comrades, to march on Zagazig; and by the Cavalry Division on the right, which was kept well in hand, to pursue the flying columns, or, in the event of defeat, to cover the retreat or threaten the enemy's rear. Every eventuality was, in short, provided for, and nothing was left to chance. Like the great Trojan chief,

> 'His piercing eyes through all the battle stray.'

And, finally, when victory rewarded the skilful tactician, its fruits were fully reaped.

CONCLUSION. 481

The Press of Europe presented the most astonishing spectacle of perplexity after the victory, which, indeed, they had prophesied would be a failure, or, at least, that it would not be achieved without great losses and a prolonged campaign. The majority of the Press—German, French, Russian, Italian, and Spanish—had indulged in diatribes at what they considered the supineness and faulty strategy of the Commander; and great was their surprise when it resulted in a brilliant victory, and still more when the blow was followed up with a vigour unsurpassed in the annals of war. Their endeavours to account for this surprising success did credit to their ingenuity, if not to their intelligence or ingenuousness; and their inventive faculty was displayed in the French story of Arabi having been bribed, and in the *canard* of the importation of 2,000 bloodhounds, gravely set afloat by the Italian Press.

The Egyptian campaign was replete with startling incidents and telling situations. What could be more picturesque than the moonlight charge of the ponderous Household Cavalry? It will ever be a proud memory in the history of that *corps d'élite*, how they burst like an avalanche on the astonished Egyptians, sweeping all before them, and converting a retreat into a rout. Then the midnight march of the army, guided alone by the stars. Can any episode recorded in war appeal more powerfully to the imagination? The vast mass of 14,000 men, with 60 guns, covering a front of four miles, moved across the desert, silent and resolute, straight upon the intrenchments behind which lay an army double their strength, and their spring was like that of the tiger on its prey, so close and deadly was it. Finally, could anything be more dramatic than the scene presented at Cairo on the night of the 14th September, when 6,000 men, the garrison of a strong citadel, defiled out of its gates by torchlight before a handful of hungry and weary British Dragoons? As General Drury-

Lowe said, the forced march of his cavalry—of which the consequences were this event, and the surrender of Arabi, with the attendant results of finishing the war, and performing for civilization the priceless service of saving a city whose architectural beauties are among the most valued possessions of art—was planned before the army embarked for Egypt by the master-mind who directed the operations of one of the most rapid and brilliant of modern wars.

The eulogium passed on Cinna, the conqueror of Sylla, may be applied with equal justice to Wolseley, '*Perfecisse quæ a nullo nisi fortissimo, perfici possent.*' Only an accomplished master of the art of war could have gained the victories over man and the forces of Nature, achieved by Lord Wolseley in his campaigns in the Red River, Ashantee, South Africa and Egypt.

THE END.